BY THE EDITORS OF

CONSUMER GUIDE®

PRESCRIPTION DRUGS

Manufactured in U.S.A.

8 7 6 5 4 3 2 1

ISBN: 0-7853-0997-7

Consultant: Peggy Boucher Mullen, Pharm.D.
Cover Photos: Sam Griffith Studios, Inc.

Contents

Introduction

The right drug for the right patient in the right dose by the right path at the right time. This rule sums up the decisions made when your doctor gives you a prescription. You've helped make those decisions by giving your doctor your complete medical history, which should include any previous allergic reactions you've suffered, any other drugs you may be taking, and any chronic health problems you may have. Once you leave your doctor's office with your prescription in hand, however, you still have more to do as a responsible patient and a smart consumer.

Drug therapy is an important component of health care. When you receive a prescription, you must know how and when to properly administer your medication. You must understand and comply with your dosage schedule. You must know what to do to prevent certain side effects and how to handle any side effects that might occur. You must recognize the signals that indicate the need to call your doctor. All too often, patients leave their doctors' offices without a full understanding of the drug therapy they're about to start. This may result in a failure to comply fully with their doctors' prescriptions. For example, they may stop taking the medication too soon because it doesn't seem to work or because they feel better or because it causes bothersome side effects. They may take the drug improperly or at the wrong time or too often. They may continue drinking alcohol or using other drugs, perhaps not even realizing that taking cold pills, oral contraceptives, aspirin, or vitamins could affect the action of the prescribed drug. The end result may be that they not only fail to get better, they may get worse and may even suffer a dangerous reaction.

Few of us would buy a car without shopping around, a house or condominium without an appraisal, or an appliance without knowing how use to it. Prescription medications should be approached like these other purchases: with understanding. You will be the end user. As a good consumer you should know what you are buying and how to get the most out of your purchase.

Prescription drugs are dispensed on the basis of two assumptions: 1) instructions for proper use are provided, and 2) those instructions

CONSUMER GUIDE®

will be followed. In many states, pharmacists are required to provide drug information for each prescription medication by means of written information, verbal counseling, or both. Nevertheless, as a consumer, you have the responsibility to understand your own drug therapy. The National Council of Patient Information and Education (NCPIE) is made up of health-care professionals, lay people, and consumer advocates. It has published guidelines to provide consumers with the information they need regarding proper drug therapy. This is important since the Council estimates that **half** of all prescriptions dispensed in one year (that's approximately 900,000,000 prescriptions) are taken incorrectly. This leads to unnecessary side effects, worsening of illnesses, and, in rare cases, even death. NCPIE recommends that you ask your health-care professional the following questions about each prescription medication you receive:

1. What is the name of the drug and what is it supposed to do?
2. How and when should it be taken?
3. What foods, drinks, activities, or other medications should be avoided while taking the drug?
4. Are any side effects likely, and what should be done if they occur?

PRESCRIPTION DRUGS provides the information you need to take prescription medications safely and effectively. Along with general information on how to read a prescription and how to buy, store, and administer drugs, this publication provides an introduction to the action of drugs—how they work to stop infection, to lower blood pressure, and to relieve pain. It then provides detailed information on hundreds of the most commonly prescribed drugs. Included in the drug profiles is information on how to alleviate certain side effects, whether the drug should be taken on an empty stomach or with meals, whether it is likely to affect your ability to drive, and whether generic equivalents are available for a prescribed trade-name medication. You will discover which side effects are common to some medications and which side effects constitute danger signals that require immediate attention from your physician. Finally, the glossary will help you to sort out medical terms with which you may not be familiar, and the index will make it easy to find terms used throughout this publication.

Of course, *PRESCRIPTION DRUGS* is not a substitute for consulting your doctor, pharmacist, or other health-care provider. They are your primary reference sources on the use of prescription drugs. To assure that you receive the best health care possible, however, you, too, must be informed and knowledgeable about the prescription drugs you use.

Filling Your Prescription

The first step in filling your prescription is reading what your doctor has written.

Reading Your Prescription

You don't have to be a doctor, nurse, or pharmacist to read a prescription. Moreover, as a health-conscious consumer, you *can* and *should* learn how. After all, the prescription identifies the drug you will be taking and describes how you should be taking it. To be sure that the label on the drug container you receive from your pharmacist coincides with the prescription, you should understand what your doctor has written on the prescription form.

Prescriptions may appear to be mysterious, but they're not. They contain no secret messages, though many of the symbols and phrases used on prescriptions are abbreviated Latin words—holdovers from the days when Latin was the language of medicine and doctors actually wrote in Latin. For example, "gtt" comes from the Latin word *guttae,* which means *drops,* and "bid" is a shortened version of *bis in die,* Latin for *twice a day.* By becoming familiar with these abbreviations, you'll be able to understand your prescription.

The table below lists the symbols and abbreviations most commonly used on prescriptions. To become familiar with the table, use it to read the sample prescriptions on the following pages. Then refer to it when you read the prescriptions you receive from your doctor.

Common Abbreviations and Symbols Used in Writing Prescriptions

Abbreviation	Meaning	Derivation and Notes
A_2	both ears	*auris* (Latin)
aa	of each	*ana* (Greek)
ac	before meals	*ante cibum* (Latin)
AD	right ear	*auris dextra* (Latin)
AL	left ear	*auris laeva* (Latin)
AM	morning	*ante meridiem* (Latin)
AS	left ear	*auris sinistra* (Latin)
bid	twice a day	*bis in die* (Latin)
C	100	—
c	with	*cum* (Latin)
Cap	let him take	*capiat* (Latin)
caps	capsule	*capsula* (Latin)
disp	dispense	—
dtd#	give this number	*dentur tales doses* (Latin)

Abbreviation	Meaning	Derivation and Notes
ea	each	—
ext	for external use	—
gtt	drops	*guttae* (Latin)
gt	drop	*gutta* (Latin)
h	hour	*hora* (Latin)
HS	bedtime	*hora somni* (Latin)
M ft	make	*misce fiat* (Latin)
mitt#	give this number	*mitte* (Latin)
ml	milliliter	30 ml equals one ounce
O	pint	*octarius* (Latin)
O_2	both eyes	*oculus* (Latin)
OD	right eye	*oculus dexter* (Latin)
OJ	orange juice	—
OL	left eye	*oculus laevus* (Latin)
OS	left eye	*oculus sinister* (Latin)
OU	each eye	*oculus uterque* (Latin)
pc	after meals	*post cibum* (Latin)
PM	evening	*post meridiem* (Latin)
po	by mouth	*per os* (Latin)
prn	as needed	*pro re nata* (Latin)
q	every	*quaque* (Latin)
qd	once a day	*quaque die* (Latin)
qid	four times a day	*quater in die* (Latin)
qod	every other day	—
s	without	*sine* (Latin)
Sig	label as follows	*signa* (Latin)
sl	under the tongue	*sub lingua* (Latin)
SOB	shortness of breath	—
sol	solution	—
ss	one-half	*semis* (Latin)
stat	at once, first dose	*statim* (Latin)
susp	suspension	—
tab	tablet	—
tid	three times a day	*ter in die* (Latin)
top	apply topically	—
ung or ungt	ointment	*unguentum* (Latin)
UT	under the tongue	—
ut dict	as directed	*ut dictum* (Latin)
x	times	—

The first sample prescription is for Fiorinal analgesic. The prescription tells the pharmacist to give you 24 capsules (#24), and it tells you to take one capsule (caps i) every four hours (q4h) as needed (prn) for pain. The prescription indicates that you may receive five refills (5), that the label on the drug container should state the name of the drug (yes), and that the pharmacist may substitute (substitution) a less expensive equivalent product if one is available.

John D. Jones MD
Anytown, U.S.A.

DEA# 123456789   PHONE# 123-4567

NAME *Your Name*   AGE *47*
ADDRESS *Anytown, U.S.A.*   DATE *5/10/92*

R℞   *Fiorinal*
     #24
     Sig: caps i q̄ 4h prn pain

REFILLS *5x*   DISPENSE AS WRITTEN
LABEL *yes*   *John D. Jones M.D.*
                                   SUBSTITUTION

Look at the second prescription. It states that you will receive 100 (dtd C) tablets of Lanoxin heart drug, 0.125 mg. You will take three tablets at once (iii stat), two (ii) tomorrow morning (AM), and then one (i) every (q) morning (AM) thereafter with (c) orange juice (OJ). You will receive the specific brand noted (dispense as written), rather than a substitute. You may receive refills as needed (prn), and the name of the drug will be on the package (✔).

John D. Jones MD
Anytown, U.S.A.

DEA# 123456789   PHONE# 123-4567

NAME *Your Name*   AGE *55*
ADDRESS *Anytown, U.S.A.*   DATE *5/23/92*

R℞   *Lanoxin 0.125*
     dtd C
     Sig: iii stat, ii tomorrow AM,
     then i q̄ AM c̄ OJ

                             John D. Jones, M.D.
                             DISPENSE AS WRITTEN
REFILLS *prn*
LABEL *✔*
                                   SUBSTITUTION

Remember to compare your prescription with the label on the drug container. If the two are not the same, question your pharmacist. Make doubly sure that you are receiving the right medication and that the instructions for taking it are correct.

Talking to Your Pharmacist

Once you have read the prescription, the directions may seem clear enough, but will they seem clear when you get home? While you're having your prescription filled, you should make sure you understand your dosage schedule, what kinds of precautions to take to prevent or reduce side effects, whether you should restrict your diet or drinking habits while taking the drug, which side effects are expected or un-avoidable, and which side effects indicate the need for a doctor's at-tention. For example, a prescription may state that you are to "take one tablet every four to six hours as needed." But how many tablets can you take each day—four, five, six? The phrase "as needed" is ambiguous, and unless you understand what it means, you don't know how much medication you can take per day. What if your pre-scription instructs you to take "one tablet four times a day"? What does "four times a day" mean? For some antibiotics, it may mean one tablet every six hours around the clock. For other medications, it may mean one tablet in the morning, one at noon, one in the early evening, and one at bedtime. For still others, it may mean one tablet every hour for the first four hours after you get up in the morning. Don't leave the pharmacy without answers to your questions: Understand that you have the right to know about your prescription. Don't hesitate to ask your pharmacist for an explanation of any terms on your prescription that are not clear to you.

Pharmacists constitute a valuable resource in your health-care in-ventory. They should maintain a record of all the prescription drugs you receive in order to detect any possible life-threatening drug inter-actions. Pharmacists will be able to tell you if your therapy may be af-fected by smoking tobacco, eating certain foods, or drinking alcohol. They can tell you what to expect from the medication and about how long you may have to take it. Of course, treatments vary tremendously from one person to another, but you should know whether you are ex-pected to take medication for five to ten days (to treat a mild respira-tory infection, for example), for a few months (perhaps for a a kidney infection), or, possibly, for the rest of your life. Your pharmacist should tell you how many refills you may have and why you need them.

Your pharmacist should advise you of possible side effects and de-scribe the symptoms in terms you can understand. For instance, you should be informed if a drug is likely to cause nausea or drowsiness. The pharmacist should also tell you which side effects require prompt attention from your physician. For example, one of the major side ef-fects from the drug Zyloprim is a blood disorder, and one of the first symptoms of a blood disorder is a sore throat. Accordingly, your phar-macist should alert you to consult with your physician if you develop a sore throat.

Your pharmacist should also explain how and when to take your medicine. Does the liquid need to be shaken well before pouring each dose? Should the tablet be swallowed whole, or can it be crushed? What is the right way to user the oral inhaler? These are questions the pharmacist can answer. Also refer to the section in this book that describes how to administer medication correctly. You should know whether to take the drug before a meal, after a meal, or with a meal. Your pharmacist should explain the meaning of terms like "as needed," "as directed," and "take with fluid." Some medication may be taken with water but not with milk. For other drugs, milk is preferred. The time of day or night at which you take a drug can make an important difference. Keep in mind that the effectiveness of each drug depends on you to follow the directions for its proper use.

Over-the-Counter Drugs

Drugs that can be purchased without a prescription are referred to as over-the-counter (OTC) or nonprescription drugs. They are sold in a wide variety of settings, such as supermarkets and convenience food stores, airports, even service stations, but the largest selection is found on the open shelves of drug stores. No legal requirements or limitations are in effect as to who may buy or sell them. Products sold OTC contain amounts of active ingredients considered to be safe for self-treatment by consumers when labeling instructions are followed.

Many people visit a doctor for ailments that can be treated effectively by taking nonprescription drugs. Actually, prescriptions are sometimes written for such drugs. Your pharmacist will also be able to guide you on the appropriate use of OTC drugs.

If your pharmacist recommends that you not take certain OTC drugs, follow the advice. For one thing, OTC drugs may affect the way your body reacts to prescription drugs you may be taking. As an example, people using tetracycline antibiotic should avoid taking antacids or iron-containing products at the same time; administration of these two medications should be separated by at least two hours. Antacids and iron interfere with the body's absorption of tetracycline, making the antibiotic less effective.

OTC drugs may also compound certain ailments if not used carefully. For example, many cough and cold remedies contain ingredients that can increase blood pressure. If you have high blood pressure, ask your pharmacist to recommend products that will not cause this effect. It is important that your health-care provider is aware of all the medication you take, prescription and nonprescription (OTC) alike.

Generic Drugs

Drugs are given two names: a generic name and a trade name. The generic name of a drug is usually a shortened form of its chemical name. A trade name, on the other hand, is registered, and only the manufacturer who holds the trademark can use the trade name when marketing that drug.

The company that develops a new medication is granted a patent that lasts for seven years. This patent limits the exclusive and legal right to sell the drug during the patent time to the developing company. Once the patent expires, however, other companies may make and sell the drug, using the generic name or a different trade name. Any manufacturer can use the generic name when marketing a drug after the seven-year period. For example, many manufacturers make a drug called tetracycline. But only Lederle Laboratories can call their tetracycline product by the trade name Achromycin, and only E. R. Squibb can use the trade name Sumycin for their tetracycline. Most trade names are easy to remember, are capitalized in print, and usually include the registration symbol (®) when the name appears in advertisements or on a package.

Many people think that drugs with trade names are made by large manufacturers and that generic drugs are made by smaller companies. In fact, a single manufacturer may market large quantities of a drug under a trade name and then sell the base chemical to several other companies. Those companies, in turn, may market the drug under the generic name, their own trade name, or both. The antibiotic ampicillin, for example, is produced by only a few dozen drug companies, yet it is the base for more than two hundred different products.

Generic drugs are usually priced lower than their trademarked equivalents, largely because less money is spent on advertising. Still, generic drugs must meet the stringent, regular inspections of the Food and Drug Administration (FDA). When a generic drug is approved by the FDA it is considered to be equivalent to its trade-name counterpart in terms of its therapeutic value as well as its safety and effectiveness. Although the FDA has stated that there is no evidence to suspect serious differences between trade name and generic drugs, differences have been shown among brands of certain drugs. This is especially true for the various digoxin, nitroglycerin, insulin, and phenytoin products. It is therefore important to discuss the advantages and disadvantages of any particular product with your doctor or pharmacist. In some cases, switching between brands is not advisable.

For many medications, consumers may be able to realize substantial savings with generic alternatives. For example, 100 tablets of Inderal (40 mg) may cost from $40 to $50, while 100 tablets of propranolol, the generic equivalent, may cost between $10 and $20, for a potential saving of 50 percent or more. Similarly, Lasix diuretic (40 mg) costs about $12 for 50 tablets, but the generic equivalent, Furosemide, is roughly half that amount.

All states have some form of substitution law that allows pharmacists to fill prescriptions with the least expensive equivalent product. And in many cases federal and state government health insurance programs will finance or reimburse only cost-effective medication, making generic drugs a desirable alternative. Your doctor can authorize the use of a specific brand by signing on the appropriate line or otherwise noting on the prescription form (see sample) that a particular brand is medically necessary. You should be aware that certain patients can respond in different ways to various equivalent products, and your doctor may have good reasons for being specific. Discuss these matters with your doctor.

Please note that not every drug is available generically, and not every generic is less expensive than its trademarked equivalent. In some cases the generic is more costly. Before filling your prescription, most pharmacists will generally offer you the choice between a drug that carries a trademark and its generic equivalent, if one is available. If you are not offered this option, ask for it. Remember, you are the consumer. Request a price comparison as you would for any other important purchase.

How Much to Buy

Your doctor specifies on a prescription form exactly how much medication you will receive and its form (tablets, capsules, liquid, and so on). If you must take a drug for a long time, however, or if you are very sensitive to drugs, you may want to purchase more or less than the prescribed quantity.

The amount of medication to buy at one time depends on several factors. One of the most basic is the flexibility of your budget. For those who have a comprehensive insurance program, the question is how much the insurance company will pay for each purchase. You must also consider the kind of medication you will be taking. Medication to treat heart disease, high blood pressure, diabetes, or a thyroid condition may be purchased in large quantities without much risk of loss of potency if properly stored. Patients with such chronic conditions take medication for long periods of time, perhaps for the rest of their lives, and they will very likely pay less per dose by purchasing them in large quantities. In other words, a drug that normally costs six cents per tablet may cost only four or five cents per tablet if you buy in quantities of 100 at a time. It is also important to make sure that you have enough medication on hand to cover vacation travel and long holidays. Remember, too, that serious side effects could occur if you miss even a few doses of such drugs as propranolol, prednisone, or Clonidine. Many doctors prescribe just enough medication to last for a single month. If you wish to buy more, check with your pharmacist.

On the other hand, you should understand that pharmacists cannot take back prescription drugs once they have left the pharmacy. Thus, if you have been plagued by annoying side effects or have had allergic reactions to some drugs on initial prescriptions, ask your pharmacist to dispense only enough medication to last a few days or a week. This will allow you to determine whether the drug agrees with you. You may have to pay more per dose by asking for a small amount of the drug, but at least you will be able to protect yourself from paying for a supply of useless medication. Be aware, too, that with some drugs, after you have received part of the intended amount, you cannot receive more without obtaining another prescription. So be sure you can get the remainder of the prescribed amount if the drug does agree with you.

CONSUMER GUIDE®

Storing Your Drugs

If drugs are stored in containers that do not protect them from heat or moisture, they may lose potency. So before you leave the pharmacy, find out how you should store your drug. Most prescription medication can be safely stored at room temperature and out of direct sunlight. Even drugs dispensed in colored bottles or containers that reflect light should be kept out of direct sunlight.

Definitions of Storage Temperatures

Cold	Any temperature less than 46°F (8°C)
Refrigerator	Any cold place where the temperature is between 36°- 46°F (2°- 8°C)
Cool	Any temperature between 46°- 59°F (8°-15°C)
Room temperature	Temperature usually between 59°- 86°F (15°- 30°C)
Excessive heat	Any temperature more than 104°F (40°C)

Some drugs are supposed to be stored in the refrigerator. But if mistakenly kept in the freezer and frozen, then thawed, sugar-coated tablets may crack. Some liquid medications may separate into layers that cannot be remixed.

In contrast, other drugs should not be stored in the refrigerator. Some liquid cough suppressants will thicken as they become cold and will not pour from the bottle. Nitroglycerin tablets are kept in the refrigerator by some people because they believe the drug will be more stable. This is not correct, however: Nitroglycerin should not be stored in the refrigerator.

The bathroom medicine cabinet would seem to be an appropriate place to keep prescription drugs and other medications, and many people use it for that purpose, but it is actually one of the worst places to keep drugs. For one thing, small children can easily climb onto the sink and reach drugs stored in the cabinet above it. For another, the changes in temperature and humidity in the bathroom may adversely affect prescription drugs.

Keep all drugs away from children. Do not keep unused prescription medication. Destroy any leftover medication by flushing it down the toilet or pouring it down the sink; then wash and discard the empty container. Regularly clean out your medicine cabinet and dispose of any drugs that are no longer in use. These drugs can be dangerous for children, and even adults might be tempted to take them in the future if symptoms occur that appear to be similar to a past illness for which the medication was prescribed. Though apparently similar, the new symptoms may not be due to the same disorder at all, and the condition may be complicated by taking the wrong medication.

Administering Medication Correctly

In order to obtain the maximum benefits from your medication, both in terms of health and cost, you must use that medication correctly. Not only can improperly administered medications waste your money and fail to improve your health, they can actually present a threat to your well-being.

Capsules and Tablets

Capsules and tablets are the most common means of packaging drugs, and there are many different types of each. Caplets, for instance, are tablets shaped like capsules so they are easier to swallow than regular tablets. It is worthwhile to be aware of these differences and similarities, since such knowledge may influence the way the various forms are used. For example, chewable tablets must be thoroughly chewed before they are swallowed, while effervescent tablets must first be dissolved in a glass of water.

Sustained-release, controlled-release, or long-acting tablets and capsules are designed to deliver the drug slowly, over a period of time. In most cases, the drugs packaged in these forms must be swallowed whole or the prolonged action will not be obtained, and the risk of potential side effects may increase. Some capsules that contain beads are called sprinkles; they are made to be opened so that the contents can be shaken onto food the way salt and pepper are used. Other capsules are filled with liquid but are designed to be opened so the liquid can be removed from the capsule and administered. Such capsules are useful for children and others who may have trouble swallowing whole capsules.

If you find it difficult to swallow a tablet or capsule, first rinse your mouth with water, or at least wet your mouth. Then place the tablet or capsule on the back of your tongue, take a drink of water, and swallow. Follow with a glass of water to help move the drug down your throat and into your stomach. If, despite these measures, you continue to experience difficulty swallowing tablets or capsules, ask your doctor to prescribe your medication in the form of a liquid or as a chewable tablet.

If you cannot swallow a tablet or capsule because it is too large or because it seems to stick in your throat, you may be able to empty the capsule or crush the tablet with a spoon and mix it with applesauce, soup, or even chocolate syrup, then take it immediately. But BE SURE TO CHECK WITH YOUR PHARMACIST FIRST. Some tablets and capsules must be swallowed whole. Chewing, crushing, or breaking certain tablets or capsules, especially those designed for long action, can change the way they are absorbed and potentially increase the risk of side effects. With other drugs, hard coatings are used to cover an unpleasant taste. If the coating is destroyed, the taste would be unacceptable. Once again, however, be sure to ask your pharmacist if your medication can be taken this way.

Examples of Drugs that
Must Be Swallowed Whole

Cardizem	E-Mycin	Phenergan
Compazine	Entex LA	Procardia
Depakote	Isordil Tembids	Tagamet
Dolobid	Micro-K	Theobid
Elavil	Norpace CR	Valrelease

Examples of Different
Capsule and Tablet Forms

Compazine Spansule	slow release
Dilantin Infatab	chewable tablet
E-Mycin	special coated
K-Lyte	effervescent tablets
Lanoxicaps	liquid filled capsule
Mycostatin	oral troche
Valium	sustained release capsule

Sublingual Tablets

Some drugs, such as nitroglycerin, are prepared as tablets that must be placed under the tongue (sublingually) because they are absorbed into the bloodstream faster this way, and thus they go to work faster. To take a sublingual tablet properly, place it under your tongue, close your mouth, and hold the saliva under your tongue for as long as you can before swallowing, but for at least five minutes. If you have a bitter taste in your mouth after five minutes, the drug has not been completely absorbed. Wait five minutes longer before drinking water. Drinking water too soon may wash the medication into the stomach before it has been absorbed thoroughly.

Ear Drops

Ear drops must be administered so that they fill the ear canal. To administer ear drops properly, tilt the head to one side; this will turn the affected ear upward. Then grasp the earlobe and gently pull it up and back to straighten the ear canal. (When administering ear drops to a child, gently pull the child's earlobe down and back.) Fill the dropper and place the prescribed number of drops—usually a dropperful—in the ear, but be careful to avoid touching the ear canal. The dropper can be easily contaminated by such contact.

Keep the ear tilted upward for five to ten seconds while continuing to hold the earlobe. Then gently insert a small piece of clean cotton into the ear to be sure the drops remain in the ear canal. Do not wash or wipe the dropper after use; replace it in the bottle and tightly close it to keep out moisture.

Before administering the medication, you may warm a bottle of ear drops by rolling it back and forth between your hands to bring the solution to body temperature. Do not place the bottle in boiling water; that might cause the drops to become so hot that they will cause pain when placed in the ear. The boiling water might also loosen the label and could possibly destroy the medication itself.

Eye Drops, Eye Ointments, and Eye Inserts

Eye medications easily and conveniently provide local therapeutic benefit with minimal systemic effects (that is, with minimal effects on other parts of the body, as distinguished from the specific part to which the medication is directly applied). Most eye medications are not absorbed into the bloodstream, so side effects are reduced. Eye medications are available as drops, ointments, or devices such as inserts (described below). Eye ointments are particularly useful for children, who may dilute the solution or drops with tears. Inserts are long acting, thus they avoid the need for frequent doses. Before administering any eye medication, wash your hands.

Some eye drops require that the container be shaken before use. To administer drops or ointments to the eye, sit down and tilt your head back or lie down. Using your thumb and index finger, gently and carefully pull your lower eyelid down to form a pouch.

If you're applying eye drops, place your second or middle finger alongside your nose near the inside corner of your eye and apply gentle pressure to your nose. This will close a duct that drains fluid from the eye. If you don't close this duct, the drops are likely to drain away too soon. Hold the dropper close to the eyelid without touching it. Place the prescribed number of drops into the pouch. Do not place the drops directly on the eyeball; doing so may cause you to blink and lose medication. Close your eye and keep it shut for a few moments. Do not blink or rub the eye. Avoid washing or wiping the dropper before replacing it in the bottle. Tightly close the bottle to keep out moisture. If more than one type of eye drop is to be used, wait at least five minutes before administering any other eye medication.

To administer an ointment to the eye, roll the tube in your hands or simply hold it for a few minutes. This will warm it and make it easier to apply. Then squeeze a one-quarter- to one-half-inch line of ointment into the pouch formed as described in the last paragraph, and close your eye. Roll your eye for one to two minutes to spread the ointment. With a tissue, wipe away any excess ointment around the eye or on the ointment tube. As long as you don't squeeze the ointment directly onto the eyeball, you should feel no stinging or pain. Eye ointments temporarily blur the vision. This is normal and should be expected. If more than one type of eye ointment is to be used, wait at least ten minutes before applying the second type. Eye drops should be applied before eye ointments.

Inserts are placed in the eye sac using a special applicator. The proper way to use and remove an eye insert should be explained by your health-care professional. Inserts are designed to slowly release the drug so that frequent drug applications are not necessary.

Regardless of which medication you use, be sure it is intended for the eye (manufacturers must sterilize all eye medication). Also check the expiration date on the label or container. Do not use a drug product after that date, and never use any eye product that has changed color. If you find particles that weren't in the container when you bought your medication, don't use it.

Liquids

Many types of liquid medications are available. Some liquids are used externally on the skin, or topically; others are placed into the eye, ear, or nose; still others are taken by mouth and either swallowed or used as a mouth rinse, then spit out.

Before taking or using any liquid medication, look at the label to see if there are any specific directions for its use. First, identify how the liquid is administered: Is it taken by mouth, or applied to the skin? Next, check for special instructions, such as shaking the container before measuring the dose. This may be necessary because some liquid products contain particles that settle to the bottom of the container. If you don't shake them well each time, you may not get the correct amount of the active ingredient. Moreover, if not shaken regularly, as the amount of liquid remaining in the container is reduced by use, the drug becomes more concentrated. As a result, you will be getting more of the active ingredient with each dose. The concentration may even reach toxic or harmful levels.

When opening the bottle, point it away from you. Some liquid medications may build up pressure inside the bottle (especially after being shaken). The liquid could spurt out quickly and stain your clothing.

If the medication is intended for application on the skin and intended for a small area, it can be spread with a finger or a cotton-tipped applicator. But never dip cotton-tipped applicators or pieces of cotton or gauze into a container of liquid medication, since any foreign substance could enter the container and contaminate the medication. For larger areas of skin, first pour a small quantity onto a cotton pad or a piece of gauze. Don't use a large piece of cotton or gauze: Larger applicators are likely to absorb more of the liquid than is necessary and result in waste. And don't pour the medication into your cupped hand where it may easily be spilled.

Liquid medications that are to be swallowed must be measured accurately. When your doctor prescribes one teaspoonful of medication, he is thinking of a five-milliliter (ml) medical teaspoon. The teaspoons you have at home may hold anywhere from two milliliters to ten milliliters of liquid. If you use one of these to measure your medication, you may get too little or too much with each dose. Ask your pharmacist for a medical teaspoon or for one of the other plastic devices for accurately measuring liquid medications. Most of these cost only a few cents, and they are well worth their cost to assure accurate dosages. These plastic measuring devices have another advantage: While many children balk at medication taken from an ordinary teaspoon, they seem to enjoy taking it from a "special" spoon.

Nose Drops, Inhalers, and Sprays

Before using nose drops, inhalers, and sprays, gently blow your nose if you can. To administer nose drops, fill the dropper, tilt your head back, and place the prescribed number of drops in your nose. Do not touch the dropper to the nasal membranes. Avoiding contact will prevent contamination of the medicine in the container when the dropper is replaced. Keep your head tilted for five to ten seconds, and inhale gently through the nose two or three times.

Do not tilt your head back when using a nasal spray or inhaler. Instead, tilt your head forward slightly and insert the sprayer into one of your nostrils. Avoid touching the inner nasal membranes, and keep the container in an upright position. Close the other nostril. Then squeeze the canister as you breath in gently through the open nostril. Continue to squeeze the sprayer until you have withdrawn it from your nose: This will prevent nasal mucus and bacteria from entering the plastic bottle and contaminating its contents. Breathe out through your mouth. After you have sprayed the prescribed number of times in one or both nostrils, gently sniff two or three times. Wipe the applicator clean with a tissue or rinse it under cold water if so directed.

Most nose drops and sprays should not be used for more than two or three days at a time unless your doctor has told you otherwise. If they have been prescribed for a longer period, don't administer nose drops or sprays from the same container for more than one week. Bacteria from your nose can easily enter the container and contaminate the solution. Nasal inhalers, on the other hand, are usually used for a longer period of time. Never allow other people to use your nose medication.

Oral Inhalers

Oral aerosol inhalers are used for asthma and other breathing disorders. The proper use of such devices assures that a drug gets deep into the lungs, where it is most effective. The medication is contained in a pressurized canister with a mouthpiece attached. The drug is actually inhaled into the lungs. Have your health-care professional demonstrate the correct way to use the inhaler.

The inhaler must be used properly for maximum benefit. To begin with, take a drink of water to moisten the throat. Shake the canister well immediately before using it. Hold the inhaler about two inches from your open mouth, and tilt your head back slightly. Exhale fully, but don't force it. Now bring the inhaler to your mouth and close your mouth around the mouthpiece. Breathe in deeply and slowly for a period of four to five seconds and at the same time fully depress the top of the canister. After inhaling, hold your breath for five to ten seconds to allow the drug to settle in the lungs. If another inhalation is prescribed, wait two to five minutes before repeating the procedure. After each use, rinse your mouth with water to help prevent dry mouth and hoarseness.

Clean the inhaler under warm running water at least once a day unless it is not used during that day. Because the contents of the inhaler are pressurized, do not store inhalers near heat or open flame.

Rectal Suppositories and Enemas

Drugs are administered rectally to place them at the site of action. They work locally in the intestine and rectum to relieve inflammation of certain intestinal disorders; to lessen the itching, swelling, and pain of hemorrhoids; or as laxatives to ease constipation. Before using a suppository, remove any aluminum wrappings. Rubber finger coverings or disposable rubber gloves may be worn when inserting a suppository, but they are not really necessary unless your fingernails are unusually long or sharp. In extremely hot weather, a suppository may become too soft to handle properly. If this happens, place it inside the refrigerator or in a glass of cool water until it becomes firm. A few minutes is usually sufficient. Manufacturers of many suppositories used in the treatment of hemorrhoids suggest that the suppositories be stored in the refrigerator. Check with your pharmacist.

To insert a suppository, lie on your left side, with the lower leg extended and the upper knee bent, and push the suppository into the rectum as far as is comfortable, pointed end first. An alternative position is to crouch forward on your knees, bringing your knees to your chest. Hold the drug in the rectum for as long as prescribed. You may feel like defecating almost immediately, but lie still until the urge has passed to give the medication a chance to work.

To use an enema, shake the container well and remove the wrapper around the applicator. Lying on your left side, with the lower leg extended and the upper knee bent, gently push the applicator tip of the enema into the rectum, pointed toward the navel. Squeeze the container firmly and steadily to release its contents. Remove the enema and discard the container in an appropriate manner. Hold the drug in the rectum for as long as prescribed.

Throat Lozenges and Troches

Lozenges are made of crystalline sugar; troches are not. Both contain medication that is released in the mouth to soothe a sore throat, reduce coughing, treat laryngitis, or treat a mouth infection. Lozenges and troches must be allowed to dissolve slowly while in the mouth; neither should be chewed. After the lozenge or troche has dissolved, try not to swallow or drink any fluids for at least thirty minutes.

Throat Sprays

To administer a throat spray, open your mouth wide and spray the medication into the throat as far back as possible. Try not to swallow: Hold the spray in your mouth for as long as you can and don't drink any fluids for several minutes. Swallowing a throat spray is not harmful, but if you find that a throat spray upsets your stomach, don't swallow it; just spit it out.

Topical Aerosol Sprays

Many topical items are packaged as pressurized aerosol sprays. They are useful on very tender or hairy areas of the body where it is difficult to apply a cream or ointment, but they usually cost more than the cream or ointment form of the same product.

Before using an aerosol spray, shake the can. Then hold it in an upright position, four to six inches from the skin. Press the nozzle for a few seconds, then release.

Never use an aerosol around the face or eyes. If your doctor tells you to apply such medication to a part of your face, spray it on your hand first, then rub it onto the appropriate area. If you happen to get some in an eye or on a mucous membrane, it can be very painful and may even damage the eye. Aerosol sprays may feel cold when applied. If this sensation bothers you, ask your pharmacist or doctor whether another form of the same product is available.

Topical Ointments, Creams, and Lotions

Most ointments, creams, and lotions have only local effects—that is, they are not absorbed into the bloodstream but affect only the area to which they have been directly applied. Most topical drugs (especially steroid products, such as Lidex and Valisone) should be applied to the skin as thinly as possible. A thin layer is as effective as a thick layer, and some steroid-containing creams and ointments can cause toxic side effects if excessive amounts are applied.

Before applying the medication, clean the affected area, then blot the skin dry and apply the medication as directed. Some drugs are simply rubbed on. Others are gently massaged into the skin until they disappear. You should feel no greasiness after applying a cream or lotion, but after applying an ointment, the skin will feel slightly greasy.

If your doctor has not specified whether you should receive a cream or an ointment, ask for the one you prefer at the pharmacy. Creams are greaseless and will not stain your clothing; they are best to use on the scalp or other hairy areas of the body. If your skin is dry, ask for an ointment; it will help to keep the skin soft.

If your doctor tells you to place a wrap on top of the skin after the drug has been applied, you may use a wrap of transparent plastic film like that used for wrapping food. A wrap will hold the medication close to the skin and help keep the skin moist so the drug can be absorbed. To use a wrap correctly, apply the drug as directed, then simply wrap the area with a layer of transparent plastic film. Be careful to follow your doctor's directions. Do not leave a wrap in place longer than prescribed. If you keep it on too long, more of the drug may be absorbed than is needed, which may cause side effects. Don't use a wrap without your doctor's approval and never use one on an oozing lesion.

Transdermal Patches

Transdermal patches allow for controlled, continuous release of medication. They have become popular because of their convenience and ease of use. Drugs administered as transdermal patches include pain relievers, antismoking drugs, estrogen hormone, and motion-sickness drugs. For best results the patch should be applied to a hairless or clean-shaven area of skin, avoiding scars and wounds. Choose a site (such as the upper arm or chest) that is not subject to excessive movement. Bathing or showering with the patch in place is allowed. And in the event that a patch becomes dislodged, simply discard it and put on a new one. To allow for uninterrupted drug therapy, apply a new patch before removing the old one, if possible. Changing the site of application each time will minimize skin irritation. If redness or irritation develops at the application site, consult your physician. Some people are sensitive to the materials used to make the patches.

Vaginal Medications

Drugs to be administered vaginally are available as ointments, creams, suppositories, tablets, and tampons. Most vaginal products contain complete instructions for use, so read the directions carefully. If questions remain, ask your pharmacist.

To use a vaginal ointment or cream, attach the applicator provided to the top of the tube and squeeze the tube from the bottom until the applicator is completely filled. Unwrap vaginal tablets and suppositories and place them into the applicator provided. Lie on your back with your knees drawn up. Hold the applicator horizontally or pointed slightly downward, and insert it into the vagina as far as it will go comfortably. Depress the plunger to release the medication into the vagina. Withdraw the applicator and wash it in warm, soapy water. Rinse it thoroughly and allow it to dry completely. Once it is dry, return the applicator to its package.

Use the drugs for the full time prescribed, even during your menstrual period. For some medications, the use of a sanitary napkin is recommended to prevent staining undergarments.

Unless your doctor has told you otherwise, do not douche within the two to three weeks prior to or following the use of vaginal tablets or suppositories. Be sure to ask your doctor for specific recommendations on douching.

Coping with Side Effects

Drugs have certain desirable effects, which is precisely why they are taken. These desirable effects are known as the drug's activity or its therapeutic effects. Unfortunately, drugs have undesirable effects as well, which are referred to as side effects or adverse reactions. These effects and reactions can range from minor inconveniences, such as dry mouth or headache, to more serious consequences that amount to life-threatening events.

Common Minor Side Effects

Side Effect	Management
Blurred vision	Avoid operating machinery
Decreased sweating	Avoid working or exercising in the sun; avoid saunas, hot baths, and hot showers
Diarrhea	Drink lots of water; if diarrhea lasts longer than three days, call your doctor
Dizziness	Avoid operating machinery, including automobiles; do not participate in any activity requiring alertness
Drowsiness	Avoid operating machinery, including automobiles; do not participate in any activity requiring alertness
Dry mouth	Suck on candy or ice chips, or use a stick of chewing gum
Dry nose and throat	Use a humidifier or vaporizer
Fluid retention	Avoid adding salt to foods
Headache	Remain quiet; take aspirin or acetaminophen*
Insomnia	Take last dose of the drug earlier in the day*; drink a glass of warm milk at bedtime; ask your doctor about an exercise program
Itching	Take frequent baths or showers, or use wet soaks (apply a cool, damp cloth)
Nasal congestion	If necessary, use nose drops or spray*
Palpitations (mild)	Rest often; avoid tension; do not drink coffee, tea, or cola; stop smoking
Upset stomach	Take the drug with milk or food

Consult your doctor first.

Some side effects are expected and unavoidable, but others may surprise the doctor as well as the patient. Unexpected reactions may be due to a person's individual response to the drug.

Side effects may fall into one of two major groups—those that are obvious and those that can be detected only through laboratory testing. The discussion of side effects from a drug should not be restricted only to those that are easily recognizable; other, less obvious, side effects may also be harmful.

If you realize that a particular side effect is expected from a given drug, you can relax somewhat. Most expected side effects are temporary and need not cause alarm. You'll merely experience discomfort or inconvenience for a short time. For example, you may become drowsy after taking an antihistamine or develop a stuffy nose after taking Hytrin or certain other drugs that lower blood pressure. Of course, if you find minor side effects especially bothersome, you should discuss them with your doctor, who may be able to prescribe another drug or at least assure you that the benefits of the drug far outweigh its side effects. Side effects can sometimes be minimized or eliminated by changing your dosing schedule or taking the drug with meals. Consult your doctor or pharmacist before making such a change.

Some side effects, however, indicate a serious problem—perhaps even a dangerous one. If such side effects appear, consult your doctor immediately. The following discussion should help you determine whether or not your side effects require attention from your physician.

OBVIOUS SIDE EFFECTS

Some side effects are obvious to the patient; others can be discerned only through laboratory testing. We have arranged the following discussion according to the affected system or part of the body.

Circulatory System

Drugs may speed up or slow down the heartbeat. If a drug slows the heartbeat, you may feel drowsy and tired or even dizzy. On the other hand, if a drug accelerates the heartbeat, you will probably experience palpitations (a rapid, pounding heartbeat or thumping in the chest). You may feel as if your heart skips a beat occasionally, and you may develop a headache. For most people, these symptoms do not indicates a serious problem, but if they bother you, consult your doctor. An adjustment in the dosage of the drug may be arranged or another drug may be prescribed.

Some drugs can cause edema, which occurs when fluid from the blood collects outside the blood vessels, causing swelling. Ordinarily, edema is not serious. But if you are steadily gaining weight, have gained more than two or three pounds a week since taking the drug, or experience swelling of the feet, ankles or hands—especially during the end of the day—talk to your doctor. To help prevent fluid retention, limit salt intake; to minimize ankle swelling, when possible, sit with your feet raised.

Examples of Drugs
that May Cause Fluid Retention*

Compazine	Naprosyn	prednisone
Lodine	Norpace	Premarin
Medrol	oral contraceptives	Tolectin

Indicated by a weight gain of two or more pounds a week.

Drugs may increase or decrease blood pressure. When blood pressure increases, you may feel dizzy, have a headache or blurred vision, or hear ringing or buzzing in your ears. On the other hand, when blood pressure decreases, you may feel drowsy and tired. You may also become dizzy and even faint, especially if you rise suddenly from a sitting or reclining position. If you develop any of these symptoms, contact your doctor.

Ear

Although a few drugs may cause loss of hearing if taken in large quantities, hearing loss is uncommon. Drugs that are used to treat problems of the ear may cause dizziness; and many drugs produce tinnitus, a sensation of ringing, buzzing, thumping, or hollowness in the ear. If it persists for more than three days, discuss any problem concerning your hearing or your ears with your doctor.

Eye

Blurred vision is a common side effect from many drugs. Medication such as digitalis (a common heart medication) may cause a halolike image to appear around lighted objects (such as a street or traffic light), and other drugs may cause night blindness. Indocin anti-inflammatory (used in the treatment of arthritis) may cause impaired vision. Klonopin (an anticonvulsant) makes it difficult to accurately judge distance while driving and makes the eyes sensitive to sunlight. While the effects on the eye caused by digitalis and Indocin are dangerous signs of toxicity, the effects caused by Klonopin are to be expected. In any case, if you have difficulty with your vision while taking drugs, contact your doctor.

Gastrointestinal System

The gastrointestinal system includes the mouth, esophagus (the tube between the mouth and stomach), stomach, small and large intestines, and rectum. A side effect can be expected from almost any drug that affects the gastrointestinal system. Many drugs produce dry mouth, mouth sores, difficulty in swallowing, heartburn, nausea, vomiting, diarrhea, constipation, loss of appetite, or abnormal cramping. Other medications cause bloating and gas as well as rectal itching.

Examples of Drugs
that May Cause Ulcers

aspirin	Indocin	Medrol
Dolobid	Lodine	prednisone

Diarrhea can be expected after taking many drugs, some of which can create localized reactions in intestinal tissue. Usually a more rapid rate of contraction occurs, which leads to diarrhea, though usually it is only a temporary condition.

The arrival of diarrhea can also signal a problem, however. For example, some antibiotics may bring on severe diarrhea. When this happens, the intestine may become ulcerated and begin bleeding. If you develop diarrhea while taking antibiotics, contact your doctor.

Diarrhea produced by a drug should be self-limiting; that is, it should stop within three days. During this time do not take any diarrhea remedy; instead, drink liquids to replace the fluid you lose. If diarrhea continues for more than three days, call your doctor.

Examples of Drugs
that May Cause Diarrhea

ampicillin	Indocin	sulfa drugs
Coumadin	Lanoxin	Tagamet
Dyazide	oral contraceptives	tetracycline
erythromycin	penicillins	Zyloprim

As a side effect of drug use, constipation is more common than diarrhea but less serious. Constipation occurs when a drug, such as morphine (which relieves severe pain), slows down the activity of the bowel. It also results when drugs absorb moisture from the bowel, resulting in a loss of moisture from the stool. Further, if a drug acts on the nervous system and decreases nerve impulses to the intestine—an effect produced by a drug such as Inderal antihypertensive—constipation may develop. In any case, constipation produced by a drug may last several days. Try to relieve it by drinking at least eight glasses of water a day, exercising, and eating foods high in fiber and roughage. Do not take laxatives unless your doctor directs you to do so. If constipation lasts for more than three days, call your doctor.

Examples of Drugs
that May Cause Constipation

Ativan	Dyazide	Percodan
Catapres	Inderal	Pravachol
Compazine	Librium	Valium
Dilantin	morphine	

Nervous System

Drugs that act on the nervous system may cause drowsiness or stimulation. If a drug causes drowsiness, you may become dizzy or your coordination may be impaired. If a drug causes stimulation, you may become nervous or have insomnia or tremors. Neither drowsiness nor stimulation is cause for concern for most people. When you are drowsy, however, you should avoid driving and operating potentially dangerous equipment. If possible, take the drug before bedtime so you sleep through these side effects. Some drugs cause throbbing headaches; others produce tingling in the fingers or toes. These symptoms are generally expected and should disappear in a few days to a week. If they don't, call your doctor.

Examples of Drugs that May Cause Dizziness

Ativan	Medrol	oral antidiabetics
Hytrin	Nitro-Bid	Procardia
Keflex	Nitrostat	Tagamet
Klonopin	Norpace	

Respiratory System

Side effects common to the respiratory system include stuffy nose, dry throat, shortness of breath, and slowed breathing. A stuffy nose and dry throat usually disappear within a few days, but you may use nose drops (consult your doctor first), throat lozenges, or a warm salt-water gargle to relieve them. Shortness of breath and coughing are characteristic side effects of some drugs (for example, Inderal antihypertensive and antianginal). Shortness of breath may continue, but it is usually not serious. Barbiturates or drugs that promote sleep may retard breathing. Slowed breathing is to be expected: You should not be concerned as long as your doctor knows about it.

Sexual Function

Many drugs can have an influence on the ability to function sexually for both men and women. The very awareness of potential problems is important in itself because many people are reluctant to talk about sexual difficulties. Some drugs may decrease, or increase, your sexual desire; other drugs may hinder your ability to perform by drug-induced impotence. In most cases the effects on sexual function cease when the dose is decreased or when administration of the drug stops. Antihypertensive drugs used to treat high blood pressure, antidepressant drugs, and antipsychotic drugs are all known to cause sexual difficulties. Problems brought on by one type of high blood pressure medication may not occur if you switch to another drug. Again, consult with your doctor if a problem of this kind arises.

Skin

Skin reactions include rash, swelling, itching, and sweating. Rash, swelling, and itching are signs that you may be allergic to the drug, and a drug allergy usually means that you should stop taking the drug. Be sure to consult your doctor before stopping the medication, however. Some drugs increase sweating; others decrease it. Drugs that decrease sweating may cause problems during hot weather, when the body must sweat to reduce body temperature. Avoid working or exercising in the sun or in a warm, unventilated area. Also avoid saunas, hot tubs, and hot showers.

If you have a minor skin reaction not diagnosed as an allergy, ask your pharmacists to recommend a soothing cream. They may also suggest that you take frequent baths and dust the sensitive area with a suitable powder.

Examples of Drugs
that May Cause a Mild Rash

ampicillin	Dyazide	Prozac
Ativan	Indocin	Tagamet
Compazine	penicillins	Valium

Another type of skin reaction to medication is photosensitivity (or phototoxicity or sun toxicity)—that is, unusual sensitivity to the sun. For example, tetracyclines can cause photosensitivity. If, after taking such a drug, you remain exposed to the sun for even a brief period of time—say 10 or 15 minutes—you may develop a severe sunburn. This doesn't mean that you have to stay indoors while taking these drugs, but you should be fully clothed when outside, and you should use a protective sunscreen while in the sun. Ask your pharmacist to help you choose a protective lotion. Since these drugs may remain in the bloodstream for a time after use, you should continue to follow these precautions for two days after therapy has ended.

Examples of Drugs
that May Cause Photosensitivity

Accutane	hydrochlorothiazide	Retin-A
Bactrim	oral antidiabetics	sulfa drugs
Compazine	Phenergan	tetracycline

SUBTLE SIDE EFFECTS

Some side effects are subtle and difficult to detect. You may not notice any symptoms at all, or what you do notice may seem too minor for concern. In fact, laboratory testing may be necessary to confirm their existence. As a result, drugs known to cause certain subtle side effects will be monitored by your doctor with periodic laboratory tests.

Blood

A great many drugs affect the blood and the circulatory system but do not produce noticeable symptoms for some time. For example, if a drug lowers the level of sugar in the blood (a condition known as hypoglycemia), you may not have any symptoms for several minutes to an hour. If symptoms develop, they may include tiredness, muscular weakness, and perhaps tinnitus (ringing or buzzing in the ears) or palpitations. Low blood levels of potassium produce dry mouth, thirst, and muscle cramps, whereas high blood-potassium levels cause listlessness, mental confusion, tingling of the hands or feet, and irregular heartbeat.

Examples of Drugs
that May Cause Blood Disorders*

Accutane	Elavil	Orinase
Depakote	Nolvadex	steroids
Dyazide	oral contraceptives	sulfa drugs

*Indicated by a sore throat that doesn't go away in one or two days.

Some drugs decrease the number of red blood cells, which carry oxygen and nutrients throughout the body. If you have too few red blood cells, you have anemia: You may appear pale and feel tired, weak, dizzy, and perhaps hungry.

Some drugs decrease the number of white blood cells, which combat bacteria. Having too few white blood cells increases susceptibility to infection and may prolong illness. If a sore throat or a fever develops after you begin taking a drug, and if this condition continues for a few days, you may have an infection with too few white blood cells to fight it. Call your doctor.

Kidneys

If one of the side effects of a drug is to reduce the ability of the kidneys to remove chemicals and other substances from the blood, these substances begin to accumulate in body tissues. Over a period of time, this accumulation may lead to vague symptoms such as itching, swelling, fluid retention, nausea, headache, or weakness. Obvious symptoms, especially pain, are rare.

Liver

Drug-induced liver damage usually occurs because the drug changes the liver's ability to metabolize other substances. Signs of liver toxicity may include muscle aches, jaundice (yellowing of the eyes or skin), weakness, or general body discomfort. Because these effects are general in nature, liver damage may be quite advanced before it is recognized; therefore, periodic tests of liver function are recommended during therapy with certain drugs, especially anticholesterol drugs (hyperlipidemics).

MANAGEMENT OF SIDE EFFECTS

Consult the drug profiles beginning on page 44 to determine whether any side effects you may experience are minor (relatively common and usually not serious) or major (rare, but important signs that something is amiss in your drug therapy). If your side effects are minor, you may be able to compensate for them without much difficulty. (See table on page 22 for suggestions.) If you find minor side effects particularly annoying, however, consult your doctor.

If you experience any major side effects, contact your doctor immediately. Your dosage may need adjustment, or you may have a sensitivity to the drug. Perhaps you should not be taking the drug at all.

Types of Drugs

Prescription drugs fall into a number of categories according to the conditions for which they are prescribed. In the following pages we will provide you with a better understanding of these categories and the types of medications that are prescribed for them. We'll describe the intended actions of drugs and the therapeutic effects you can expect from different types of common medications.

ANTIBACTERIALS

Antibiotics

Antibacterials are used to treat many bacterial infections. Antibiotics, a specific kind of antibacterial, can be derived from molds or produced synthetically. They have the ability to destroy or inhibit the growth of bacteria and fungi, and when used properly they are usually effective in eliminating bacteria. Antibiotics do not counteract viruses, however, and viruses are the major cause of the common cold. Using antibiotics in cold therapy, therefore, is of no help.

To adequately treat an infection, antibiotics must be taken regularly for a specific period of time. If they are not taken for the prescribed period, the infection may not be resolved, and microorganisms resistant to the antibiotic may appear. Such a development would require further therapy. Antibiotics include aminoglycosides, cephalosporins, erythromycins, penicillins (including ampicillin and amoxicillin), quinolones, and tetracyclines.

Antivirals

Antiviral drugs are used to combat virus infections. Over the past few years, new antiviral drugs have been identified to help in the treatment of human immunodeficiency virus (HIV) infections. People who are HIV-positive may go on to develop acquired immunodeficiency syndrome (AIDS) and AIDS-related illness. Antiviral drugs such as Virex and Hivid help to prolong the survival rate and decrease development of infections from AIDS and HIV, but these medications are not cures for AIDS.

The antiviral drug called Zovirax is used in the management of herpes. Zovirax reduces the reproduction of the herpes virus in initial outbreaks, lessens the number of recurring outbreaks, and speeds the healing of herpes blisters. This antiviral drug does not actually cure herpes, however.

Symmetrel and Flumadine are also antiviral drugs. It is not clear exactly how they work, but they are effective in preventing and treating respiratory infections caused by the influenza A virus, commonly known as "the flu".

CONSUMER GUIDE®

Vaccines

Vaccines were used long before antibiotics. A vaccine contains weakened or dead disease-causing microorganisms that activate the body's defense mechanisms to produce a natural immunity against a particular illness, such as polio, measles, or influenza.

Other Anti-Infectives

Another group of drugs commonly used to treat infections, especially infections of the urinary tract, includes the synthetically produced sulfonamides (sulfa drugs) and nitrofurantoins (Macrodantin).

Fungal infections are treated with antifungals, such as Mycostatin, which destroy and prevent the growth of fungi. Drugs called anthelmintics are used to treat worm infestations. A pediculicide is a drug used to treat a person infested with lice, and a scabicide is a preparation used to treat a person with scabies.

ANTINEOPLASTICS

Also referred to as chemotherapeutics, these drugs are used primarily in the treatment of cancer, but they may be used to treat viral illnesses and other immune-related disorders. Without exception, these drugs are extremely toxic and may cause serious side effects. To many patients, however, the benefits of drug therapy far outweigh the risks. Cancer patients may be treated with one or several anticancer drugs at one time. Treatment with more than one drug is called combination chemotherapy and is more effective than treatment with a single drug.

Some of the antineoplastic drugs currently available include methotrexate, cisplatin, interferon, and Nolvadex. Most of these drugs act by disrupting the growth of cells. Others, like interferon, help to boost the immune system response, thus helping the body to fight the illness. If you will be undergoing chemotherapy, it is important that you discuss the use of antineoplastic drugs in detail with your doctor. You should fully understand the medications you will be taking and what you can expect from therapy.

CARDIOVASCULAR DRUGS

Antianginals

The chest pain known as angina occurs when there is an insufficient supply of blood to the heart, and consequently of the oxygen contained in that blood. Antianginal drugs are used to relieve or prevent angina. They allow an increased amount of oxygen to enter certain parts of the heart; they also cause a sudden drop in blood pressure. Nitroglycerin is the most frequently prescribed antianginal. Calcium channel blockers (Isoptin, Calan) are often used to treat angina. They may also be used to lower blood pressure.

Antiarrhythmics

If the heart fails to beat regularly or smoothly (a condition called arrhythmia), its rate of contraction must be regulated. Antiarrhythmic drugs, including Norpace and Pronestyl, prevent or alleviate cardiac arrhythmias. Dilantin (phenytoin), though most frequently used as an anticonvulsant in the treatment of epilepsy, can also act as an antiarrhythmic agent when injected intravenously.

Anticoagulants

Drugs that prevent blood clotting are called anticoagulants, or blood thinners. Anticoagulants fall into two categories: injectable and oral.

The injectable anticoagulants are heparin and enoxaparin. Their use is generally restricted to patients in the hospital.

Oral anticoagulants are principally derivatives of the drug warfarin, which is used to treat conditions such as stroke, heart disease, or abnormal blood clotting. Warfarin is also used to prevent the movement of a clot, a development that could cause serious problems.

People taking warfarin must avoid many other drugs (including aspirin), because interaction with the anticoagulant could cause internal bleeding. In fact, those on warfarin should check with their physician or pharmacist before using any other medications, including over-the-counter products. They must also have their blood checked frequently to ensure that the dose of anticoagulant is appropriate.

Antihyperlipidemics

Antihyperlipidemics are drugs used to reduce the cholesterol and/or triglycerides (fats) in the blood that form plaques on the walls of the arteries. This plaque formation can play a major role in the development of coronary artery disease by narrowing blood vessels and restricting the amount of oxygen-rich blood that reaches the heart. Antihyperlipidemic drugs are generally prescribed only after dietary therapy (usually for a minimum of six months) and lifestyle changes have failed to lower blood cholesterol to a desirable level. And even when cholesterol-lowering drugs are prescribed, dietary therapy must be continued. Periodic blood tests during therapy monitor the drug's effectiveness and prevent side effects. Examples of cholesterol-lowering drugs include Lopid, Mevacor, Pravachol, and Zocor.

Antihypertensives

Briefly stated, high blood pressure, or hypertension, is a condition in which the pressure of the blood against the walls of the blood vessels is higher than what is considered normal. High blood pressure is sometimes controllable with lifestyle changes alone, such as weight loss, increased exercise, reduced salt intake, and limited alcohol intake. When these lifestyle modifications are not enough, however, drug therapy is advised for keeping blood pressure under control and to help prevent other diseases, such as coronary heart disease. Drugs that counteract or reduce high blood pressure can effectively prolong the life of a hypertensive patient.

The actions of several different drugs produce an antihypertensive effect. Some drugs block nerve impulses that cause arteries to constrict; others slow the heart's rate and force of contraction; still others reduce the amount of a certain hormone in the blood that causes blood pressure to rise. Because they vary in how they work and the side effects they can cause, various antihypertensives may have to be tried in order to find the best drug type for an individual patient. Diuretics, beta blockers, vasodilators, and calcium channel blockers are among the types of drugs that may be used to reduce blood pressure. Examples of antihypertensive drugs include Catapres, Dyazide, Hytrin, Inderal, Lopressor, Tenex, and Tenormin.

Beta Blockers

Beta-blocking drugs stop the response to nerve stimulation in order to increase blood flow, slow heart rate, and reduce blood pressure. They are used in the treatment of angina (chest pain), hypertension (high blood pressure), and arrhythmias (irregular heartbeats). Some beta-blockers are also used topically on the eyes of people with glaucoma to reduce pressure there. Propranolol (Inderal) is a beta blocker that may also be used to prevent migraine headache and to treat anxiety and tremors. Atenolol (Tenormin), timolol (Blocadren), and metoprolol (Lopressor) are other examples of beta blockers.

Calcium Channel Blockers

Calcium channel blocking agents affect muscle contraction and nerve impulses in the heart. They dilate (expand) the coronary arteries and inhibit spasms, thus allowing greater amounts of oxygen to reach the heart. This, in turn, reduces angina and hypertension. The slowing of nerve transmission to the heart helps to slow heart rhythm, which relieves arrhythmias. Adalat, Calan, Cardizem, Dynacirc, Isoptin, and Procardia are examples of calcium channel blockers.

Digitalis

The digitalis plant is the source of drugs (Digoxin and Lanoxin) that affect the heart rate, though they are not strictly antiarrhythmics. Digitalis slows the rate of the heart but increases the force of contraction. Thus, digitalis acts as both a heart depressant and stimulant: to regulate erratic heart rhythm or to increase heart output in heart failure.

Diuretics

Diuretic drugs (sometimes referred to as water pills), such as Bumex, Dyazide, hydrochlorothiazide, HydroDIURIL, Lasix, and Lozol, promote the loss of water and salt from the body by increasing the production of urine. They also lower blood pressure by causing blood vessels to expand. Most diuretics act directly on the kidneys, but there are different types of diuretics, each with different actions. Therapy for high blood pressure can therefore be individualized for each patient's specific needs.

Thiazide diuretics are popular because they are generally well tolerated and can be taken once or twice a day. Thiazide diuretics are also effective all day, whereas some diuretics act over a shorter time frame. Patients do not develop a tolerance for the antihypertensive effects of these drugs, so they can be taken for long periods.

A major drawback to thiazide diuretics is that they often deplete potassium. But this depletion can be offset by a potassium supplement, such as K-Lor or Slow-K. Potassium-rich foods and liquids—bananas, apricots, and orange juice—can be used to correct the potassium deficiency; salt substitutes are also sources of potassium. Your doctor will direct you to an appropriate potassium source.

Loop diuretics, such as Bumex or Lasix, act more vigorously than thiazide diuretics. They promote more water loss, but they deplete more potassium as well.

To remove excess water from the body while retaining its store of potassium, manufacturers developed potassium-sparing diuretics, which are effective in the treatment of potassium loss, heart failure, and hypertension. Potassium-sparing diuretics have been combined with thiazide diuretics in medications such as Dyazide. Such combinations enhance the antihypertensive effect and reduce the loss of potassium.

Combinations of an antihypertensive with a diuretic are popular. To be sure of the effects and the dose, each drug should be tried separately before using a combination. Examples of antihypertensive-diuretic combinations are Dyazide, Inderide, Lotensin, Maxzide, and Vaseretic. Combinations like these make it easier for the patient to comply with the treatment since only one medication is taken instead of two separate ones.

Vasodilators

Vasodilating drugs cause the blood vessels to widen. Some vasodilators, such as Apresoline and Lonitenact, act directly on the heart muscle to reduce blood pressure. Other vasodilators, including cyclandate (Cyclospasmol), isoxsuprine (Vasodilan), and nylidrin, are used to treat stroke and diseases characterized by poor circulation.

CENTRAL NERVOUS SYSTEM DRUGS

Analgesics

Pain is not a disease but a symptom. The drugs used to relieve pain are called analgesics. We do not fully understand how most analgesics work: Whether they all act in the brain or some act outside the brain is not known. Because most analgesics are more effective in preventing pain rather than stopping it once it begins, pain relievers are usually prescribed to be taken periodically (typically every four to eight hours) as needed for pain. The phrase "as needed for pain" means that medication should be taken at the first indication that pain will recur. In other words, the time to take your analgesic medicine is as soon as the pain begins: Don't think it is desirable or brave to wait until the pain is already upon you and too intense. Therefore, if your prescription reads, "Every four to six hours as needed for pain," and you know from experience that a single dose lasts for about five hours, don't wait for the full six hours to elapse before administering another dose.

Analgesics may be narcotic or nonnarcotic. Narcotics, which are derived from the opium poppy, are used to relieve moderate to severe pain. They act on the brain to cause deep analgesia, or relief from pain, and often drowsiness. They also produce euphoria—a feeling of well-being. But narcotics can be addictive, especially if abused or as the result of long-term or excessive use. Consequently, narcotics are available by prescription only. Attempts by manufacturers to produce nonaddictive synthetic derivatives of narcotics have failed. Many cough syrups use narcotics such as codeine in low doses because they relieve coughing spasms.

Nonnarcotic pain relievers are used to treat mild to moderate painful conditions. Salicylates are among the most commonly used pain relievers in the United States today, and aspirin is the most widely used salicylate. Aspirin also acts as an analgesic (pain reliever), anti-inflammatory (reduces inflammation) and antipyretic (fever reducer). While aspirin does not require a prescription, many doctors prescribe or recommend it on a regular, long-term basis in nonstandard doses to treat diseases such as arthritis.

Acetaminophen is an aspirin substitute that may be used in place of aspirin in most cases. It cannot relieve inflammation caused by arthritis, however, and it is much more toxic if overdoses are taken.

A number of analgesics contain codeine or other narcotics combined with nonnarcotic analgesics, such as aspirin or acetaminophen. Fiorinal with Codeine, Phenaphen with Codeine, and Lorcet are examples. These analgesics are not as potent as pure narcotics, but frequently they are just as effective. Because these medications contain narcotics, they have the potential of becoming habit-forming. Therefore, they must be used with caution, only for the prescribed condition, and only by the person for whom prescribed.

Anesthetics

Anesthetics are another kind of pain-relieving drug. There are two types: general and local. General anesthetics are administered by a trained anesthesiologist prior to surgery or other painful procedures in order to relax muscles and block feelings. In contrast, local anesthetics are applied directly to a painful area to relieve such localized pain as that caused by toothaches, earaches, and hemorrhoids. Local anesthetics do not relieve major, generalized pain, however, and many people are allergic to them. When given by intravenous or intramuscular injection, some local anesthetics, such as lidocaine, are also useful in the treatment of heart disease because they restore the heartbeat to normal.

Anorectics

Amphetamines are commonly used as anorectics, which are drugs used to reduce the appetite. These drugs quiet the part of the brain that causes hunger, but they also keep people awake, speed up the heart rate, and raise blood pressure. They lose their effectiveness after two to three weeks. Anorectics are also available that do not use amphetamines.

Amphetamines stimulate most people, but they have the opposite effect on hyperkinetic children. Hyperkinesis, or attention deficit disorder (the condition of being highly overactive), is difficult to diagnose and define and must be treated by a specialist. When hyperkinetic children take amphetamines or the stimulant Ritalin, their activity slows down. It is not known why amphetamines affect such children this way. It is most likely that hyperkinetic children are relaxed by selective stimulation of the parts of the brain that ordinarily control levels of activity.

Antianxiety Agents

Antianxiety drugs act in the brain to relieve nervousness and tension. They are mainly used in the management of anxiety and panic disorders, and to treat symptoms of anxiety. Drowsiness is a common side effect. Atarax, BuSpar, Centrax, Librium, Tranxene, Valium, and Xanax are examples of antianxiety drugs.

Anticonvulsants

Drugs such as phenobarbital or Phenytoin can effectively control most symptoms of epilepsy or seizure disorders. They selectively reduce excessive stimulation in the brain, thus reducing the number and intensity of seizures. Many new anticonvulsant drugs (Effexor, Felbalol, and Neurontin) have been introduced in the past year. They are as effective as Phenytoin but are believed to cause fewer side effects.

Antidepressants

Antidepressants are mood-elevating drugs. They act in the brain to change the chemical balance to bring about an improvement in mood.

Many new antidepressant drugs have recently become available, such as Janimine, Prozac, and Tofranil. Although they appear to be tolerated better by most people than older type antidepressants, they are not without serious side effects. In addition to relieving depression, antidepressants such as Prozac are used to treat eating disorders and to affect personalities. Prozac has received a great deal of media attention because of its positive as well as its negative effects.

Tricyclic antidepressants are used for more than just the treatment of depression; they are effective for anxiety, bed-wetting, bulimia, chronic pain, and panic disorder as well. Examples of this type of drug include Aventyl, Elavil, and Tofranil.

Monoamine oxidase inhibitors are effective in relieving symptoms of depression, but they may interact with other drugs or foods. For example, they greatly increase blood pressure when taken with certain kinds of cheese or other foods and beverages that contain the chemical tyramine, so follow any recommended dietary guidelines. Parnate is an example. As a result of these interactions, their use is being limited by newer antidepressants.

Anti-Inflammatories

Inflammation, or swelling, is the body's response to injury; it causes pain, fever, redness, and itching. Common aspirin is one of the most effective anti-inflammatory drugs. Ibuprofen is one of the most popular anti-inflammatory drugs, since it is available without a prescription in low-strength forms. Other drugs—Indocin, Ketoprofen Lodine, Naprosyn, Oruvail, Tolectin, and Toradol—relieve inflammation, but none is more effective than aspirin. Steroids are also used to treat inflammatory diseases.

Gout is one inflammatory disease that can be treated more effectively with other agents, such as probenecid uricosuric, or antigout remedies like colchicine or Zyloprim. Gout is caused by excessive uric acid, which causes swelling and pain in the toes and joints. Probenecid stimulates excretion of the uric acid in urine, colchicine prevents swelling, and Zyloprim decreases the production of uric acid. Both probenecid and Zyloprim guard against attacks of gout; they do not relieve the pain of an attack, as does colchicine.

When sore muscles tense up, they cause pain and inflammation. Skeletal muscle relaxants such as Flexeril can relieve these symptoms. They are often given with an anti-inflammatory drug, such as aspirin. Some doctors believe that aspirin and rest alleviate the pain and inflammation of muscle strain more effectively than do skeletal muscle relaxants.

Antiparkinson Agents

Parkinson's disease is a progressive disease that is due to a chemical imbalance in the brain. Victims of Parkinson's disease have uncontrollable tremors, develop a characteristic stoop, and eventually become unable to walk. Drugs such as levodopa and Sinemet are commonly used to correct the chemical imbalance and thereby relieve the symptoms of the disease, but they may lose effectiveness after five years or so with continued use. Levodopa and carbidopa along with Symmetrel are examples of the other drugs that help relieve Parkinson's symptoms, such as drooling and tremor. Eldepryl is a new drug that is gaining popularity in the treatment of Parkinson's disease because it has been found to help slow down progression of the disease.

Antipsychotics

Antipsychotic agents are also classified as major tranquilizers or psychotherapeutic drugs. These drugs calm certain areas of the brain but permit the rest of the brain to function normally. They act as a screen that allows the transmission of some nerve impulses while restricting others. They are useful in the management of psychotic disorders (mental illness). Haldol, Loxitane, Navane, Permital, Prolixin, and Serentil are among the commonly prescribed antipsychotics.

Sedatives

All drugs used in the treatment of insomnia have a calming effect and cause drowsiness. They selectively reduce activity in the central nervous system; thus they are referred to as central nervous system depressants. These drugs are used as sleep aids for short periods (one to two weeks). Examples of sedatives include Ativan, Halcion, Lorazepam, Q-Pam, and Restoril.

DRUGS FOR THE EARS (OTICS)

For an ear infection, a physician usually prescribes an antibiotic and a steroid—Cortisporin Otic, for example. The antibiotic attacks infecting bacteria, and the steroid reduces inflammation and pain. A local anesthetic such as benzocaine or lidocaine may also be prescribed to relieve pain.

DRUGS FOR THE EYES (OPHTHALMICS)

Almost all drugs that are used to treat eye problems can be used to treat disorders of other parts of the body as well.

Glaucoma is caused by increased pressure within the eyeball and is one of the major disorders of the eye, especially for people past the age of 40. Although sometimes treated surgically, glaucoma often can be resolved—and blindness prevented—through the use of eye drops. Two drops frequently used are epinephrine and pilocarpine. Epinephrine is an adrenergic agent. Drugs with adrenergic properties have actions similar to those of adrenaline, which is secreted in the body when one must flee from danger, resist attack, or combat stress. Adrenaline increases the blood-sugar level, accelerates the heartbeat, and dilates the pupils. Isopto Carpine (pilocarpine) is a cholinergic drug. Such drugs act by stimulating the body's parasympathetic nerve endings (the nerve endings that assist in the control of the heart, lungs, bowels, and eyes). Beta-blocking drugs also reduce intraocular pressure (pressure within the eyeball) and are often used to treat glaucoma.

Antibiotics usually resolve eye infections. Steroids can be used to treat eye inflammations as long as they are not used for too long. Pharmacists carefully monitor requests for eye drop refills—particularly for drops that contain steroids—and may refuse to refill such medication until the patient has revisited the doctor.

Antiallergy eye drops are fairly new to the market. These drugs reduce the itching and tearing of the eye that is associated with seasonal allergies. Livostin and Alomide are examples.

GASTROINTESTINAL DRUGS

Anticholinergics

Anticholinergic drugs slow the action of the bowel and reduce the amount of stomach acid. Because these drugs slow bowel action by relaxing the muscles and relieving spasms, they are said to have an antispasmodic action.

Antidiarrheals

Diarrhea may be caused by many conditions, including influenza and ulcerative colitis, and can sometimes occur as a side effect of drug therapy. Narcotics and anticholinergics are used in the treatment of diarrhea because they slow the action of the bowel. A medication such as Lomotil antidiarrheal combines a narcotic with an anticholinergic.

Antiemetics

Antiemetics prevent or relieve nausea and vomiting. Phenothiazine derivatives such as Compazine have been the mainstay of antiemetic therapy. Compazine is often administered rectally (in suppository form) and usually alleviates acute nausea and vomiting within a few minutes to an hour. Marinol and Zofran are example of new drugs that have recently been introduced to prevent the nausea and vomiting associated with cancer therapy.

Antihistamines are often used to prevent nausea and vomiting, especially when those symptoms are due to motion sickness.

Antiulcer Medications

Antiulcer medications are prescribed to relieve the symptoms and promote the healing of an ulcer. The antisecretory ulcer medications Axid, Pepcid, Tagamet, and Zantac work by suppressing the production of excess stomach acid. Prilosec is a new type of antisecretory drug used to treat ulcers and reflux disease where stomach acid backs up and causes heartburn. Another antiulcer drug, Carafate, works by forming a chemical barrier over an exposed ulcer—rather like a bandage—thus protecting the ulcer from stomach acid. Antacids are also commonly used to help relieve the pain and heartburn associated with ulcers.

HORMONES

A hormone is a substance that is produced and secreted by a gland. Hormones stimulate body functions. Hormone drugs are given to mimic the effects of the hormones naturally produced by the body.

Diabetic Drugs

Insulin, which is secreted by the pancreas, regulates the level of sugar in the blood and the metabolism of carbohydrates and fats.

Insulin's counterpart, glucagon, stimulates the liver to produce glucose, a kind of sugar. Both insulin and glucagon must be present in the right amounts to maintain a proper blood-sugar level in the body.

Treatment of diabetes (a condition in which the body is unable to supply and/or utilize insulin) may involve an adjustment of diet and/or the administration of insulin. Glucagon is given only in an emergency, such as insulin shock, when the blood-sugar level must be raised quickly.

Oral antidiabetic drugs, including Glucotrol, Micronase, and Orinase, induce the pancreas to secrete more insulin. They do this by acting on small groups of cells within the pancreas that make and store insulin. Oral antidiabetics are used by diabetics in addition to a diet program. These drugs cannot be used by insulin-dependent (juvenile-onset) diabetics, who can control their diabetes only with injections of insulin.

Sex Hormones

Sex hormones are produced mainly by the sex glands, though small amounts are also secreted by the adrenal glands. Estrogens (Estrace, Ogen, Premarin) are the female hormones responsible for the secondary sex characteristics, such as the development of the breasts, maintenance of the lining of the uterus, and enlargement of the hips at puberty. Progesterone is produced in females and prepares the uterus for pregnancy. Testosterone (also called androgen) is the corresponding male hormone. It is responsible for secondary sex characteristics, such as beard growth and muscle enlargement.

Testosterone causes retention of protein in the body, thereby producing an increase in muscle size. Anabolic steroids, which are similar to testosterone, are sometimes taken by athletes for this muscle-enhancing effect, but using such drugs is dangerous. In fact, the improper use of anabolic steroids can adversely affect the heart, liver, nervous system, and kidneys. With long-term abuse, death might result. On the other hand, testosterone is given to males therapeutically when the body fails to produce enough naturally for proper growth and development. In females, androgens, or testosterone, are used to treat breast and other cancers. This hormone is used in males when the body does not produce enough for proper growth and development. In females, androgens are used to treat breast cancer.

Most oral contraceptives, or birth control pills, combine estrogen and progesterone, but some contain only progesterone. The estrogen in birth control pills prevents egg production. Progesterone aids in preventing ovulation, alters the lining of the uterus, and thickens cervical mucus—processes that help to prevent conception. Oral contraceptives have many side effects; discuss them thoroughly with a doctor.

Estrace, Ogen, and Premarin estrogen hormones are used to treat symptoms of menopause. Provera progesterone hormone is used for uterine bleeding and menstrual problems.

Steroids

The pituitary gland secretes adrenocorticotropic hormone (ACTH), which directs the adrenal glands to produce glucocorticoids, such as hydrocortisone and other steroids. Steroids have many effects on the body. Two major results are boosting the body's ability to treat illness and helping to fight inflammation. In addition, ACTH may be injected to treat inflammatory diseases.

Oral steroid preparations (for example, Medrol and prednisone) are used in the treatment of a wide variety of illnesses, such as skin conditions, allergic reactions, blood disorders, cancers, and nervous system diseases. They may also be used to treat inflammatory diseases, such as arthritis, and to treat poison ivy, hay fever, and insect bites.

Steroids can even be inhaled through the mouth or nose. Intranasal steroids are used to relieve allergy symptoms, such as a runny nose. Orally inhaled steroids are used to control asthma. As mentioned previously, steroids are also used in the eye to reduce itching, redness, and inflammation due to allergic conditions.

Thyroid Drugs

The thyroid gland secretes thyroid hormone, which helps regulate body metabolism, body temperature, breathing rate, and heart rate. It also affects every organ system of the body. Thyroid hormone was one of the first hormone drugs to be produced synthetically. Originally, thyroid preparations were made by drying the thyroid glands of animals and pulverizing them into tablets. Such preparations are still used today in the treatment of patients who have reduced levels of thyroid hormone production, though a synthetic thyroid hormone (Synthroid) is also available.

Radioactive-iodine therapy and drugs such as propylthiouracil are used to slow down the production of thyroid hormones in patients who have excessive amounts.

RESPIRATORY DRUGS

Allergy Medication

Antihistamines counteract the symptoms of an allergy by blocking the effects of histamine, a chemical released in the body that typically causes swelling and itching. For mild respiratory allergies, such as hay fever, slow-acting oral antihistamines like Seldane can be used. Injectable epinephrine, which is fast-acting, will often be prescribed for severe allergy attacks.

Antitussives

Antitussives are used to suppress a dry, hacking cough. Coughs that help to clear mucous are productive coughs and should not be totally blocked. Dextromethorphan is a nonnarcotic antitussive medication that controls the cough from a cold. Another antitussive drug is the narcotic codeine. In small doses, codeine blocks the cough center of the brain. Most cough drops and syrups must be absorbed into the blood and must circulate through the brain before they act on a cough. Thus they do not coat the throat, as might be assumed, and should be taken with a glass of water.

Bronchodilators

Bronchodilators (agents that relax airways in the lungs) and smooth muscle relaxants (agents that relax smooth muscle tissue, such as the tissue in the lungs) are also used to improve breathing. Theophylline is commonly used to relieve the symptoms of asthma, pulmonary emphysema, and chronic bronchitis. Alupent and Brethine are other popular bronchodilators.

Decongestants

Decongestants constrict the blood vessels in the nose and sinuses in order to open up air passages. Decongestants can be taken by mouth, as nose drops, or in a spray. Oral decongestants are slow-acting but do not interfere with the production of mucus or the movement of the cilia in the respiratory tract. They do increase blood pressure. Many cough, cold, and allergy formulations contain decongestants. Topical decongestants (nose drops or spray) provide almost immediate relief. They do not increase blood pressure as much as oral decongestants, but they do slow the movement of the cilia. People who use these topical products may develop a tolerance for them. Consequently, they should not be used for more than a few days at a time. Entex LA and phenylpropanolamine are decongestants.

Expectorants

Expectorants are used to change a nonproductive cough to a productive one (one that brings up phlegm) and are supposed to increase the amount of mucus brought up. The effectiveness of some expectorants has been questioned, however. Drinking water or using a vaporizer or humidifier may be just as effective in thinning and breaking up mucus. Guaifenesin is a popular OTC expectorant.

TOPICAL DRUGS

Topical drugs are intended to treat problems of the skin. Dry skin is a very common complaint. One method of treatment is to add moisture to the air with a humidifier. Other methods include soaking in water; blotting the skin dry after washing rather than rubbing; and applying a lotion, cream, or oil in order to seal in moisture.

Dermatologic, or skin-related, problems, such as infection or inflammation, are also common ailments. Antibiotics are used to treat skin infections; steroids are used to treat inflammations.

Another common dermatologic problem is acne. Acne is often treated with over-the-counter drugs, but sometimes prescription medications are required. Over-the-counter drugs generally contain agents that open blocked skin pores. Antibiotics, such as the tetracyclines, erythromycin, or clindamycin, are used orally or applied topically to prevent pimple formation. Keratolytics, agents that soften the skin and cause the outer cells to peel off, are also sometimes prescribed. Tretinoin (Retin-A), a skin irritant derived from vitamin A, is also used topically in the treatment of acne.

Isotretinoin, also related to vitamin A, is available in an oral form called Accutane and is used to treat severe cystic acne that has not responded to other treatment.

Topical products are used to treat psoriasis, burns, pain, and many other skin problems. Lotions, creams, ointments, oils, gels, sprays, shampoos, medicated bandages, patches, and powders are some of the forms in which topical products have been made available.

VITAMINS AND MINERALS

Vitamins and minerals are chemical substances vital to the maintenance of normal body functions. Vitamin deficiencies do occur, but most people get enough vitamins and minerals in their diet. Serious nutritional deficiencies, such as pellagra (a disease caused by a lack of a B-complex vitamin) and beriberi (a disease caused by a lack of thiamine), are uncommon these days, but if they appear they must be treated by a physician. People who have an inadequate or restricted diet, those with certain disorders or debilitating illnesses, women who are pregnant or breast-feeding, and some others may benefit from taking supplemental vitamins and minerals. Even these people, however, should consult a doctor to see if a true vitamin deficiency exists.

Drug Profiles

On the following pages are drug profiles for the most commonly prescribed drugs in the United States. These profiles are arranged alphabetically.

A drug profile summarizes the most important information about a particular drug. By studying a drug profile, you will learn what to expect from your medication, when to be concerned about possible side effects, which drugs interact with the drug you are taking, and how to take the drug to achieve its maximum benefit. You may notice that some drugs have longer lists of side effects than do other drugs. This may indicate that one drug has the potential to cause a greater number of side effects than another drug. On the other hand, an extensive listing of possible side effects may simply be a result of the drug having been on the market for a greater length of time and having been used by a greater number of people. In other words, the more people who take a drug and the longer it's been in use, the greater the chance that new side effects will be identified.

Each drug profile includes the following information:

Name. Most of the drugs profiled in this book are listed by trade name; those drugs commonly known or prescribed by their generic names (such as insulin, tetracycline, penicillin) are listed generically. All trade name drugs can be identified by an initial capital letter; generics, by an initial lower-case letter. The chemical or pharmacological class is listed for each drug after its name. To help understand these classifications, refer to the previous chapter, Types of Drugs.

Ingredients. The components of each drug product are itemized. Many drugs contain several active chemical components, all of which are included in this category.

Equivalent Products. Products with the same chemical formulation as the profiled drug, including both trade name and generic drugs, are listed as equivalent products. For more information about generic and equivalent products, see the section on Generic Drugs on page 10.

Dosage Forms. The most common forms (i.e., tablets, capsules, liquid, suppositories) of each profiled drug are listed. Strengths or concentrations are also included.

Uses. This category includes the most important and most common clinical uses for each profiled drug. Your doctor may prescribe a drug for a reason that does not appear in this category. This does not mean that your doctor has made an error. If the use for which you are taking a drug does not appear in this category, and if you have any questions concerning the reason for which the drug was prescribed, consult your doctor.

Minor Side Effects. The most common and least serious reactions to a drug are found in this category. Most of these side effects, if they occur at all, should disappear or subside as your body adjusts to the drug. You should not expect to experience these minor side effects, but if they occur and are particularly annoying, don't hesitate to seek medical advice. For information on coping with these side effects, read the Comments section in the drug profile.

Major Side Effects. Should the reactions listed as Major Side Effects occur, call your doctor. These reactions indicate that something may be going wrong with your drug therapy. You may have developed an allergy to the drug, or some other problem could have developed. If you experience a major side effect, it may be necessary to adjust your dosage or substitute a different medication. Major side effects are less common than minor side effects, and you will probably never experience them; if you do, consult your doctor immediately.

Contraindications. Some drugs are counterproductive when taken by people in certain circumstances or people with specific symptoms and should not be used. These conditions are listed under Contraindications. If the profiled drug has been prescribed for you, yet you have a condition listed in this category, consult your doctor before taking the medication.

Warnings. This category lists the precautions necessary for safe use of the profiled drug. For example, certain conditions, while not contraindicating use of the drug, do demand close monitoring. Pregnant women, children under 12, the elderly, people with liver or kidney disease, and those with heart problems must exercise caution when taking medication. In some cases, these people will have to have frequent lab tests while taking drugs; in other cases, the doctor will monitor dosages carefully. The Warnings category also lists drugs that can interact with the profiled drug. Certain drugs are safe when used alone but may cause serious reactions when taken with other drugs or chemicals, or with certain foods. In this category, you'll also find out whether the profiled drug is likely to affect your ability to drive, whether you are likely to become tolerant to its effects, and whether any laboratory tests are included in the usual course of therapy.

Comments. The information in the Comments section is more general and concerns use of the profiled drug. For example, you'll find out if you can avoid stomach upset by taking the drug with meals or if you can avoid sleeplessness by taking the drug early in the day. You'll find out how to deal with certain side effects, such as dizziness or light-headedness or mouth dryness. You may also find out whether you should take the drug around the clock or only during waking hours. Other information included might concern supplemental therapy, such as wearing an effective sunscreen and protective clothing while taking a drug that increases sensitivity to sunlight. Information about the price of the drug, equivalent products, methods of administering the drug, or special storage requirements may be found in this part of the profile. Never be reluctant to ask your doctor or pharmacist for further information about any drug you are taking.

Accupril antihypertensive

Ingredient: quinapril
Dosage Form: Tablet: 5 mg; 10 mg; 20 mg; 40 mg
Use: Treatment of high blood pressure
Minor Side Effects: Cough; decreased sexual desire; diarrhea; dizziness; fatigue; flushing; headache; insomnia; light-headedness; nasal congestion; nausea; sleep disturbances; stomach upset; sweating; taste disturbances. Most of these side effects, if they occur, should subside as your body adjusts to the medication. Tell your doctor about any that are persistent or particularly bothersome.
Major Side Effects: Blood disorders; blurred vision; breathing difficulties; chest pain; decreased sexual ability; depression; fever; impotence; irregular pulse; itching; low blood pressure; muscle aches or cramps; nervousness; rapid, pounding heartbeat; rash; sore throat; swelling of face, lips, and tongue; tingling in fingers and toes; vomiting. Notify your doctor if you notice any major side effects.
Contraindications: This drug should not be used by any woman who is pregnant, who thinks she is pregnant, or who intends to become pregnant. Use of this drug during pregnancy has resulted in fetal abnormalities. Notify your doctor immediately if you suspect you are pregnant. • This drug should not be used by persons who are allergic to it or to similar drugs such as captopril or lisinopril. Remind your doctor that you have such an allergy if this drug has been prescribed for you.
Warnings: This drug should be used cautiously by nursing mothers, persons with kidney disease, and diabetics. Be sure your doctor knows if any of these conditions applies to you. • Persons taking this drug in conjunction with other antihypertensive or heart medications should use it cautiously, especially during initial therapy. Dosage adjustments may be required to prevent blood pressure from dropping too low. • This drug must be used cautiously with agents that increase serum potassium, such as spironolactone, triamterene, amiloride, potassium supplements, and salt substitutes containing potassium. If you are currently taking any drugs of these types, consult your doctor about their use. Dosages may need to be adjusted. Your doctor may wish to test your blood periodically to check the potassium level. While taking this drug, you should limit your consumption of alcoholic beverages, which can increase dizziness and other side effects. • It is recommended that persons taking this drug for a prolonged period have periodic blood tests to monitor the effects of therapy. • Contact your doctor immediately if you notice swelling of the face, lips, tongue, or eyes, or have breathing difficulties while taking this drug. • If this medication makes you dizzy, avoid driving a car or operating potentially dangerous equipment. • Notify your doctor if you develop signs of an infection (sore throat, fever) while taking this drug. • Notify your doctor if you develop severe or persistent vomiting or diarrhea while taking this drug, since they can lead to dehydration. • If you have high blood pressure, do not take any nonprescription item for weight control, cough, cold, or sinus problems without consulting your doctor or pharmacist; such items can increase blood pressure. • Avoid prolonged work or exercise in hot weather, since excessive sweating can intensify the effects of this drug.
Comments: Take this drug as prescribed. Do not skip doses or take extra doses without consulting your doctor. • This drug may be taken with food if stomach upset occurs. • Do not stop taking this drug without consulting your doctor. It is important to continue taking this medication even if you do not feel sick. Most people with high blood pressure do not have symptoms and do not feel ill; therefore, it is easy to forget to take the medication. • Side effects of this

drug are usually mild and transient. During the first few days you may experience light-headedness, which should subside as therapy continues. If light-headedness continues or becomes more pronounced, contact your doctor. • To avoid dizziness or light-headedness, contract and relax the muscles of your legs for a few moments before rising. Do this by pushing one foot against the floor while raising the other foot slightly, alternating feet so that you are pumping your feet in a pedaling motion. • Learn how to monitor your pulse and blood pressure while taking this drug. As with all antihypertensive medications, they are most effective when used in conjunction with diet and lifestyle changes, such as exercise and stress reduction to control blood pressure. The medication does not cure high blood pressure.

Accurbron bronchodilator, see theophylline bronchodilator.

Accutane acne preparation

Ingredient: isotretinoin (13-*cis*-retinoic acid)
Dosage Form: Capsule: 10 mg; 20 mg; 40 mg
Use: Treatment of severe cystic acne
Minor Side Effects: Changes in skin color; conjunctivitis; dry lips, nose, and mouth; fatigue; flushing; increased susceptibility to herpes simplex virus; increased susceptibility to sunburn; indigestion; inflammation of lips; muscle pain and stiffness; peeling of palms and soles; rash; swelling; thinning of hair. Most of these side effects, if they occur, should subside as your body adjusts to the medication. Tell your doctor about any side effects you experience that are persistent or particularly bothersome.

Major Side Effects: Abdominal pain; black stools; bruising; burning or tingling sensation of the skin; changes in the menstrual cycle; dizziness; headache; hives; increased susceptibility to bone changes; nausea; respiratory infections; severe diarrhea; skin infection; visual disturbances; vomiting; weight loss. Notify your doctor if you notice any major side effects.

Contraindications: This drug should not be used by any woman who is pregnant, who thinks she is pregnant, or who intends to become pregnant. Use of this drug in any amount for even short periods during pregnancy is associated with an extremely high risk of fetal abnormalities and spontaneous abortion. Women of childbearing age should use contraception during therapy with this drug; use of contraception should begin one month prior to starting therapy and should not be discontinued until one month after therapy is completed. Notify your doctor immediately if you suspect that you are pregnant. • You should receive both oral instructions and a patient information sheet with this drug; you may also be asked to sign a consent form prior to therapy. • This drug should not be used by women who are breast-feeding. Be sure your doctor knows if you are breast-feeding a baby. • This drug should not be used by people who are allergic to parabens (preservative). Consult your doctor immediately if this drug has been prescribed for you and any of these conditions applies to you.

Warnings: This drug may increase blood fat levels (triglycerides, lipoproteins), especially in overweight or diabetic persons, in persons with increased alcohol intake, and in persons with a family history of high blood fat levels. • Avoid alcohol consumption while taking this drug. Some persons have had trouble controlling their blood sugar while taking this medication. Diabetics should monitor their blood sugar levels closely. • This drug may cause sun sensitivity. Avoid sun exposure, and use an effective sunscreen. • Do not take vitamin A supplements while taking Accutane. • Inform your doctor if you wear contact lenses. This drug may reduce your tolerance to them. • This drug may interfere with blood transfusions. If you give or receive blood, tell your doctor you are taking this drug. It is recommended that you not donate blood until at least 30 days after stopping Accutane therapy. • This drug may affect the results of blood and urine tests. If you are scheduled to have any such tests, remind your doctor that you are taking this drug.

Comments: This drug is most effective when taken with meals. • Do not crush or chew the capsules. • During treatment, there may be an apparent increase in skin lesions with crusting, especially during the first few weeks. This is usually not a reason to discontinue its use. • This drug is usually used only after other acne treatments have failed. • Store this medication away from light.

acetaminophen with codeine analgesic

Ingredients: acetaminophen; codeine phosphate
Equivalent Products: Aceta with Codeine; Capital with Codeine; Margesic; Phenaphen with Codeine; Tylenol with Codeine
Dosage Forms: Capsule (various dosages; see Comments). Liquid (content per 5 ml teaspoon): acetaminophen, 120 mg and codeine, 12 mg. Tablet (various dosages; see Comments)
Use: Symptomatic relief of mild to severe pain, depending on strength
Minor Side Effects: Blurred vision; constipation; dizziness; drowsiness; dry mouth; flushing; light-headedness; loss of appetite; nausea; sweating; vomiting. Most of these side effects, if they occur, should subside as your body adjusts to the drug. Tell your doctor about any that are persistent or bothersome.
Major Side Effects: Anxiety; bleeding or bruising; breathing difficulties; dark urine; difficulty in urinating; excitation; false sense of well-being; fatigue; light-colored stools; low blood sugar; palpitations; rapid or slow heartbeat; rash; restlessness; sore throat; weakness; yellowing of the eyes or skin. Notify your doctor if you notice any major side effects.
Contraindication: This drug should not be taken by people who are allergic to either acetaminophen or narcotic pain relievers. Consult your doctor immediately if this drug has been prescribed for you and you have such an allergy.
Warnings: This drug should be used cautiously by children under 12; by the elderly; by people who have heart or lung disease, blood disorders, asthma or other respiratory problems, epilepsy, head injuries, liver or kidney disease, colitis, gallbladder disease, thyroid disease, acute abdominal conditions, or prostate disease; and by pregnant or nursing women. Be sure your doctor knows if any of these conditions applies to you. • This drug may cause drowsiness; avoid tasks that require alertness, such as driving a car or operating potentially dangerous equipment. • To prevent oversedation, avoid the use of alcohol or other drugs that have sedative properties. • Because this product contains codeine, a narcotic analgesic, it has the potential for abuse and must be used with caution. It usually should not be taken for more than ten days. Tolerance may develop quickly; do not increase the dose without consulting your doctor. • Notify your doctor if you develop signs of jaundice (yellowing of the eyes or skin, dark urine). • Avoid use of any other drugs that contain acetaminophen, codeine, or other narcotics. If you have any questions about the contents of your medications, consult your doctor or pharmacist.
Comments: Side effects caused by this drug may be somewhat relieved by lying down. • This medication may be taken with food if stomach upset occurs. • Eat a high-fiber diet, and drink plenty of water to prevent constipation. This medication is more effective in preventing pain than treating it once it occurs. • The name of this drug is often followed by a number that refers to the amount of codeine prescribed. Hence #1 contains 1/8 grain (gr) or 7.5 mg codeine; #2 has 1/4 gr (15 mg); #3 has 1/2 gr (30 mg); #4 contains 1 gr (60 mg) codeine.

acetaminophen with oxycodone analgesic, see Percocet analgesic.

Aceta with Codeine analgesic, see acetaminophen with codeine analgesic.

Achromycin V antibiotic, see tetracycline hydrochloride antibiotic.

Adalat antihypertensive and antianginal, see Procardia, Procardia XL antihypertensive and antianginal.

Adsorbocarpine ophthalmic glaucoma preparation, see Isopto Carpine ophthalmic glaucoma preparation.

Aerolate bronchodilator, see theophylline bronchodilator.

Akarpine ophthalmic glaucoma preparation, see Isopto Carpine ophthalmic glaucoma preparation.

AK-Spore H.C. ophthalmic steroid and antibiotic, see Cortisporin ophthalmic steroid and antibiotic.

AK-Spore H.C. Otic steroid and antibiotic, see Cortisporin Otic steroid and antibiotic.

AK-Spore ophthalmic antibiotic, see Neosporin ophthalmic antibiotic.

Ala-Tet antibiotic, see tetracycline hydrochloride antibiotic.

Albuterol bronchodilator, see Ventolin broncholidator.

Aleve anti-inflammatory, see Naprosyn anti-inflammatory.

Allopurinol antigout drug, see Zyloprim antigout drug.

Alprazolam antianxiety, see Xanax antianxiety.

Alupent bronchodilator

Ingredient: metaproterenol sulfate
Equivalent Products: Arm-a-Med; Metaprel
Dosage Forms: Inhaler (metered dose). Oral syrup (content per 5 ml teaspoon): 10 mg. Solution for inhalation: 0.4%; 0.6%; 5%. Tablet: 10 mg; 20 mg
Use: For symptomatic treatment of asthma and bronchospasm associated with bronchitis or emphysema
Minor Side Effects: Bad taste in mouth; dry mouth and throat; fear; flushing; headache; hoarseness; insomnia; nausea; nervousness; restlessness; sweating; tension; trembling; vomiting; weakness. Most of these side effects, if they occur, should subside as your body adjusts to the medication. Tell your doctor about any that are persistent or particularly bothersome.
Major Side Effects: Breathing difficulties; chest pain; confusion; difficulty in urinating; dizziness; muscle cramps; palpitations. Notify your doctor if you notice any major side effects.
Contraindications: This drug should not be used by persons allergic to it or by persons with heart arrhythmias. Consult your doctor if this drug has been prescribed for you and you have either of these conditions.

Warnings: This drug must be used with caution by diabetics; by persons with high blood pressure, certain types of heart disease, glaucoma, enlarged prostate, or hyperthyroidism; and by pregnant or nursing women. Be sure your doctor knows if any of these conditions applies to you. • The inhaler forms of this drug should not be used by children under 12 years of age. The tablet form of this drug is not recommended for children under six years of age. • This drug has been shown to interact with monamine oxidase inhibitor antidepressants, antihistamines, beta blockers, and anesthetics. If you are currently taking any of these drugs, consult your doctor about their use. If you are unsure about the type or contents of your medications, ask your doctor or pharmacist. While taking this drug, do not take any nonprescription item for cough, cold, or sinus problems without first checking with your doctor; these items may contain a sympathomimetic amine (a decongestant, for example), which can cause additive side effects with this medication. • Prolonged or excessive use of this drug may reduce its effectiveness. Take this drug as prescribed. Do not take it more often than prescribed, increase your dose, or stop taking it without first consulting your physician. It may be necessary to temporarily stop using this drug for a short period to ensure its effectiveness. • If your symptoms do not improve, or if they worsen while taking this drug, or if dizziness or chest pain develops, contact your doctor.

Comments: Make sure you know how to use the inhaler properly. Ask your pharmacist for a demonstration and a patient instruction sheet. In addition, check the section entitled Administering Medications Correctly in this book to ensure that you are using the inhaler properly. • If more than one inhalation is prescribed, wait at least ten minutes between inhalations for maximum effectiveness. • If stomach upset occurs while taking the tablets or solution, take the drug with food or milk. • To help relieve dry mouth, chew gum or suck on ice chips or hard candy. • Do not use the solution for inhalation if it has turned brown in color. • Store the inhaler away from heat and open flame. Do not puncture, break, or burn the container. The 5 ml inhaler contains approximately 100 doses and the 10 ml canister approximately 200 doses. It is best not to change from one brand of the inhaler to another without consulting your doctor or pharmacist.

Amacodone analgesic, see Vicodin, Vicodin ES analgesics.

Amantadine HCl antiviral and antiparkinson, see Symmetrel antiviral and antiparkinson.

Amen progesterone hormone, see Provera progesterone hormone.

Ami-Tex LA decongestant and expectorant, see Entex LA decongestant and expectorant.

amitriptyline antidepressant

Ingredient: amitriptyline hydrochloride
Equivalent Products: Elavil; Endep
Dosage Form: Tablet: 10 mg; 25 mg; 50 mg; 75 mg; 100 mg; 150 mg
Uses: Relief of depression. This drug may also be used in the treatment of bulimia, migraine or cluster headache, or chronic pain syndromes.
Minor Side Effects: Agitation; anxiety; blurred vision; constipation; cramps; diarrhea; dizziness; drowsiness; dry mouth; fatigue; headache; heartburn; increased sensitivity to light; insomnia; loss of appetite; nausea; peculiar tastes; restlessness; vomiting; weakness; weight gain or loss. Most of these side ef-

fects, if they occur, should subside as your body adjusts to the medication. Notify your doctor in the event that any side effects appear that are persistent or particularly bothersome.

Major Side Effects: Chest pain; confusion; convulsions; dark urine; delusions; difficulty in urinating; enlarged or painful breasts (in both sexes); fainting; fever; fluid retention; hair loss; hallucinations; high or low blood pressure; imbalance; impotence; incoordination; mood changes; mouth sores; muscle stiffness; nervousness; nightmares; numbness in fingers or toes; palpitations; problems concentrating; rapid pulse; ringing in the ears; seizures; skin rash; sleep disorders; sore throat; sweating; tremors; unusual bleeding or bruising; yellowing of the eyes or skin. Notify your doctor if you develop any major side effects.

Contraindications: This drug should not be taken by people who are allergic to it, by those who have had a heart attack, or by those who are taking monoamine oxidase inhibitors (ask your pharmacist if you are unsure of the contents of your medications). Consult your doctor immediately if this drug has been prescribed for you and any of these conditions applies. This drug is not recommended for use by children under age 12.

Warnings: This drug should be used cautiously by pregnant or nursing women and by people with glaucoma (certain types), heart disease (certain types), high blood pressure, enlarged prostate, epilepsy, urine retention, liver disease, asthma, kidney disease, alcoholism, or hyperthyroidism. Be sure your doctor knows if any of these conditions applies to you. • Elderly persons should use this drug with caution because they are more sensitive to its effects. • This drug should be used cautiously by patients who are receiving electroshock therapy or by those who are about to undergo surgery. • This drug interacts with alcohol, antihypertensives, amphetamine, barbiturates, cimetidine, clonidine, epinephrine, monoamine oxidase inhibitors, oral anticoagulants, phenylephrine, and depressants; if you are currently taking any drugs of these types, consult your doctor about their use. If you are unsure of the type or contents of your medications, ask your doctor or pharmacist. • To prevent oversedation, avoid the use of alcohol or other drugs that have sedative properties. • While taking this drug, do not take any nonprescription item for weight control, cough, cold, or sinus problems without first checking with your doctor. Be sure your doctor is aware of every medication you use; do not stop or start any other drug without your doctor's approval. • This drug may cause changes in blood sugar levels. Diabetics should monitor their blood sugar levels more frequently when first taking this medication. • This drug may cause drowsiness; avoid tasks that require alertness, such as driving a car or operating potentially dangerous equipment. • Report any sudden mood changes to your doctor. • Notify your doctor if you develop signs of jaundice (yellowish discoloration of the eyes or skin, dark urine) or if you experience incoordination, muscle stiffness, or difficulty urinating.

Comments: Take this medicine exactly as your doctor prescribes. Do not stop taking it without first checking with your doctor. • This drug may cause the urine to turn blue-green; this is harmless. • The effects of therapy with this drug may not be apparent for two to four weeks. Your doctor may adjust your dosage frequently during the first few months of therapy to find the dose best for you. • Chew gum or suck on ice chips or a piece of hard candy to reduce mouth dryness. • This drug causes increased sensitivity to sunlight. Avoid long exposure to the sun, and wear protective clothing and an effective sunscreen while taking this drug. • To avoid dizziness or light-headedness when you stand, contract and relax the muscles of your legs for a few moments before rising. Do this by pushing one foot against the floor while raising the other foot slightly, alternating feet so that you are pumping your legs in a pedaling motion. • Many people receive as much benefit from taking a single dose of this drug at bedtime as from taking multiple doses throughout the day. Talk to your doctor about this. • This drug is very similar in action to other tricyclic antidepressants (desipramine, imipramine). If one of these antidepressants is ineffective or not well tolerated, your doctor may want you to try one of the others to find the one best for you.

amoxicillin antibiotic

Ingredient: amoxicillin
Equivalent Products: Amoxil; Biomox; Polymox; Trimox 250; Trimox 500; Utimox; Wymox
Dosage Forms: Capsule: 250 mg; 500 mg. Chewable tablet: 125 mg; 250 mg. Drop (content per ml): 50 mg. Oral suspension (content per 5 ml teaspoon): 125 mg; 250 mg
Use: Treatment of a wide variety of bacterial infections
Minor Side Effects: Diarrhea; gas; loss of appetite; nausea. Most of these side effects, if they occur, should subside as your body adjusts to the drug. Tell your doctor about any minor side effects that are persistent or particularly bothersome.
Major Side Effects: Abdominal pain; black tongue; breathing difficulties; fever; joint pain; mouth sores; rash; rectal and vaginal itching; severe diarrhea; sore throat; superinfection; unusual bleeding or bruising; vomiting. Notify your doctor if you notice any major side effects.
Contraindication: This drug should not be taken by people who are allergic to penicillin-type drugs or cephalosporin antibiotics. Consult your doctor immediately if this drug has been prescribed for you and you have such an allergy.
Warnings: This drug should be used cautiously by pregnant or nursing women and by people who have kidney or liver disease, asthma, severe hay fever, or other significant allergies. Be sure your doctor knows if you have any of these conditions. • Complete blood cell counts and liver and kidney function tests are advisable if you take this drug for a prolonged period of time. • This drug should not be used in conjunction with allopurinol, chloramphenicol, erythromycin, or tetracycline; if you are currently taking any drugs of these types, consult your doctor about their use. If you are unsure of the contents of your medications, ask your doctor or pharmacist. • Severe allergic reactions to this drug (indicated by breathing difficulties and a drop in blood pressure) have been reported with the injectable form but are rare when the drug is taken orally. Notify your doctor if a rash develops. • Prolonged use of this drug may allow uncontrolled growth of organisms that are not susceptible to it. Do not use this drug unless your doctor has specifically told you to do so. Be sure to follow directions carefully and report any unusual reactions to your doctor at once. • In some women, use of certain antibiotics can cause vaginal yeast infections. Contact your doctor if vaginal itching occurs while taking this drug. • This drug may affect the potency of oral contraceptives. Consult your doctor about using supplementary contraceptive measures while you are taking this drug. • Diabetics using Clinitest urine test may get a false reading while taking this drug. Change to Clinistix, Diastix, Chemstrip UG, or Tes-Tape urine test.
Comments: Amoxicillin can be taken either on an empty stomach or with food or milk (in order to prevent stomach upset). • Finish all of the medication, even if you begin to feel better. Stopping therapy too soon may lead to reinfection. • This medication works best if a constant level of the drug is kept in the body. To do this, take each dose as prescribed at evenly spaced intervals around the clock. Your doctor or pharmacist can help you establish a dosing schedule. • The liquid form of this drug should be stored in the refrigerator.

Shake well before using. Discard any unused portion after 14 days. • This drug is similar in nature to penicillin and ampicillin.

Amoxil antibiotic, see amoxicillin antibiotic.

ampicillin antibiotic

Ingredient: ampicillin

Equivalent Products: D-Amp; Marcillin; Omnipen; Polycillin; Principen; Totacillin

Dosage Forms: Capsule: 250 mg; 500 mg. Oral suspension (content per 5 ml teaspoon): 100 mg; 125 mg; 250 mg; 500 mg

Use: Treatment of a wide variety of bacterial infections

Minor Side Effects: Diarrhea; gas; loss of appetite; nausea. Most of these side effects, if they occur, should subside as your body adjusts to the medication. Tell your doctor about any that are persistent or particularly bothersome.

Major Side Effects: Abdominal pain; black tongue; breathing difficulties; bruising; cough; fever; mouth irritation; rash; rectal and vaginal itching; severe diarrhea; sore throat; superinfection; vomiting. Notify your doctor if you notice any major side effects.

Contraindication: This drug should not be taken by people who are allergic to penicillin-type drugs or cephalosporin antibiotics. Consult your doctor immediately if this drug has been prescribed for you and you have such an allergy.

Warnings: This drug should be used cautiously by pregnant women and by people who have liver or kidney disease, mononucleosis, asthma, severe hay fever, or other significant allergies. Be sure your doctor knows if any of these conditions applies to you. • This drug should not be used in conjunction with allopurinol, chloramphenicol, erythromycin, or tetracycline; if you are currently taking any of these drugs, consult your doctor about their use. If you are unsure about the contents of your medication, ask your doctor or pharmacist. • Complete blood cell counts and liver and kidney function tests are advisable if you take this drug for an extended period of time. • Severe allergic reactions to this drug (indicated by breathing difficulties and a drop in blood pressure) have been reported with the injectable form but are rare when this drug is taken orally. Notify your doctor if a rash develops. • Prolonged use of this drug may allow uncontrolled growth of organisms that are not susceptible to it. Do not use this drug unless your doctor has specifically told you to do so. Be sure to follow directions carefully and report any unusual reactions to your doctor at once. • In some women, use of certain antibiotics can cause vaginal yeast infections. Contact your doctor if vaginal itching occurs while taking this drug. • This drug may affect the potency of oral contraceptives. Consult your doctor about using supplementary contraceptive measures while you are taking this drug. • Diabetics using Clinitest urine test may get a false high sugar reading while taking this drug. Change to Clinistix, Diastix, Chemstrip UG, or Tes-Tape urine test to avoid this problem.

Comments: Take the drug on an empty stomach (one hour before or two hours after a meal). • Finish all the medication, even if you begin to feel better. Stopping therapy too soon may lead to reinfection. • This medication works best if a constant level of the drug is kept in the body. To do this, take each dose as prescribed at evenly spaced intervals around the clock. Your doctor or pharmacist can help you establish a dosing schedule. • The liquid form of this drug should be stored in the refrigerator. Shake well before using. Any unused portion should be discarded after 14 days. • This drug should be taken as long as prescribed, even if symptoms disappear. • This drug is similar in nature and action to penicillin and amoxicillin.

Analpram-HC topical steroid and anesthetic, see Pramosone topical steroid and anesthetic.

Anaprox anti-inflammatory, see Naprosyn anti-inflammatory.

Anexsia analgesic, see Vicodin, Vicodin ES analgesics.

Anodynos-DHC analgesic, see Vicodin, Vicodin ES analgesics.

Ansaid anti-inflammatory

Ingredient: flurbiprofen
Dosage Form: Tablet: 50 mg; 100 mg
Use: Relief of pain and swelling due to arthritis
Minor Side Effects: Bloating; blurred vision; constipation; diarrhea; dizziness; drowsiness; gas; headache; heartburn; insomnia; nausea; nervousness; stomach upset; vomiting; weakness. Most of these side effects, if they occur, should subside as your body adjusts to the medication. Tell your doctor about any that are persistent or particularly bothersome.
Major Side Effects: Black or tarry stools; breathing difficulties; chest pain; depression; difficulty urinating; easy bruising or bleeding; fluid retention; itching; rapid weight gain; rash; ringing in the ears; sore throat; swelling of the hands or feet, especially at night; ulcers; visual disturbances. Notify your doctor if you notice any major side effects.
Contraindications: This drug should not be taken by people who are allergic to it or to aspirin or similar drugs. Consult your doctor immediately if this drug has been prescribed for you and you have such an allergy.
Warnings: This drug should be used with extreme caution by patients with upper gastrointestinal tract disease, peptic ulcer, heart disease (certain types), high blood pressure, kidney disease, or bleeding diseases. Be sure your doctor knows if any of these conditions applies to you. • Use of this drug by pregnant women, nursing mothers, and children under two years of age is not recommended. • This drug should be used cautiously in conjunction with aspirin, diuretics, oral anticoagulants, oral antidiabetics, phenytoin, and probenecid. If you are currently taking any drugs of these types, consult your doctor. If you are unsure of the type or contents of your medications, ask your doctor or pharmacist. • Do not take aspirin or alcohol while taking this drug without first consulting your doctor. • This drug may cause drowsiness; avoid tasks that require alertness, such as driving a car or operating potentially dangerous equipment. • Notify your doctor if skin rash; itching; black, tarry stools; swelling of the hands or feet; or persistent headache occur. • Persons taking this drug for prolonged periods should have regular eye examinations.
Comments: If this drug upsets your stomach, take it with food, milk, or antacids. • You should note improvement of your condition soon after you start using this drug; however, full benefit may not be obtained for one to two weeks. It is important not to stop taking this drug even though symptoms have diminished or disappeared. Do not take it only when you feel pain. Its benefit is based on continued, regular use. • This drug is not a substitute for rest, physical therapy, or other measures recommended by your doctor to treat your condition. • This drug is similar in action to other anti-inflammatory agents, such as Indocin, Naprosyn, Lodine, and ibuprofen. If one of these drugs is not well tolerated, your doctor may have you try the others to find the best drug for you.

Antibiotic ear solution otic steroid and antibiotic, see Cortisparin Otic steroid and antibiotic.

AntibiOtic steroid and antibiotic, see Cortisporin Otic steroid and antibiotic.

Antivert antiemetic

Ingredient: meclizine hydrochloride
Equivalent Products: Antrizine; Bonine; Meclizine HCl; Meni-D; Ru-Vert-M; see Comments
Dosage Forms: Chewable tablet: 25 mg. Tablet: 12.5 mg; 25 mg; 50 mg
Uses: To provide symptomatic relief of dizziness due to ear infections, to prevent or relieve dizziness and nausea due to motion sickness
Minor Side Effects: Blurred vision; drowsiness; dry mouth; headache; insomnia; loss of appetite; nervousness; restlessness; ringing in the ears; upset stomach. Most of these side effects, if they occur, should subside as your body adjusts to the medication. Tell your doctor about any that are persistent or particularly bothersome.
Major Side Effects: Breathing difficulties; double vision; fever; painful urination; palpitations; rapid heart rate; skin rash; sore throat. Notify your doctor if you notice any major side effects.
Contraindications: This drug should be used by pregnant or nursing women only when clearly necessary. If you are pregnant or nursing, discuss the use of this drug with your doctor or pharmacist. • This drug should not be taken by people who are allergic to it. Consult your doctor immediately if this drug has been prescribed for you and you have such an allergy. • This drug is not recommended for use by children under 12.
Warnings: This drug should be used cautiously by people with asthma, glaucoma, heart rhythm disorder, stomach ulcer, urinary tract blockage, or prostate trouble. Be sure your doctor knows if you have any of these conditions. • This drug may cause drowsiness. Avoid tasks that require alertness, such as driving a car or operating potentially dangerous equipment. • To prevent oversedation, avoid the use of other sedative drugs or alcohol.
Comments: When used for motion sickness, this drug should be taken thirty minutes to one hour before travel, then once every 24 hours during travel. • Chew gum or suck on ice chips or a piece of hard candy to reduce mouth dryness. • Although most brands of this drug require a prescription, nonprescription forms are also available. Ask your doctor or pharmacist about them.

Antrizine antiemetic, see Antivert antiemetic.

Anxanil antianxiety and antihistamine, see Atarax antianxiety and antihistamine.

Aquaphyllin bronchodilator, see theophylline bronchodilator.

Arm-a-Med bronchodilator, see Alupent bronchodilator.

Armour Thyroid hormone, see thyroid hormone.

Asmalix bronchodilator, see theophylline bronchodilator.

Atarax antianxiety and antihistamine

Ingredient: hydroxyzine hydrochloride
Equivalent Products: Anxanil; Hydroxyzine HCl; Vistaril (see Comments)

Dosage Forms: Syrup (content per 5 ml teaspoon): 10 mg. Tablet: 10 mg; 25 mg; 50 mg; 100 mg. See Comments

Uses: Symptomatic relief of anxiety and tension; treatment of itching caused by allergic conditions; as a sedative before or after surgery

Minor Side Effects: Dizziness; drowsiness; dry mouth. These side effects, if they occur, should subside as your body adjusts to the medication. Tell your doctor about any that are persistent or particularly bothersome.

Major Side Effects: Breathing difficulties; chest tightness; convulsions; skin rash; sore throat; tremors. Notify your doctor if you notice any of these.

Contraindications: Do not take this drug if you are allergic to it or if you are pregnant. Consult your doctor immediately if either condition applies.

Warnings: Use of this drug by nursing mothers is not recommended. • This drug should not be used in conjunction with central nervous system depressants, alcohol, or other sedative-type drugs; consult your doctor about their use. If you are unsure of the type or contents of your medications, ask your doctor or pharmacist. • This drug may cause drowsiness, especially during the first few days of therapy; avoid tasks that require alertness, such as driving a car or operating potentially dangerous equipment.

Comments: Take this drug as directed. Do not increase your dose or take it more often than prescribed. • Chew gum or suck on ice chips or a piece of hard candy to reduce mouth dryness. • The generic name for Vistaril is hydroxyzine pamoate. Vistaril is available in capsule form (25 mg; 50 mg; 100 mg); Vistaril is also available in suspension form (25 mg per 5 ml teaspoon). Shake the suspension well before pouring each dose. Although not generically identical to each other, these products have the same therapeutic effects as Atarax antianxiety and other hydroxyzine hydrochloride products.

Atenolol antihypertensive and antianginal, see Tenormin antihypertensive and antianginal.

Ativan antianxiety

Ingredient: lorazepam
Equivalent Product: Lorazepam
Dosage Form: Tablet: 0.5 mg; 1 mg; 2 mg
Uses: Relief of anxiety symptoms and anxiety disorder

Minor Side Effects: Blurred vision; change in appetite; constipation; depression; diarrhea; dizziness; drowsiness; dry mouth; headache; increased salivation; nausea; rash; weakness. Most of these side effects, if they occur, should subside as your body adjusts to the medication. Tell your doctor about any that are persistent or particularly bothersome.

Major Side Effects: Breathing difficulties; chest pain; confusion; dark urine; decreased hearing; difficulty in urinating; disorientation; fever; hallucinations; memory loss; menstrual irregularities; mood changes; mouth sores; palpitations; rapid heart rate; slurred speech; sore throat; uncoordinated movements; yellowish discoloration of the eyes or skin. Notify your doctor if you notice any major side effects.

Contraindications: This drug should not be used by people who are allergic to it. Consult your doctor immediately if this drug has been prescribed for you and you have such an allergy. • This drug should not be used by people with acute narrow-angle glaucoma. Be sure your doctor knows if you have either of these conditions.

Warnings: This drug should be used cautiously by the elderly; children under 12; pregnant or nursing women; and people with impaired liver or kidney function, psychotic illness, or with certain diseases of the heart, stomach, or lungs. Be sure your doctor knows if any of these conditions applies to you. • This drug is safe when used alone. When it is combined with other sedatives, serious adverse reactions may develop. This drug may also interact with cimetidine, phenytoin, levodopa, lithium, and anticoagulants. If you are currently taking any drugs of these types, consult your doctor about their use. If you are unsure about the type or contents of your medications, ask your doctor or pharmacist. • This drug has the potential to be habit-forming and must be used with caution. Tolerance may develop quickly; do not increase the dose without first consulting your doctor. • Persons taking this drug for long periods should have periodic blood and liver function tests. • Do not stop taking this drug suddenly without consulting your doctor; if you have been taking this drug for long periods or in high doses, withdrawal symptoms may occur with abrupt cessation. It will be necessary to reduce your dosage gradually. • This drug may cause drowsiness; avoid tasks that require alertness, such as driving a car or operating potentially dangerous equipment. • To prevent oversedation, avoid the use of alcohol or other drugs that have sedative properties. • Notify your doctor if you develop signs of jaundice (yellowish discoloration of the eyes or skin, dark urine).

Comments: Take with food or a full glass of water if stomach upset occurs. • It may take two or three days before this drug's full effects become apparent. • Chew gum or suck on ice chips or a piece of hard candy to reduce mouth dryness. • This drug is used by many people to relieve anxiety. It is effective for this purpose, but it is important to make an effort to understand the cause of anxiety as well.

Atrovent bronchodilator

Ingredient: ipratropium bromide
Dosage Form: Inhaler: (content per inhalation): 18 mcg
Use: For symptomatic treatment of bronchospasm associated with bronchitis or emphysema
Minor Side Effects: Bad taste in mouth; dry mouth and throat; headache; hoarseness; nausea; nervousness; restlessness; sweating; tension; trembling; vomiting; weakness. Most of these side effects, if they occur, should subside as your body adjusts to the medication. Tell your doctor about any that are persistent or particularly bothersome.
Major Side Effects: Blurred vision; breathing difficulties; chest pain; difficulty in urinating; dizziness; muscle cramps; palpitations. Notify your doctor if you notice any major side effects.
Contraindications: This drug should not be used by persons allergic to it or to atropinelike drugs. Consult your doctor if this drug has been prescribed for you and you have such an allergy.
Warnings: This drug must be used with caution by persons with certain types of heart disease, glaucoma, enlarged prostate, or urinary tract problems; and by pregnant or nursing women. Be sure your doctor knows if any of these conditions applies to you. • This drug is not recommended for use by children under 12 years of age. • This drug has been shown to interact with antihistamines, beta blockers, and anesthetics. If you are currently taking any of these drugs, consult your doctor about their use. If you are unsure about the type or contents of your medications, ask your doctor or pharmacist. While taking this drug, do not take any nonprescription item for cough, cold, or sinus problems without first checking with your doctor; these items may contain a sympathomimetic amine (a decongestant, for example) that can cause additive side effects with this medication. • Prolonged or excessive use of this drug may reduce its effectiveness. Take this drug as prescribed. Do not take it more often

than prescribed, increase your dose, or stop taking it without first consulting your physician. It may be necessary to temporarily stop using this drug for a short period to ensure its effectiveness. This medication is not effective in stopping an acute asthma attack. It is used continuously to prevent episodes of bronchospasm. • If your symptoms do not improve, or if they worsen while taking this drug, or if dizziness or chest pain develops, contact your doctor.

Comments: Make sure you know how to use the inhaler properly. Ask your pharmacist for a demonstration and a patient instruction sheet. In addition, check the section entitled Administering Medications Correctly in this book to ensure that you are using the inhaler properly. • If more than one inhalation is prescribed, wait at least five minutes between inhalations for maximum effectiveness. • To help relieve dry mouth, chew gum or suck on ice chips or hard candy. • Do not use the solution for inhalation if it has turned brown in color. • Store the inhaler away from heat and open flame. Do not puncture, break, or burn the container. The inhaler contains approximately 200 doses.

Augmentin antibiotic

Ingredients: amoxicillin; clavulanic acid

Dosage Forms: Chewable tablet: Augmentin 125: amoxicillin, 125 mg and clavulanic acid, 31.25 mg; Augmentin 250: amoxicillin, 250 mg and clavulanic acid, 62.5 mg. Oral suspension (content per 5 ml teaspoon): Augmentin 125: amoxicillin, 125 mg and clavulanic acid, 31.25 mg; Augmentin 250: amoxicillin, 250 mg and clavulanic acid, 62.5 mg. Tablet: Augmentin 250: amoxicillin, 250 mg and clavulanic acid, 125 mg; Augmentin 500: amoxicillin, 500 mg and clavulanic acid, 125 mg

Use: Treatment of a wide variety of bacterial infections

Minor Side Effects: Diarrhea; gas; loss of appetite; nausea. Most of these side effects, if they occur, should subside as your body adjusts to the medication. Tell your doctor about any that are persistent or particularly bothersome.

Major Side Effects: Abdominal pain; black tongue; breathing difficulties; fever; joint pain; mouth sores; rash; rectal or vaginal itching; severe diarrhea; sore throat; superinfection; vomiting. Notify your doctor if you notice any major side effects.

Contraindication: This drug should not be taken by people who are allergic to penicillin-type drugs or cephalosporin antibiotics. Consult your doctor immediately if this drug has been prescribed for you and you have such an allergy.

Warnings: This drug should be used cautiously by people who have kidney or liver disease, asthma, severe hay fever, or other significant allergies. Be sure your doctor knows if you have any of these conditions. • Complete blood cell counts and liver and kidney function tests are advisable if you take this drug for a prolonged period of time. • This drug should not be used in conjunction with allopurinol, chloramphenicol, erythromycin, or tetracycline; if you are currently taking any drugs of these types, consult your doctor about their use. If you are unsure of the contents of your medications, ask your doctor or pharmacist. • Severe allergic reactions to this drug (indicated by breathing difficulties and a drop in blood pressure) have been reported but are rare. Notify your doctor if you develop a rash or experience breathing trouble while taking this medication. • Prolonged use of this drug may allow organisms that are not susceptible to it to grow wildly. Do not use this drug unless your doctor has specifically told you to do so. Be sure to follow directions carefully and report any unusual reactions to your doctor at once. • In some women, use of certain antibiotics can cause vaginal yeast infections. Contact your doctor if vaginal itching occurs while taking this drug. • This drug may affect the potency of oral contraceptives. Consult your doctor about using supplementary contraceptive measures while you are taking this drug. • Diabetics using Clinitest urine tests may get a false high sugar reading while taking this drug. Change to Clinistix, Diastix, Chemstrip UG, or Tes-Tape urine test to avoid this problem.

Comments: • Finish all of the medication, even if you begin to feel better. Stopping therapy too soon may lead to reinfection. • This medication works best if a constant level of the drug is kept in the body. To do this, take each dose as prescribed at evenly spaced intervals around the clock. Your doctor or pharmacist can help you establish a dosing schedule. • The liquid form of this drug should be stored in the refrigerator. Shake well before using. Discard the unused portion after ten days. • This drug is similar in nature to penicillin, ampicillin, and amoxicillin. • The clavulanic acid enables the amoxicillin to be more effective in treating certain infections.

Aventyl HCl antidepressant, see Pamelor antidepressant.

Axid antisecretory and antiulcer

Ingredient: nizatidine
Dosage Form: Capsule: 150 mg; 300 mg
Uses: Treatment of ulcer; prevention of recurrent ulcers; management of heartburn and ulcerations associated with gastroesophageal reflux disease

Minor Side Effects: Constipation; diarrhea; dizziness; dry mouth; dry skin; fatigue; headache; nausea; sweating; stomach upset; vomiting. Most of these side effects, if they occur, should subside as your body adjusts to the medication. Tell your doctor about any that are persistent or particularly bothersome.

Major Side Effects: Blood disorders; confusion; decreased sexual ability; itchy skin; rapid heart rate; skin rash; trouble sleeping. Notify your doctor if you notice any major side effects.

Contraindication: This drug should not be taken by anyone who is allergic to it. Consult your doctor immediately if you have such an allergy.

Warnings: This drug should be used cautiously by pregnant or nursing women, people with kidney trouble, and children. Be sure your doctor knows if any of these conditions applies to you. • This drug should be used with caution in conjunction with high doses of aspirin; if you are currently taking aspirin for arthritis, consult your doctor about its use. • This drug has not been shown to affect the use of other medications. However, check with your doctor or pharmacist before taking other drugs.

Comments: This drug is usually taken twice a day or once daily at bedtime. • For best results, this drug must be taken continuously for as long as your doctor prescribes, even if you feel better during that time. Lab tests may be scheduled to check on the effectiveness of the medication. • Lifestyle changes may be recommended in addition to this medication to assist in the prevention and treatment of ulcers. Dietary changes, exercise programs, smoking cessation, and stress-reduction programs may be beneficial. • This drug is very similar in action to Pepcid, Tagamet, and Zantac. Discuss these medications with your doctor to determine if there is a less expensive alternative.

Azmacort inhaled antiasthmatic

Ingredient: triamcinolone acetonide
Dosage Form: Pressurized inhaler for oral use (content per one actuation from mouthpiece): 100 mcg
Use: Control of chronic asthma
Minor Side Effects: Coughing; dry mouth and throat; hoarseness; wheezing. Most of these side effects, if they occur, should subside as your body ad-

justs to the medication. Tell your doctor about any that are persistent or particularly bothersome.

Major Side Effects: Breathing difficulties; depression; muscle aches and pains; nosebleeds; skin rash; sore throat or infections of the mouth or throat; swelling of the face; weakness. Notify your doctor if you notice any major side effects.

Contraindications: This drug is a steroid. It should not be used in the initial treatment of severe asthma attacks where immediate measures are required since it does not produce immediate effects. • This drug should not be taken by persons allergic to it or who have reacted adversely to other steroids or by persons with systemic fungal infections. Inform your doctor if any of these conditions applies to you.

Warnings: This drug should be used cautiously by pregnant women, nursing mothers, women of childbearing age, and children under the age of six. Be sure your doctor knows if any of these conditions applies to you. • If you have been taking oral steroids to control your asthma, conversion to therapy with this inhaled drug will be accomplished slowly. Follow your doctor's instructions closely and report any side effects immediately. • If you develop an infection, need to have surgery, or experience other injury, it may be necessary for you to take supplemental oral steroids. Talk to your doctor about this, and make sure you understand what you must do in the event of a medical complication. This drug is not for rapid relief of an asthma attack (bronchospasm). If you have an asthma attack and your dilator drugs do not help, call your doctor. • The dosage of this drug should be monitored very carefully. Taking more of this drug than is recommended will probably not give you more relief over the long term. • Call your doctor if you develop mouth sores or a sore throat while taking this medication.

Comments: Use this drug exactly as prescribed. Do not use it more often than prescribed. Full benefit from this drug may not be apparent for two to four weeks. • Shake the canister well before use. • Rinsing your mouth before and after inhalation of this drug is advised in order to reduce irritation and dryness of mouth and throat. To use the inhaler, place the inhaler device two fingerwidths away from the mouth. With your head tipped back slightly, depress the inhaler while taking a slow, deep breath. Hold it for ten seconds, then breathe out slowly. If more than one inhalation is used, wait at least one minute between inhalations. • Your pharmacist should dispense patient instructions with this drug that explain administration technique. • If you use a bronchodilator with this drug, use the bronchodilator first, wait a few minutes, then use this drug. This method has been shown to be the most effective and to have the least potential for toxicity. • The contents of one canister of this drug should provide at least 200 oral inhalations. • This drug is sealed in the canister under pressure. Do not puncture the canister. Do not store the canister near heat or an open flame. • This drug is not useful during acute asthma attacks. It is used to prevent attacks.

Bacitracin Neomycin Polymyxin B ophthalmic antibiotic ointment, see Neosporin ophthalmic antibiotic.

Bacitracin Zinc/Neomycin Sulfate/Polymyxin B Sulfate/Hydrocortisone ophthalmic steroid and antibiotic, see Cortisporin ophthalmic steroid and antibiotic.

Bacticort Suspension ophthalmic steroid and antibiotic, see Cortisporin ophthalmic steroid and antibiotic.

CONSUMER GUIDE®

Bactrim, Bactrim DS antibacterials

Ingredients: sulfamethoxazole; trimethoprim

Equivalent Products: Cotrim; Cotrim DS; Septra; Septra DS; sulfamethoxazole and trimethoprim; sulfamethoxazole and trimethoprim DS; Sulfatrim; Sulfatrim DS; Uroplus DS; Uroplus SS

Dosage Forms: Double-strength (DS) tablet: trimethoprim, 160 mg and sulfamethoxazole, 800 mg. Liquid (content per 5 ml teaspoon): trimethoprim, 40 mg and sulfamethoxazole, 200 mg. Tablet: trimethoprim, 80 mg and sulfamethoxazole, 400 mg

Uses: Treatment of urinary or intestinal tract infections, certain respiratory infections, and middle-ear infections; prevention of traveler's diarrhea; reduction of risk of infections in persons with compromised immune systems

Minor Side Effects: Abdominal pain; diarrhea; dizziness; headache; loss of appetite; nausea; sore mouth; sun sensitivity; vomiting. Most of these side effects, if they occur, should subside as your body adjusts to the medication. Tell your doctor about any that are persistent or particularly bothersome.

Major Side Effects: Anemia; arthritis; blood disorders; breathing difficulties; chills; convulsions; dark urine; depression; difficulty in urinating; easy bruising; fever; fluid retention; hallucinations; hives; itching; joint pain; muscle aches; rash; ringing in the ears; sore throat; tingling in hands or feet; unusual bleeding; weakness; yellowing of the eyes or skin. Notify your doctor if you notice any major side effects.

Contraindications: This drug should not be taken by people who are allergic to either ingredient or to sulfa medications, by those with folate deficiency anemia, or by women who are nursing. Consult your doctor immediately if any of these conditions applies to you. • This drug should not be used by infants under two months old.

Warnings: This drug may cause allergic reactions and should, therefore, be used cautiously by people who have asthma, severe hay fever, or other significant allergies. People who have certain vitamin deficiencies or who have liver or kidney disease should also use this drug with caution. This drug should be used cautiously by elderly patients. • Be sure your doctor knows if any of these conditions applies to you. • This drug should be used during pregnancy only if clearly needed. Discuss the risks and benefits with your doctor. • This drug must be used cautiously in conjunction with barbiturates, cyclophosphamide, diuretics ("water pills"), isoniazid, local anesthetics, methenamine hippurate, methenamine mandelate, methotrexate, oral anticoagulants, oral antidiabetics, oxacillin, para-aminobenzoic acid (PABA), penicillins, phenylbutazone, phenytoin, or probenecid; if you are currently taking any drugs of these types, consult your doctor or pharmacist. • This drug may interfere with blood and urine laboratory tests. If you are scheduled to take any such tests, remind your doctor that you are taking this drug. • Long term use of this drug can cause blood diseases; notify your doctor immediately if you experience fever, sore throat, or skin discoloration, as these can be early signs of blood disorders. • Complete blood cell counts and liver and kidney function tests should be done if you take this drug for a prolonged period. • Notify your doctor if you develop signs of jaundice (yellowing of the eyes or skin, dark urine).

Comments: This drug is best taken on an empty stomach, but it may be taken with food if stomach upset occurs. Take this drug with at least one full glass of water. Drink at least nine or ten glasses of water each day. Shake the liquid well before pouring each dose. Store the liquid at room temperature. It does not require refrigeration. • This drug should be taken for as long as prescribed, even if symptoms disappear within that time. • To be most effective, this drug should be taken at even intervals around the clock. Your doctor or pharmacist can help you set up a dosing schedule. • This drug may cause you to be especially sensitive to the sun, so avoid prolonged exposure to the sun and use an effective sunscreen.

Bactroban topical antibiotic

Ingredient: mupirocin
Dosage Form: Ointment: 2%
Use: Treatment of impetigo (a skin infection)
Minor Side Effects: Burning, stinging, and itching at the application site; dry skin; nausea; redness; tenderness. Most of these side effects, if they occur, should subside as your body adjusts to the medication. Tell your doctor about any that are persistent or particularly bothersome.
Major Side Effect: Irritation, pain, or swelling at application site. Notify your doctor if you notice a major side effect.
Contraindication: This drug should not be taken by anyone allergic to it. Be sure your doctor is aware if you have such an allergy.
Warnings: Pregnant or nursing women should use this drug only if it is clearly needed. • This medication is for use on the skin only. Avoid contact with the eyes or mouth. • If a rash or pain and swelling occur at the application site, wash the area and call your doctor.
Comments: Apply this medication to the affected area as directed. It is usually applied three times a day. Apply a small amount to the affected area and rub it in gently. Cover with gauze or a bandage if needed. • If no improvement is noticed after three to five days, notify your doctor. • Do not use this medication longer than prescribed since prolonged use can lead to development of other skin infections.

Bancap HC analgesic, see Vicodin, Vicodin ES analgesics.

Beclovent inhaled antiasthmatic, see Vanceril inhaled antiasthmatic.

Beconase, Beconase AQ intranasal steroid and antiallergy, see Vancenase, Vancenase AQ intranasal steroid and antiallergy.

Beepen VK antibiotic, see penicillin V potassium (penicillin VK) antibiotic.

betamethasone valerate topical steroid hormone, see Valisone topical steroid hormone.

Betapen-VK antibiotic, see penicillin V potassium (penicillin VK) antibiotic.

Betatrex topical steroid hormone, see Valisone topical steroid hormone.

Beta-Val topical steroid hormone, see Valisone topical steroid hormone.

Biaxin antibiotic

Ingredient: clarithromycin
Dosage Form: Tablet: 250 mg; 500 mg
Use: Treatment of a wide variety of bacterial infections
Minor Side Effects: Altered taste; diarrhea; headache; nausea; stomach upset. Most of these side effects, if they occur, should subside as your body

adjusts to the medication. Tell your doctor about any that are persistent or particularly bothersome.

Major Side Effects: Dark urine; fungal infections in the mouth or vagina; pale stools; rash; rectal and vaginal itching; severe diarrhea; stomach cramps; weakness; yellowing of the eyes or skin, vomiting. Notify your doctor if you notice any major side effects.

Contraindication: This drug should not be taken by people who are allergic to it or to erythromycin antibiotic. Consult your doctor immediately if you have such an allergy.

Warnings: This drug should be used cautiously by people who have liver disease and by pregnant or nursing women. • This drug may affect the potency of theophylline: If you are currently taking theophylline, consult your doctor about its use. This drug may interact with digoxin, antihistamines; anticoagulants (blood thinners), and carbamazepine. If you are taking any of these medications, consult your doctor about their use. If you are unsure about the contents of your medications, ask your doctor or pharmacist. • Notify your doctor if you develop signs of jaundice (yellowing of the eyes or skin, dark urine). • Call your doctor if diarrhea, vomiting, or stomach cramps persist or if your urine turns dark, your stools turn pale, or unusual weakness develops.

Comments: Take this drug as directed. If stomach upset occurs, take this drug with food. Take each dose with a full glass of water. • It is best to take this medication at evenly spaced intervals around the clock. Your doctor or pharmacist will help you choose the best schedule. • Finish all the medication prescribed, even if your symptoms disappear after a few days. Stopping treatment early may lead to reinfection. This medication is similar in action to erythromycin antibiotic, but studies suggest that Biaxin causes less stomach discomfort.

Biocef antibiotic, see Keflex antibiotic.

Biomox antibiotic, see amoxicillin antibiotic.

birth control pills, see oral contraceptives.

Blocadren antihypertensive

Ingredient: timolol maleate
Equivalent Product: Timolol Maleate
Dosage Form: Tablet: 5 mg; 10 mg; 20 mg
Uses: Treatment of high blood pressure (hypertension); prevention of heartbeat irregularities following heart attack; prevention of migraine headaches

Minor Side Effects: Abdominal pain; bloating; blurred vision; constipation; dizziness (slight); drowsiness; dry eyes, mouth, or skin; gas or heartburn; headache; insomnia; loss of appetite; nasal congestion; nausea; sweating; tiredness; vivid dreams; vomiting. Most of these side effects, if they occur, should subside as your body adjusts to the medication. Tell your doctor about any that are persistent or particularly bothersome.

Major Side Effects: Chest pain; cold hands and feet; confusion; decreased sexual ability; depression; diarrhea; difficulty in urination; dizziness (severe); earache; fever; hair loss; hallucinations; irregular heartbeat; mouth sores; night cough; nightmares; numbness and tingling in the fingers and toes; rash; ringing in the ears; shortness of breath; slowed heart rate; swelling in the hands and feet; unusual bleeding or bruising. Notify your doctor if you notice any of these major side effects.

Contraindications: This drug should not be used by people who are allergic to timolol maleate or any other beta blocker. This drug should not be taken by people who suffer from certain types of heart disease or lung disease or anyone who has taken any monoamine oxidase inhibitors within the past two weeks. Consult your doctor immediately if this drug has been prescribed for you and any of these conditions applies.

Warnings: This drug should be used with caution by persons with certain respiratory problems, diabetes, certain heart problems, liver or kidney diseases, hypoglycemia, or thyroid disease. Be sure your doctor knows if you have any of these conditions. • This drug should be used cautiously by persons taking other medications, such as theophylline, insulin, calcium channel blockers, salicylates, and other antihypertensive agents. • This drug should be used cautiously when reserpine is taken. • Inform your doctor of all the medications you are taking so that effects can be monitored. • This drug should be used cautiously by pregnant women and by women of childbearing age. • This drug should be used with care during anesthesia and by patients undergoing major surgery. If possible, this drug should be stopped 48 hours prior to surgery. • Do not abruptly stop taking this drug unless directed to do so by your doctor; usually the dose must be gradually reduced over one to two weeks. • Diabetics taking this drug should watch for signs of altered blood-glucose levels. • While taking this drug, do not take any nonprescription item for weight control, cough, cold, or sinus problems without first checking with your doctor; such medications may contain ingredients that can increase blood pressure. • Notify your doctor if severe dizziness, diarrhea, or shortness of breath develops, or if a slow pulse is noticed.

Comments: Take this drug as directed. Be sure to take your medication doses at the same time each day. It is important to continue taking this medication even if you do not feel sick. Most people with high blood pressure do not have symptoms and do not feel ill; therefore, it is easy to forget to take the medication. • Your doctor may want you to take your pulse and monitor your blood pressure every day while you take this medication. Ask your doctor about what your normal pulse and blood pressure values are and what they should be. • This drug may cause you to be sensitive to the cold. Dress warmly. As with all antihypertensive medications, they are most effective when used in conjunction with diet and lifestyle changes such as exercise and stress reduction to control blood pressure. The medication does not cure high blood pressure. • There are many different beta blockers available. Your doctor may want you to try different ones in order to find the best one for you. • Timolol maleate is also available as Timoptic, an eye drop used in the management of glaucoma.

Bonine antiemetic, see Antivert antiemetic.

Brethaire oral inhaler bronchodilator, see Brethine bronchodilator.

Brethine bronchodilator

Ingredient: terbutaline sulfate
Equivalent Products: Brethaire (oral inhaler only); Bricanyl
Dosage Forms: Tablet: 2.5 mg; 5 mg. Oral inhaler (content per one metered dose): 0.2 mg
Use: Relief of bronchial asthma and bronchospasm associated with bronchitis or emphysema
Minor Side Effects: Anxiety; dry mouth; flushing; headache; increased heart rate; insomnia; loss of appetite; nausea; nervousness; peculiar taste in

CONSUMER GUIDE®

the mouth; restlessness; sweating; tension; tremors; vomiting; weakness. Most of these side effects, if they occur, should subside as your body adjusts to the medication. Tell your doctor about any that are persistent or particularly bothersome.

Major Side Effects: Breathing difficulties; chest pain; confusion; difficulty in urinating; dizziness; muscle cramps; palpitations. Notify your doctor if you notice any major side effects.

Contraindications: This drug should not be taken by people who are allergic to any sympathomimetic amine drug. Consult your doctor immediately if this drug has been prescribed for you and you have an allergy of this type. • This drug is not recommended for use by children under age 12.

Warnings: This drug should be used cautiously by pregnant or nursing women and by people who have diabetes, high blood pressure, thyroid disease, glaucoma, enlarged prostate, Parkinson's disease, heart disease (certain types), or epilepsy. Be sure your doctor knows if any of these conditions applies to you. • This drug should not be used in conjunction with guanethidine, beta blockers, or monoamine oxidase inhibitors; if you are currently taking any drugs of these types, consult your doctor about their use. If you are unsure of the type or contents of your medications, ask your doctor or pharmacist. • While taking this drug, do not take any nonprescription item for cough, cold, or sinus problems without first checking with your doctor; these items may contain a sympathomimetic amine (a decongestant, for example), which can cause additive side effects with this medication. • Prolonged or excessive use of this drug may reduce its effectiveness. Take this drug as prescribed. Do not take it more often than prescribed without first consulting your physician. Do not increase your dose or stop taking this without consulting your doctor. It may be necessary to temporarily stop using this drug for a short period to ensure its effectiveness. • If your symptoms do not improve, or if they worsen while taking this drug, or if dizziness or chest pain develops, contact your doctor.

Comments: Make sure you know how to use the inhaler properly. Ask your pharmacist for a demonstration and a patient instruction sheet. In addition, check the section entitled Administering Medications Correctly in this book to ensure that you are using the inhaler properly. If more than one inhalation is prescribed, wait at least one full minute between inhalations for maximum effectiveness. • Store the inhaler away from heat and open flame. Do not puncture, break, or burn the container. Each inhaler canister contains approximately 300 doses. • If stomach upset occurs while taking the tablets, take the drug with food or milk. • To help relieve dry mouth, chew gum or suck on ice chips or hard candy.

Bricanyl bronchodilator, see Brethine bronchodilator.

Bronkodyl bronchodilator, see theophylline bronchodilator.

Bumex diuretic

Ingredient: bumetanide
Dosage Form: Tablet: 0.5 mg; 1 mg; 2 mg
Use: Removal of fluid from body tissues to treat edema due to heart disease, liver disease, or kidney disease
Minor Side Effects: Abdominal pain; blurred vision; decreased sexual desire; diarrhea; dizziness; fatigue; headache; loss of appetite; nausea; stomach upset; sun sensitivity; weakness. Most of these side effects, if they occur, should subside as your body adjusts to the medication. Tell your doctor about any that are persistent or particularly bothersome.

Major Side Effects: Blood disorders; chest pain; dark urine; dehydration; dry mouth; easy bruising or bleeding; excessive thirst; hives; impaired coordination; impotence; loss of hearing; low blood pressure; muscle cramps; rash; sweating; tingling of fingers and toes; vomiting; yellowing of the eyes or skin. Notify your doctor if you notice any major side effects.

Contraindications: This drug should not be used by persons allergic to it, by persons with anuria (inability to urinate), or by those with severe liver or kidney disease. Consult your doctor immediately if this drug has been prescribed for you and you have any of these conditions.

Warnings: This drug should be used with caution by persons with cirrhosis of the liver or other liver problems and by persons with kidney disease. This drug should be used cautiously by children and by pregnant or nursing women. Be sure your doctor knows if any of these conditions applies to you. • Persons who are allergic to sulfa drugs may also be allergic to this drug. If this drug has been prescribed for you and you are allergic to sulfa drugs, consult your doctor immediately. • This drug interacts with aspirin, indomethacin, digitalis, lithium carbonate, steroids, and probenecid. If you are currently taking any drugs of these types, consult your doctor about their use. If you are unsure of the type or contents of your medications, ask your doctor or pharmacist. • This drug should be used with caution in conjunction with other high blood pressure drugs. If you are taking other such medications, the dosages may require adjustment. • If you have high blood pressure, do not take any nonprescription item for weight control, cough, cold, or sinus problems without first checking with your doctor. Such medications may contain ingredients that can increase blood pressure. • When taking this drug (or other drugs for high blood pressure), limit the use of alcohol to avoid dizziness or light-headedness. • Use of this drug may cause gout, diabetes, hearing loss, and loss of potassium, calcium, water, and salt. Persons taking this drug should have periodic drug tests to monitor for these effects. • Whenever reactions to this drug are moderate to severe, this drug should be reduced or discontinued. Consult your doctor promptly if such side effects occur. • Notify your doctor if you develop signs of jaundice (yellowing of the eyes or skin, dark urine). • This drug can cause potassium loss. Signs of such loss include dry mouth, thirst, muscle cramps, weakness, and nausea or vomiting. If you experience any of these side effects, notify your doctor. • This drug can increase your skin's sensitivity to the sun. Avoid prolonged sun exposure, and use a sunscreen when outdoors.

Comments: Take this drug exactly as directed. It is usually taken in the morning with food. Do not take extra doses or skip a dose without first consulting your doctor. • Diuretics are also called water pills. Diuretics help eliminate extra fluid that may build up, especially in the feet, causing swelling. As a result, this drug causes frequent urination. Expect this effect; it should not alarm you. Try to plan your dosage schedule to avoid taking this drug at night. • To help avoid potassium loss, take this drug with a glass of fresh or frozen orange juice. You may also eat a banana each day. The use of a salt substitute helps prevent potassium loss. Do not change your diet, however, without consulting your doctor. Too much potassium may also be dangerous. • To avoid dizziness or light-headedness when you stand, contract and relax the muscles of your legs for a few moments before rising. Do this by pushing one foot against the floor while raising the other foot slightly, alternating feet so that you are pumping your legs in a pedaling motion. • This drug has potent activity. If another drug to decrease blood pressure is also prescribed, your doctor may decide to decrease the dose of one of the drugs to avoid an excessive drop in blood pressure. You should learn how to monitor your pulse and blood pressure; discuss this with your doctor. As with all antihypertensive medications, they are most effective when used in conjunction with diet and lifestyle changes, such as exercise and stress reduction to control blood pressure. The medication does not cure high blood pressure.

BuSpar antianxiety

Ingredient: buspirone hydrochloride
Dosage Form: Tablet: 5 mg; 10 mg
Use: For short-term relief of anxiety or anxiety disorders
Minor Side Effects: Change in appetite; dizziness; dream disturbances; drowsiness; dry mouth; dry skin; excitement; fatigue; flushing; hair loss; headache; insomnia; light-headedness; menstrual irregularity; muscle aches; nasal congestion; nausea; nervousness; red or itchy eyes; sleeplessness; stomach distress; sweating; weight gain. Most of these side effects, if they occur, should subside as your body adjusts to the medication. Tell your doctor about any that are persistent or particularly bothersome.
Major Side Effects: Chest pain; confusion; depression; easy bruising; eye pain; hyperventilation; incoordination; increased heart rate; involuntary or abnormal movements, especially of the face and head; muscle spasms; numbness; pain or difficulty in urinating; palpitations; restlessness; ringing in the ears; shortness of breath; skin rash; stiff muscles; tremors. Notify your doctor if you notice any major side effects.
Contraindications: This drug should not be used by people who are allergic to it. Consult your doctor immediately if this drug has been prescribed for you and you have such an allergy. • This drug is not recommended for use in children under 18 years of age, since safety and efficacy have not been established in this age group.
Warnings: This drug should be used cautiously by people who have severe liver or kidney disease. Be sure your doctor knows if either of these conditions applies to you. • This drug should only be used during pregnancy if clearly needed. Discuss the risks and benefits with your doctor. It is not known if this drug appears in breast milk. Consult your doctor before breast-feeding while taking this medication. • This drug has been found to interact with antidepressants, monoamine oxidase inhibitors, psychotropic drugs, trazodone, alcohol, and digoxin. To prevent oversedation, avoid the use of alcohol or other drugs that have sedative properties. If you are currently taking any medications of these types, consult your doctor about their use. If you are unsure about the types or contents of your medications, ask your doctor or pharmacist. Inform your doctor of any medications (prescription or nonprescription) that you are currently taking or are planning to take during the course of your treatment with this drug. • This drug may cause drowsiness and dizziness; avoid tasks that require alertness, such as driving a car or operating potentially dangerous equipment. • This medication may cause restlessness, stiff muscles, or involuntary repetitive movements of the face or neck muscles. If you experience any of these symptoms, inform your doctor.
Comments: Take this drug with food or a full glass of water if stomach upset occurs. • Continue taking this medication as prescribed. Do not suddenly stop taking this drug without your doctor's approval. • Nausea, dizziness, headache, light-headedness, and excitement are common during the first few days of therapy. These effects should subside as your body adjusts to the drug. • Chew gum or suck on ice chips to help relieve dry mouth. • Some improvement in your condition should be noticeable within one week of beginning therapy with this drug, but it may take as long as three to four weeks before optimal results are achieved.

butalbital, acetaminophen, and caffeine analgesic, see Fioricet analgesic.

butalbital, aspirin, and caffeine analgesic, see Fiorinal analgesic.

butalbital compound analgesic, see Fiorinal analgesic.

Calan and Calan SR antianginal and antihypertensive, see Isoptin, Isoptin SR antianginal, antihypertensive, and antiarrhythmic.

Capital with Codeine analgesic, see acetaminophen with codeine analgesic.

Capoten antihypertensive

Ingredient: captopril
Dosage Form: Tablet: 12.5 mg; 25 mg; 50 mg; 100 mg
Uses: Treatment of high blood pressure; treatment of heart failure; may be used for other conditions as deemed appropriate by your doctor
Minor Side Effects: Cough; decreased sexual desire; diarrhea; dizziness; fatigue; frequent urination; gas; gastrointestinal upset; headache; impairment or loss of taste perception; insomnia; light-headedness; nasal congestion; nausea. Most of these side effects, if they occur, should subside as your body adjusts to the medication. Tell your doctor about any that are persistent or particularly bothersome.
Major Side Effects: Blood disorders; blurred vision; breathing difficulties; chest pain; chills; decreased sexual ability; fainting; fast or irregular heartbeat; fever; itching; mouth sores; muscle aches; skin rash; sore throat; swelling or tingling of face, hands, or feet; weakness; yellowing of the eyes or skin. Notify your doctor if you notice any major side effects.
Contraindications: This drug should not be taken by people who are allergic to it. Consult your doctor if this drug has been prescribed for you and you have such an allergy. • This drug should not be used by any woman who is pregnant, who thinks she is pregnant, or who intends to become pregnant. Use of this drug during pregnancy has resulted in fetal abnormalities. Notify your doctor immediately if you suspect you are pregnant.
Warnings: This drug should be used cautiously by the elderly, nursing women, and people with kidney diseases or blood disorders. Be sure your doctor knows if any of these conditions applies to you. • This drug should be used with caution with other medicines. Inform your doctor if you are taking any cancer medicines, diuretics, antihypertensive drugs, steroids, indomethacin, or potassium supplements. The effectiveness of Capoten may be reduced by aspirin and by indomethacin. Check with your doctor before taking any product containing either of these drugs. • While taking this drug, do not take any nonprescription item for weight control, cough, cold, or sinus problems without first checking with your doctor; these items may contain ingredients that can increase blood pressure. • While taking this drug, you should limit your consumption of alcoholic beverages in order to minimize dizziness and light-headedness. • Because this medicine may initially cause dizziness or fainting, your doctor may start you on a low dose and gradually increase it. Do not discontinue taking this drug unless directed to do so by your doctor because high blood pressure can return quickly. • Do not use salt substitutes or low-salt milk that contains potassium without first checking with your doctor. • Periodic kidney function tests and blood tests are recommended if this drug is prescribed for a long time. Tests will be used to monitor the drug's effectiveness and to

prevent side effects. • Notify your physician if you develop mouth sores, sore throat, fever, chest pains, or swelling of hands or feet.

Comments: For maximum effect, take this drug on an empty stomach one hour before meals. Take this drug exactly as directed. Do not take extra doses or skip doses without consulting your physician. • Do not discontinue taking this medication unless your doctor directs you to do so. It is important to continue taking this medication even if you do not feel sick. Most people with high blood pressure do not have symptoms and do not feel ill; therefore, it is easy to forget to take the medication. • To avoid dizziness or light-headedness when you stand, contract and relax the muscles of your legs for a few moments before rising. Do this by pushing one foot against the floor while raising the other foot slightly, alternating feet so that your legs are pumping in a pedaling motion. • Mild side effects (e.g., nasal congestion) are noticeable during the first few weeks of therapy and become less bothersome after this period. • Have your blood pressure checked regularly, and learn how to monitor your pulse and blood pressure. As with all antihypertensive medications, they are most effective when used in conjunction with diet and lifestyle changes, such as exercise and stress reduction to control blood pressure. The medication does not cure high blood pressure. • This drug may cause drowsiness, especially during the first days of use; avoid tasks that require alertness, such as driving a car or operating potentially dangerous equipment. • Taking this medication before bedtime may make the side effects more tolerable.

Carafate antiulcer

Ingredient: sucralfate
Dosage Form: Tablet: 1g
Use: Treatment and prevention of ulcers
Minor Side Effects: Back pain; constipation; diarrhea; dizziness; drowsiness; dry mouth; gas; headache; indigestion; nausea; sleepiness; stomach upset. Most of these side effects, if they occur, should subside as your body adjusts to the medication. Tell your doctor about any that are persistent or particularly bothersome.
Major Side Effects: Itching; rash.
Contraindication: This drug should not be used by people who are allergic to it. Consult your doctor immediately if this drug has been prescribed for you and you have such an allergy.
Warnings: This drug should be used with caution by pregnant women, nursing mothers, and persons with kidney trouble. Be sure your doctor knows if any of these conditions applies to you. • If you are also taking tetracycline, phenytoin, cimetidine, ranitidine, theophylline, warfarin "blood thinner", ciprofloxacin, or digoxin, it is best to separate dosing of these drugs and Carafate by two hours. Consult your doctor if these drugs have been prescribed for you. • Do not take antacids within 30 minutes before or after taking this drug. • Notify your doctor if you develop red or black stools or cough up or vomit red or "coffee grounds" material. These are signs that an ulcer may be bleeding and needs immediate attention.
Comments: Take this drug with water on an empty stomach at least one hour before or two hours after a meal and at bedtime. • Continue taking this medication for the full time prescribed by your doctor, even if your symptoms disappear. • Sucralfate forms a protective layer at the ulcer site. It is virtually not absorbed into the body, so side effects are minimal.

Carbamazepine anticonvulsant, see Tegretol anticonvulsant.

Carbidopa & Levodopa antiparkinson drug, see Sinemet, Sinemet CR antiparkinson drug.

Cardizem, Cardizem CD, Cardizem SR
antianginal and antihypertensive

Ingredient: diltiazem hydrochloride
Equivalent Products: Dilacor XR; Diltiazem HCl
Dosage Forms: Sustained-release capsule (Cardizem SR): 60 mg; 90 mg; 120 mg. Tablet: 30 mg; 60 mg; 90 mg; 120 mg. Controlled release capsule (Cardizem CD, Dilacor XR): 120 mg; 180 mg; 240 mg; 300 mg.
Uses: Treatment of various types of angina (chest pain). Sustained release and controlled release only: used in the management of high blood pressure.
Minor Side Effects: Constipation; diarrhea; dizziness (mild); drowsiness; fatigue; flushing; gastric upset; headache; increased frequency of urination; indigestion; light-headedness; nausea; nervousness; sexual difficulties; sweating; weakness. Most of these side effects, if they occur, should subside as your body adjusts to the medication. Tell your doctor about any that are persistent or particularly bothersome.
Major Side Effects: Blurred vision; breathing trouble; confusion; depression; dizziness (severe); fainting; hallucinations; low blood pressure; rapid or pounding heartbeat; skin rash; swelling of the feet, ankles, or lower legs; tingling of hands or feet; tremor. Notify your doctor if you notice any major side effects.
Contraindications: This drug should not be used by people who are allergic to it or by people with very low blood pressure or certain heart diseases. Consult your doctor immediately if this drug has been prescribed for you and either of these conditions applies.
Warnings: This drug should be used cautiously by pregnant or nursing women and by people with low blood pressure, certain heart diseases, kidney disease, or liver disease. Be sure your doctor knows if any of these conditions applies to you. • This drug may interact with beta blockers, theophylline, lithium, cimetidine, calcium supplements, antihypertensive medications, and digoxin. If you are taking any of these medicines, consult your doctor about their use. If you are unsure about the type or contents of your medications, ask your doctor or pharmacist. • This drug may make you dizzy, especially during the first few days of use. Avoid activities that require alertness, such as driving a car or operating potentially dangerous equipment. Avoid alcohol, which may exaggerate this effect. • Contact your doctor if this drug causes severe or persistent dizziness, constipation, nausea, swelling of hands and feet, shortness of breath, or irregular heartbeat.
Comments: This drug must be taken as directed. It is important that you continue to take Cardizem even if you feel well. This drug is not effective in treating an attack of angina already in progress. Do not suddenly stop taking this drug unless you contact your doctor first as chest pain can occur if this drug is stopped suddenly. This drug is not effective in treating an attack of angina already in progress. • Cardizem SR, Cardizem CD, and Dilacor XR are sustained-release formulations. Cardizem SR is usually taken twice a day, while Cardizem CR and Dilacor XR are usually taken only once a day. Do not crush or chew the sustained-release forms of this drug; they must be swallowed whole. Crushing or chewing the drug will destroy the prolonged action, increasing the risk of side effects. • Your physician may want to see you regularly when you begin taking this drug in order to check your response to the therapy. You should learn how to monitor your pulse and blood pressure; discuss this with your doctor. As with all antihypertensive medications, they are most effective when used in conjunction with diet and lifestyle changes, such

CONSUMER GUIDE®

as exercise and stress reduction to control blood pressure. The medication does not cure high blood pressure.

Cardura antihypertensive

Ingredient: doxazosin
Dosage Form: Tablet: 1 mg; 2 mg; 4 mg; 8 mg
Use: Treatment of high blood pressure
Minor Side Effects: Abdominal pain; constipation; cough; diarrhea; dizziness; drowsiness; dry mouth; frequent urination; gas; headache; itching; nausea; nervousness; runny nose; sweating; tiredness; vivid dreams; vomiting; weakness. Most of these side effects, if they occur, should subside as your body adjusts to the medication. Tell your doctor about any that are persistent or particularly bothersome.
Major Side Effects: Breathing trouble; chest pain; depression; fast pulse; fever; fluid retention; hallucinations; joint pain; muscle aches; nosebleed; rapid, pounding heartbeat; rash; ringing in the ears; shortness of breath; tingling of the fingers or toes; vision changes; weight gain. Notify your doctor if you notice any major side effects.
Contraindications: This drug should not be taken by people who are allergic to it or to prazosin or terazosin antihypertensives. Consult your doctor immediately if you have such an allergy.
Warnings: This drug should be used very cautiously by pregnant or nursing women, by children, and by persons with kidney disease. Be sure your doctor knows if any of these conditions applies to you. • This drug should be used with caution in conjunction with other antihypertensive drugs such as calcium channel blockers and beta blockers; if you are currently taking any drugs of these types, consult your doctor about their use. If you are unsure of the type or contents of your medications, ask your doctor or pharmacist. • While taking this drug, do not take any nonprescription item for weight control, cough, cold, allergy, or sinus problems without first checking with your doctor; such items may contain ingredients that can increase blood pressure. • While taking this drug, you should limit your consumption of alcoholic beverages, which can increase dizziness and other side effects. • Because initial therapy with this drug may cause dizziness, the first dose is usually taken at bedtime. In addition, your doctor will probably start you on a low dose and gradually increase your dosage. • Do not drive a car or operate potentially dangerous equipment for a few hours after the first dose or when your dose is increased if you experience dizziness.
Comments: Take this drug exactly as directed. Do not take extra doses or skip a dose without consulting your doctor first. • Do not discontinue taking this medication unless your doctor directs you to do so. It is important to continue taking this medication even if you do not feel sick. Most people with high blood pressure do not have symptoms and do not feel ill; therefore, it is easy to forget to take the medication. • Mild side effects (e.g., nasal congestion, headache) are most noticeable during the first two weeks of therapy and become less bothersome as your body adjusts to the medication. • To avoid dizziness or light-headedness when you stand, contract and relax the muscles of your legs for a few moments before rising. Do this by pushing one foot against the floor while raising the other foot slightly, alternating feet so that you are pumping your legs in a pedaling motion. • If you are taking this drug and begin therapy with another antihypertensive drug, your doctor may adjust your dose over the next couple of weeks. Dosage adjustments will be made based on your response. • Learn how to monitor your pulse and blood pressure while taking this drug; discuss this with your doctor or pharmacist. As with all antihy-

pertensive medications, they are most effective when used in conjunction with diet and lifestyle changes such as exercise and stress reduction to control blood pressure. The medication does not cure high blood pressure.

Catapres antihypertensive

Ingredient: clonidine hydrochloride
Equivalent Product: Clonidine
Dosage Forms: Tablet: 0.1 mg; 0.2 mg; 0.3 mg. Transdermal patch (see Comments)
Uses: Treatment of high blood pressure; may also be used for alcohol withdrawal, smoking cessation, opiate withdrawal, menopausal flushing, and other conditions as deemed appropriate by your doctor
Minor Side Effects: Anxiety; constipation; decreased sexual desire; depression; dizziness; drowsiness; dry eyes; dry mouth; fatigue; headache; increased sensitivity to alcohol; insomnia; itching; jaw pain; loss of appetite; nasal congestion; nausea; nervousness; nightmares; vision changes; vomiting. Most of these side effects, if they occur, should subside as your body adjusts to the medication. Tell your doctor about any that are persistent or particularly bothersome.
Major Side Effects: Breathing difficulties; chest pain; cold feeling in fingertips or toes; dark urine; difficult urination; enlarged breasts (in both sexes); hair loss; heart failure; hives; impotence; pain; rash; rise in blood sugar; tiredness; weakness; weight gain; yellowing of the eyes or skin. Notify your doctor if you notice any major side effects.
Contraindications: This drug should not be used by people who are allergic to it. The transdermal patch should not be used by people allergic to the adhesive layer. Consult your doctor if this drug has been prescribed for you and you have any such allergies.
Warnings: This drug is not recommended for use by women who are pregnant or who may become pregnant. • This drug should be used cautiously by children. • This drug should be used with caution by persons with severe heart disease, depression, or chronic kidney failure and by those who have had a stroke or heart attack. Be sure your doctor knows if any of these conditions applies to you. • This drug should not be used with alcohol, barbiturates, or other sedatives. If you are currently taking any drugs of these types, consult your doctor about their use. If you are unsure of the type or contents of the medications you are taking, ask your doctor or pharmacist. • While taking this drug, do not take any nonprescription item for weight control, cough, cold, or sinus problems without first checking with your doctor; such products often contain ingredients that may increase blood pressure. • Tolerance to this drug develops occasionally; consult your doctor if you feel the drug is becoming less effective. Do not stop using this drug without consulting your doctor first. Your doctor will advise you on how to discontinue the drug gradually. • You should receive periodic eye examinations while taking this drug. • This drug can cause drowsiness; avoid tasks that require alertness, such as driving a car or operating potentially dangerous equipment. • Notify your doctor if you develop signs of jaundice (yellowing of the eyes or skin, dark urine) while taking this drug.
Comments: Take this drug exactly as directed. Do not take extra doses or skip a dose without first consulting your doctor. Persons unable to swallow the tablets may benefit by placing them under their tongue. Discuss the sublingual use of this drug with your doctor if swallowing the tablets is a problem. • Your physician may want to see you regularly when you first begin taking this drug in order to check your response. Dosage adjustments may be made frequently. It is important to continue taking this medication even if you do not feel sick.

CONSUMER GUIDE®

Most people with high blood pressure do not have symptoms and do not feel ill; therefore, it is easy to forget to take the medication. You should learn how to monitor your pulse and blood pressure; discuss this with your doctor or pharmacist. As with all antihypertensive medications, they are most effective when used in conjunction with diet and lifestyle changes, such as exercise and stress reduction to control blood pressure. The medication does not cure high blood pressure. • Mild side effects from this drug (e.g., nasal congestion) are most noticeable during the first two weeks of therapy and become less bothersome as your body adjusts to the medication. • To avoid dizziness or lightheadedness when you stand, contract and relax the muscles of your legs for a few moments before rising. Do this by pushing one foot against the floor while raising the other foot slightly, alternating feet so that you are pumping your legs in a pedaling motion. • Chew gum or suck on ice chips or a piece of hard candy to reduce mouth dryness. • The transdermal patches (called Catapres-TTS) are designed to continually release the medication over a seven-day period. The patch should be applied to a hairless area (shaving may be necessary) on the upper arm or chest. Do not apply a patch to the lower arm or to the legs. Change the site of application with each new patch. Avoid placing the patch on irritated or damaged skin. It is safe to bathe and shower with a patch in place. If it loosens, apply a new one. Store the patches in a cool, dry place. Do not refrigerate. Patient instructions for application are available. Ask your pharmacist for them if they are not provided with your prescription. For maximum benefit, read and follow the instructions carefully. If you are currently taking clonidine tablets, discuss the use of transdermal patches with your doctor.

Ceclor antibiotic

Ingredient: cefaclor

Dosage Forms: Capsule: 250 mg; 500 mg. Liquid (content per 5 ml teaspoon): 125 mg; 187 mg; 250 mg; 375 mg

Use: Treatment of a wide variety of bacterial infections, including ear, respiratory, skin, and urinary tract infections

Minor Side Effects: Diarrhea; fatigue; heartburn; loss of appetite; mouth sores; nausea; vomiting. Most of these side effects, if they occur, should subside as your body adjusts to the medication. Tell your doctor about any that are persistent or particularly bothersome.

Major Side Effects: Breathing difficulties; dark urine; fever; kidney disease; rash; rectal or vaginal itching; severe diarrhea; superinfection; tingling in hands and feet; unusual bleeding and bruising; yellowing of the eyes or skin. Notify your doctor if you notice any major side effects.

Contraindication: This is a cephalosporin antibiotic. This drug should not be used by people who are allergic to it or to other cephalosporin antibiotics. It is generally believed that about ten percent of all people who are allergic to penicillin will be allergic to an antibiotic like this as well. Consult your doctor immediately if this drug has been prescribed for you and you have such an allergy.

Warnings: This drug should be used cautiously by people who are allergic to penicillin or who have other allergies; by women who are pregnant or nursing; and by people with kidney disease. Be sure your doctor knows if any of these conditions applies to you. • This drug should be used cautiously in newborns. • Prolonged use of this drug may allow organisms that are not susceptible to it to grow wildly. Do not use this drug unless your doctor has specifically told you to do so. Be sure to follow directions carefully and report any unusual reactions to your doctor at once. • This drug should be used cautiously in conjunction with diuretics, oral anticoagulants, and probenecid. • This drug may interfere with some blood tests. Be sure your doctor knows you are taking it. • Notify your doctor if you develop signs of jaundice (yellowing of the eyes or skin, dark urine) while taking this drug. • Diabetics using Clinitest urine test may get a false high sugar reading. Change to Clinistix urine test or Tes-Tape urine test to avoid this problem.

Comments: Take this drug with food or milk if stomach upset occurs. • Finish all of the medication, even if you begin to feel better. Stopping therapy too soon may lead to reinfection. • This medication works best if a constant level of the drug is kept in the body. To do this, take each dose as prescribed at evenly spaced intervals around the clock. Your doctor or pharmacist can help you establish a dosing schedule. • The liquid form of this drug should be stored in the refrigerator. Any unused portion should be discarded after 14 days. Shake well before using. • This drug is usually prescribed after unsuccessful treatment with another antibiotic, such as penicillin or Bactrim. Ceclor is more potent and more expensive, so it is generally reserved for second-line use.

Cefadroxil antibiotic, see Duricef antibiotic.

Cefanex antibiotic, see Keflex antibiotic.

Ceftin antibiotic

Ingredient: cefuroxime axetil
Dosage Form: Tablet: 125 mg; 250 mg; 500 mg
Use: Treatment of various bacterial infections, including tonsillitis and ear, respiratory, skin, and urinary tract infections
Minor Side Effects: Abdominal pain; diarrhea; gas; headache; heartburn; loss of appetite; nausea; stomach upset; vomiting. Most of these side effects, if they occur, should subside as your body adjusts to the medication. Tell your doctor about any that are persistent or particularly bothersome.
Major Side Effects: Breathing difficulties; dark urine; fever; hives; mouth sores; muscle pain; rectal or vaginal itching; severe diarrhea; skin rash; superinfection; unusual bleeding or easy bruising; yellowing of the eyes or skin. Notify your doctor if you notice any major side effects.
Contraindication: This is a cephalosporin antibiotic. This drug should not be used by people who are allergic to it or to other cephalosporin antibiotics. Persons with severe allergies to penicillin should not take this drug. It is believed that ten percent of people with penicillin allergies may also be allergic to this type of antibiotic. Be sure your doctor knows if you have such allergies.
Warnings: This drug should be used cautiously by persons with severe liver or kidney disease or those with a history of stomach or intestinal disease. Be sure your doctor knows if any of these conditions applies to you. • This drug should be used only if clearly needed during pregnancy or while nursing. Discuss the risks and benefits with your doctor. • This drug should be used cautiously in conjunction with diuretics or other antibiotics. If you are currently taking any medications of these types, consult your doctor about their use. If you are unsure about the type or contents of your medications, ask your doctor or pharmacist. • Notify your doctor if you experience breathing difficulties, fever, skin rash, or severe diarrhea while taking this medication. • Nausea, stomach upset, diarrhea, or headache may occur during the first few days of therapy. These effects should subside as your body adjusts to the drug. If they become severe or bothersome, notify your doctor.
Comments: Take this drug with food or milk if stomach upset occurs. • Finish all of the medication, even if you begin to feel better. Stopping therapy too soon may lead to reinfection. • This medication works best if a constant level of

the drug is kept in the body. To do this, take each dose as prescribed at evenly spaced intervals around the clock. Your doctor or pharmacist can help you establish a dosing schedule. • If you have difficulty swallowing the tablets, they may be crushed and mixed with applesauce, ice cream, pudding, or beverages, such as juice or chocolate milk, but you must eat or drink all of the food or beverage in which the medication is mixed to receive the full dose. When crushed, the tablets have a strong, bitter taste that may not be disguised by the food or drink. If you are unable to take this medication because of the taste, call your doctor or pharmacist.

Cefzil antibiotic

Ingredient: cefprozil

Dosage Forms: Tablets: 250 mg; 500 mg. Liquid (content per 5 ml teaspoon): 125 mg; 250 mg

Use: Treatment of a wide variety of bacterial infections, including ear, respiratory, skin, and urinary tract infections

Minor Side Effects: Diarrhea; fatigue; heartburn; loss of appetite; mouth sores; nausea; vomiting. Most of these side effects, if they occur, should subside as your body adjusts to the medication. Tell your doctor about any that are persistent or particularly bothersome.

Major Side Effects: Breathing difficulties; dark urine; fever; kidney disease; rash; rectal or vaginal itching; severe diarrhea; superinfection; tingling in hands and feet; unusual bleeding and bruising; yellowing of the eyes or skin. Notify your doctor if you notice any major side effects.

Contraindication: This is a cephalosporin antibiotic. This drug should not be used by people who are allergic to it or to other cephalosporin antibiotics. It is generally believed that about ten percent of all people who are allergic to penicillin will be allergic to an antibiotic like this as well. Consult your doctor immediately if this drug has been prescribed for you and you have such an allergy.

Warnings: This drug should be used cautiously by people who are allergic to penicillin or who have other allergies, by women who are pregnant or nursing, and by people with kidney disease. Be sure your doctor knows if any of these conditions applies to you. • This drug should be used cautiously in newborns. • Prolonged use of this drug may allow organisms that are not susceptible to it to grow wildly. Do not use this drug unless your doctor has specifically told you to do so. Be sure to follow directions carefully and report any unusual reactions to your doctor at once. • This drug should be used cautiously in conjunction with diuretics, oral anticoagulants, and probenecid. • This drug may interfere with some blood tests. Be sure your doctor knows you are taking it. • Notify your doctor if you develop signs of jaundice (yellowing of the eyes or skin, dark urine) while taking this drug. • Diabetics using Clinitest urine test may get a false high sugar reading. Change to Clinistix, Tes-Tape, Diastix, or Chomstrip UG urine test to avoid this problem.

Comments: Take this drug with food or milk if stomach upset occurs. • Finish all of the medication, even if you begin to feel better. Stopping therapy too soon may lead to reinfection. • This medication works best if a constant level of the drug is kept in the body. To do this, take each dose as prescribed at evenly spaced intervals around the clock. Your doctor or pharmacist can help you establish a dosing schedule. The liquid form of this drug should be stored in the refrigerator. Any unused portion should be discarded after 14 days. Shake well before using.

Cena-K potassium replacement, see potassium replacement.

Centrax antianxiety

Ingredient: prazepam
Dosage Forms: Capsule: 5 mg; 10 mg; 20 mg. Tablet: 10 mg
Use: Treatment of anxiety and its symptoms
Minor Side Effects: Constipation; decrease or increase in sex drive; depression; diarrhea; dizziness; drowsiness; dry mouth; excess saliva; fatigue; headache; heartburn; loss of appetite; menstrual irregularities; nausea; sweating; vomiting. Most of these side effects, if they occur, should subside as your body adjusts to the medication. Tell your doctor about any that are persistent or particularly bothersome.
Major Side Effects: Blood disorders; blurred vision; breathing difficulties; confusion; dark urine; difficulty in urinating; double vision; excitation; fever; fluid retention; hallucinations; low blood pressure; mouth sores; rapid, pounding heartbeat; rash; slurred speech; sore throat; stimulation; tremors; uncoordinated movements; yellowing of the eyes or skin. Notify your doctor if you notice any major side effects.
Contraindications: This drug should not be given to children under six months of age. This drug should not be taken by persons with certain types of glaucoma or severe mental disorder, by pregnant or nursing women, or by people who are allergic to it. Consult your doctor immediately if any of these conditions applies to you.
Warnings: This drug should be used cautiously by the elderly or debilitated and by people with epilepsy, respiratory problems, myasthenia gravis, porphyria, a history of drug abuse, or impaired liver or kidney function. Be sure your doctor knows if any of these conditions applies to you. • This drug should not be taken simultaneously with alcohol or other central nervous system depressants that exaggerate its effects; serious adverse reactions may develop. • This drug should be used cautiously with phenytoin, cimetidine, and oral anticoagulants. If you are unsure about the type or contents of your medications, talk to your doctor or pharmacist. • This drug may cause drowsiness, especially during the first few days of therapy, as your body is adjusting to the medication; avoid tasks that require alertness, such as driving a car or operating potentially dangerous equipment. • Do not stop taking this drug without informing your doctor. If you have been taking the drug regularly and wish to discontinue use, you must decrease the dose gradually, according to your doctor's instructions. • This drug has the potential to be habit forming and must be used with caution. Tolerance may develop quickly; do not increase the dose without first consulting your doctor. • Persons taking this drug for a prolonged period of time should have periodic blood counts and liver function tests. • Notify your doctor if you develop signs of jaundice (yellowing of the eyes or skin, dark urine).
Comments: To lessen stomach upset, take with food or a full glass of water. • Chew gum or suck on ice chips or a piece of hard candy to reduce mouth dryness. • The full effects of this drug may not be apparent until it has been taken for two to three days. • Drowsiness is common during the first few days of therapy and should subside with continued use. Because this drug causes drowsiness, it may be best to take Centrax at bedtime. Discuss this with your doctor. This drug is used by many people to relieve anxiety. It is effective for this purpose, but it is important to try to understand the cause of anxiety as well.

Cephalexin antibiotic, see Keflex antibiotic.

Chlordiazepoxide HCl antianxiety, see Librium antianxiety.

Cipro antibiotic

Ingredient: ciprofloxacin
Dosage Form: Tablet: 250 mg; 500 mg; 750 mg
Use: Treatment of bacterial infections, including urinary tract, skin, and respiratory infections
Minor Side Effects: Abdominal pain; bad taste in mouth; constipation; diarrhea; dizziness; gas; headache; heartburn; lack of energy; loss of appetite; nausea; sensitivity to sunlight; stomach upset; vomiting. Most of these side effects, if they occur, should subside as your body adjusts to the medication. Tell your doctor about any that are persistent or particularly bothersome.
Major Side Effects: Blurred vision; breathing difficulties; chest pain; chills; confusion; fever; hives; nightmares; restlessness; ringing in the ears; skin rash; tremors; vaginal itching. Notify your doctor if you notice any major side effects.
Contraindications: This drug should not be used by people who are allergic to it or to other quinolone antibiotics. Be sure your doctor knows if you have such an allergy. • This drug is not recommended for use in children or by pregnant or nursing women.
Warnings: Persons with certain kidney problems should use this drug cautiously. Lower than normal doses may be necessary. • This drug must be used with caution by persons with epilepsy or central nervous system disorders and by those with a history of seizure disorders. Tremor, restlessness, confusion and, very rarely, hallucinations or convulsions may occur. Make sure your doctor knows if you have any of these conditions or experience any of these effects. • This drug has been shown to interact with blood thinners, cimetidine, cyclosporine, nitrofurantoin, phenytoin, probenecid, and theophylline. If you are currently taking any drugs of these types, consult your doctor. If you are unsure about the type or contents of your medications, ask your doctor or pharmacist. • Antacids can interfere with the absorption of this drug. Avoid taking an antacid within two hours of taking this drug. Wait at least two to four hours after taking ciprofloxacin before taking an antacid. • Notify your doctor if you experience breathing difficulties, fever, skin rash, chest pain, tremor, restlessness, or confusion while taking this medication. • This drug may cause dizziness or light-headedness; avoid tasks that require alertness, such as driving a car or operating potentially dangerous equipment.
Comments: This drug may be taken with or without food; however, the preferred dosing time is two hours after a meal. If stomach upset occurs, it may be taken with food or milk. Drink plenty of fluids while taking this medication. • This medication works best if a constant level of the drug is kept in the body. To do this, take each dose as prescribed at evenly spaced intervals around the clock. Your doctor or pharmacist can help you establish a dosing schedule. • Finish all of this medication, even if you begin to feel better. Stopping therapy too soon can cause ineffective treatment, and the infection may reappear. • Nausea, stomach upset, diarrhea, or headache may occur during the first few days of therapy. These effects should subside as your body adjusts to the drug. If they become severe or bothersome, notify your doctor. • This drug can increase sensitivity to sunlight. Avoid prolonged sun exposure, and wear protective clothing and an effective sunscreen when outdoors.

Claritin antihistamine

Ingredient: loratadine
Dosage Form: Tablet: 10 mg
Use: Relief of allergy symptoms (including insect stings), such as watery eyes, sneezing, itching, hives

Minor Side Effects: Blurred vision; constipation; diarrhea; drowsiness; dry mouth, nose, and throat; excitation; headache; increased frequency of urination; insomnia; loss of appetite; muscle pain; nasal stuffiness; nausea; nightmares; sedation; sun sensitivity; sweating; vomiting; weight gain. Most of these side effects, if they occur, should subside as your body adjusts to the medication. Notify your doctor in the event that any side effects appear that are persistent or particularly bothersome.

Major Side Effects: Breathing difficulties; chest pain; confusion; depression; difficulty in urinating; dizziness; faintness; irregular heartbeat; menstrual disorders; rapid, pounding heartbeat; rash; ringing in the ears; tingling of hands and feet; thinning of hair; tremors. Notify your doctor if you notice any major side effects.

Contraindications: This drug should not be taken by people who are allergic to it, by persons taking monoamine oxidase inhibitors, or by nursing mothers. Consult your doctor immediately if any of these conditions applies to you. • This drug is not recommended for use in infants or children under 12 years of age. • This drug should not be used to treat asthma or lower respiratory tract symptoms.

Warnings: This drug must be used cautiously by persons with glaucoma (certain types), ulcers (certain types), thyroid disease, liver disease, certain urinary difficulties, enlarged prostate, or heart disease (certain types). Be sure your doctor knows if any of these conditions applies to you. • Elderly persons may be more likely than others to experience side effects, especially sedation, and should use this drug with caution. • The sedative effects of this drug are enhanced by alcohol and other central nervous system depressants. This drug can effect your response to erythromycin, theophylline, heart medications, and antibiotics. If you are currently taking drugs of these types, consult your doctor about their use. If you are unsure about the type or contents of your medications, ask your doctor or pharmacist. • This medication may cause irregular heart rhythms, especially at high doses. Do not increase your dose or take other drugs with this medication without consulting your doctor. Notify your doctor if you experience faintness, dizziness, or an irregular heartbeat. • Because this drug may cause drowsiness, avoid tasks requiring alertness, such as driving a car or operating potentially dangerous equipment. • While taking this medication, do not take any nonprescription item for weight control, cough, cold, or sinus problems without first consulting your doctor or pharmacist. • If taken for prolonged periods, you may become tolerant to the effects of this drug. Do not increase your dose. Another type of antihistamine may be substituted if necessary for a short period.

Comments: Take this medication as directed on an empty stomach. Do not crush or chew the tablet; swallow it whole. Because this medication has prolonged action, do not increase your dose or take this more often than prescribed. • Chew gum or suck on ice chips or a piece of hard candy to relieve mouth dryness. • This drug may make you more sensitive to the effects of the sun. Wear protective clothing and use a sunscreen when outdoors. • This medication is similar to Seldane and Hismanal. As with all medications, store properly and keep out of the reach of children.

Clonidine antihypertensive, see Catapres antihypertensive.

Clorazepate Dipotassium antianxiety and anticonvulsant, see Tranxene antianxiety and anticonvulsant.

Co-Gesic analgesic, see Vicodin, Vicodin ES analgesics.

Compazine antiemetic and antipsychotic

Ingredient: prochlorperazine
Equivalent Product: Prochlorperazine
Dosage Forms: Suppository: 2.5 mg; 5 mg; 25 mg. Syrup (per 5 ml teaspoon): 5 mg. Tablet: 5 mg; 10 mg; 25 mg. Time-release capsule: 10 mg; 15 mg; 30 mg
Uses: Control of severe nausea and vomiting; relief of certain kinds of anxiety, tension, agitation, psychiatric disorders
Minor Side Effects: Constipation; diarrhea; dizziness; drowsiness; dry mouth; fatigue; headache; insomnia; jitters; loss of appetite; nasal congestion; nausea; reduced sweating; sun sensitivity; weakness. Most of these side effects, if they occur, should subside as your body adjusts to the medication. Tell your doctor about any that are persistent or particularly bothersome.
Major Side Effects: Blurred vision or vision changes; breast enlargement (in both sexes); breathing difficulty; chest pain; convulsions; difficulty in urinating; drooling; eye changes; fever; fluid retention; heart attack; involuntary or unusual movements of the mouth, face, neck, and tongue; joint pain; liver damage; low blood pressure; menstrual irregularities; mouth sores; muscle spasms; muscle stiffness; palpitations; rapid heart rate; rash; restlessness; skin darkening; sexual difficulties; sore throat; tremors; uncoordinated movements; unusual bruising or bleeding. Notify your doctor of any major side effects.
Contraindications: This drug should not be taken by people who are suffering from drug-induced depression or by those who have blood diseases, severe high or low blood pressure, Parkinson's disease, or liver disease. This drug should not be taken by those who are allergic to it. Consult your doctor immediately if this drug has been prescribed for you and any of these conditions applies to you. • This drug should not be given to people who are comatose or to children undergoing surgery.
Warnings: This drug should be used cautiously by people with glaucoma; heart, lung, brain, or kidney disease; diabetes; epilepsy; breast cancer; ulcers; or an enlarged prostate gland. This drug should be used cautiously by pregnant women and by people who have previously had an allergic reaction to any phenothiazine. Be sure your doctor knows if any of these conditions applies to you. • Children and the elderly, especially those with acute illnesses, should take this drug only under close supervision. Their dosage may need adjustment since they are more sensitive to its effects. • This drug interacts with oral antacids, antidepressants, antihypertensives, anticonvulsants, and anticholinergics; if you are currently taking any drugs of these types, consult your doctor about their use. If you are unsure of the type or contents of your medications, ask your doctor or pharmacist. • When taking this drug, do not take any nonprescription item for weight control, cough, cold, or sinus problems without first checking with your doctor. • This drug may interfere with certain blood and urine laboratory tests. If you are scheduled for any such tests, remind your doctor that you are taking this medication. • This drug may cause drowsiness; avoid tasks that require alertness, such as driving a car or operating potentially dangerous equipment. • To prevent oversedation, avoid the use of alcohol or other drugs that have sedative properties. • This drug may cause motor restlessness, uncoordinated movements, and muscle spasms. If you notice any of these effects, contact your doctor immediately—the drug may need to be stopped or the dosage may need to be adjusted • If you take this drug for a prolonged period of time, it may be desirable for you to stop taking it for a while in order to see if you still need it. Do not stop taking this drug, however, without talking to your doctor first. You may have to reduce your dosage gradually. • Because this drug reduces sweating, avoid excessive work or exercise in hot

weather and drink plenty of fluids. • If you notice a sore throat, darkening vision, or fine tremors of your tongue, call your doctor.

Comments: The capsule form of this drug has sustained action. Never take it more frequently than your doctor prescribes; a serious overdose may result. The capsules are to be swallowed whole. Do not crush or chew them. • When used in the treatment of anxiety or psychotic illness, the effects of this drug may not be apparent for at least two weeks. • This drug may cause urine to turn pink or red-brown; this is harmless. • Chew gum or suck on ice chips or a piece of hard candy to reduce mouth dryness. • To avoid dizziness or lightheadedness when you stand, contract and relax the muscles in your legs for a few moments before rising. Do this by pushing one foot against the floor while raising the other foot slightly, alternating feet so that you are pumping your legs in a pedaling motion. • Some side effects caused by this drug can be controlled by taking an antiparkinson drug. Discuss this with your doctor. • This drug can increase your sensitivity to the sun. Avoid prolonged sun exposure, and wear protective clothing and a sunscreen when outdoors.

Conjugated Estrogens hormone, see Premarin estrogen hormone.

Constant-T bronchodilator, see theophylline bronchodilator.

contraceptives (oral), see oral contraceptives.

Corgard antihypertensive and antianginal

Ingredient: nadolol
Dosage Form: Tablet: 20 mg; 40 mg; 80 mg; 120 mg; 160 mg
Uses: Treatment of chest pain (angina) and high blood pressure (hypertension)
Minor Side Effects: Abdominal pain; bloating; blurred vision; constipation; drowsiness; dry eyes, mouth, or skin; gas or heartburn; headache; insomnia; loss of appetite; nasal congestion; nausea; sweating; tiredness; vivid dreams; vomiting. Many of these side effects, if they occur, should subside as your body adjusts to the medication. Tell your doctor about any that are persistent or particularly bothersome.
Major Side Effects: Chest pain; cold hands and feet; confusion; decreased sexual ability; depression; diarrhea; difficulty in urination; dizziness; earache; fever; hair loss; hallucinations; irregular heart rate; mouth sores; night cough; nightmares; numbness and tingling in the fingers and toes; rash; ringing in the ears; shortness of breath; slow pulse; swelling in the hands or feet; unusual bleeding or bruising. Notify your doctor if you notice any major side effects.
Contraindications: This drug should not be used by people who are allergic to nadolol or any other beta blocker. This drug should not be taken by people who suffer from certain types of heart disease or lung disease or by anyone who has taken any monoamine oxidase inhibitors within the past two weeks. Consult your doctor immediately if this drug has been prescribed for you and any of these conditions applies.
Warnings: This drug should be used with caution by persons with certain respiratory problems, diabetes, certain heart problems, liver disease, kidney disease, hypoglycemia, or thyroid disease. Be sure your doctor knows if you have any of these conditions. • Diabetics should watch for signs of altered blood glucose levels. • This drug should be used cautiously by pregnant women and by women of childbearing age. • This drug should be used with care during anesthesia and by patients undergoing major surgery. If possible, this drug should be stopped 48 hours prior to surgery. • This drug should be

CONSUMER GUIDE®

used cautiously when reserpine is taken. • This drug may interact with cimetidine, chlorpromazine, oral contraceptives, salicylates, phenytoin, and theophyllines. If you are currently taking any of these types of drugs, consult your doctor about their use. If you are unsure about the type or contents of your medications, ask your doctor or pharmacist. • While taking this drug, do not take any nonprescription item for weight control, cough, cold, or sinus problems without first checking with your doctor; such items may contain ingredients that may increase blood pressure. • Do not abruptly stop taking this medication unless directed to do so by your doctor. Chest pain—even heart attacks—can occur when this drug is suddenly stopped. Your doctor will gradually reduce the dosage or substitute another medication. • Notify your doctor if you develop dizziness, diarrhea, or a slow pulse, or if you are having breathing difficulties while on this medication.

Comments: Take this medication as directed. Be sure to take this medication at the same time each day. It is important to continue taking this medication even if you do not feel sick. Most people with high blood pressure do not have symptoms and do not feel ill; therefore, it is easy to forget to take the medication. • This drug may make you more sensitive to the cold. Dress warmly. • Your doctor may want you to take your pulse and monitor your blood pressure every day while you take this medication. Discuss with your doctor what your normal pulse and blood pressure values are and what they should be. As with all antihypertensive medications, they are most effective when used in conjunction with diet and lifestyle changes, such as exercise and stress reduction to control blood pressure. The medication does not cure high blood pressure. • There are many different beta blockers available. Your doctor may have you try different ones to find the one that's best for you.

Cortatrigen Modified Otic steroid and antibiotic, see Cortisporin Otic steroid and antibiotic.

Cortisporin ophthalmic steroid and antibiotic

Ingredients: polymyxin B sulfate; neomycin sulfate; hydrocortisone; thimerosal (drops only); bacitracin (ointment only)

Equivalent Products: AK-Spore H.C.; Bacticort Suspension; Neomycin/Polymyxin B Sulfate/Hydrocortisone (drops only); Bacitracin Zinc/Neomycin Sulfate/Polymyxin B Sulfate/Hydrocortisone (ointment only)

Dosage Forms: Drop (content per ml): polymyxin B sulfate, 10,000 units; neomycin sulfate, 0.35%; hydrocortisone, 1%; thimerosal, 0.001%. Ointment (content per gram): polymyxin B sulfate, 10,000 units; neomycin sulfate, 0.35%; hydrocortisone, 1%; bacitracin, 400 units.

Use: Short-term treatment of bacterial infections of the eye

Minor Side Effects: Burning; eye redness; stinging; temporary blurred vision. Most of these side effects, if they occur, should subside as your body adjusts to the medication. Tell your doctor about any effects that are persistent or particularly bothersome.

Major Side Effects: Disturbed or reduced vision; eye pain; headache; severe irritation. Notify your doctor if you notice any major side effects.

Contraindications: This product should not be used for fungal or viral infections of the eye or for eye infections with pus. Nor should this product be used for conditions involving the back part of the eye. This drug should not be used by people who are allergic to any of its ingredients or by those with tuberculosis. Consult your doctor immediately if this drug has been prescribed for you and any of these conditions applies.

Warnings: Frequent eye examinations are advisable while this drug is being used, particularly if it is necessary to use the drug for an extended period of time. • This drug should be used cautiously by people with inner ear disease, kidney disease, or myasthenia gravis. • Prolonged use of this drug may result in secondary infection, cataracts, and eye damage. Contact your doctor immediately if you notice any visual disturbances (dimming or blurring of vision, reduced night vision, halos around lights), eye pain, or headache. • Consult your doctor if symptoms reappear.

Comments: Use this drug as prescribed. Do not use more often or longer than directed. For best results, use this medication at evenly spaced intervals throughout the day and night. As with all eye medications, this drug may cause minor, temporary clouding or blurring of vision when first applied. • When you have used this product for the prescribed amount of time, discard any unused portion. • The suspension should be shaken well before using. • Be careful about the contamination of medications used for the eyes. Do not touch the dropper or ointment tube to the eye surface. Wash your hands before administering eye medications. Do not wash or wipe the dropper before replacing it in the bottle. Close the bottle tightly to keep out moisture. • See the chapter on Administering Medication Correctly for instructions on using eye medications.

Cortisporin Otic steroid and antibiotic

Ingredients: hydrocortisone; neomycin sulfate; polymyxin B sulfate

Equivalent Products: AK-Spore H.C. Otic; Antibiotic ear solution; Antibi-Otic; Cortatrigen Modified; Drotic; Ear-Eze; LazerSporin-C; Octicair; Otic-Care; OtiTricin; Otobiotic; Otocort; Otomycin-HPN Otic; Otosporin; Pediotic; UAD Otic.

Dosage Forms: Solution (per ml): hydrocortisone, 1%; neomycin sulfate, 5 mg; polymyxin B sulfate, 10,000 units. Suspension (per ml): hydrocortisone, 1%; neomycin sulfate, 5 mg; polymyxin B sulfate, 10,000 units

Use: Treatment of superficial bacterial infections of the outer ear

Minor Side Effects: Itching; rash; temporary burning sensation when first applied. These side effects, if they occur, should subside as your body adjusts to the medication. Tell your doctor if they persist or are particularly bothersome.

Major Side Effects: Ear pain; red, swollen skin around the ear.

Contraindications: This drug should not be used to treat viral or fungal infections. This drug should not be used by people who are allergic to it. Consult your doctor immediately if you have such a condition or allergy.

Warnings: Do not use this drug for more than ten days, unless your doctor directs you to do so. • This drug should be used cautiously if there is a possibility that the patient has a punctured eardrum. • This drug should be used cautiously by persons with myasthenia gravis or kidney disease. • Notify your doctor if your skin becomes red and swollen, scaly, or itchy; allergic reactions to neomycin are common.

Comments: To administer ear drops, tilt your head to one side with the affected ear turned upward. Grasp the earlobe and pull it upward and back to straighten the ear canal. (If administering ear drops to a child, gently pull the earlobe downward and back.) Fill the dropper and place the prescribed number of drops in the ear. Be careful not to touch the dropper to the ear canal, as the dropper can easily become contaminated this way. Keep the ear tilted upward for five to ten seconds, then gently insert a small piece of cotton into the ear to prevent the drops from escaping. • Do not wash or wipe the dropper after use. Close the bottle tightly to keep out moisture. • Discard any remaining medicine after treatment has been completed so that you will not be tempted to use the medication for a subsequent ear problem without consulting a doctor. • If you wish to warm the drops before administration, roll the bottle back and forth between your hands. Do not place the bottle in boiling water.

Cotrim, Cotrim DS antibacterials, see Bactrim, Bactrim DS antibacterials.

Coumadin anticoagulant

Ingredient: warfarin sodium
Equivalent Products: Panwarfin; Sofarin
Dosage Form: Tablet: 1 mg; 2 mg; 2.5 mg; 5 mg; 7.5 mg; 10 mg
Use: A blood thinner used in the prevention of blood clot formation
Minor Side Effects: Blurred vision; cramps; decreased appetite; nausea; red-orange colored urine. Most of these side effects, if they occur, should subside as your body adjusts to the medication. Tell your doctor about any that are persistent or particularly bothersome.
Major Side Effects: Black stools; coughing up blood; dark urine; diarrhea; fever; hemorrhage; loss of hair; mouth sores; nausea; rash; severe headache; unusual bleeding or bruising; yellowing of the eyes or skin. Notify your doctor if you notice any major side effects.
Contraindications: This drug should not be taken if any condition or circumstance exists in which bleeding is likely to be worsened by taking the drug (such as ulcers or certain surgeries). Be sure that you have given your doctor a complete medical history. • This drug should not be taken by people who are allergic to it or by pregnant women. Consult your doctor immediately if this drug has been prescribed for you and either of these conditions applies.
Warnings: This drug should be used cautiously by people who have any condition where bleeding is an added risk, including those suffering malnutrition, and by people who have liver disease, kidney disease, intestinal infection, wounds or injuries, severe high blood pressure, blood disease (certain types), severe diabetes, menstrual difficulties, indwelling catheters, or congestive heart failure. The drug should be used cautiously by nursing mothers. Be sure your doctor knows if any of these conditions applies to you. • This drug interacts with alcohol, allopurinol, aminosalicylic acid, anabolic steroids, antibiotics, antidepressants, antipyrine, Bactrim/Septra, barbiturates, bromelains, chloral hydrate, chloramphenicol, chlordiazepoxide, chlorpropamide, cholestyramine, chymotrypsin, cimetidine, cinchophen, clofibrate, dextran, dextrothyroxine, diazoxide, disulfiram, diuretics, ethacrynic acid, ethchlorvynol, glucagon, glutethimide, griseofulvin, haloperidol, indomethacin, mefenamic acid, meprobamate, methyldopa, methylphenidate, metronidazole, monoamine oxidase inhibitors, nalidixic acid, neomycin, oral antidiabetics, oral contraceptives, oxyphenbutazone, paraldehyde, phenylbutazone, phenytoin, primidone, quinidine, quinine, rifampin, salicylates, steroids, sulfinpyrazone, sulfonamides, sulindac, thyroid drugs, tolbutamide, triclofos sodium, and vitamin C. If you are currently taking any drugs of these types, consult your doctor about their use. If you are unsure of the type or contents of your medications, ask your doctor. • Because this drug affects the actions of many other drugs, do not start or stop taking any other medication, including aspirin, without checking with your doctor. • Notify your doctor if you develop signs of jaundice (yellowing of the eyes or skin, dark urine), diarrhea, red or tar-black stools. • Regular blood coagulation tests are essential while you are taking this drug. Diet, environment, exercise, and other medications may affect your response to this drug, so blood tests will need to be repeated often, and your dose may be changed often based on the results. • Avoid eating large amounts of leafy green vegetables and avoid drastic dietary changes. • If clots fail to form over cuts and bruises or

if purple or brown spots appear under bruised skin, call your doctor immediately. • Avoid drinking alcoholic beverages. • A change in urine color may or may not be serious; if you notice a change, contact your doctor.

Comments: It is important that you take this drug as prescribed and that you take it at the same time each day. Never take more than the prescribed dose, as spontaneous bleeding can occur. Your doctor or pharmacist may have a special calendar or chart you can use to keep track of your doses. Ask them about it. • Do not increase your dose or take this drug more frequently than your doctor prescribes. • Be sure all of your health care professionals know you are taking this drug. It is advisable to wear a medical alert bracelet and to carry a medical information card that states that you are taking this drug. • Although there are many equivalent products, you should not change brands. If you must switch brands, discuss the impact with your doctor or pharmacist.

Curretab progesterone hormone, see Provera progesterone hormone.

Cycrin progesterone hormone, see Provera progesterone hormone.

D-Amp antibiotic, see ampicillin antibiotic.

Darvocet-N analgesic

Ingredients: propoxyphene napsylate; acetaminophen
Equivalent Products: Propacet 100; propoxyphene napsylate and acetaminophen analgesic
Dosage Form: Tablet: Darvocet-N 50: propoxyphene napsylate, 50 mg and acetaminophen, 325 mg; Darvocet-N 100: propoxyphene napsylate, 100 mg and acetaminophen, 650 mg
Use: Relief of moderate to severe pain
Minor Side Effects: Blurred vision; constipation; dizziness; drowsiness; fatigue; headache; light-headedness; loss of appetite; nausea; restlessness; sedation; vomiting; weakness. Most of these side effects, if they occur, should subside as your body adjusts to the medication.
Major Side Effects: Abdominal pain; breathing difficulties; dark urine; diarrhea; false sense of well-being; hives; palpitations; rash; ringing in the ears; seizures; sore throat; stomach cramps; yellowing of the eyes or skin. Notify your doctor if you notice any major side effects.
Contraindications: This drug should not be used by persons allergic to either of its ingredients. Consult your doctor immediately if this drug has been prescribed for you and you have such an allergy. • This drug is not recommended for use by children under 12 years of age.
Warnings: This drug should be used cautiously by people with blood disorders or heart, lung, liver, or kidney disease; it should be used cautiously by pregnant or nursing women. Be sure your doctor knows if any of these conditions applies to you. • This drug should be used with extreme caution by patients taking sedative, antianxiety, or antidepressant drugs. If you are currently taking any drugs of these types, consult your doctor about their use. If you are unsure of the type or contents of your medications, ask your doctor or pharmacist. • This drug may interfere with certain urine laboratory tests. Tell your doctor you are taking this drug before undergoing any urine tests. • To prevent oversedation, avoid alcohol and other drugs that have sedative properties. • Due to the propoxyphene component (a narcotic analgesic), this drug can be habit-forming with long-term or excessive use. This drug has the potential for abuse and must be used with caution. Tolerance to the effects of this drug may develop quickly; do not increase you dose without consulting your doctor. •

CONSUMER GUIDE®

This drug can cause drowsiness; avoid tasks that require alertness, such as driving a car or operating potentially dangerous equipment.

Comments: If stomach upset occurs, take this medication with food. • Side effects from this drug may be somewhat relieved by lying down. • This medication works best to prevent pain rather than relieve pain that has become intense. • Aspirin or acetaminophen should be tried before therapy with this drug is undertaken. If aspirin or acetaminophen alone does not relieve pain, this drug may be effective. • Store this and all medications out of reach of children.

Deltasone steroid hormone, see prednisone steroid hormone.

Depakote anticonvulsant

Ingredient: divalproex sodium
Dosage forms: Tablet, delayed-released: 125 mg; 250 mg; 500 mg. Sprinkle capsule: 125 mg
Use: Treatment of seizure disorders
Minor Side Effects: Abdominal cramps; breast enlargement (in both sexes); constipation; diarrhea; drowsiness; headache; increased sensitivity to sunlight; indigestion; irregular menstruation; loss of appetite; nausea; temporary hair loss; tremor; vomiting. Most of these side effects, if they occur, should subside as your body adjusts to the medication. Tell your doctor about any that are persistent or particularly bothersome.

Major Side Effects: Behavior changes; blood disorders; depression; double vision; incoordination; restlessness; skin rash; swelling of the feet or ankles; weakness. Notify your doctor if you notice any major side effects.

Contraindications: This drug should not be taken by persons allergic to it or to valproic acid or by persons with severe liver disease. Be sure your doctor is aware if any of these conditions applies to you.

Warnings: This drug should be used cautiously by persons with liver disease, children, and nursing women. This drug should be used during pregnancy only if clearly needed. • Diabetics should carefully monitor blood sugar since this drug can interfere with urine tests for ketones. • This drug should be used in conjunction with other anticonvulsant or depressant drugs; if you are currently taking any drugs of these types, consult your doctor about their use. If you are unsure of the type or contents of your medications, ask your doctor or pharmacist. • To prevent excessive sedation, avoid alcohol while taking this drug. • This drug can cause drowsiness, especially during the first few days of therapy. If you feel drowsy, avoid tasks requiring alertness, such as operating machinery. Talk to your doctor about taking this at bedtime to eliminate daytime problems. • This drug may cause you to become sensitive to sunlight. Avoid prolonged sun exposure, and use a sunscreen when outdoors. • While you are taking this drug your doctor will periodically schedule laboratory tests to check the effectiveness of the medication and to monitor for side effects.

Comments: Take this drug exactly as prescribed. Do not stop taking this without first consulting your doctor. • If stomach upset occurs, this may be taken with food. • Tablets must be swallowed whole. Do not crush or chew them since the drug can be irritating to the mouth. • Sprinkle capsules can be swallowed whole or opened and the contents sprinkled on a spoonful of soft food, such as applesauce or pudding. Do not chew the food; swallow it immediately. • Carry a medical identification card in your wallet or wear a medical alert bracelet indicating you are taking this drug. • This medication is identical in action to Depakene (valproic acid) except that Depakote causes less stomach upset.

Deponit transdermal antianginal, see nitroglycerin transdermal antianginal.

Desipramine HCl antidepressant, see Norpramin antidepressant.

Despic decongestant and expectorant, see Entex LA decongestant and expectorant.

DiaBeta oral antidiabetic, see Micronase oral antidiabetic.

Diazepam antianxiety, anticonvulsant, and muscle relaxant, see Valium antianxiety, anticonvulsant, and muscle relaxant.

Digoxin heart drug, see Lanoxin heart drug.

Dilacor XR, see Cardizem, Cardizem CD, Cardizem SR antianginal and antihypertensive.

Dilantin anticonvulsant

Ingredient: phenytoin sodium
Equivalent Products: Diphenylan Sodium; Phenytoin Sodium (see Comments)
Dosage Forms: Capsule: 30 mg; 100 mg. Chewable tablet: 50 mg. Liquid (content per 5 ml teaspoon): 30 mg; 125 mg
Use: Control of seizure disorders
Minor Side Effects: Bleeding or tender gums; blurred vision; constipation; drowsiness; headache; insomnia; joint pain; muscle pain; muscle twitching; nausea; vomiting. Most of these side effects, if they occur, should subside as your body adjusts to the medication. Tell your doctor about any that are persistent or particularly bothersome.
Major Side Effects: Blood disorders; chest pain; clumsiness; confusion; dizziness; enlarged lips; excessive hair growth; fever; gland swelling; gum enlargement; liver damage; nervousness; numbness; rash; red, itchy eyes; slurred speech; sore throat; uncoordinated movements; unusual bleeding or bruising. Notify your doctor if you notice any major side effects.
Contraindication: This drug should not be taken by people who are allergic to it. Consult your doctor immediately if this drug has been prescribed for you and you have such an allergy.
Warnings: This drug should be used cautiously by the elderly, by people who have impaired liver function, and by pregnant women. Be sure your doctor knows if any of these conditions applies to you. • Diabetics who need to take this drug should check their urine sugar more frequently than usual, as this medication may raise blood sugar levels. • This drug should not be used to treat seizures if they are due to hypoglycemia. Careful diagnosis is essential before this drug is prescribed. • While taking this drug, you should see your doctor regularly for blood tests to monitor effectiveness and to prevent side effects. Talk to your doctor about these blood-level tests and gain an understanding of what they mean. You should be aware of the test results. • Because the metabolism of this drug may be significantly altered by the use of other drugs, great care must be taken when this drug is used concurrently with other drugs. Be sure your doctor is aware of every medication you take. Do not start or stop taking any other medication, either prescription or nonprescription, without first consulting your doctor. This drug interacts with barbiturates, carbamazepine, chloramphenicol, cimetidine, disulfiram, doxycycline, isoniazid, oral

anticoagulants, oral antidiabetics, oral contraceptives, phenylbutazone, quinidine, steroids, sulfaphenazole, and tricyclic antidepressants; if you are currently taking any drugs of these types, consult your doctor about their use. If you are unsure of the type or contents of your medications, ask your doctor or pharmacist. • The results of certain lab tests may be altered if you are taking this drug. If you need any lab tests, remind your doctor that you are taking this drug. • Depending on the type of seizure being treated, this drug may be used in combination with other anticonvulsants. • Do not abruptly stop taking this drug or change your dosage without your doctor's advice; you may start to convulse. • This drug may cause drowsiness, especially during the first few weeks of therapy; avoid tasks that require alertness, such as driving a car or operating potentially dangerous equipment. • To prevent oversedation, avoid the use of alcohol or other drugs that have sedative properties. • Notify your doctor if any of the following symptoms develop: fever; impaired coordination; mouth and gum sores; persistent headache; prolonged weakness; rash; slurred speech; sore throat; or unusual bleeding or bruising.

Comments: Take this drug with food to minimize stomach upset. • Do not use this drug to treat headaches unless your doctor specifically recommends it. • It is important to take all doses of this medicine on time. • The liquid form of this drug must be shaken thoroughly before pouring each dose. • Some phenytoin products are taken once a day (e.g., Phenytoin Sodium and Dilantin Kapseals). Other products are generally taken in three daily doses. • Therapy with this drug may cause your gums to enlarge enough to cover the teeth. Gum enlargement can be minimized, at least partially, by good dental care—frequent brushing and massaging the gums with the rubber tip of a good toothbrush. Inform your dentist if you are taking this drug. • It is recommended you carry a medical alert card or wear a medical alert bracelet indicating that you are taking phenytoin. • Although several generic versions of this drug are available, you should not switch from one to another without your doctor's complete approval and careful assessment. • If you take phenobarbital in addition to this drug, you may be able to take them together in a single product, Dilantin with Phenobarbital anticonvulsant. Consult your doctor or pharmacist.

Dilatrate-SR antianginal, see Isordil antianginal.

Diltiazem HCl antianginal and antihypertensive, see Cardizem, Cardizem CD, Cardizem SR antianginal and antihypertensive.

Diphenylan Sodium anticonvulsant, see Dilantin anticonvulsant.

Dipyridamole anticoagulant, see Persantine anticoagulant.

Disopyramide Phosphate antiarrhythmic, see Norpace, Norpace CR antiarrhythmics.

Dolacet analgesic, see Vicodin, Vicodin ES analgesics.

Dolobid anti-inflammatory analgesic

Ingredient: diflunisal
Dosage Form: Tablet: 250 mg; 500 mg
Uses: Symptomatic treatment of mild to moderate pain; treatment of osteoarthritis and rheumatoid arthritis
Minor Side Effects: Constipation; diarrhea; dizziness; drowsiness; gas; heartburn; insomnia; loss of appetite; nausea; vomiting. Most of these side ef-

fects, if they occur, should subside as your body adjusts to the medication. Tell your doctor about any that are persistent or particularly bothersome.

Major Side Effects: Anemia; blood disorders; blood in stools, urine, or mouth; blurred vision; breathing difficulties; confusion; dark urine; depression; fatigue; fluid retention; headache; high blood pressure; itching; loss of hair; loss of hearing; numbness or tingling in fingers or toes; rash; ringing in the ears; severe abdominal pain; sore throat; stomach ulcer; weight gain; wheezing; yellowing of the eyes or skin. Notify your doctor if you notice any major side effects.

Contraindications: This drug should not be used by people who are allergic to it or to aspirin or other nonsteroidal anti-inflammatory drugs. Consult your doctor immediately if this drug has been prescribed for you and you have such an allergy. • This drug should not be used by pregnant or nursing women. If this drug has been prescribed for you and either of these conditions applies, consult your doctor immediately.

Warnings: This drug should be used cautiously by elderly people; children under 14; people with a history of gastrointestinal disorders; and people with mental illness, epilepsy, Parkinson's disease, infections, bleeding disorders, kidney or liver disease, high blood pressure, or heart failure. Be sure your doctor knows if any of these conditions applies to you. • Nursing women who must use this drug should stop nursing. • This drug interacts with aspirin, acetaminophen, other anti-inflammatories, probenecid, lithium, phenytoin, anticoagulants, steroids, sulfa drugs, diabetes drugs, and diuretics. If you are currently taking any drugs of these types, talk to your doctor about their use. Do not take aspirin or acetaminophen with this drug unless told to do so by your doctor. If you are not sure about the type or contents of your medications, talk to your doctor or pharmacist. • The severity of the side effects caused by this drug depends upon the dosage taken. Use the least amount possible and watch carefully for side effects. • This drug may cause ulcers. Call your doctor if you experience stomach pain or if your stools are black and tarry. • Notify your doctor if you develop signs of jaundice (yellowing of the eyes or skin, dark urine). • If you notice changes in your vision or if you experience headaches while taking this drug, call your doctor. • This drug may cause drowsiness; avoid tasks that require alertness, such as driving a car or operating potentially dangerous equipment. • Side effects are more likely to occur in the elderly. • This drug may cause discoloration of the urine or feces. If you notice a change in color, call your doctor. • Regular medical checkups, including blood tests, are required of persons taking this drug for prolonged periods.

Comments: This drug may be taken with food or milk immediately after meals, or with antacids (other than sodium bicarbonate). Never take this drug on an empty stomach or with aspirin or alcohol. Do not crush or chew the tablets; swallow them whole. • It may take a month before you feel the full effect of this drug. If you are taking diflunisal to relieve osteoarthritis, you must take it regularly, as directed by your doctor. Do not take it only when you feel pain. This drug is not a substitute for rest, physical therapy, or other measures recommended by your doctor. • This drug is not intended for general aches and pains.

Drotic otic steroid and antibiotic, see Cortisporin Otic steroid and antibiotic.

Duocet analgesic, see Vicodin, Vicodin ES analgesics.

Duradyne DHC analgesic, see Vicodin, Vicodin ES analgesics.

Duricef antibiotic

Ingredient: cefadroxil
Equivalent Products: Cefadroxil; Ultracef
Dosage Forms: Capsule: 500 mg. Liquid (content per 5 ml teaspoon): 125 mg; 250 mg; 500 mg. Tablet: 1 g
Use: Treatment of various bacterial infections
Minor Side Effects: Diarrhea; dizziness; flushing; headache; heartburn; loss of appetite; nausea; stomach upset; vomiting. Most of these side effects, if they occur, should subside as your body adjusts to the medication. Tell your doctor about any that are persistent or particularly bothersome.
Major Side Effects: Breathing difficulties; dark urine; hypersensitivity reactions such as skin rash, itching, muscle aches, and fever; severe diarrhea; vaginal itching; superinfection, unusual bruising or bleeding. Notify your doctor if you notice any major side effects.
Contraindications: This is a cephalosporin antibiotic. This drug should not be used by people who are allergic to it or to other cephalosporin antibiotics. Persons with severe allergies to penicillin should not take this drug. It is believed that ten percent of people with penicillin allergies may also be allergic to this type of antibiotic as well. Be sure your doctor knows of any such allergies.
Warnings: This drug should be used cautiously by persons with severe liver or kidney disease or a history of stomach or intestinal disease. Be sure your doctor knows if any of these conditions applies to you. • This drug should be used only if clearly needed during pregnancy or while nursing. Discuss the risks and benefits with your doctor. • This drug should be used cautiously in conjunction with diuretics or other antibiotics. If you are currently taking any medications of these types, consult your doctor about their use. If you are unsure about the type or contents of your medications, ask your doctor or pharmacist. • Notify your doctor if you experience breathing difficulties, fever, skin rash, or severe diarrhea while taking this medication. • Diabetics using Clinitest urine test may get a false high sugar reading while taking this drug. Change to Clinistix, Diastix, Chemstrip UG, or Tes-Tape while taking this drug to avoid this problem.
Comments: Take this drug with food or milk if stomach upset occurs. • The liquid form must be stored in the refrigerator and shaken well before using. Discard any unused portion after 14 days. • Finish all of the medication, even if you begin to feel better. Stopping therapy too soon may lead to reinfection. • This medication works best if a constant level of the drug is kept in the body. To do this, take each dose as prescribed at evenly spaced intervals around the clock. Your doctor or pharmacist can help you establish a dosing schedule. • Nausea, stomach upset, diarrhea, or headache may occur during the first few days of therapy. These effects should subside as your body adjusts to the drug. If they become severe or bothersome, notify your doctor.

Dyazide diuretic and antihypertensive

Ingredients: hydrochlorothiazide; triamterene
Equivalent Product: Triamterene with hydrochlorothiazide
Dosage Form: Capsule: hydrochlorothiazide, 25 mg and triamterene, 50 mg
Uses: Treatment of high blood pressure; removal of fluid from the tissues
Minor Side Effects: Constipation; decreased sexual desire; diarrhea; dizziness; drowsiness; fatigue; headache; itching; loss of appetite; nausea; restlessness; sun sensitivity; upset stomach; vomiting. Most of these side effects, if they occur, should subside as your body adjusts to the medication. Tell your doctor about any that are persistent or particularly bothersome.

Major Side Effects: Blood disorders; breathing difficulties; bruising; chest pain; confusion; dark urine; dry mouth; elevated blood sugar; elevated uric acid; kidney stones; mood changes; mouth sores; muscle cramps or spasms; palpitations; rash; sore throat; tingling in fingers or toes; weak pulse; weakness; yellowing of the eyes or skin. Notify your doctor if you notice any major side effects.

Contraindications: This drug should not be used by persons with severe liver or kidney disease, hyperkalemia (high blood levels of potassium), or anuria (inability to urinate). Be sure your doctor knows if you have any of these conditions. • This drug should not be used routinely during pregnancy in otherwise healthy women, since mother and fetus are being exposed unnecessarily to possible hazards. • This drug should not be used by persons allergic to it or to sulfa drugs. Consult your doctor immediately if this drug has been prescribed for you and you have such an allergy.

Warnings: This drug should be used cautiously by pregnant women; children; and people with diabetes, allergy, asthma, liver disease, anemia, blood diseases, high calcium levels, gout, or a history of kidney stones. Nursing mothers who must take this drug should stop nursing. Be sure your doctor knows if any of these conditions applies to you. • This drug may affect the results of thyroid function tests. Be sure your doctor knows you are taking this drug if you must have such tests. • Persons who take this drug with digitalis should watch for signs of increased toxicity (e.g., nausea, blurred vision, palpitations). Call your doctor if such symptoms develop. • If you must undergo surgery, remind your doctor that you are taking this drug. • This drug interacts with curare, digitalis, lithium carbonate, oral antidiabetics, potassium salts, steroids, and spironolactone. If you are currently taking any drugs of these types, consult your doctor about their use. If you are unsure of the type or contents of your medications, ask your doctor or pharmacist. • When taking this drug, do not take any nonprescription item for weight control, cough, cold, or sinus problems without first checking with your doctor; such items may contain ingredients that can increase blood pressure. • Regular blood tests should be performed if you must take this drug for a long time. You should also be tested for kidney function. • If you develop a sore throat, bleeding, bruising, dry mouth, weakness, or muscle cramps, call your doctor. • Notify your doctor if you develop signs of jaundice (yellowing of the eyes or skin, dark urine). • While taking this drug (as with many drugs that lower blood pressure), you should limit your consumption of alcoholic beverages in order to prevent dizziness or light-headedness. • This drug may cause you to become especially sensitive to the sun. Avoid prolonged sun exposure, and use an effective sunscreen outdoors. • Unlike many diuretic drugs, this drug usually does not cause the loss of potassium. Do not take potassium supplements while taking this drug unless directed to do so by your doctor. Too much potassium can be dangerous.

Comments: Take this drug with food or milk. • Take this drug exactly as directed. Do not skip a dose or take extra doses without first consulting your doctor. • Diuretics are also called water pills. Diuretics help eliminate extra fluid that may build up, especially in the feet, causing swelling. As a result, this drug causes frequent urination. Expect this effect; it should not alarm you. Try to plan your dosage schedule to avoid taking this drug at bedtime. • To avoid dizziness or light-headedness when you stand, contract and relax the muscles of your legs for a few moments before rising. Do this by pushing one foot against the floor while raising the other foot slightly, alternating feet so that you are pumping your legs in a pedaling motion. • Have your blood pressure checked regularly. Learn how to monitor your pulse and blood pressure. • Combination or fixed-dose products are usually not prescribed as the first

CONSUMER GUIDE®

choice in the treatment of high blood pressure. Persons should receive each of the individual ingredients singly, and if the response is adequate to the fixed doses contained in Dyazide, it can be substituted. The advantage of a combination product such as this drug is increased convenience to the patient. As with all antihypertensive medications, they are most effective when used in conjunction with diet and lifestyle changes, such as exercise and stress reduction to control blood pressure. The medication does not cure high blood pressure. • This drug has the same ingredients as Maxzide, but the strengths of the ingredients are different. Note that Maxzide and Dyazide cannot be used interchangeably.

Dynacin antibiotic, see Minocin antibiotic.

DynaCirc antihypertensive

Ingredient: isradipine
Dosage Form: Capsule: 2.5 mg; 5 mg
Use: Treatment of hypertension (high blood pressure)
Minor Side Effects: Bloating; blurred vision; constipation; cough; diarrhea; dizziness (mild); drowsiness; dry mouth; flushing; frequent urination; headache; heartburn; loss of balance; muscle cramps; nausea; nervousness; sweating; weakness. Most of these side effects, if they occur, should subside as your body adjusts to the medication. Tell your doctor about any that are persistent or particularly bothersome.
Major Side Effects: Breathing difficulties; chills; dizziness (severe); fainting; fever; rapid, pounding heart rate; sexual difficulties; skin rash; sore throat; swelling of ankles, feet, or lower legs. Notify your doctor if you notice any major side effects.
Contraindication: This drug should not be used by people who are allergic to it. Consult your doctor immediately if this drug has been prescribed for you and you have such an allergy.
Warnings: This drug should be used cautiously by people who have low blood pressure or heart disease (certain types) and by pregnant or nursing women. Be sure your doctor knows if any of these conditions applies to you. • This drug may interact with beta blockers, digoxin, phenytoin, quinidine, warfarin, calcium supplements, and digitalis. If you are taking antihypertensive medication, the dose may have to be adjusted. If you are currently taking any of these drug types, consult your doctor about their use. If you are unsure of the type or contents of your medications, ask your doctor or pharmacist. • This drug may make you dizzy, especially during the first few days of therapy; this should subside as your body adjusts to the medication. If it does make you dizzy, avoid activities that require alertness, such as driving a car or operating potentially dangerous equipment, and limit your consumption of alcohol, which exaggerates this side effect. • Your doctor may want to see you regularly while you are taking this drug to check your response and to conduct liver function tests. • Contact your doctor if this drug causes severe or persistent dizziness, constipation, breathing difficulties, swelling of hands and feet, or irregular heartbeat.
Comments: Take this drug as directed, even if you feel well. Compliance is necessary to manage high blood pressure. • Swallow the capsule whole without breaking or chewing it unless otherwise instructed by your physician. • Do not suddenly stop taking this drug, unless you consult with your doctor first. Your dosage may have to be decreased gradually. • It may take several days before the effects of this drug are noticed. • Learn how to monitor your pulse and blood pressure; discuss this with your doctor. • If you feel dizzy or light-

headed, sit or lie down for a while; get up slowly from a sitting or reclining position, and be careful on stairs. • Protect this drug from light and moisture. As with all antihypertensive medications, they are most effective when used in conjunction with diet and lifestyle changes, such as exercise and stress reduction to control blood pressure. The medication does not bring about a cure for high blood pressure.

Ear-Eze Otic steriod and antibiotic, see Cortisporin Otic steroid and antibiotic.

E-Base antibiotic, see erythromycin antibiotic.

E.E.S. antibiotic, see erythromycin antibiotic.

Effer-K potassium replacement, see potassium replacement.

Effervescent Potassium replacement, see potassium replacement.

Elavil antidepressant, see amitriptyline antidepressant.

Elixomin bronchodilator, see theophylline bronchodilator.

Elixophyllin bronchodilator, see theophylline bronchodilator.

Elocon topical steroid

Ingredient: mometasone furoate
Dosage Forms: Cream; Lotion; Ointment: 0.1%
Uses: For temporary relief of discomfort, irritation and itching due to skin disorders caused by minor wounds, bruises, prickly heat, diaper rash, sunburn, insect bites, plant poisoning (poison ivy), eczema, psoriasis, allergies, and other skin conditions
Minor Side Effects: Burning or stinging sensation; redness of skin. Most of these side effects, if they occur, should subside as your body adjusts to the medication. Tell your doctor about any that are persistent or particularly bothersome.
Major Side Effects: Blistering; itching; peeling of skin; rash; swelling or tenderness of skin. Notify your doctor if you notice any major side effects.
Contraindications: This drug should not be used by persons allergic to it. Consult your doctor immediately if this drug has been prescribed for you and you have such an allergy. • This drug should not be used in or near the eyes. • This drug should not be used for treatment of most bacterial, fungal, or viral infections of the skin or in areas where blood circulation is markedly impaired. Be sure your doctor knows if any of these conditions applies to you. This medication should not be used on burns or infections, unless directed, as it may slow the healing process.
Warnings: Use this medication sparingly and with caution on children and the elderly. • Pregnant women should use this medication with caution and only if clearly necessary. • Use this medication with caution in persons with known drug sensitivities or when the skin in the area is severely traumatized or broken. If irritation, rash, or swelling occur, discontinue use and notify your doctor. • Use of an occlusive dressing or bandage will increase the absorption of the drug. Use a dressing only if directed to do so by your doctor. If this medication is being used on a child's diaper area, avoid tight-fitting diapers and plastic pants, which increase absorption of the drug. • This product is for exter-

nal use only. • Do not apply this medication to large areas of the body. Avoid using this medication for prolonged periods and do not apply it more frequently than directed. Additional benefits are not achieved with larger amounts of medication. If the condition does not improve after three days, discontinue use of the product and contact your doctor.

Comments: Wash or soak the affected area before applying the medication; this helps increase penetration. Wash your hands immediately after applying this medication. Avoid contact with the eyes. • The cream or lotion may be applied to gauze or a bandage before being applied to the skin. A thin layer of medication rubbed into the skin lightly is all that is necessary to achieve benefit; do not use a bandage or wrap unless directed to do so. • The ointment form is best for use on dry skin. The lotion is preferred for application to hairy areas.

E-Mycin antibiotic, see erythromycin antibiotic.

Endep antidepressant, see amitriptyline antidepressant.

Entex LA decongestant and expectorant

Ingredients: phenylpropanolamine hydrochloride; guaifenesin
Equivalent Products: Ami-Tex LA; Despic; Gentab LA; Guaipax; Nolex LA; Partuss LA; Phenylfenesin LA; Phenylpropanolamine HCl and Guaifenesin; Rymed-TR; ULR-LA; Vanex LA
Dosage Form: Sustained-release tablet (see Comments): phenyl-propanolamine hydrochloride, 75 mg and guaifenesin, 400 mg
Use: For relief of cough and nasal congestion
Minor Side Effects: Dizziness; headache; insomnia; loss of appetite; nausea; nervousness; restlessness; stomach upset. Most of these side effects, if they occur, should subside as your body adjusts to the medication. Tell your doctor about any that are persistent or particularly bothersome.
Major Side Effects: Breathing difficulty; chest pain; difficulty in urinating; fainting; palpitations; rapid heart rate; skin rash; tremors. Notify your doctor if you notice any major side effects.
Contraindications: This drug should not be used by persons with an allergy to either of its components or to sympathomimetic drugs or by persons with severe high blood pressure. This drug should not be used in conjunction with monoamine oxidase inhibitors. Contact your doctor immediately if this drug has been prescribed for you and any of these conditions applies. If you are unsure about the types or contents of your medications, consult your doctor or pharmacist. • This drug is not recommended for use in children under 12.
Warnings: This drug must be used cautiously by persons with high blood pressure, diabetes, certain types of heart disease, glaucoma, hyperthyroidism, or enlarged prostate and by pregnant or nursing women. Be sure your doctor knows if any of these conditions applies to you. • This drug may affect the results of certain laboratory tests. Be sure to remind your doctor you are taking this drug if you are scheduled for any tests. • Contact your physician if chest pain, tremor, or dizziness occur while taking this medication. • Do not take any nonprescription item for weight control, cough, cold, or sinus problems without first checking with your doctor or pharmacist; such items may contain similar ingredients to this drug.
Comments: This drug must be swallowed whole. Do not crush or chew the tablets, because the sustained action will be eliminated and the side effects will be increased. • If stomach upset occurs, this may be taken with food. • While taking this drug, you should drink at least six to eight glasses of fluid each day. • To relieve dry mouth, chew gum or suck on ice chips or hard candy. • This

drug is also available in liquid and capsule forms under the name Entex, which contains phenylephrine HCl (another decongestant agent) and must be dosed more frequently. • There are many drugs of this type on the market that vary slightly in ingredients and amounts. Some are available without a prescription. Your doctor or pharmacist can help select an antihistamine and decongestant medication best for you.

Enzone topical steroid and anesthetic, see Pramosone topical steroid and anesthetic.

Epifoam topical steroid and anesthetic, see Pramosone topical steroid and anesthetic.

Epitol anticonvulsant, see Tegretol anticonvulsant.

Eramycin antibiotic, see erythromycin antibiotic.

Eryc antibiotic, see erythromycin antibiotic.

EryPed antibiotic, see erythromycin antibiotic.

Ery-Tab antibiotic, see erythromycin antibiotic.

Erythrocin Stearate antibiotic, see erythromycin antibiotic.

Erythromycin and Sulfisoxazole antibiotic, see Pediazole antibiotic.

erythromycin antibiotic

Ingredient: erythromycin

Equivalent Products: E-Base; E.E.S.; E-Mycin; Eramycin; Eryc; EryPed; Ery-Tab; Erythrocin Stearate; Ilosone; PCE; Robimycin; Wyamycin S (see Comments)

Dosage Forms: Capsule; Chewable tablet; Drops; Liquid; Tablet (various dosages)

Use: Treatment of a wide variety of bacterial infections

Minor Side Effects: Cough; diarrhea; fatigue; irritation of the mouth; loss of appetite; nausea; stomach upset. Most of these side effects, if they occur, should subside as your body adjusts to the medication. Tell your doctor about any that are persistent or particularly bothersome.

Major Side Effects: Dark urine; fever; fungal infections in the mouth or vagina; hearing loss; pale stools; rash; rectal and vaginal itching; severe diarrhea; stomach cramps; weakness; yellowing of the eyes or skin; vomiting. Notify your doctor if you notice any major side effects.

Contraindication: This drug should not be taken by people who are allergic to it. Consult your doctor immediately if you have such an allergy.

Warnings: This drug should be used cautiously by people who have liver disease and by pregnant or nursing women. • This drug may affect the potency of theophylline; if you are currently taking theophylline, consult your doctor about its use. This drug may interact with digoxin, antihistamines, anticoagulants (blood thinners), and carbamazepine. If you are taking any of these medications, consult your doctor about their use. If you are unsure about the contents of your medications, ask your doctor or pharmacist. • Notify your doctor if you develop signs of jaundice (yellowing of the eyes or skin, dark urine). • Call your doctor if diarrhea, vomiting, or stomach cramps persist or if your urine turns dark, your stools turn pale, or unusual weakness develops.

Comments: It is best to take this drug on an empty stomach (one hour before or two hours after a meal); however, if stomach upset occurs, take this drug with food. Take each dose with a full glass of water. • It is best to take this medication at evenly spaced intervals around the clock. Your doctor or pharmacist will help you choose the best schedule. • Finish all the medication prescribed, even if your symptoms disappear after a few days. Stopping treatment early may lead to reinfection. • The liquid forms of this drug can be stored in the refrigerator to improve taste. Shake well before each dose is poured. • Not all erythromycin products are chemically equivalent. However, most produce the same therapeutic effect. The different salts of erythromycin are base, estolate, ethylsuccinate, and stearate. Doses may vary between products due to differences in absorption. Discuss with your doctor or pharmacist which products are appropriate for you, and then choose among those recommended.

Eryzole antibiotic, see Pediazole antibiotic.

Esgic analgesic, see Fioricet analgesic.

Esidrix diuretic, see hydrochlorothiazide diuretic.

Estrace estrogen hormone

Ingredient: estradiol
Dosage Forms: Oral tablet: 1 mg; 2 mg. Vaginal cream (per gram): 0.1 mg
Uses: Estrogen replacement therapy, treatment of symptoms of menopause, treatment of some cases of breast cancer or prostrate cancer, and prevention of osteoporosis (tablets only)
Minor Side Effects: Abdominal cramps; bloating; breast tenderness; change in sexual desire; diarrhea; dizziness; headache (mild); increased sensitivity to sunlight; loss of appetite; nausea; swelling of the feet or ankles; vomiting; weight loss or gain. Most of these side effects, if they occur, should subside as your body adjusts to the medication. Tell your doctor about any that are persistent or particularly bothersome.
Major Side Effects: Allergic rash; breathing difficulties; cervical changes; change in menstrual patterns; chest pain; dark urine; depression; fluid retention; fungal infections; increased blood pressure; loss of coordination; migraine; pain in calves; painful urination; severe headache; skin irritation; slurring of speech; vaginal itching; vaginal bleeding; vision changes; yellowing of the eyes or skin. Notify your doctor if you notice any major side effects.
Contraindications: This drug should not be taken by persons who have experienced an allergic reaction to estrogen. This drug should not be used by pregnant or nursing women, by persons with blood clotting disorders or a history of such disorders because of estrogen use, or by those persons with certain cancers or vaginal bleeding. Consult your doctor immediately if this drug has been prescribed for you and you have any of these conditions.
Warnings: Your pharmacist has a brochure that describes the benefits and risks involved with estrogen therapy. Your pharmacist is required by law to give you a copy each time you have your prescription filled. Read this material carefully. Discuss any concerns or questions you may have with your doctor or pharmacist. • This drug should be used cautiously by people who have asthma, diabetes, epilepsy, gallbladder disease, heart disease, high blood levels of calcium, high blood pressure, kidney disease, liver disease, migraine, porphyria, uterine fibroid tumors, or a history of depression and by nursing

women. Be sure your doctor knows if any of these conditions applies to you. • This drug may retard bone growth and therefore should be used cautiously by young patients who have not yet completed puberty. • This drug interacts with oral anticoagulants, barbiturates, rifampin, ampicillin, some antibiotics, anticonvulsants, and steroids; if you are currently taking any drugs of these types, consult your doctor about their use. If you are unsure of the type or contents of your medications, ask your doctor or pharmacist. • This drug may alter the body's tolerance to glucose. Diabetics should monitor urine sugar or blood glucose and report any changes to their doctors. • Notify your doctor immediately if you experience abnormal vaginal bleeding, breast lumps, pain in the calves or chest, sudden shortness of breath, coughing up of blood, severe headaches, loss of coordination, changes in vision or skin color, or dark urine. • This drug may affect a number of laboratory tests; remind your doctor that you are taking it if you are scheduled for any tests. • This drug may increase your sensitivity to sun. Avoid prolonged sun exposure, and wear a sunscreen outdoors. • You should have a complete physical examination at least once a year while you are on this medication.

Comments: This drug is usually taken for 21 days followed by a seven-day rest. • Compliance is mandatory with this drug. Take it exactly as prescribed. If you miss a dose, take it as soon as it is remembered, unless it is near the time for the next dose. If so, skip the missed dose and resume your normal dosing schedule. Do not double the dose in order to catch up. If more than one dose is missed, contact your doctor to establish a new dosing schedule. • Special applicators are available with the vaginal cream to ensure proper dosing. Fill the applicator with the cream. Insert the applicator high into the vagina unless otherwise directed, and gently depress the plunger to release the medication. Remove the applicator and wash it in warm, soapy water. Refer to the chapter on Administering Medication for details on the use of vaginal drug products. This drug is helpful in preventing estrogen-deficiency osteoporosis when used in conjunction with calcium supplements and exercise. It is important to ensure adequate intake of calcium while on estrogen therapy to reduce the risk of osteoporosis. Make sure your diet contains 1,000 to 1,500 mg calcium per day. If not, a calcium supplement may be recommended. Discuss the use of calcium with your doctor or pharmacist.

Estraderm transdermal estrogen hormone

Ingredient: estradiol
Dosage Form: Transdermal patch system (various strengths)
Uses: To relieve vasomotor symptoms of menopause, such as hot flashes or flushes, or symptoms due to deficient estrogen production. This drug is not used to relieve emotional or nervous symptoms associated with menopause.
Minor Side Effects: Abdominal cramps; bloating; breast tenderness; change in sexual desire; diarrhea; dizziness; headache (mild); increased sensitivity to sunlight; loss of appetite; nausea; swelling of the ankles or feet; vomiting; weight loss or gain. Most of these side effects, if they occur, should subside as your body adjusts to the medication. Tell your doctor about any that are persistent or particularly bothersome.
Major Side Effects: Allergic rash; breathing difficulties; cervical changes; change in menstrual patterns; chest pain; dark urine; depression; excessive hair growth; fluid retention; increase in blood pressure; migraine; pain in calves; painful urination; skin irritation; slurring of speech; sudden or severe headache; vaginal infection; vision changes; yellowing of the eyes or skin. Notify your doctor if you notice any major side effects.

Contraindications: Do not use this drug if you have ever experienced an allergic reaction to estrogens. This drug should not be used by pregnant or nursing women, by persons with blood clotting disorders or a history of such disorders due to estrogen use, or by persons with certain cancers or vaginal bleeding. Consult your doctor immediately if this drug has been prescribed for you and any of these conditions applies.

Warnings: Prolonged estrogen use is associated with many side effects. Your pharmacist has a brochure that should be included with your medication; it describes the benefits and risks involved with estrogen therapy. Read this information carefully. Discuss any questions or concerns you may have with your doctor or pharmacist. • This drug should be used cautiously by people with asthma, diabetes, epilepsy, gallbladder disease, heart disease, high blood pressure, kidney disease, liver disease, migraines, porphyria, uterine fibroid tumors, or a history of depression. Be sure your doctor knows if any of these conditions applies to you. • There is an increased risk of developing gallbladder disease in postmenopausal women treated with estrogen. • This drug may retard bone growth and therefore should be used cautiously by young persons who have not yet completed puberty. • This drug has been shown to interact with oral anticoagulants, barbiturates, rifampin, steroids, anticonvulsants, and some antibiotics and antidepressants. Consult your doctor if you are taking any drugs of these types. If you are unsure about the type or contents of your medications, ask your doctor or pharmacist. • This drug may alter the body's tolerance to glucose. If you are diabetic, you should monitor your urine sugar and blood glucose closely and report any changes to your doctor. • Notify your doctor immediately if you experience abnormal vaginal bleeding, breast lumps or secretions, pain in the calves or chest, sudden shortness of breath, unexplained coughing, sudden severe headaches, dizziness, faintness, change in skin color, or vision changes. • This drug may alter results of laboratory tests; remind your doctor that you are taking this drug if you are scheduled for any tests. • This drug may increase your sensitivity to the sun. Avoid prolonged exposure to the sun, and wear a sunscreen outdoors. • It is recommended that you schedule a medical examination once a year while you are taking this medication.

Comments: This medication is usually used on a cyclic schedule—three weeks of using the drug followed by one week off. Make sure you are clear on when to use this medication. Use this medication exactly as prescribed. • Transdermal patches are designed to continually release the drug at a constant rate. The medication is absorbed through the skin into the bloodstream. • To use the transdermal patch, open the pouch and remove the protective liner. Place the patch, adhesive side down, on a clean, dry, nonhairy area of the skin of the torso—preferably on the abdomen. Avoid placing the patch on the legs, arms, breasts, or waistline, where clothing may rub the patch off. Do not apply the patch to irritated, oily, or damaged skin. Press the patch in place firmly, and hold for ten seconds. Make sure the patch is securely in place, especially around the edges. It is recommended that you apply a new patch immediately before removing the old one. If a patch falls off, try to reapply it. If necessary, a new patch may be used. In either case, continue with your original treatment schedule. To minimize skin irritation, rotate the application site. Do this by allowing at least one week to go by before you apply a new patch to the same area. It is important to ensure adequate intake of calcium while on estrogen therapy to reduce the risk of osteoporosis. Make sure your diet contains 1,000 to 1,500 mg calcium per day. If not, a calcium supplement may be recommended. Discuss the use of calcium with your doctor or pharmacist.

Estropipate estrogen hormone, see Ogen estrogen hormone.

Ezide diuretic, see hydrochlorothiazide diuretic.

Fiorgen PF analgesic, see Fiorinal analgesic.

Fioricet analgesic

Ingredients: butalbital; acetaminophen; caffeine

Equivalent Products: butalbital, acetaminophen, and caffeine; Esgic; Repan

Dosage Form: Tablet: butalbital, 50 mg; acetaminophen, 325 mg; caffeine, 40 mg (see Comments)

Use: For relief of headache pain associated with tension

Minor Side Effects: Anxiety; blurred vision; dizziness; drowsiness; gas; light-headedness; loss of appetite; nausea; sedation; stomach upset; vomiting. Most of these side effects, if they occur, should subside as your body adjusts to the medication. Tell your doctor about any that are persistent or particularly bothersome.

Major Side Effects: Dark urine; depression; false sense of well-being; loss of coordination; mental confusion; rapid heartbeat; stomach cramps; tremors; yellowing of the eyes or skin. Notify your doctor if you notice any major side effects.

Contraindications: This drug should not be taken by anyone who is allergic to any of the ingredients or by people who have porphyria. Consult your doctor immediately if this drug has been prescribed for you and either of these conditions applies.

Warnings: This drug should be used cautiously by people who have severe liver or kidney disease, are mentally depressed, or have a history of drug abuse. Be sure your doctor knows if any of these conditions applies to you. • Elderly persons may be more sensitive to the effects of this drug. Excitement, depression, or confusion may occur. Notify your doctor if you experience any of these symptoms. • This drug should be used only if clearly needed during pregnancy or while nursing. Discuss the risks and benefits with your doctor. • This drug is not recommended for use in children under 12 years of age since safety and efficacy have not been established in this age group. • This drug interacts with alcohol, central nervous system depressants, antidepressants, and anticonvulsants. If you are currently taking any drugs of these types, consult your doctor about their use. If you are unsure about the type or contents of your medications, consult your doctor or pharmacist. • While using this medication, avoid the use of nonprescription medication containing acetaminophen or caffeine, and limit your consumption of caffeine-containing beverages. • To prevent oversedation, avoid the use of alcohol or other sedative-type drugs while taking this medication. • Because of the butalbital (barbiturate) content, this drug can be habit-forming; do not take this drug unless absolutely necessary. Tolerance to this drug can develop, making it less effective over time. Do not increase the dose or take this medication more often than prescribed without consulting your doctor. No more than six tablets of this drug should be taken in one day. • This drug may cause drowsiness and dizziness; avoid tasks requiring alertness, such as driving a car or operating potentially dangerous equipment. Notify you doctor if you develop any signs of jaundice (yellowing of the eyes or skin, dark urine).

Comments: Take this drug with food or a full glass of water if stomach upset occurs. • Many headaches are believed to be caused by nervousness, tension, or prolonged contraction of the head and neck muscles. This drug is reported to relieve these conditions to control headache. This medication is also available in capsule form containing butalbital, 50 mg; acetaminophen, 325 mg; caffeine, 40 mg; under the names of Anaphen, Anoquan, Butace, Endolor, Femcet, G-1, Medgesic, and Two-dyne. • This drug is very similar in action to Fiorinal. Fiorinal contains aspirin instead of acetaminophen.

Fiorinal analgesic

Ingredients: aspirin; butalbital; caffeine
Equivalent Products: butalbital, aspirin, and caffeine; butalbital compound; Fiorgen PF; Isollyl Improved; Lanorinal; Marnal
Dosage Forms: Capsule; Tablet: aspirin, 325 mg; butalbital, 50 mg; caffeine, 40 mg
Use: Relief of headache pain associated with tension
Minor Side Effects: Blurred vision; dizziness; drowsiness; gas; insomnia; light-headedness; loss of appetite; nausea; nervousness; vomiting. Most of these side effects, if they occur, should subside as your body adjusts to the medication. Tell your doctor about any that are persistent or particularly bothersome.
Major Side Effects: Breathing difficulties; chest tightness; dark urine; difficulty in urinating; easy bruising or bleeding; false sense of well-being; hives; loss of coordination; rapid heartbeat; rash; ringing in the ears; shortness of breath; tremor; yellowing of the eyes or skin. Notify your doctor if you notice any major side effects.
Contraindications: This drug should not be taken by people who are allergic to aspirin or any of the other ingredients or by people who have porphyria. Consult your doctor immediately if this drug has been prescribed for you and you have such a condition or such an allergy.
Warnings: This drug should be used cautiously by people who have ulcers, coagulation problems, liver disease, gout, or kidney disease and by women who are pregnant or nursing. Be sure your doctor knows if any of these conditions applies to you. • The safety and effectiveness of this drug when used by children under the age of 12 has not been established. Do not give Fiorinal to a child or teenager who has the flu or chicken pox without first consulting your doctor or pharmacist since it contains aspirin. • This drug interacts with alcohol, aminophylline, theophylline, 6-mercaptopurine, anticoagulants (blood thinners), methotrexate, probenecid, sulfinpyrazone, central nervous system depressants (sedatives, narcotic analgesics), phenytoin, and antidepressants: If you are currently taking any drugs of these types, consult your doctor about their use. If you are unsure of the type or contents of your medications, ask your doctor or pharmacist. • While using this medication, avoid the use of nonprescription medicines containing aspirin or caffeine and limit your consumption of caffeine-containing beverages. • Because of the butalbital (barbiturate) content, this drug may be habit-forming; do not take this drug unless absolutely necessary. This drug has the potential for abuse and must be used with caution. Tolerance may develop quickly; do not increase the dose without first consulting your doctor. • No more than six tablets or capsules of this drug should be taken in one day. • This drug may cause drowsiness; avoid tasks that require alertness, such as driving a car or operating potentially dangerous equipment. • To prevent oversedation, avoid the use of alcohol or other drugs that have sedative properties. • If your ears feel strange, if you hear ringing or buzzing, or if your stomach hurts, your dosage may need adjustment. Call your doctor.
Comments: Take this drug with food or milk. • Many headaches are believed to be caused by nervousness, tension, or prolonged contraction of the head and neck muscles. This drug is reported to relieve these conditions to help control headache. • This drug is very similar in action to Fioricet. Fioricet contains acetaminophen instead of aspirin.

Fiorinal with Codeine analgesic

Ingredients: aspirin; butalbital; caffeine; codeine phosphate

Dosage Form: Capsule #3: aspirin, 325 mg; butalbital, 50 mg; caffeine, 40 mg; codeine phosphate, 30 mg

Use: Relief of pain associated with tension

Minor Side Effects: Blurred vision; constipation; dizziness; drowsiness; flushing; headache; indigestion; insomnia; loss of appetite; nausea; nervousness; sweating; tiredness; vomiting; weakness. Most of these side effects, if they occur, should subside as your body adjusts to the medication. Tell your doctor about any that are persistent or particularly bothersome.

Major Side Effects: Abdominal pain; breathing difficulties; chest tightness; confusion; dark urine; easy bruising and bleeding; false sense of well-being; hallucination; kidney disease; nightmares; ringing in the ears; skin rash; sore throat; ulcer; yellowing of the eyes or skin. Notify your doctor if you notice any major side effects.

Contraindications: This drug should not be taken by people who are allergic to aspirin or any of its ingredients or to narcotic analgesics. Consult your doctor immediately if this drug has been prescribed for you and you have any such allergies.

Warnings: The use of this drug may be habit-forming, due to the presence of codeine and butalbital. This drug has the potential for abuse and must be used with caution. Tolerance to this drug may develop quickly; do not increase the dose of this drug without consulting your doctor. • No more than six capsules of this product should be taken in one day. • This drug should be used cautiously by pregnant or nursing women and by people who have ulcers, coagulation problems, liver disease, gout, brain disease, porphyria, thyroid disease, gallstones or gallbladder disease, or kidney disease. Be sure your doctor knows if any of these conditions applies to you. • The safety and effectiveness of this drug when used by children under the age of 12 has not been established. Do not give this drug to a child or teenager who has the flu or chicken pox without first consulting your doctor or pharmacist. • This drug interacts with alcohol, ammonium chloride, anticoagulants, methotrexate, oral antidiabetics, oral contraceptives, probenecid, quinidine, steroids, sulfinpyrazone, vitamin C, central nervous system depressants, griseofulvin, phenytoin, sulfonamides, tetracyclines, and antidepressants; if you are currently taking any drugs of these types, consult your doctor about their use. If you are unsure of the type or contents of your medications, ask your doctor or pharmacist. • While using this medication, avoid the use of nonprescription medicines containing aspirin or caffeine and limit your consumption of caffeine-containing beverages. • This drug may cause drowsiness; avoid tasks that require alertness, such as driving a car or operating potentially dangerous equipment. • To prevent oversedation, avoid the use of alcohol or other drugs that have sedative properties. • If your ears feel strange, if you hear ringing or buzzing, or if your stomach hurts, your dosage may need adjustment. Call your doctor. • Notify your doctor if you develop signs of jaundice (yellowing of the eyes or skin, dark urine).

Comments: Take this drug with food or milk. Nausea caused by this drug may be relieved by lying down. • Many headaches are believed to be caused by nervousness, tension, or prolonged contraction of the head and neck muscles. This drug is reported to relieve these conditions to help control headache. • For this and other preparations containing codeine, the number that follows the drug name always refers to the amount of codeine present. Hence, #3 has 1/2 grain (30 mg); #4 has 1 grain (60 mg). These numbers are standard for the amounts of codeine contained in any codeine product.

Floxin antibiotic

Ingredient: ofloxacin
Dosage Form: Tablet: 200 mg; 300 mg; 400 mg
Use: Treatment of bacterial infections including urinary tract, respiratory, and skin infections; and sexually transmitted diseases
Minor Side Effects: Abdominal pain; altered taste sensations; constipation; cough; diarrhea; dizziness; dry mouth; gas; headache; heartburn; loss of appetite; nausea; sensitivity to sunlight; stomach upset; thirst; tiredness; vomiting; weakness. Most of these side effects, if they occur, should gradually subside over a period of time as your body makes an adjustment to the medication. Be sure to inform your doctor about any that are persistent or particularly bothersome.
Major Side Effects: Blurred vision; breathing difficulty; chest pain; chills; confusion; depression; fever; hallucinations; hives; itchy skin; rapid, pounding heartbeat; restlessness; skin rash; trouble sleeping; tremor; vaginal discharge; vaginal itching. Notify your doctor if you notice any major side effects.
Contraindications: This drug is a quinolone antibiotic. It should not be taken by people who are allergic to it or to other quinolone antibiotics. Be sure your doctor knows if you have such an allergy. • This drug is not recommended for use in children or by pregnant or nursing women. Discuss the risks and benefits of this drug with your doctor.
Warnings: Persons with kidney problems should use this drug with caution. Lower than normal doses may be necessary. • This drug should be used cautiously by persons with epilepsy, central nervous system disorders, or seizure disorders because tremor, confusion, restlessness, and, very rarely, hallucinations and seizures have occurred. Make sure your doctor knows if you have any of these conditions or experience any of these effects. • This drug may interact with cyclosporine, nitrofurantoin, probenecid, and theophylline. If you are currently taking any drugs of these types, consult your doctor about their use. If you are unsure of the type or contents of your medications, ask your doctor or pharmacist. • Antacids can interfere with the absorption of this drug. Avoid taking an antacid at least two hours before or after taking this drug. • Notify your doctor if you experience breathing difficulties, fever, skin rash, chest pain, tremor, restlessness, or confusion while taking this medication. • This drug may cause dizziness or light-headedness; avoid tasks that require alertness, such as driving a car or operating potentially dangerous equipment. • This drug can increase sensitivity to sunlight. Avoid prolonged sun exposure and wear protective clothing and an effective sunscreen when outdoors.
Comments: This drug is best taken on an empty stomach two hours before or after a meal. Drink plenty of fluids while taking this medication. • Antibiotics work best if a constant level of the drug is kept in the body. To do this, take each dose as prescribed at evenly spaced intervals around the clock. Your doctor or pharmacist can help you establish a dosing schedule. • Finish all of this medication, even if you begin to feel better. Stopping therapy too soon can lead to ineffective treatment and the infection may reappear. • Nausea, stomach upset, diarrhea, or headache may occur during the first few days of therapy. These effects should subside as your body adjusts to the medication. If they become severe or bothersome, notify your doctor. • Drink plenty of fluids while taking this drug. Try to drink eight to ten glasses of water, unless your doctor directs you otherwise.

Fluocinonide topical steroid hormone, see Lidex, Lidex-E topical steroid hormone.

Fluonex topical steroid hormone, see Lidex, Lidex-E topical steroid hormone.

Furadantin antibacterial, see nitrofurantoin antibacterial.

Furalan antibacterial, see nitrofurantoin antibacterial.

Furan antibacterial, see nitrofurantoin antibacterial.

Furanite antibacterial, see nitrofurantoin antibacterial.

Furosemide diuretic, see Lasix diuretic.

Gastrocrom antiasthmatic and antiallergic, see Intal antiasthmatic and antiallergic.

Gen-K potassium replacement, see potassium replacement.

Gentab LA decongestant and expectorant, see Entex LA decongestant and expectorant.

Gen-XENE antianxiety and anticonvulsant, see Tranxene antianxiety and anticonvulsant.

Glucotrol oral antidiabetic

Ingredient: glipizide
Dosage Form: Tablet: 5 mg; 10 mg
Use: Treatment of diabetes mellitus not controlled by diet and exercise alone

Minor Side Effects: Dizziness; fatigue; headache; heartburn; loss of appetite; nausea; stomach upset; sun sensitivity. Most of these side effects, if they occur, should subside as your body adjusts to the medication. Tell your doctor about any that are persistent or particularly bothersome.

Major Side Effects: Blood disorders; breathing difficulties; dark urine; diarrhea; fluid retention; itching; light-colored stools; low blood sugar; muscle cramps; rash; ringing in the ears; sore throat and fever; thirst; tingling in the hands and feet; unusual bleeding or bruising; vomiting; weakness; yellowing of the eyes or skin. Notify your doctor if you notice any major side effects.

Contraindications: This drug should not be used for the treatment of juvenile (insulin dependent) or unstable diabetes. This drug should not be used by diabetics subject to acidosis or ketosis or those with a history of diabetic coma. Persons with severe liver, kidney, heart, or thyroid disorders should not use this drug. Avoid using this drug if you are allergic to sulfonylureas or sulfa drugs. Be sure your doctor knows if any of these conditions applies to you.

Warnings: This drug should be used cautiously during pregnancy. If you are currently pregnant or become pregnant while taking this drug, talk to your doctor about its use. • This drug should be used with caution by nursing women, children, and persons with liver, kidney, or thyroid disorders. • Thiazide diuretics and beta-blocking drugs commonly used to treat high blood pressure may interfere with your control of diabetes. • This drug interacts with alcohol, steroids, estrogens, oral contraceptives, antipsychotics, phenytoin, isoniazid, thyroid hormones, salicylates, and certain diuretics and antibiotics. If you are taking any drugs of these types, talk to your doctor about your use of Glucotrol. If you are not sure about the types or contents of your medications, talk to your doctor or pharmacist. • Do not drink alcohol or take any other medications unless directed to do so by your doctor. Flushing or breathlessness can occur with the combination of alcohol and Glucotrol. Be especially careful with nonprescription cough and cold remedies. Learn how to monitor your blood sugar (glucose). Discuss this with your health-care provider. When starting this drug, your blood sugar should be tested frequently as directed and your doctor should review the results at least once a week. Your doctor may also want you to have frequent laboratory blood tests and tests of liver function to check for side effects. • Be sure you can recognize signs of low blood sugar (hypoglycemia) and know what to do if you begin to experience these symptoms. Signs of low blood sugar include chills, cold sweat, drowsiness, headache, nausea, nervousness, rapid pulse, tremors, and weakness. If these symptoms develop, eat or drink something containing sugar and call your doctor. Poor diet, malnutrition, strenuous exercise, and alcohol may lead to low blood sugar. • Call your doctor if you develop an infection, fever, sore throat, rash, excessive thirst or urination, unusual bleeding or bruising, dark urine, light-colored stools, or yellowing of the eyes or skin.

Comments: Take this drug at the same time every day. It is usually taken 30 minutes before breakfast unless otherwise directed. • Do not discontinue taking this medication without consulting your doctor. • It is advised that persons taking this drug carry a medical alert card or wear a medical alert bracelet. • Studies have shown that a good diet and exercise program are extremely important in controlling diabetes. Discuss the use of this drug with your doctor. Persons taking this drug must carefully watch their diet, exercise regularly, and should practice good personal hygiene. • Avoid prolonged or unprotected exposure to sunlight while taking this drug, as it makes you more sensitive to the sun's burning rays. • You may have to switch to insulin therapy if you require surgery or if complications such as ketoacidosis, severe trauma, or infection develop. There are other drugs similar to this (see Orinase, Diabinese, Micronase) that vary slightly in their activity. Certain persons who do not benefit from one type of these oral antidiabetic agents may find another one more effective. Discuss this with your doctor.

Glynase PresTab oral antidiabetic, see Micronase oral anatidiabetic.

Guaipax decongestant and expectorant, see Entex LA decongestant and expectorant.

G-well pediculicide and scabicide, see Kwell pediculicide and scabicide.

Habitrol transdermal smoking deterrent, see Nicoderm transdermal smoking deterrent.

Halcion sedative and hypnotic

Ingredient: triazolam
Dosage Form: Tablet: 0.125 mg; 0.25 mg
Use: Short-term relief of insomnia

Minor Side Effects: Blurred vision; constipation; decreased sexual drive; diarrhea; dizziness; drowsiness; dry mouth; headache; lethargy; light-headedness; loss of appetite; nausea; nervousness; relaxed feeling; vomiting. Most of these side effects, if they occur, should subside as your body adjusts to the medication. Tell your doctor about any that are persistent or bothersome.

Major Side Effects: Confusion; depression; hallucinations; impaired coordination; memory loss; nightmares; rapid heartbeat; ringing in the ears; tremors; weakness. Notify your doctor if you notice any major side effects.

Contraindications: This drug should not be used by persons allergic to it or by pregnant or nursing women. Consult your doctor immediately if this drug has been prescribed for you and either condition applies.

Warnings: This drug should be used with caution by depressed people, persons under the age of 18, elderly patients, and people with liver or kidney disease, narrow-angle glaucoma, or psychosis. Be sure your doctor knows if any of these conditions applies to you. • Because this drug has the potential to be habit-forming, it must be used with caution, especially by those with a history of drug dependence. Tolerance may develop quickly; do not increase the dose or take this drug more often than prescribed without first consulting your physician. Do not abruptly discontinue taking this drug if you have been taking it for a long time. Your dosage may need to be decreased gradually. • This drug is safe when taken alone; when it is combined with other sedative drugs or alcohol, serious adverse reactions may develop. Avoid the use of alcohol, other sedatives, or central nervous system depressants. This drug may interact with anticonvulsants, antihistamines, cimetidine, and erythromycin. If you are currently taking any drugs of these types, consult your doctor about their use. If you are unsure of the type or contents of your medications, ask your doctor or pharmacist. • This drug causes drowsiness; avoid tasks that require alertness, such as driving a car or operating potentially dangerous equipment. • The elderly are more sensitive to this drug, so smaller doses are prescribed for them.

Comments: Take this drug one-half to one hour before bedtime unless otherwise prescribed. • After you stop taking this drug, your sleep may be disturbed for a few nights. If you feel groggy the day after taking this drug, talk to your doctor about using a smaller dose or different sedative so you get a restful night's sleep but can still function alertly the next day.

Hismanal antihistamine

Ingredient: astemizole
Dosage Form: Tablet: 10 mg
Use: Relief of symptoms of allergy (including insect stings), such as watery eyes, sneezing, itching, hives

Minor Side Effects: Blurred vision; constipation; diarrhea; drowsiness; dry mouth, nose, and throat; excitation; headache; increased frequency of urination; insomnia; loss of appetite; muscle pain; nasal stuffiness; nausea; nightmares; sedation; sun sensitivity; sweating; vomiting; weight gain. Most of these side effects, if they occur, should subside as your body adjusts to the medication. Tell your doctor about any that are persistent or particularly bothersome.

Major Side Effects: Breathing difficulties; chest pain; confusion; depression; difficulty in urinating; dizziness; faintness; irregular heartbeat; menstrual disorders; rapid, pounding heartbeat; rash; ringing in the ears; tingling of hands and feet; thinning of hair; tremors. Notify your doctor of any major side effects.

Warnings: This drug must be used cautiously by persons with glaucoma (certain types), ulcers (certain types), thyroid disease, certain urinary difficulties, enlarged prostate, or heart disease (certain types). Be sure your doctor knows if any of these conditions applies to you. • Elderly persons may be more likely than others to experience side effects, especially sedation, and should use this drug with caution. • The sedative effects of this drug are enhanced by alcohol and other central nervous system depressants. This drug can affect your response to theophylline, heart medications, and antibiotics. If you are currently taking drugs of these types, consult your doctor about their use. If you are unsure about the type or contents of your medications, ask your doctor or pharmacist. • This medication may cause irregular heart rhythms, especially at high doses. Do not increase your dose or take other drugs along with this without consulting your doctor. Notify your doctor if you experience faintness, dizziness, or an irregular heartbeat. • Because this drug may cause drowsiness, avoid tasks requiring alertness, such as driving a car or operating potentially dangerous equipment. • While taking this medication, do not take any nonprescription item for weight control, cough, cold, or sinus problems without first consulting your doctor or pharmacist.

Comments: Hismanal is best taken on an empty stomach, either one hour before or two hours after meals. • Chew gum or suck on ice chips or a piece of hard candy to relieve mouth dryness. • This drug may make you more sensitive to the effects of the sun. Wear protective clothing and use a sunscreen when outdoors. • Hismanal offers the advantage of causing less drowsiness and sedation than other antihistamines. Hismanal is similar to Seldane.

Hydrocet analgesic, see Vicodin, Vicodin ES analgesics.

hydrochlorothiazide diuretic

Ingredient: hydrochlorothiazide
Equivalent Products: Esidrix; Ezide; HydroDIURIL; Hydro-Par; Oretic
Dosage Forms: Tablet: 25 mg; 50 mg; 100 mg. Liquid (content per 5 ml teaspoon): 50 mg. Concentrated solution (content per 1 ml): 100 mg.
Uses: Prevention of fluid accumulation and removal of fluid from tissue; treatment of high blood pressure
Minor Side Effects: Abdominal pain; constipation; decreased sexual desire; diarrhea; dizziness; drowsiness; headache; heartburn; increased cholesterol and triglyceride levels in the blood; itching; loss of appetite; nausea; restlessness; sun sensitivity; vomiting. Most of these side effects, if they occur, should subside as your body adjusts to the medication. Tell your doctor about any that are persistent or particularly bothersome.
Major Side Effects: Blood disorders; blurred vision; bruising; chest pain; dark urine; dry mouth; elevated blood sugar; fever; gout; muscle cramps or spasm; palpitations; skin rash; sore throat; thirst; tingling in fingers and toes; weakness; yellowing of the eyes or skin. Notify your doctor if you notice any major side effects.
Contraindications: This drug should not be used by people who are allergic to it or to sulfa drugs, by people with kidney disease, or by people who are unable to urinate. Consult your doctor immediately if this drug has been prescribed for you and any of these conditions applies.
Warnings: This drug should be used cautiously by pregnant women and by people who have diabetes, liver disease, a history of allergy, or asthma. Be sure your doctor knows if any of these conditions applies to you. • Nursing mothers who must take this drug should stop nursing. • This drug may affect the potency of, or your need for, other blood pressure drugs and antidiabetics; dosage adjustment may be necessary. • This drug interacts with colestipol hydrochloride, cholestyramine, digitalis, lithium, quinidine, and steroids. If you are currently taking any drugs of these types, consult your doctor about their use. If you are unsure about the type or contents of your medications, ask your doctor or pharmacist. • If you are taking digitalis in addition to this drug, watch carefully for symptoms of increased digitalis toxicity (e.g., nausea, blurred vision, palpitations), and notify your doctor immediately if they occur. • This drug may affect thyroid and other laboratory tests; be sure your doctor knows that you are taking this drug if you are having any tests done. • This drug can cause potassium loss. Signs of such loss include dry mouth, thirst, weakness, muscle pain or cramps, nausea, and vomiting. Call your doctor if you experience any of these symptoms. • While taking this product, limit your consumption of alco-

holic beverages in order to prevent dizziness or light-headedness. • If you have high blood pressure, do not take any nonprescription item for weight control, cough, cold, or sinus problems without first checking with your doctor; such medications may contain ingredients that can increase blood pressure. • Notify your doctor if you develop signs of jaundice (yellowing of the eyes or skin, dark urine). • This drug may cause gout, high blood levels of calcium, or the onset of diabetes that has been latent. To help prevent these problems, you should have blood tests done periodically. • This medication can increase your skin's sensitivity to the sun. Avoid prolonged sun exposure and use a sunscreen.

Comments: This drug must be taken as directed. Do not take extra doses or skip a dose without first consulting your doctor. • Diuretics are also called water pills. Diuretics help eliminate extra fluid that may build up, especially in the feet, causing swelling. As a result, this drug causes frequent urination. Expect this effect; it should not alarm you. Try to plan your dosage schedule to avoid taking this drug at bedtime. • You should learn how to monitor your pulse and blood pressure while you are taking this drug; discuss this with your doctor or pharmacist. • To avoid dizziness or light-headedness when you stand, contract and relax the muscles of your legs for a few moments before rising. Do this by pushing one foot against the floor while raising the other foot slightly, alternating feet so that you are pumping your legs in a pedaling motion. • To help avoid potassium loss, take this product with a glass of fresh or frozen orange juice, or eat a banana every day. The use of a salt substitute also helps prevent potassium loss. Do not change your diet, however, without consulting your doctor. Too much potassium can also be dangerous.

hydrocodone bitartrate and acetaminophen analgesic, see Vicodin, Vicodin ES analgesic.

HydroDIURIL diuretic, see hydrochlorothiazide diuretic.

Hydrogesic analgesic, see Vicodin, Vicodin ES analgesics.

Hydro-Par diuretic, see hydrochlorothiazide diuretic.

Hydroxyzine HCl antianxiety and antihistamine, see Atarax antianxiety and antihistamine.

Hy-Phen analgesic, see Vicodin, Vicodin ES analgesics.

Hytrin antihypertensive

Ingredient: terazocin
Dosage Form: Tablet: 1 mg; 2 mg; 5 mg; 10 mg
Use: Treatment of high blood pressure
Minor Side Effects: Abdominal pain; constipation; cough; diarrhea; dizziness; drowsiness; dry mouth; frequent urination; gas; headache; itching; nasal congestion; nausea; nervousness; sweating; tiredness; vivid dreams; vomiting; weakness. Most of these side effects, if they occur, should subside as your body adjusts to the medication. Tell your doctor about any that are persistent or particularly bothersome.
Major Side Effects: Blurred vision; breathing trouble; chest pain; decreased sexual ability; depression; difficulty urinating; fainting; fast pulse; fever; fluid retention; hallucinations; joint pain; muscle aches; nosebleed; rapid, pounding heartbeat; rash; ringing in the ears; shortness of breath; tingling of the fingers or toes; weight gain. Notify your doctor if you notice any major side effects.

Contraindication: This drug should not be taken by people who are allergic to it. Consult your doctor immediately if you have such an allergy.

Warnings: This drug should be used very cautiously by pregnant or nursing women, by children, and by persons with kidney disease. Be sure your doctor knows if any of these conditions applies to you. • This drug should be used with caution in conjunction with other antihypertensive drugs such as calcium channel blockers and beta blockers; if you are currently taking any drugs of these types, consult your doctor about their use. If you are unsure of the type or contents of your medications, ask your doctor or pharmacist. • While taking this drug, do not take any nonprescription item for weight control, cough, cold, allergy, or sinus problems without first checking with your doctor; such items may contain ingredients that can increase blood pressure. • While taking this drug, you should limit your consumption of alcoholic beverages, which can increase dizziness and other side effects. • Because initial therapy with this drug may cause dizziness and fainting, the first dose is usually taken at bedtime. In addition, your doctor will probably start you on a low dose and gradually increase your dosage. • Do not drive a car or operate potentially dangerous equipment for a few hours after the first dose or when your dose is increased if dizziness occurs.

Comments: Take this drug exactly as directed. Do not take extra doses or skip a dose without consulting your doctor first. • Do not discontinue taking this medication unless your doctor directs you to do so. It is important to continue taking this medication even if you do not feel sick. Most people with high blood pressure do not have symptoms and do not feel ill; therefore, it is easy to forget to take the medication. • Mild side effects (e.g., nasal congestion, headache) are most noticeable during the first two weeks of therapy and become less bothersome as your body adjusts to the medication. • To avoid dizziness or light-headedness when you stand, contract and relax the muscles of your legs for a few moments before rising. Do this by pushing one foot against the floor while raising the other foot slightly, alternating feet so that you are pumping your legs in a pedaling motion. • If you are taking this drug and begin therapy with another antihypertensive drug, your doctor may reduce the dose of Hytrin and recalculate your dose over the next couple of weeks. Dosage adjustments will be made based on your response. • Learn how to monitor your pulse and blood pressure while taking this drug; discuss this with your doctor or pharmacist. As with all antihypertensive medications, they are most effective when used in conjunction with diet and lifestyle changes, such as exercise and stress reduction to control blood pressure. The medication does not cure high blood pressure.

Ilosone antibiotic, see erythromycin antibiotic.

Imipramine HCl antidepressant, see Tofranil antidepressant.

Inderal antihypertensive and antianginal, see propranolol antihypertensive and antianginal.

Inderide, Inderide LA diuretic and antihypertensive

Ingredients: propranolol; hydrochlorothiazide
Equivalent Product: Propranolol and Hydrochlorothiazide
Dosage Forms: Sustained-action tablet (see Comments): propranolol, 80 mg and hydrochlorothiazide, 50 mg; propranolol, 120 mg and hydrochlorothiazide, 50 mg; propranolol, 160 mg and hydrochlorothiazide, 50 mg. Tablet:

propranolol, 40 mg and hydrochlorothiazide, 25 mg; propranolol, 80 mg and hydrochlorothiazide, 25 mg

Uses: Treatment of high blood pressure and removal of fluid from tissues

Minor Side Effects: Abdominal cramps; blurred vision; constipation; drowsiness; elevated levels of cholesterol and triglycerides in the blood; fatigue; gas; headache; heartburn; insomnia; light-headedness; loss of appetite; muscle spasm; nasal congestion; nausea; restlessness; sun sensitivity; sweating; vomiting; weakness. Most of these side effects, if they occur, should subside as your body adjusts to the drug. Tell your doctor about any that are persistent or bothersome.

Major Side Effects: Blood disorders; breathing difficulties; bruises; cold hands and feet; dark urine; depression; diarrhea; difficulty in urinating; dizziness; dry mouth; elevated uric acid; fever; hair loss; hallucinations; heart failure; nightmares; rash; ringing in the ears; slow pulse; sore throat; tingling in the fingers; visual disturbances; yellowing of the eyes or skin. Notify your doctor if you notice any major side effects.

Contraindications: This drug should not be used by persons with bronchial asthma, severe hay fever, certain types of heart problems, or allergies to either of the active ingredients of this medication or to sulfa drugs. Be sure your doctor knows if any of these conditions applies to you. • This drug should not be used concurrently with monoamine oxidase inhibitors or during the two-week withdrawal period from such drugs. If you are currently taking any drugs of this type, consult your physician. If you are unsure of the type or contents of your medications, ask your doctor or pharmacist.

Warnings: This drug should be used with caution by persons undergoing major surgery and by persons with certain types of heart problems, thyroid disease, certain respiratory disorders, severe kidney disease, severe liver disease, diabetes, gout, or hypoglycemia. Be sure your doctor knows if any of these conditions applies to you. • This drug must be used with extreme caution in pregnancy. Discuss the risks and benefits with your doctor. • Nursing mothers who must take this drug should stop nursing. • This drug may interact with reserpine, digitalis, cimetidine, theophylline, aminophylline, indomethacin, colestipol, lithium, and corticosteroids. If you are currently taking any drugs of these types, consult your doctor about their use. If you are unsure about the type or contents of your medications, ask your doctor or pharmacist. • This drug may affect thyroid and other laboratory tests; be sure your doctor knows that you are taking this drug if you are having any tests done. • Because this drug may add to the effect of other blood pressure drugs, the doses may need to be adjusted if taken concurrently. • If you are taking digitalis in addition to this drug, watch for symptoms of increased digitalis toxicity (e.g., nausea, blurred vision, palpitations), and notify your doctor immediately if they occur. • Because of the hydrochlorothiazide component, this drug may cause gout or increased blood levels of calcium. It may also cause the onset of diabetes that has been latent. • This drug can cause potassium loss. Some of the symptoms of potassium loss are thirst, dry mouth, and muscle cramps. Notify your doctor if you experience such symptoms. • Notify your doctor if you develop signs of jaundice (yellowing of the eyes or skin, dark urine). • Do not suddenly stop taking this drug without your doctor's approval. Some of the symptoms may become worse when the drug is stopped abruptly. • While you are taking this drug, do not take any nonprescription item for weight control, cough, cold, or sinus problems without first checking with your doctor or pharmacist. Such items may contain ingredients that can increase blood pressure. • Notify your doctor if dizziness or diarrhea develops. • While taking this drug, limit your consumption of alcohol-containing beverages.

Comments: Take this drug exactly as directed. Be sure to take your medication doses at the same time each day. Do not take extra doses or skip a dose without first consulting your doctor. It is important to continue taking this medication even if you do not feel sick. Most people with high blood pressure do not have symptoms and do not feel ill; therefore, it is easy to forget to take the medication. The sustained-action tablets are designed for convenient once-a-day dosing; they are called Inderide LA. Do not crush or chew these tablets; they must be swallowed whole. Diuretics help eliminate extra fluid that may build up, especially in the feet, causing swelling. As a result, this drug causes frequent urination. Expect this effect; it should not alarm you. Try to plan your dosage schedule to avoid taking this at bedtime. • To avoid dizziness or light-headedness when you stand, contract and relax the muscles of your legs for a few moments before rising. Do this by pushing one foot against the floor while raising the other foot slightly, alternating feet so you are pumping your legs in a pedaling motion. • To help prevent potassium loss, take this drug with a glass of fresh or frozen orange juice, or eat a banana every day. The use of a salt substitute also helps prevent potassium loss. Do not change your diet, however, without consulting your doctor. Too much potassium may also be dangerous. • This drug may make you more sensitive to the cold. Dress warmly. This drug may also make you more sensitive to the sun. Avoid prolonged sun exposure, and wear a protective sunscreen when outdoors. • Your doctor may want you to take your pulse and blood pressure every day while you are on this medication. Discuss this with your doctor. • Combination or fixed-dose products are usually not prescribed as the first choice in the treatment of high blood pressure. Persons should receive each of the individual ingredients singly, and if the response is adequate to the fixed doses contained in Inderide, it can be substituted. The advantage of a combination product such as this drug is increased convenience to the patient. As with all antihypertensive medications, they are most effective when used in conjunction with diet and lifestyle changes, such as exercise and stress reduction to control blood pressure. The medication does not cure high blood pressure.

Indocin anti-inflammatory

Ingredient: indomethacin
Equivalent Product: Indomethacin
Dosage Forms: Capsule: 25 mg; 50 mg. Suppository: 50 mg. Suspension (content per 5 ml teaspoon): 25 mg. Sustained-release capsule (see Comments): 75 mg
Uses: Reduction of pain, redness, and swelling due to arthritis, bursitis, or tendinitis
Minor Side Effects: Bloating; constipation; diarrhea; dizziness; drowsiness; gas; headache; heartburn; insomnia; loss of appetite; nausea; vomiting. Most of these side effects, if they occur, should subside as your body adjusts to the medication. Tell your doctor about any that are persistent or particularly bothersome.
Major Side Effects: Black or tarry stools; bleeding gums; blood disorders; blood in urine; blurred vision; breathing difficulties; chest tightness; confusion; dark urine; depression; difficulty in urinating; easy bruising or bleeding; fatigue; fluid retention; itching; loss of hair; loss of hearing; numbness or tingling in fingers or toes; ringing in the ears; severe abdominal pain; skin rash; sore throat; ulcer; weight gain; yellowing of the eyes or skin. Notify your doctor if you notice any major side effects.
Contraindications: This drug should not be used by people who are allergic to it or to aspirin or other nonsteroidal anti-inflammatory drugs. Consult your

doctor immediately if this drug has been prescribed for you and you have such an allergy. • This drug should not be used by persons with nasal polyps associated with swelling. • The suppository form of this drug should not be used by persons with a history of proctitis or rectal bleeding. If you have either of these conditions, consult your doctor immediately.

Warnings: This drug should be used cautiously by elderly people; pregnant women; children under 14; people with a history of gastrointestinal disorders; and people with mental illness, epilepsy, Parkinson's disease, bleeding disorders, colitis, kidney or liver disease, high blood pressure, or heart failure. Be sure your doctor knows if any of these conditions applies to you. • Nursing women who must use this drug should stop nursing. • This drug interacts with aspirin, probenecid, oral antidiabetics, lithium, anticoagulants, furosemide, and certain antihypertensive medications. If you are currently taking any drugs of these types, consult your doctor about their use. If you are not sure about the type or contents of your medications, talk to your doctor or pharmacist. • If you are taking an anticoagulant (blood thinner), remind your doctor. • The severity of the side effects caused by this drug depends upon the dosage taken. Use the least amount possible and watch carefully for side effects. • Side effects are more likely to occur in the elderly. • This drug may irritate the stomach or intestines. Call your doctor if you experience stomach pain or if your stools are black and tarry. • If you notice changes in your vision or if you experience headaches while taking this drug, notify your doctor. • This drug may cause drowsiness; avoid tasks that require alertness, such as driving a car or operating potentially dangerous equipment. • Notify your doctor if you develop signs of jaundice (yellowing of the eyes or skin, dark urine). • Regular medical check-ups, including blood tests, are required of persons taking this drug for prolonged periods. • Never take this drug with aspirin or alcohol.

Comments: This drug must be taken with food or milk, immediately after meals, or with antacids (except sodium bicarbonate). Never take this drug on an empty stomach. It may take a month before you feel the full effect of this drug. • The sustained-release capsules (Indocin SR) must be swallowed whole. Do not crush or chew them. These capsules are taken less frequently than Indocin. Talk to your doctor about their use. • This drug is potent and is not intended for general aches and pains. • If you are taking this drug for the treatment of arthritis, an improvement in your condition should be noted within the first week. However, full benefits may not be obtained for several weeks. It is important to take this drug regularly. Do not to stop taking this drug even if symptoms have diminished or disappeared. • Do not take it only when you feel pain. This drug is not a substitute for rest, physical therapy, or other measures your doctor recommends. • This drug is similar in action to ibuprofen, tolmentin (Tolectin), piroxicam (Feldene), and other anti-inflammatory medications. If one anti-inflammatory drug is not well tolerated, your doctor may prescribe another one to find the best drug for you.

Indomethacin anti-inflammatory, see Indocin anti-inflammatory.

insulin antidiabetic

Ingredient: insulin

Equivalent Products: This drug is usually prescribed according to time of onset and duration of action, rather than by trade name.

Dosage Form: This drug is available only as an injection. Various types of insulin provide different times of onset and duration of action. The types of insulin and their times of onset and duration are as follows:

	Onset (hr.)	Duration (hr.)
regular insulin	½	6-8
insulin zinc suspension, prompt (Semilente)	1	14
isophane insulin (NPH)	1	24
insulin zinc suspension (Lente)	1-2	24
protamine zinc insulin (PZI)	6	36
insulin zinc suspension, extended (Ultralente)	6	over 36

Use: Treatment of insulin-dependent diabetes and diabetes mellitus not controlled by diet alone

Minor Side Effects: Low blood sugar (hypoglycemia) level characterized by confusion, fatigue, headache, hunger, nausea, rapid pulse, sweaty skin, tremor; vision changes, and weakness.

Major Side Effects: Difficulty breathing; rash.

Contraindications: There are no specific contraindications to the use of insulin, but before you begin therapy, your doctor must determine your specific needs and carefully work out your dosage regimen.

Warnings: This drug should be used only under the direction of a doctor, and a prescribed diet should be followed precisely. • Do not substitute one type of this drug for another. Your doctor may put you on a regimen of two or more types of insulin based on the onset and duration of action of each type to get the best effect. Stick to your prescribed regimen. • Roll insulin vial in hands to mix gently before withdrawing a dose in the syringe. • Purchase disposable syringes, do not reuse them, and remember to dispose of them properly. Once you have started using a particular brand of disposable insulin syringe and needle, do not switch brands without first talking with your doctor or pharmacist. • Injection sites for this drug should be rotated so as to avoid skin reactions due to repeated injections. It is important that this be done. Be sure to follow your doctor's instructions carefully. • When using this drug, be on guard for signs of low blood sugar—fatigue, nervousness, nausea, rapid heartbeat, and a cold sweat. If signs of low blood sugar are evident, eat a piece of candy or drink a glass of orange juice and try to contact your doctor who will instruct you on what to do in such a situation. • Also, be on the alert for signs of too much sugar. These signs include thirst, excess urination, and vision changes. Call your doctor if you experience any of these symptoms. • Allergy to insulin is unusual, but it may happen. Symptoms of such an allergy are similar to those of other allergies, including rash and difficulty breathing. If these symptoms occur, call your doctor. • If you become ill—if you catch a cold or the flu or become nauseated, for example—your insulin requirement may change. Consult your doctor. • This drug interacts with guanethidine, monoamine oxidase inhibitors, propranolol, steroids, tetracycline, and thyroid hormone. If you are currently taking any drugs of these types, consult your doctor about their use. If you are unsure of the type or contents of your medications, ask your doctor or pharmacist. • While taking this drug, do not take any nonprescription item for weight control, cough, cold, or sinus problems without first checking with your doctor.

Comments: It is best to store this drug in the refrigerator. Once the bottle has been opened, most forms (except U-500 strength) may be kept at room temperature if the contents are used within a month. Store in a cool, dry place. Avoid heat and sunlight. Do not freeze. • Special injection kits are available for blind diabetics. Ask your doctor for help in obtaining them. • Doses of this drug may be prepared in advance. Ask your pharmacist for advice. • Most insulin products are composed of a mixture of both pork and beef insulins. However, products are available that contain all beef insulin or all pork insulin. Human insulin is also available. Never switch from one form to another unless your doctor tells you to do so. • For best results, it is important that you understand diabetes. Insulin is used in conjunction with a proper diet and exercise program. Frequent monitoring of your urine or blood to check sugar levels is important. Various tests are available. Find the one that best suits your needs (check with your doctor or pharmacist), and learn how to use it. • If you are diabetic, you should wear a medical I.D. alert bracelet or carry a medical I.D. alert card in your wallet.

Intal antiasthmatic and antiallergic

Ingredient: cromolyn sodium
Equivalent Products: Gastrocrom; Nasalcrom respiratory inhalant
Dosage Forms: Aerosol spray (per actuation): 800 mcg. Inhaled solution (per 2 ml amp): 20 mg. Inhaled capsule: 20 mg. Oral capsule: 100 mg. Nasal solution: 5.2 mg per actuation
Uses: Prevention and the management of bronchial asthma and allergic symptoms
Minor Side Effects: Bad taste in mouth; cough; dizziness; dry throat; headache; hoarseness; increased frequency of urination; itchy nose; nasal congestion; nasal irritation; nausea; postnasal drip; sneezing; stomach upset; teary eyes. Most of these side effects, if they occur, should subside as your body adjusts to the medication. Tell your doctor about any that are persistent or bothersome.
Major Side Effects: Breathing difficulties; joint pain and swelling; nosebleed; painful urination; rash; wheezing. Notify your doctor if you notice any major side effects.
Contraindication: This drug should not be taken by anyone who is allergic to it. Consult your doctor if this drug has been prescribed for you and you have such an allergy.
Warning: The safety of this drug for use in pregnant or nursing women has not been established. Discuss the risks and benefits with your doctor. This drug will not stop an acute asthma attack. This drug must be taken continuously to prevent asthma symptoms.
Comments: For best results in the management of asthma, this drug must be taken continuously, at regular intervals throughout the day and night, even if you feel better. Do not stop taking this drug without consulting your doctor. To prevent exercise-induced bronchospasm, use this drug as directed no more than one hour before exercising. • Notify your doctor if chronic coughing or wheezing occurs while you are taking this medication. • It may take two to four weeks for the full effect of this drug to become apparent. • Rinsing your mouth before and after inhalation of this drug is advised in order to reduce irritation and dryness of mouth and throat. • To use the oral inhaler device, breathe out deeply, then place the inhaler between your lips. Compress inhaler and inhale deeply and steadily, then hold your breath for a few seconds. Remove the inhaler from your lips, then exhale. Repeat this procedure as directed. Ask your doctor or pharmacist to demonstrate the proper use of the inhaler; be sure you know how to use it correctly to get the most benefit from this medication. Be sure to clean the inhaler device weekly. • Nasalcrom nasal solution is used with a special nasalmatic spray device. Each spray measures the proper amount of the drug. Make sure you understand how to use the nasal device properly. The nasal spray is best used at regular intervals throughout the day. The pump should be replaced every six months. • Before using the nasal solution, blow your nose to clear the nasal passages. Sneezing or slight stinging may occur when it is first used. To avoid contamination, be sure to replace the nasal solution every six months, even if you have not finished all of it. Do not keep outdated medication. • Gastrocrom is the name for the oral capsule form.

It is best taken one-half hour before meals. The capsules are NOT to be swallowed. Open the capsule, and pour contents into one-half glass of hot water. Stir until it dissolves. Then add cold water, and drink all the liquid. Do not mix the capsule contents with juice, foods, or milk.

Iodinated glycerol and codeine cough suppressant and expectorant, see Tussi-Organidin cough suppressant and expectorant.

Iophen-C cough suppressant and expectorant, see Tussi-Organidin cough suppressant and expectorant.

Iotuss cough suppressant and expectorant, see Tussi-Organidin cough suppressant and expectorant.

Iso-Bid antianginal, see Isordil antianginal.

Isollyl Improved analgesic, see Fiorinal analgesic.

Isoptin, Isoptin SR antianginal, antihypertensive, and antiarrhythmic

Ingredient: verapamil hydrochloride
Equivalent Products: Calan and Calan SR; Verapamil HCl; Verelan
Dosage Forms: Sustained-release tablet (see Comments): 120 mg; 180 mg; 240 mg. Tablet: 40 mg; 80 mg; 120 mg
Uses: Prevention and control of angina pectoris (chest pain) or irregular heartbeat (arrhythmia); management of high blood pressure. This drug may also be used for other medical conditions as determined by your doctor.
Minor Side Effects: Abdominal pain; constipation; dizziness; fatigue; fever; headache; loss of balance; muscle cramps; nausea; sexual difficulties; shakiness; sleeplessness; sweating. Most of these side effects, if they occur, should subside as your body adjusts to the medication. Tell your doctor about any that are persistent or particularly bothersome.
Major Side Effects: Blurred vision; breathing trouble; changes in menstruation; confusion; depression; dizziness (severe); fainting; hair loss; itching; shortness of breath; slow or irregular heartbeat; swelling of the hands and feet; swollen or bleeding gums; unusual weakness. Notify your doctor if you notice any major side effects.
Contraindications: This drug should not be taken by people who are allergic to it or by those who have certain types of heart disease or extremely low blood pressure. Contact your doctor immediately if this drug has been prescribed for you and any of these conditions applies. • This drug should not be used during pregnancy unless clearly needed. • Women who are breast-feeding should not take this drug. • Do not take this drug until at least two days after stopping the drug disopyramide (Norpace).
Warnings: This drug should be used with caution by people who have cardiogenic shock, AV block, sick sinus syndrome, congestive heart failure, or liver or kidney disease. • This drug may interact with beta blockers, antihypertensive drugs, theophylline, lithium, cimetidine, digitalis, diuretics, calcium supplements, and quinidine. If you are currently using any of these types of drugs, consult your doctor about their use; dosage adjustments may be needed. If you are unsure about the type or contents of your medications, ask your doctor or pharmacist. • This medication causes dizziness, especially during the first few days of therapy. Avoid activities that require alertness, such as driving a car or operating potentially dangerous equipment. Limit consumption of alco-

hol, which can exaggerate this dizziness. • Contact your doctor if this drug causes severe or persistent dizziness, constipation, or nausea, or if it causes swelling of hands and feet, shortness of breath, or irregular heartbeat.

Comments: Take this drug as directed. • It may take several weeks before any effect from the drug is noticed. It is important that you continue to take the medication even if you feel well. Do not suddenly stop taking this medication, as chest pain can occur. This drug is not effective in treating an attack of angina already in progress. • Isoptin SR, Calan SR, and Verelan are sustained-release formulations that are usually taken only once a day with food. Do not crush or chew the sustained-release forms of this drug; they must be swallowed whole. Crushing or chewing the drug will destroy the prolonged action, increasing the risk of side effects. • Your doctor may want to see you regularly when you first start taking this drug in order to check your response. Your doctor may also want you to monitor your pulse and blood pressure; discuss this with your doctor. As with all antihypertensive medications, they are most effective when used in conjunction with diet and lifestyle changes, such as exercise and stress reduction to control blood pressure. The medication does not cure high blood pressure.

Isopto Carpine ophthalmic glaucoma preparation

Ingredient: pilocarpine hydrochloride

Equivalent Products: Adsorbocarpine; Akarpine; Ocu-Carpine; Ocusert Pilo-20; Ocusert Pilo-40; Pilocar; Pilocarpine HCl; Piloptic 1; Piloptic 2; Pilostat

Dosage Forms: Drops: 0.25%; 0.5%; 1%; 2%; 3%; 4%; 6%; 8%; 10%. Gel: 4%. Ocular therapeutic system (see Comments): 20 mcg; 40 mcg

Use: Treatment of glaucoma

Minor Side Effects: Aching in the brow; blurred vision; headache; decreased night vision; salivation; tearing; temporary burning or stinging on application; twitching of eyelids. Most of these side effects, if they occur, should subside as your body adjusts to the medication. Tell your doctor about any that are persistent or particularly bothersome.

Major Side Effects: Diarrhea; frequent urination; muscle tremors; nausea; nearsightedness or other changes in vision; stomach cramps; sweating. Notify your doctor if you notice any major side effects.

Contraindication: This drug should not be used by people who are allergic to pilocarpine. Consult your doctor immediately if this drug has been prescribed for you and you have such an allergy.

Warnings: This drug should be used cautiously by people who have certain types of heart disease, asthma, peptic ulcer, thyroid disease, spasms of the gastrointestinal tract, blockage of the urinary tract, seizures, or Parkinson's disease. Alert your doctor if you have any of these conditions. • Soft contact lenses may become discolored by this drug. Avoid wearing them while using this drug. • This drug may cause sensitivity to bright light and impair night vision. Use extra caution performing hazardous tasks or driving, especially at night.

Comments: To administer eye drops, lie or sit down and tilt your head back. Carefully pull your lower eyelid down to form a pouch. Hold the dropper close to, but not touching, the eyelid, and place the prescribed number of drops into the pouch. Do not place the drops directly on the eyeball; you probably will blink and lose the medication. Close your eye and keep it shut for a few moments. To administer eye gel, lie or sit down and tilt your head back. Carefully pull your lower eyelid down to form a pouch. Gently squeeze the tube to release a small amount of the gel. With a sweeping motion, place the gel into the pouch. Do not place it directly on the eyeball; you probably will blink and lose medication. Slowly roll your eyeball around to spread the gel. If you are using other eye medications in addition to the gel, use eye drops at least five minutes before using the gel. If you miss a dose, apply it as soon as it is remembered unless it is near the time for the next dose. In that case, skip the missed dose and resume your usual dosing schedule. Do not double the dose to catch up. • This drug may sting when first administered; this sensation usually goes away quickly. • Be careful about the contamination of solutions used for the eyes. Wash your hands before using eye drops. Do not touch dropper to your eye. Do not wash or wipe the dropper before replacing it in the bottle. Close the bottle tightly to keep out moisture. Store at room temperature away from heat and direct sunlight. If the eye drops or gel become discolored or contain particles, discard the unused medication and begin using a fresh bottle or tube. Check the expiration date on the drug label and discard any unused drug after that date. • The ocular therapeutic system (Ocusert Pilo) is an oval ring of plastic that contains pilocarpine. This ring is placed in the eye by the patient, and the drug is released gradually over a period of seven days. It offers the convenience of once-a-week dosing versus frequent application (four to six times a day) of the drops. If you are having trouble controlling glaucoma, ask your doctor about the possibility of using one of these devices.

Isordil antianginal

Ingredient: isosorbide dinitrate

Equivalent Products: Dilatrate-SR; Iso-Bid; Isosorbide Dinitrate; Isotrate Timecelles; Sorbitrate

Dosage Forms: Sublingual tablet: 2.5 mg; 5 mg; 10 mg. Sustained-action capsule: 40 mg. Sustained-action tablet: 40 mg. Tablet: 5 mg; 10 mg; 20 mg; 30 mg; 40 mg; Chewable tablet: 5 mg; 10 mg.

Use: Prevention (all dosage forms) and relief (chewable and sublingual tablets only) of chest pain (angina) due to heart disease

Minor Side Effects: Anxiety; blurred vision; dizziness; flushing; headache; loss of appetite; nausea; vomiting. Most of these side effects, if they occur, should subside as your body adjusts to the medication. Tell your doctor about any that are persistent or particularly bothersome.

Major Side Effects: Fainting spells; low blood pressure; rapid, pounding heart rate; rash; restlessness; sweating; weakness. Notify your doctor if you notice any major side effects.

Contraindications: This drug should not be taken by people who are allergic to it or by people with low blood pressure or head injury. Sublingual tablets should not be used by persons who are recovering from a heart attack. Consult your doctor if this drug has been prescribed for you and any of these conditions applies.

Warnings: This drug should be used cautiously by those with glaucoma, severe anemia, thyroid disease, or frequent diarrhea. • This drug should be used by pregnant and nursing women only if clearly necessary. Discuss the risks and benefits with your doctor. • This drug interacts with nitroglycerin; if you are currently using nitroglycerin, consult your doctor about its use. • Alcoholic beverages should be avoided or used with caution, as they may enhance the severity of this drug's side effects. • With continued use, you may develop a tolerance to this drug. Many adverse side effects disappear after two to three weeks of drug use, but you may also become less responsive to the drug's beneficial effects. Consult your doctor if you feel that the drug is losing its effectiveness or if you have a persistent headache. • Before using this drug to relieve chest pain, be certain that the pain arises from the heart. • If your chest pain is not relieved by use of this drug or if pain arises from a different location or differs in severity, consult your doctor immediately.

Comments: Take this medication as directed. Do not suddenly stop taking this medication without consulting your doctor. Oral tablets are best taken on an empty stomach with a full glass of water. The sustained-action forms must be swallowed whole. Crushing or chewing them will destroy the sustained action and may increase side effects. Chewable tablets are to be chewed thoroughly before swallowing. • To take a sublingual tablet, first sit down, then place the tablet under your tongue, close your mouth, and hold the saliva in your mouth and under your tongue as long as you can before swallowing it. (If you have a bitter taste in your mouth after five minutes, the drug has not been completely absorbed. Wait five minutes before drinking water.) It may be necessary to take another tablet as directed if the pain still exists. If the pain continues or it worsens, immediately call your doctor, medical rescue service, or report directly to the nearest emergency treatment facility. • Side effects generally disappear as your body adjusts to the medication. • Headache is a common side effect. It generally occurs after taking a dose and lasts a short time. Headaches should be less noticeable with continued treatment. If they persist, contact your doctor. Aspirin or acetaminophen may help to relieve headaches, but do not take either without first consulting your doctor. • To avoid dizziness or light-headedness, contract and relax the muscles of your legs for a few moments before rising. Do this by pushing one foot against the floor while raising the other foot slightly, alternating feet so that you are pumping your legs. • The tablets and capsules should be stored in their original containers, and the containers should be kept tightly closed. Do not keep outdated medication. • Although the sublingual tablets are effective in relieving chest pain, there is some question about the effectiveness of the other forms in preventing pain. Discuss the possible benefits with your doctor.

Isosorbide Dinitrate antianginal, see Isordil antianginal.

Isotrate Timecelles antianginal, see Isordil antianginal.

Janimine antidepressant, see Tofranil antidepressant.

K + 8 potassium replacement, see potassium replacement.

K + 10 potassium replacement, see potassium replacement.

Kaochlor potassium replacement, see potassium replacement.

Kaon potassium replacement, see potassium replacement.

Kaon-Cl potassium replacement, see potassium replacement.

Kato potassium replacement, see potassium replacement.

Kay Ciel potassium replacement, see potassium replacement.

Kaylixir potassium replacement, see potassium replacement.

K + Care potassium replacement, see potassium replacement.

K-Dur potassium replacement, see potassium replacement.

Keflet antibiotic, see Keflex antibiotic.

Keflex antibiotic

Ingredient: cephalexin

Equivalent Products: Biocef; Cefanex; Cephalexin; Keflet; Keftab; Lartan; Zartan

Dosage Forms: Capsule: 250 mg; 500 mg. Drops (content per ml): 100 mg. Liquid (content per 5 ml teaspoon): 125 mg; 250 mg. Tablet (see Comments): 250 mg; 500 mg; 1 g

Use: Treatment of a variety of bacterial infections

Minor Side Effects: Diarrhea; dizziness; fatigue; flushing; gas; headache; heartburn; loss of appetite; nausea; vomiting. Most of these side effects, if they occur, should subside as your body adjusts to the medication. Tell your doctor about any that are persistent or particularly bothersome.

Major Side Effects: Breathing difficulties; dark urine; fever; itching; rash; rectal and vaginal itching; severe diarrhea; sore mouth; stomach cramps; superinfection; tingling in the hands or feet; unusual bruising or bleeding. Notify your doctor if you notice any major side effects.

Contraindications: This is a cephalosporin antibiotic. This drug should not be used by people who are allergic to it or to other cephalosporin antibiotics or to other antibiotics similar to it (such as penicillins). It is generally believed that about ten percent of all people who are allergic to penicillin will be allergic to an antibiotic like this as well. Be sure your doctor knows if you have such an allergy.

Warnings: This drug should be used cautiously by women who are pregnant or nursing and by people with kidney disease or a history of colitis or stomach disorders. Be sure your doctor knows if any of these conditions applies to you. • This drug should be used cautiously in newborns. • Prolonged use of this drug may allow organisms that are not susceptible to it to grow wildly. Do not use this drug unless your doctor has specifically told you to do so. Be sure to follow directions carefully and report any unusual reactions to your doctor at once. • This drug should be used cautiously in conjunction with diuretics, probenecid, and aminoglycoside antibiotics. If you are unsure of the type or contents of your medications, ask your doctor or pharmacist. • This drug may interfere with some blood tests. Be sure your doctor knows you are taking it. • Diabetics using Clinitest urine test may get a false high sugar reading. Change to Clinistix, Diastix, Chemstrip UG, or Tes-Tape urine test to avoid this problem.

Comments: Take this drug with food or milk if stomach upset occurs. • The capsule and tablet forms of this drug should be stored at room temperature. The liquid form of this drug should be refrigerated and any unused portion should be discarded after 14 days. Shake well before using. This medication should never be frozen. • This medication works best if a constant level of the drug is kept in the body. To do this, take each dose as prescribed at evenly spaced intervals around the clock. Your doctor or pharmacist can help you establish a dosing schedule. Finish all the medication even if you feel better, to ensure complete elimination of the infection. Stopping therapy too soon may lead to reinfection. • Nausea, stomach upset, diarrhea, or headache may occur during the first few days of therapy. These effects should subside as your body adjusts to the drug. If they become severe or bothersome, notify your doctor.

Keftab antibiotic, see Keflex antibiotic.

Ketoprofen anti-inflammatory, see Orudis anti-inflammatory.

K-G potassium replacement, see potassium replacement.

K-Lease potassium replacement, see potassium replacement.

Klonopin anticonvulsant

Ingredient: clonazepam
Dosage Form: Tablet: 0.5 mg; 1 mg; 2 mg
Uses: Treatment of seizure disorders or other conditions as determined appropriate by your doctor

Minor Side Effects: Blurred vision; change in sex drive; constipation; diarrhea; dizziness; drowsiness; dry mouth; fatigue; headache; heartburn; irritability; nervousness; stomach pains; sweating; weakness. Most of these side effects, if they occur, should subside as your body adjusts to the medication. Tell your doctor about any that are persistent or particularly bothersome.

Major Side Effects: Breathing difficulties; clumsiness; confusion; dark urine; depression; difficulty in urinating; hallucinations; menstrual changes; nervousness; rapid heartbeat; rash; shakiness; sleeping difficulties; slurred speech; sore throat; uncoordinated movements; yellowing of the eyes or skin. Notify your doctor if you notice any major side effects.

Contraindications: This drug should not be used by persons allergic to it or to other benzodiazepines or by persons with acute narrow-angle glaucoma. Consult your doctor immediately if this drug had been prescribed for you and either condition applies.

Warnings: This drug should be used cautiously by pregnant or nursing women, elderly people, children, and people with a history of kidney or liver disease. Be sure your doctor knows if any of these conditions applies to you. • This drug should be used cautiously with antipsychotic medications, pain medications, anticonvulsants, antihistamines, alcohol, sedatives, antianxiety drugs, or other central nervous system depressants. If you are currently taking any drugs of these types, consult your doctor about their use. If you are unsure of the type or contents of your medications, ask your doctor or pharmacist. • Depending on the type of seizure being treated, this drug may be used in combination with other anticonvulsants. • To prevent oversedation, avoid the use of alcohol or other drugs with sedative properties. • Do not stop taking this drug suddenly without first consulting your doctor. If you have been taking this drug for a long time, your dosage should gradually be reduced, according to your doctor's directions. • This drug has the potential to become habit-forming and must be used with caution. Tolerance may develop; do not increase the dose of this medication without first consulting your doctor. • If you are taking this drug for an extended duration, your doctor may require you to have periodic blood and liver-function tests to monitor for side effects. • This drug may cause drowsiness, especially during the first few weeks of therapy; avoid tasks that require alertness, such as driving a car or operating potentially dangerous equipment. • Notify your doctor if you develop signs of jaundice (yellowing of the eyes or skin, dark urine).

Comments: To lessen stomach upset, take this medication with food or with a full glass of water. • It is important to take all doses of this medicine on time. • The full effects of this drug may not become apparent for three to four days. • Chew gum or suck on ice chips or a piece of hard candy to reduce mouth dryness. It is recommended you carry a medical alert card or wear a medical alert bracelet indicating that you are taking this medication for a seizure disorder.

K-Lor potassium replacement, see potassium replacement.

Klor-Con potassium replacement, see potassium replacement.

Klor-Con/EF potassium replacement, see potassium replacement.

Klorvess potassium replacement, see potassium replacement.

Klotrix potassium replacement, see potassium replacement.

K-Lyte potassium replacement, see potassium replacement.

K-Lyte/Cl potassium replacement, see potassium replacement.

K-Lyte DS potassium replacement, see potassium replacement.

K-Norm potassium replacement, see potassium replacement.

Kolyum potassium replacement, see potassium replacement.

K-Tab potassium replacement, see potassium replacement.

Kwell pediculicide and scabicide

Ingredient: lindane (gamma benzene hexachloride)
Equivalent Products: G-well; Lindane; Scabene
Dosage Forms: Cream; Lotion; Shampoo: 1%
Uses: Elimination of crab lice, head lice and their nits, and scabies
Minor Side Effects: Rash; skin irritation (see Warnings)
Major Side Effects: See Warnings.
Contraindications: This drug should not be used by people who are allergic to it or by those with known seizure disorders. Consult your doctor immediately if this drug has been prescribed for you and you have such an allergy or condition. This medication should not be used by pregnant women or by women who are breast-feeding.
Warnings: Side effects of this drug are rare if the directions for use are followed. However, convulsions and even death can result if the drug is swallowed or otherwise misused. If swallowed, do not take mineral oil; call the poison control center, your doctor, or your pharmacist immediately. • Do not use this drug with other skin products. • Special caution must be used in treating infants and children with this drug. • If you get any of this product in your eyes, flush them immediately with water. • Do not use this product over a longer period or more often than recommended by your doctor. • Do not use this product on your face. • Be sure to rinse this product off completely, as is stated in the directions. • Avoid unnecessary skin contact. • Wear rubber gloves when applying this product. • Avoid using this medication on open cuts.
Comments: Complete directions for the use of this drug are supplied by the manufacturer. Ask your pharmacist for these directions if they are not supplied with the drug. • To equalize the doses of lindane, the lotion and shampoo forms of this medication should be shaken before each dose is measured. • After using this product, you must remove the dead nits (eggs). Use a fine-tooth comb to remove them from your hair, or mix a solution of equal parts of water and vinegar and apply it to the affected area. Rub the solution in well. After several minutes, shampoo with your regular shampoo and then brush your hair. This process should remove all nits. • If required, a second application may be repeated in seven to nine days. Do not use lindane products routinely as shampoo. • A lice infestation can be treated just as effectively with a nonprescription product as with this product. However, this product is effective for scabies; the nonprescription medication is not. Consult your pharmacist. •

Lice are easily transmitted from one person to another. All family members should be carefully examined. Personal items (clothing, towels) need only be machine-washed on the "hot" temperature cycle and dried. No unusual cleaning measures are required. Combs, brushes, and other such washable items may be soaked in boiling water for one hour.

Lanophyllin bronchodilator, see theophylline bronchodilator.

Lanorinal analgesic, see Fiorinal analgesic.

Lanoxicaps heart drug, see Lanoxin heart drug.

Lanoxin heart drug

Ingredient: digoxin
Equivalent Products: Digoxin; Lanoxicaps; (see Comments)
Dosage Forms: Capsule: 0.05 mg; 0.1 mg; 0.2 mg. Elixir, pediatric (content per ml): 0.05 mg. Tablet: 0.125 mg; 0.25 mg; 0.5 mg
Use: To strengthen heartbeat and improve heart rhythm
Minor Side Effects: Apathy; drowsiness; headache; muscle weakness. Most of these side effects, if they occur, should subside as your body adjusts to the medication. Tell your doctor about any that are persistent or particularly bothersome.
Major Side Effects: Breast enlargement (in both sexes); depression; diarrhea; disorientation; hallucinations; loss of appetite; nausea; palpitations; skin rash; slow heart rate; stomach pain; unusual tiredness or weakness (extreme); visual disturbances (such as blurred or yellow vision); vomiting. Notify your doctor if you notice any major side effects.
Contraindications: People who have suffered heart stoppage, have a history of rheumatic fever, or who are allergic to this drug should not take it. Consult your doctor immediately if this drug has been prescribed for you and any of these conditions applies.
Warnings: This drug should be used cautiously by people who have kidney disease, thyroid disease, certain heart diseases, lung disease, potassium depletion, or calcium accumulation. Be sure your doctor knows if any of these conditions applies to you. • This drug should be used cautiously in infants. • Some people develop toxic reactions to this drug. If you suffer any side effects that are prolonged or especially bothersome, contact your doctor. • The elderly are more sensitive to this drug. Regular checkups are recommended while taking this drug. • This drug interacts with aminoglycosides, amphotericin B, amrinone, antacids, antibiotics, cholestyramine, colestipol hydrochloride, diltiazem, diuretics, flecainide, nifedipine, propranolol, quinidine, spironolactone, and verapamil; if you are currently taking any drugs of these types, consult your doctor about their use. If you are unsure of the type or contents of your medications, ask your doctor or pharmacist. • The pharmacologic activity of the different brands of this drug varies widely depending on how well the tablets or capsules dissolve in the stomach and bowels. Because of this variation, it is important not to change brands of the drug without consulting your doctor. • Dosages of this drug must be carefully adjusted to the needs and responses of the individual patient. Your doctor may find it necessary to adjust your dosage of this drug frequently. To do so, blood tests may be done to measure the amount of the drug in your blood. Ask your doctor to explain the test and your results. • While taking this drug, do not take any nonprescription item for weight control, cough, cold, or sinus problems without first checking with your doctor. • Notify your doctor if you experience a loss of appetite, pain in the stomach,

nausea, vomiting, diarrhea, unusual and extreme tiredness or weakness, blurred or yellow vision, or mental depression.

Comments: Your doctor may want you to take your pulse daily while you are using this drug. • Take this drug at the same time every day. Do not skip any doses, and do not stop taking this medication without consulting your doctor. • There are no products exactly equivalent to Lanoxin heart drug. You should not switch to another brand of digoxin unless your doctor is monitoring your condition closely. Because this product is priced inexpensively, you will probably save little money, if any, by switching to another brand. Ask your pharmacist about prices of different brands. • Do not use outdated medication.

Lartan antibiotic, see Keflex antibiotic.

Lasix diuretic

Ingredient: furosemide
Equivalent Product: Furosemide
Dosage Forms: Liquid (content per ml): 8 mg; 10 mg. Tablet: 20 mg; 40 mg; 80 mg

Uses: Removal of fluid from body tissues to treat edema due to heart disease, liver disease, or kidney disease; treatment of high blood pressure

Minor Side Effects: Blurred vision; constipation; cramping; decreased sexual desire; diarrhea; dizziness; headache; itching; loss of appetite; muscle spasm; nausea; sore mouth; stomach upset; sun sensitivity; weakness. Most of these side effects, if they occur, should subside as your body adjusts to the medication. Tell your doctor about any that are persistent or bothersome.

Major Side Effects: Anemia; blood disorders; easy bruising or bleeding; dark urine; dry mouth; gout; impotence; increase in blood sugar; irregular heartbeats; low blood pressure; muscle cramps; rash; ringing in the ears; sore throat; thirst; tingling in the fingers and toes; vomiting; yellowing of the eyes or skin. Notify your doctor if you notice any major side effects.

Contraindications: This drug should not be used by persons with anuria (inability to urinate), or by people who are allergic to it. Consult your doctor immediately if this drug has been prescribed for you and either of these conditions applies.

Warnings: This drug should be used cautiously by persons with cirrhosis of the liver or other liver problems and by those with kidney disease. This drug should be used cautiously by children and pregnant women. Discuss the risks and benefits with your doctor. Nursing mothers who must take this drug should stop nursing. Be sure your doctor knows if any of these conditions applies to you. • Persons hypersensitive to sulfa drugs may also be hypersensitive to this drug. If this drug has been prescribed for you and you are allergic to sulfa drugs, consult your doctor immediately. • This drug has potent activity and should be used with caution in conjunction with other high blood pressure drugs. If you are taking other such medications, the dosages may require adjustment. • This drug interacts with aspirin, curare, indomethacin, digitalis, lithium carbonate, steroids, antidiabetic agents, and aminoglycosides. If you are currently taking any drugs of these types, consult your doctor about their use. If you are unsure of the type or contents of your medications, ask your doctor or pharmacist. • Persons taking this product and digitalis should watch carefully for symptoms of increased digitalis toxicity (e.g., nausea, blurred vision, palpitations), and notify their doctors immediately if symptoms occur. • If you have high blood pressure, do not take any nonprescription item for weight control, cough, cold, or sinus problems without first checking with your doctor. Such items may contain ingredients that can increase blood pressure. • Use of this drug may cause gout; diabetes; hearing loss; and loss of potassium, calcium, water, and salt. Persons taking this drug should have periodic blood and urine tests to check for these effects. Signs of potassium loss include dry mouth, thirst, muscle cramps, weakness, and nausea or vomiting. If you experience any of these side effects, notify your doctor. • Use of this drug may activate the appearance of systemic lupus erythematosus. • Notify your doctor if you develop signs of jaundice (yellowing of the eyes or skin, dark urine). • When taking this drug (or other drugs for high blood pressure), limit the use of alcohol. • Whenever adverse reactions to this drug are moderate to severe, this drug should be reduced or discontinued. Consult your doctor promptly if such side effects occur. • This drug can increase your skin's sensitivity to the sun. Avoid prolonged sun exposure, and use a sunscreen when outdoors.

Comments: Take this drug exactly as directed. It is usually taken in the morning. Avoid taking this medication near bedtime since it causes frequent urination. This should not alarm you. • Diuretics are also called water pills. Diuretics help eliminate extra fluid that may build up, especially in the feet, causing swelling. As a result, this drug causes frequent urination. Lasix is best taken on an empty stomach, but if stomach upset occurs, it can be taken with food or milk. • Do not take extra doses or skip a dose without first consulting your doctor. • To avoid dizziness or light-headedness when you stand, contract and relax the muscles of your legs for a few moments before rising. Do this by pushing one foot against the floor while raising the other foot slightly, alternating feet so that you are pumping your legs in a pedaling motion. • To help avoid potassium loss, take this drug with a glass of fresh or frozen orange juice, or eat a banana each day. The use of a salt substitute helps prevent potassium loss. Do not change your diet, however, before discussing it with your doctor. Too much potassium may also be dangerous. • You should learn how to monitor your pulse and blood pressure while taking this medication; consult your doctor. • The liquid form of this drug should be stored in the refrigerator in a light-resistant container.

LazerSporin-C otic steroid and antibiotic, see Cortisporin Otic steroid and antibiotic.

Ledercillin VK antibiotic, see penicillin V potassium (penicillin VK) antibiotic.

Levodopa antiparkinson drug, see Sinemet, Sinemet CR antiparkinson drug.

Levothroid thyroid hormone, see Synthroid thyroid hormone.

Levothyroxine Sodium thyroid hormone, see Synthroid thyroid hormone.

Levoxine thyroid hormone, see Synthroid thyroid hormone.

Libritabs antianxiety, see Librium antianxiety.

Librium antianxiety

Ingredient: Chlordiazepoxide HCl
Equivalent Products: Chlordiazepoxide HCl; Libritabs; Mitran; Reposans-10
Dosage Forms: Capsule: 5 mg; 10 mg; 25 mg. Tablet (see Comments): 5 mg; 10 mg; 25 mg

Uses: Relief of anxiety symptoms and anxiety disorder; withdrawal symptoms of alcohol addiction

Minor Side Effects: Constipation; decrease or increase in sex drive; depression; diarrhea; dizziness; drooling; drowsiness; dry mouth; fainting; fatigue; fluid retention; headache; heartburn; insomnia; loss of appetite; menstrual irregularities; nausea; sweating. Most of these side effects, if they occur, should subside as your body adjusts to the medication. Tell your doctor about any that are persistent or particularly bothersome.

Major Side Effects: Blood disorders; blurred vision or other vision changes; breathing difficulties; confusion; dark urine; difficulty in urinating; excitation; fever; hallucinations; low blood pressure; rash; slow or rapid heart rate; slurred speech; sore throat; stimulation; tremors; uncoordinated movements; weakness; yellowing of the eyes or skin. Notify your doctor of any major side effects.

Contraindications: This drug should not be used by people who are allergic to it or by pregnant or nursing women. Consult your doctor immediately if this drug has been prescribed for you and any of these conditions applies.

Warnings: This drug should be used cautiously by people who have liver or kidney disease, chronic lung disease, myasthenia gravis, or porphyria; by those with acute, narrow-angle glaucoma; and by those who are depressed. Be sure your doctor knows if any of these conditions applies to you. • Elderly people should use this drug cautiously and take the smallest effective dose. • This drug has the potential to be habit-forming and must be used with caution. • This drug is not recommended for use in children under six years of age. • Do not take it with other sedative drugs, central nervous system depressants, or alcohol; serious adverse reactions may develop. • This drug should be used cautiously in conjunction with phenytoin, cimetidine, lithium, levodopa, isoniazid, rifampin, and disulfiram. • Tolerance may develop quickly; do not increase the dose of this drug without first consulting your doctor. • This drug may cause drowsiness; avoid tasks that require alertness, such as driving a car or operating potentially dangerous equipment. • Consult your doctor if you wish to discontinue use of this drug; do not stop taking the drug suddenly. If you have been using the drug for an extended period of time, it will be necessary to reduce the dosage gradually, according to your doctor's instructions. • Persons taking this drug for a long period should have periodic blood counts and liver function tests. • Notify your doctor if you develop signs of jaundice (yellowing of the eyes or skin, dark urine). • Do not take this drug with an antacid; it may retard absorption of the drug. After taking this drug, wait 30 minutes before taking an antacid if one is needed.

Comments: Take this medication with food or a full glass of water if stomach upset occurs. • Chew gum or suck on ice chips or a piece of hard candy to reduce mouth dryness. • This drug is effective in relieving anxiety symptoms, but it is important to understand the cause of the anxiety as well. • The tablet forms of this drug are available under the name Libritabs.

Lidex, Lidex-E topical steroid hormone

Ingredient: fluocinonide

Equivalent Products: Fluocinonide; Fluonex

Dosage Forms: Cream; Gel; Ointment; Solution: 0.05%; see Comments

Use: Relief of skin inflammation and irritation associated with conditions such as eczema, poison ivy, insect bites, and psoriasis

Minor Side Effects: Burning sensation; dryness; irritation of affected area; mild, temporary stinging upon application; rash. Most of these side effects, if they occur, should subside as your body adjusts to the medication. Tell your doctor about any that are persistent or particularly bothersome.

Major Side Effects: Blistering; increased hair growth; loss of skin color; pain; redness; secondary infection; skin wasting. Notify your doctor if you notice any major side effects.

Contraindications: This drug should not be taken by people who are allergic to it. This drug should not be used in the ear if the eardrum is perforated or by people who have viral or fungal skin disease, tuberculosis of the skin, or severe circulatory disorders. Consult your doctor immediately if this drug has been prescribed for you and any of these conditions applies.

Warnings: This drug should be used cautiously by pregnant women. • This drug is for external use only. It should not be used in the eyes. Wash your hands after applying this drug. • If irritation develops, consult your doctor. • If extensive areas are treated or if occlusive dressings are used, there will be increased systemic absorption of this drug; suitable precautions should be taken, especially in children and infants. If this drug is being used on a child's diaper area, avoid tight-fitting diapers or plastic pants, which can increase absorption of the drug. • Use this product to treat only the condition for which it was prescribed. Using topical steroids to treat an infection may worsen the infection.

Comments: If the affected area is dry or is scaling, the skin may be moistened before applying the product by soaking in water or by applying water with a clean cloth. The ointment form is probably the better product for dry skin. • Do not use this medication more often or for longer periods of time than recommended by your doctor. • Do not use an occlusive wrap of transparent plastic film to cover the medicated area unless directed to do so by your doctor. If it is necessary for you to use this drug under a wrap, follow your doctor's directions exactly. Do not leave the wrap in place for a longer time than specified, because the risk of side effects can be increased. • A mild, temporary stinging sensation may occur after this medication is applied. If this sensation persists, contact your doctor. • If the condition worsens while using this drug, notify your doctor. • The gel form may produce a cooling sensation on the skin. • Lidex-E topical steroid hormone contains fluocinonide in a cream form similar to Lidex but has more skin-softening ingredients. For all practical purposes, Lidex and Lidex-E are the same, as are Vasoderm and Vasoderm E.

Lindane pediculicide and scabicide, see Kwell pediculicide and scabicide.

Liquid Pred steroid hormone, see prednisone steroid hormone.

Lodine anti-inflammatory

Ingredient: etodolac
Dosage Form: Capsule: 200 mg; 300 mg
Uses: Symptomatic treatment of mild to moderate pain; treatment of symptoms of osteoarthritis

Minor Side Effects: Bloating; constipation; cramps; diarrhea; dizziness; drowsiness; dry mouth; gas; headache; nausea; nervousness; sweating; vomiting; weakness. Most of these side effects, if they occur, should subside as your body adjusts to the medication. Tell your doctor about any that are persistent or particularly bothersome.

Major Side Effects: Black, tarry stools; blood disorders; breathing difficulties; chest tightness; dark urine; hearing loss; itching; palpitations; ringing in the ears; severe stomach cramps; skin rash; sore throat; swelling of the hands or feet; unusual bleeding or bruising; unusual weight gain; vision disturbances; yellowing of the eyes of skin. Notify your doctor if you notice any major side effects.

CONSUMER GUIDE®

Contraindications: This drug should not be taken by people who are allergic to it, to aspirin, or to other nonsteroidal anti-inflammatory drugs. Consult your doctor immediately if this drug has been prescribed for you and you have such an allergy. • This drug should not be used by persons with nasal polyps associated with swelling. If you have this condition, consult your doctor immediately.

Warnings: This drug should be used with extreme caution by persons who have a history of ulcers or of stomach or intestinal disorders. • This drug must be used with caution by persons with anemia, severe allergies, bleeding disorders, high blood pressure, liver disease, certain heart diseases, or kidney disease. Be sure your doctor knows if any of these conditions applies to you. • Elderly persons must use this drug carefully as prescribed since they are more susceptible to the effects of this medication. • This drug has not been adequately studied in children; therefore its use in children is not recommended. • This drug should be used only if clearly needed by pregnant women and nursing mothers. Discuss the risks and benefits with your doctor. • This drug interacts with anticoagulants, diuretics, aspirin, oral antidiabetics, steroids, phenytoin, and sulfonamides. If you are currently taking any drugs of these types, consult your doctor about their use. If you are unsure of the type or contents of your medications, ask your doctor or pharmacist. • Do not take nonprescription medication containing aspirin or ibuprofen while taking this drug without first consulting your doctor since they are similar in action to this drug. • Avoid consuming alcohol while taking this medication. • It is recommended that persons taking this drug for prolonged periods of time have lab tests and eye tests done to monitor the effects of the medication. • This drug may cause drowsiness or blurred vision. Avoid activities that require alertness, such as driving a car or operating potentially dangerous equipment. • Notify your doctor if you develop black, tarry stools; dark urine; swelling of the hands or feet; breathing difficulties; vision problems; unusual weight gain; skin rash; or severe headaches while taking this medication. Report any signs of unusual bruising or bleeding, frequent indigestion, or if you notice a change in the appearance of your urine or stools.

Comments: This drug should be taken with food or milk to prevent stomach upset. • This drug is not a substitute for rest, physical therapy, or other measures recommended by your doctor to treat your condition. • If you are taking this drug for the treatment of arthritis, an improvement in your condition should be noted within the first week. However, full benefits may not be obtained for several weeks. It is important not to stop taking this drug even if symptoms have diminished or disappeared. • This drug is potent and is not intended for general aches and pains. • There are many anti-inflammatory medications available. If one is not effective or not well tolerated, your doctor may have you try other ones in order to find the best drug for you.

Lopid antihyperlipidemic

Ingredient: gemfibrozil
Dosage Form: Tablet: 600 mg
Use: Used in conjunction with diet to reduce elevated triglyceride and, to a lesser extent, cholesterol levels
Minor Side Effects: Abdominal pain; blurred vision; change in taste; constipation; diarrhea; dizziness; fatigue; headache; itching; muscle pain; nausea; stomach upset. Most of these side effects, if they occur, should subside as your body adjusts to the medication. Tell your doctor about any that are persistent or particularly bothersome.

Major Side Effects: Breathing trouble; chills; dark urine; decreased sexual ability; fever; irregular heartbeat; numbness or tingling of hands or feet; skin rash; sore throat; vomiting; yellowing of the eyes or skin. Notify your doctor if you notice any major side effects.

Contraindications: This drug should not be taken by anyone allergic to it or by persons with liver disease, severe kidney disease, or gallbladder disease. Consult your doctor immediately if this drug has been prescribed for you and you have any of these conditions.

Warnings: This drug should be used cautiously by people who have diabetes or hypothyroidism and by persons undergoing estrogen therapy. Be sure your doctor knows if any of these conditions applies to you. • This drug should be used only if clearly needed during pregnancy. Discuss the risks and benefits with your doctor. In breast-feeding women, either breast-feeding should be discontinued or treatment with gemfibrozil should be stopped. Discuss this with your doctor. • This drug is not recommended for use in children since safety and efficacy have not been established in this age group. • This drug interacts with oral anticoagulants and lovastatin (Mevacor). A severe inflammation of muscles has developed in some patients taking gemfibrozil with lovastatin. If you are currently taking any drugs of these types, consult your doctor about their use. If you are unsure about the type or contents of your medications, consult your doctor or pharmacist. • This drug may cause dizziness or blurred vision; use caution when engaging in activities that require alertness, such as driving a car or operating potentially dangerous equipment. • Notify your doctor if abdominal pain, diarrhea, nausea, or vomiting become bothersome or severe.

Comments: For best results, take this medication 30 minutes before morning and evening meals or as directed. • Diet therapy is considered the initial treatment of choice for high blood cholesterol levels. This drug should be used only after diet therapy has been tried. This drug is not a substitute for a proper diet. For maximum effectiveness, this drug must be used in conjunction with a diet that is low in saturated fat and cholesterol. You may be referred to a nutritionist for diet counseling. • It may take a month for this drug to develop its full effect. Periodic laboratory tests will be done while you are taking this medication to determine its effectiveness. Ask your doctor to explain what your cholesterol levels are and what the goals of therapy are. Learn to monitor your progress. • Store this medication away from heat and moisture.

Lopressor antihypertensive and antianginal

Ingredient: metoprolol tartrate
Equivalent Product: Toprol XL (see comments)
Dosage Form: Tablet: 50 mg; 100 mg
Uses: Management of high blood pressure (hypertension) or chest pain (angina); prevention of irregular heartbeat after heart attack

Minor Side Effects: Abdominal cramps; blurred vision; constipation; diarrhea; drowsiness; dry eyes; dry mouth; gas; gastric pain; headache; heartburn; insomnia; loss of appetite; nasal congestion; nausea; sweating; vivid dreams. Most of these side effects, if they occur, should subside as your body adjusts to the medication. Tell your doctor about any that are persistent or particularly bothersome.

Major Side Effects: Chest pain; cold hands and feet; confusion; decreased sexual ability; depression; dizziness; fainting; fever; hallucinations; itching; nightmares; numbness or tingling in the hands and feet; palpitations; rash; reversible loss of hair; ringing in the ears; shortness of breath; slow heart rate; slurred speech; sore throat; tiredness; unusual bleeding or bruising; visual dis-

CONSUMER GUIDE®

turbances; weak pulse; wheezing. Notify your doctor if you notice any major side effects.

Contraindications: This drug should not be used by people with certain types of heart disease (such as bradycardia, overt cardiac failure, heart block, or cardiogenic shock) or certain lung diseases, or by people with an allergy to it or to any other beta blocker. Consult your doctor if this drug has been prescribed for you and any of these conditions applies.

Warnings: This drug should be used with caution by people with thyroid disease (certain types), impaired kidney or liver function, asthma, bronchospasm, or diabetes. Be sure your doctor knows if any of these conditions applies to you. • Persons about to undergo surgery should use this drug with caution. • Pregnant women, nursing mothers, and children should take this drug only when clearly needed. • Extra care is needed if this drug is used with reserpine, phenytoin, terbutaline, aminophylline, theophylline, digitalis, phenobarbital, cimetidine, monoamine oxidase inhibitors, or oral contraceptives. If you are currently taking any drugs of these types, consult your doctor about their use. If you are unsure of the type or contents of your medications, ask your doctor or pharmacist. • This medication may mask signs of hypoglycemia, such as a change in pulse rate. Diabetics who are taking this medication should monitor glucose levels closely. • This drug should not be stopped abruptly (unless your doctor advises you to do so). Chest pain and even heart attacks have occurred when this drug has been stopped suddenly. • While taking this drug, do not take any nonprescription item for weight control, cough, cold, or sinus problems without first checking with your doctor; such items may contain ingredients that can increase blood pressure. • Notify your doctor if dizziness, rash, or breathing difficulty develops.

Comments: It is best to take this drug with food. • Be sure to take the doses of this drug at the same time each day. • Your doctor may want you to take your pulse and blood pressure every day while you are taking this drug. Discuss this with your doctor. • It is important to continue taking this medication even if you do not feel sick. Most people with high blood pressure do not have symptoms and do not feel ill; therefore, it is easy to forget to take the medication. This drug may cause you to be sensitive to the cold. Dress warmly. As with all antihypertensive medications, they are most effective when used in conjunction with diet and lifestyle changes, such as exercise and stress reduction to control blood pressure. The medication does not cure high blood pressure. Toprol XL is a long-acting form of metoprolol, which is taken only once a day. This offers convenience, but may not be suitable for all persons. Talk to your doctor about its use for your condition. • Many beta blockers are available. Your doctor may want you to try different ones in order to find the one that works best for you.

Lorazepam antianxiety, see Ativan antianxiety.

Lorcet, Lorcet HD, Lorcet Plus analgesics, see Vicodin, Vicodin ES analgesics.

Lorelco antihyperlipidemic

Ingredient: probucol
Dosage Form: Tablet: 250 mg; 500 mg
Use: In conjunction with diet to reduce elevated blood cholesterol levels
Minor Side Effects: Altered senses of taste and smell; bloating; blurred vision; diarrhea; dizziness; flatulence; headache; indigestion; itching; loss of appetite; nausea; stomach upset. Most of these side effects, if they occur, should

subside as your body adjusts to the medication. Tell your doctor about any that are persistent or particularly bothersome.

Major Side Effects: Chest pain; decreased sexual ability; irregular heartbeat; ringing in the ears; stomach cramps; swelling of ankles and feet; tingling of the hands or feet; vomiting. Notify your doctor if you notice any major side effects.

Contraindications: This drug should not be taken by anyone who is allergic to it or by persons with certain heart diseases. Consult your doctor immediately if this drug has been prescribed for you and any of these conditions applies.

Warnings: This drug must be used with caution in pregnant or nursing women. Discuss the benefits and risks with your doctor if either condition applies to you. • This drug is not recommended for use in children since safety and efficacy have not been determined in this age group. • Persons with certain types of heart disease and liver disease must be monitored closely.

Comments: For best results, take this drug with meals. • Do not stop taking this drug suddenly unless instructed to do so by your doctor. • The full effects of this drug may not be evident for up to three months. Your doctor will want to monitor the effects of this drug by doing periodic blood tests. Ask your doctor to explain what your cholesterol levels mean and what your therapy goals are. Learn to monitor your progress. • Diarrhea, gas, abdominal pain, nausea, and vomiting may occur when first taking this drug. These effects usually disappear with continued use. Notify your doctor if they persist or worsen. • Diet therapy is considered the initial treatment of choice for high blood cholesterol levels. This drug should be used only after diet therapy has been tried. This drug is not a substitute for a proper diet. For maximum effectiveness, this drug must be used in conjunction with a diet that is low in saturated fat and cholesterol. You may be referred to a nutritionist for diet counseling.

Lortab analgesic, see Vicodin, Vicodin ES analgesics.

Lotensin antihypertensive

Ingredient: benazepril
Dosage Form: Tablet: 5 mg; 10 mg; 20 mg; 40 mg
Use: Treatment of high blood pressure
Minor Side Effects: Cough; decreased sexual desire; diarrhea; dizziness; fatigue; flushing; headache; insomnia; light-headedness; nasal congestion; nausea; sleep disturbances; stomach upset; sweating; taste disturbances. Most of these side effects, if they occur, should subside as your body adjusts to the medication. Tell your doctor about any that are persistent or particularly bothersome.

Major Side Effects: Blood disorders; blurred vision; breathing difficulties; chest pain; decreased sexual ability; depression; fever; impotence; irregular pulse; itching; low blood pressure; muscle aches or cramps; nervousness; rapid, pounding heartbeat; rash; sore throat; swelling of face, lips, and tongue; tingling in fingers and toes; vomiting. Notify your doctor if you notice any major side effects.

Contraindications: This drug should not be used by any woman who is pregnant, who thinks she is pregnant, or who intends to become pregnant. Use of this drug during pregnancy has resulted in fetal abnormalities. Notify your doctor immediately if you suspect you are pregnant. • This drug should not be used by persons who are allergic to it or to similar drugs such as captopril or lisinopril. Remind your doctor that you have such an allergy if this drug has been prescribed for you.

Warnings: This drug should be used cautiously by nursing mothers, persons with kidney disease, and diabetics. Be sure your doctor knows if any of these conditions applies to you. • Persons taking this drug in conjunction with other antihypertensive or heart medications should use it cautiously, especially during initial therapy. Dosage adjustments may be required to prevent blood pressure from dropping too low. • This drug must be used cautiously with agents that increase serum potassium, such as spironolactone, triamterene, amiloride, potassium supplements, and salt substitutes containing potassium. If you are currently taking any drugs of these types, consult your doctor about their use. Dosages may need to be adjusted. Your doctor may wish to test your blood periodically to check the potassium level. While taking this drug, you should limit your consumption of alcoholic beverages, which can increase dizziness and other side effects. • It is recommended that persons taking this drug for a prolonged period have periodic blood tests to monitor the effects of therapy. • Contact your doctor immediately if you notice swelling of the face, lips, tongue, or eyes, or have breathing difficulties while taking this drug. • If this medication makes you dizzy, avoid driving a car or operating potentially dangerous equipment. • Notify your doctor if you develop signs of an infection (sore throat, fever) while taking this drug. • Notify your doctor if you develop severe or persistent vomiting or diarrhea while taking this drug, since they can lead to dehydration. • If you have high blood pressure, do not take any nonprescription item for weight control, cough, cold, or sinus problems without consulting your doctor or pharmacist: Such items can increase blood pressure. • Avoid prolonged work or exercise in hot weather, since excessive sweating can intensify the effects of this drug.

Comments: Take this drug as prescribed. Do not skip doses or take extra doses without consulting your doctor. • This drug may be taken with food if stomach upset occurs. • Do not stop taking this drug without consulting your doctor. It is important to continue taking this medication even if you do not feel sick. Most people with high blood pressure do not have symptoms and do not feel ill; therefore, it is easy to forget to take the medication. • Side effects of this drug are usually mild and transient. During the first few days you may experience light-headedness, which should subside as therapy continues. If light-headedness continues or becomes more pronounced, contact your doctor. • To avoid dizziness or light-headedness, contract and relax the muscles of your legs for a few moments before rising. Do this by pushing one foot against the floor while raising the other foot slightly, alternating feet so that you are pumping your feet in a pedaling motion. • Learn how to monitor your pulse and blood pressure while taking this drug. As with all antihypertensive medications, they are most effective when used in conjunction with diet and lifestyle changes, such as exercise and stress reduction to control blood pressure. The medication does not cure high blood pressure.

Lotrimin antifungal

Ingredient: clotrimazole
Equivalent Product: Mycelex (see Comments)
Dosage Forms: Cream (content per gram); Lotion; Solution (content per ml): 1%
Use: Treatment of superficial fungal infections of the skin
Minor Side Effects: Redness; stinging sensation. These side effects, if they occur, should subside as your body adjusts to the medication. Tell your doctor if they persist or are particularly bothersome.
Major Side Effects: Blistering; irritation; peeling of skin; swelling. Notify your doctor if you notice any major side effects.

Contraindication: This drug should not be used by people who are allergic to it. Consult your doctor immediately if this drug has been prescribed for you and you have such an allergy.

Warnings: This drug should be used with caution by pregnant women. • Do not use this drug in or near the eyes. • If irritation occurs, stop using this product, and call your doctor.

Comments: Apply this product after cleansing the area, unless your doctor has directed otherwise. This drug should be gently rubbed into the affected area and the surrounding skin. • Do not use a dressing over this drug unless instructed to do so by your doctor. • Improvement in your condition may not be seen for one week after beginning treatment with this drug. Nevertheless, be sure to complete a full course of therapy. If the condition has not improved after four weeks, or if it worsens, consult your doctor. Lotrimin AF and Mycelex OTC are available without a prescription. Talk to your doctor or pharmacist about their use. • Clotrimazole is also available as an oral troche (lozenge) for the treatment of thrush, which is a fungal infection of the mouth. It is marketed under the trade name Mycelex. • Clotrimazole is also available without a prescription in vaginal cream and vaginal tablet forms to treat certain fungal infections of the vagina. It is marketed under the names of Gyne-lotrimin and Mycelex.

Lotrisone steroid hormone and antifungal

Ingredients: betamethasone; clotrimazole
Dosage Form: Cream: betamethasone, 0.05% and clotrimazole, 1%
Use: Treatment of certain skin infections

Minor Side Effects: Burning sensation; irritation; itching; redness of skin. Most of these side effects, if they occur, should subside as your body adjusts to the medication. Tell your doctor about any that are persistent or particularly bothersome.

Major Side Effects: Blistering; peeling of skin; rash; secondary infection; swelling of extremities. Notify your doctor immediately if you notice any major side effects.

Contraindications: This drug should not be used by persons sensitive to either of its ingredients or to corticosteroids. Consult your doctor immediately if this drug has been prescribed for you and you have any such allergies. • This drug is not to be used in the eyes, nor in the ear canals of persons with a perforated eardrum.

Warnings: This drug must be used cautiously by pregnant or nursing women and on children under two years of age. • Prolonged use of large amounts of this drug should be avoided, especially in areas where the skin is damaged, as with extensive burns. If extensive areas are treated or if an occlusive dressing is used to cover the area, there will be increased absorption of this drug into the bloodstream leading to systemic side effects. Suitable precautions should be taken, especially with children, who have a greater tendency to absorb the drug. Use this drug sparingly, especially on children, and do not use an occlusive dressing unless directed to do so by your physician. Follow your doctor's directions closely, and do not leave the dressing in place longer than specified or the risk of side effects can be increased. When using this drug on children, avoid tight-fitting diapers or plastic pants, which can act as occlusive dressings.

Comments: Clean and dry the affected area. Apply a small amount and rub in gently. • Use this drug for as long as prescribed and only for the condition for which it was prescribed. Do not use it more often since the chance of side effects increases. Continue using it for the complete period prescribed even if symptoms disappear within that time. Notify your doctor if no improvement is seen after a few days or if symptoms worsen. • If irritation develops, discontinue use and notify your doctor.

Lozol diuretic

Ingredient: indapamide
Dosage Form: Tablet: 1.25 mg; 2.5 mg
Uses: Removal of fluid from tissues; treatment of high blood pressure
Minor Side Effects: Altered sense of taste; cough; decreased sexual desire; diarrhea; dizziness; dry mouth; fatigue; headache; insomnia; light-headedness; loss of appetite; nausea; somnolence; stomach upset; sweating. Most of these side effects, if they occur, should subside as your body adjusts to the medication. Tell your doctor about any that are persistent or particularly bothersome.

Major Side Effects: Anxiety; blood disorders; breathing difficulties; chest pain; dark urine; depression; easy bruising or bleeding; impotence; itching; muscle cramps or pain; palpitations; rash; sore throat; tingling in the hands and feet; vomiting; yellowing of the eyes or skin. Notify your doctor if you notice any major side effects.

Contraindication: This drug should not be taken by anyone who is allergic to it. Consult your doctor if this drug has been prescribed for you and you have such an allergy.

Warnings: This drug must be used cautiously by pregnant or nursing women, by persons with kidney disease, and by diabetics. Be sure your doctor knows if any of these conditions applies to you. • If you are taking digitalis in addition to this drug, watch carefully for increased digitalis effects (e.g., nausea, blurred vision, palpitations), and notify your doctor immediately if they occur. • Persons taking this drug along with other antihypertensive medications may need to have their dosages adjusted. Notify your doctor if you develop signs of jaundice (yellowing of the eyes or skin, dark urine). • Do not take any nonprescription item for weight control, cough, cold, or sinus problems without first consulting your doctor. Such items may contain ingredients that can increase blood pressure. • This drug may cause potassium loss, so it is often prescribed in conjunction with a potassium supplement. Your doctor may periodically test your blood to check the potassium level. Watch for signs of potassium loss (dry mouth, thirst, weakness, muscle pain or cramps, nausea, and vomiting). Call your doctor if you develop any of these signs. • This medication can increase your skin's sensitivity to the sun. Avoid sun exposure, and wear a sunscreen outdoors.

Comments: Take this drug exactly as prescribed. Do not take extra doses or skip a dose without first consulting your doctor. • Do not stop using this drug without first consulting your doctor. It is important to continue taking this medication even if you do not feel sick. Most people with high blood pressure do not have symptoms and do not feel ill; therefore, it is easy to forget to take the medication. Diuretics are also called water pills. Diuretics help eliminate extra fluid that may build up, especially in the feet, causing swelling. As a result, this drug causes frequent urination. Expect this effect; it should not alarm you. Try to plan your dosage schedule to avoid taking this at bedtime. • To avoid dizziness or light-headedness when you stand, contract and relax the muscles of your legs for a few moments before rising. Do this by pushing one foot against the floor while raising the other foot slightly, alternating feet so that you are pumping your legs in a pedaling motion. • Side effects from this drug are usually mild and transient. During the first few days of therapy, you may experience light-headedness, which should subside with continued use. If side effects continue or become bothersome, consult your doctor. • To help prevent potassium loss, take this drug with a glass of fresh or frozen orange juice, or eat a banana each day. The use of salt substitutes, which contain potassium, can also help prevent the loss of potassium. Do not change your diet, however, without first consulting your doctor. Too much potassium can also be dangerous. • Learn how to monitor your pulse and blood pressure; discuss this with your doctor. As with all antihypertensive medications, they are most effective when used in conjunction with diet and lifestyle changes, such as exercise and stress reduction to control blood pressure. The medication does not cure high blood pressure.

Ludiomil antidepressant

Ingredient: maprotiline HCl
Equivalent Product: Maprotiline HCl
Dosage Form: Tablet: 25 mg; 50 mg; 75 mg
Uses: Treatment of depression and of anxiety associated with depression
Minor Side Effects: Abdominal cramps; bitter taste in mouth; black tongue; bloating; blurred vision; constipation; diarrhea; dizziness; drooling; drowsiness; dry mouth; false sense of well-being; headache; increased appetite; increased or decreased sex drive; increased salivation; nasal congestion; nausea; nervousness; nightmares; pupil dilation; restlessness; sensitivity to sunlight; shaking; stomach distress; trouble sleeping; vomiting; weight loss or gain. Most of these side effects, if they occur, should subside as your body adjusts to the medication. Tell your doctor about any that are persistent or particularly bothersome.
Major Side Effects: Anxiety; breast enlargement (in both sexes); breathing trouble; confusion; convulsions; dark-colored urine; delusions; difficulty swallowing; disturbed concentration; eye pain; fever; frequent or difficult urination; hair loss; hallucinations; impotence; irregular heartbeat; itching; loss of memory; menstrual irregularities; muscle stiffness; palpitations; panic; ringing in the ears; seizures; severe weakness; skin rash; sore throat; sweating; swelling of the testicles; tingling in the hands or feet; unusual weakness; yellowing of the skin or eyes. Notify your doctor if you notice any major side effects.
Contraindications: This drug should not be taken by anyone who is allergic to it. This drug should not be taken by persons who have seizure disorders, persons who have recently had a heart attack, or persons who are taking or who have recently taken monoamine oxidase inhibitors. Consult your doctor immediately if this drug has been prescribed for you and any of these conditions applies. • Children and adolescents under 18 years of age should not take this drug.
Warnings: This drug should be used with caution by persons with certain types of heart disease, high blood pressure, thyroid problems, glaucoma, urinary tract problems, stomach or intestinal problems, an enlarged prostate, schizophrenia, or liver or kidney disease and by persons with a history of suicidal tendencies, alcoholism, or electroshock treatments. This drug should be used cautiously by those about to undergo surgery. Be sure your doctor knows if any of these conditions applies to you. • This drug should be used cautiously by pregnant or nursing women. • Diabetics should be cautious because this drug may cause changes in blood sugar levels. • This drug interacts with anticholinergic or sympathomimetic drugs, amphetamines, oral contraceptives, epinephrine, phenylephrine, antiparkinson drugs, methylphenidate, barbiturates, phenothiazines, oral anticoagulants, beta blockers, antiarrhythmics, thyroid drugs, blood pressure medications, and some painkillers and sedatives. If you are using any drugs of these types, consult your doctor about their use. If you are unsure of the type or contents of your medications, consult your doctor or

CONSUMER GUIDE®

pharmacist. Do not stop or start taking any medication, prescription or nonprescription, without first consulting your doctor. • Avoid drinking alcohol while taking this drug, since excessive drowsiness may result. • Report any mood changes to your doctor. • If this drug makes you feel dizzy or drowsy, avoid activities that require alertness, such as driving a car or operating potentially dangerous equipment. • If you take this drug for a prolonged period of time, you will need to see your doctor regularly for blood cell counts and liver function tests.

Comments: If this drug causes stomach upset, take it with food. • Do not stop taking this drug suddenly and do not increase the dose without first consulting your doctor. • It may take two to three weeks before the therapeutic effect of this drug is evident. Your doctor may adjust your dose frequently during the first few months of therapy to find the best dose for you. • This drug increases your sensitivity to sunlight; wear protective clothing and sunglasses, and use an effective sunscreen when outdoors. • Chew gum or suck on ice chips or a piece of hard candy to reduce mouth dryness. • To minimize dizziness and light-headedness, rise slowly from a sitting or reclining position. • This drug is similar in action to other antidepressants. If one antidepressant is not effective or well tolerated, your doctor may have you try others.

Macrobid antibacterial, see nitrofurantoin antibacterial.

Macrodantin antibacterial, see nitrofurantoin antibacterial.

Mallergan VC with Codeine expectorant, see Phenergan VC, Phenergan VC with Codeine expectorants.

Maprotiline HCl antidepressant, see Ludiomil antidepressant.

Marcillin antibiotic, see ampicillin antibiotic.

Margesic analgesic, see acetaminophen with codeine analgesic.

Margesic analgesic, see Vicodin, Vicodin ES analgesic.

Marnal analgesic, see Fiorinal analgesic.

Maxolon gastrointestinal stimulant and antiemetic, see Reglan gastrointestinal stimulant and antiemetic.

Maxzide diuretic and antihypertensive

Ingredients: hydrochlorothiazide; triamterene
Equivalent Product: Triamterene with hydrochlorothiazide
Dosage Form: Tablet: Maxzide: hydrochlorothiazide, 50 mg and triamterene, 75 mg; Maxzide-25 mg: hydrochlorothiazide, 25 mg and triamterene, 37.5 mg
Uses: Treatment of high blood pressure; removal of fluid from body tissues
Minor Side Effects: Constipation; decreased sexual desire; diarrhea; dizziness; drowsiness; fatigue; headache; itching; loss of appetite; nausea; restlessness; sun sensitivity; upset stomach; vomiting. Most of these side effects, if they occur, should subside as your body adjusts to the medication. Tell your doctor about any that are persistent or particularly bothersome.
Major Side Effects: Blood disorders; breathing difficulties; bruising; chest pain; confusion; cracking at the corners of the mouth; dark urine; dry mouth; el-

evated blood sugar; fever; kidney stones; mood changes; mouth sores; muscle cramps or spasms; palpitations; rash; sore throat; tingling in fingers or toes; weakness; weak pulse; yellowing of the eyes or skin. Notify your doctor if you notice any major side effects.

Contraindications: This drug should not be used by persons with severe liver or kidney disease, hyperkalemia (high blood levels of potassium), or anuria (inability to urinate). Be sure your doctor knows if any of these conditions applies to you. • This drug is generally not used during pregnancy, since mother and fetus may be exposed to possible hazards. • This drug should not be used by persons allergic to it or to sulfa drugs. Consult your doctor immediately if this drug has been prescribed for you and you have such an allergy.

Warnings: This drug should be used cautiously by pregnant women, by children, and by people with diabetes, allergies, asthma, liver disease, anemia, blood diseases, high calcium levels, gout, or a history of kidney stones. Be sure your doctor knows if any of these conditions applies to you. • Nursing mothers who must take this drug should stop nursing. • This drug may affect the results of thyroid function tests. Be sure your doctor knows you are taking this drug if you are scheduled to have such tests. • Persons taking this drug and digitalis should watch for signs of increased digitalis effects (e.g., nausea, blurred vision, palpitations), and notify their doctor if such signs develop. • If you must undergo surgery, remind your doctor that you are taking this drug. • This drug interacts with curare, digitalis, lithium carbonate, oral antidiabetics, potassium salts, steroids, spironolactone, enalapril, and captopril. If you are currently taking any drugs of these types, consult your doctor about their use. If you are unsure of the type or contents of your medications, consult your doctor or pharmacist. • While taking this drug, do not take any nonprescription item for weight control, cough, cold, or sinus problems without first consulting your doctor. Such items may contain ingredients that can increase blood pressure. • Regular blood tests should be performed if you must take this drug for a long time. You should also be tested for kidney function. • If you develop a sore throat, bleeding, bruising, dry mouth, weakness, or muscle cramps, call your doctor. • Notify your doctor if you develop signs of jaundice (yellowing of the eyes or skin, dark urine). • This medication may cause you to become especially sensitive to the sun. Avoid sun exposure and use a sunscreen outdoors. • While taking this drug, you should limit your consumption of alcoholic beverages in order to prevent dizziness or light-headedness. • This drug usually does not cause the loss of potassium. Do not take potassium supplements unless directed to do so by your doctor.

Comments: Take this drug with food or milk. • Take this drug exactly as directed. Do not skip a dose or take extra doses without first consulting your doctor. Do not stop using this medication without first consulting your doctor. It is important to continue taking this medication even if you do not feel sick. Most people with high blood pressure do not have symptoms and do not feel ill; therefore, it is easy to forget to take the medication. • Diuretics are also called water pills. Diuretics help eliminate extra fluid that may build up, especially in the feet, causing swelling. As a result, this drug causes frequent urination. Expect this effect; it should not alarm you. If a single daily dose is prescribed, take the medication in the morning to prevent frequent urination from disturbing your sleep. If you are to take more than one dose each day, take the last dose no later than six P.M. unless otherwise directed by your physician. • To avoid dizziness or light-headedness, contract and relax the muscles of your legs for a few moments before rising. Do this by pushing one foot against the floor while raising the other foot slightly, alternating feet so that you are pumping your legs in a pedaling motion. • You should learn how to monitor your pulse and blood pressure; consult your doctor. • Combination or fixed-dose products are usually not prescribed as the first choice in the treatment of high blood pressure. Persons should receive each of the individual ingredients singly, and if the response is adequate to the fixed dose in Maxzide, it can then be substituted. The advantage of a combination product such as this drug is increased convenience. • As with all antihypertensive medications, they are most effective when used in conjunction with diet and lifestyle changes, such as exercise and stress reduction to control blood pressure. The medication does not cure high blood pressure. • This medication has the same ingredients as Dyazide but the strengths of the two drugs are different. Maxzide and Dyazide cannot be used interchangeably.

Meclizine HCl antiemetic, see Antivert antiemetic.

Medipain 5 analgesic, see Vicodin, Vicodin ES analgesics.

Medrol steroid hormone

Ingredient: methylprednisolone
Equivalent Product: Methylprednisolone
Dosage Form: Tablet: 2 mg; 4 mg; 8 mg; 16 mg; 24 mg; 32 mg
Uses: Treatment of endocrine or rheumatic disorders; asthma; blood diseases; certain cancers; eye disorders; gastrointestinal disturbances, such as ulcerative colitis; respiratory diseases; inflammations, such as arthritis, dermatitis, and poison ivy; allergic conditions
Minor Side Effects: Dizziness; headache; increased appetite; increased hair growth; increased susceptibility to infection; increased sweating; indigestion; insomnia; menstrual irregularities; muscle weakness; reddening of the skin on the face; restlessness; thin skin. Most of these side effects, if they occur, should subside as your body adjusts to the medication. Tell your doctor about any that are persistent or particularly bothersome.
Major Side Effects: Abdominal enlargement; blurred vision; bone loss; bruising; cataracts; convulsions; diabetes; false sense of well-being; fluid retention; fungal infections of the mouth and vagina; glaucoma; growth impairment in children; heart failure; high blood pressure; impaired healing of wounds; mood changes; muscle wasting; peptic ulcer; potassium loss; salt retention; weakness. Notify your doctor if you notice any major side effects.
Contraindications: This drug should not be taken by people who are allergic to it or by those who have systemic fungal infections. Consult your doctor if this drug has been prescribed for you and either of these conditions applies. • This drug has not been proven safe for use during pregnancy.
Warnings: This drug should be used very cautiously by people who have had tuberculosis and by those who have thyroid disease, liver disease, severe ulcerative colitis, history of ulcers, kidney disease, high blood pressure, bone disease, or myasthenia gravis. Be sure your doctor knows if any of these conditions applies to you. • Growth of children may be affected by this drug. • This drug may cause high blood pressure, high blood sugar, fluid retention, and potassium loss. Diabetics who are taking this drug should monitor blood glucose carefully. • This drug interacts with aspirin, barbiturates, digitalis, diuretics, estrogens, indomethacin, oral anticoagulants, antidiabetics, and phenytoin; if you are currently taking any drugs of these types, consult your doctor about their use. If you are unsure of the type or contents of your medications, ask your doctor or pharmacist. • While you are taking this drug, you should not be vaccinated or immunized without your doctor's approval. • It is best to limit alcohol consumption while taking this drug. Alcohol may aggravate stomach

problems. • Long-term use of this drug has been associated with glaucoma and cataracts. Periodic eye examinations are recommended during long-term use. • This drug may mask signs of an infection or cause new infections to develop. • Blood pressure, body weight, and vision should be checked at regular intervals if you are taking this drug for a prolonged period. Stomach X rays are advised for persons with suspected or known peptic ulcers. • Notify your doctor if you are scheduled to have any skin tests, surgery, or dental work or if you develop a serious infection while on this medication. • Notify your doctor if you develop a sore throat, fever, unusual bleeding or bruising, yellowing of the skin, or impaired vision while you are taking this drug. • Report mood swings or depression to your doctor. • If you are using this drug for longer than a week and are subjected to stress, such as serious infection, injury, or surgery, you may need to receive higher dosages. • If you have been taking this drug for more than a week, do not stop taking it suddenly. Talk to your doctor about tapering off slowly. Never increase the dose or take the drug for a longer time than prescribed without consulting your doctor.

Comments: Take this drug exactly as directed. Do not take extra doses or skip a dose without first consulting your doctor. For long-term treatment, this drug may be taken on an alternate-day dosing schedule to minimize side effects. Talk to your doctor about this. • To prevent stomach upset, take this drug with food or a snack. • This drug is often taken on a decreasing-dosage schedule (four times a day for several days, then three times a day, etc.). • Often, taking the entire dose at one time (about eight A.M.) gives the best results. Ask your doctor. • To help avoid potassium loss while using this drug, it is recommended that you take your dose with a glass of fresh or frozen orange juice, or eat a banana each day. The use of a salt substitute also helps prevent potassium loss. Do not change your diet, however, without consulting your doctor. Too much potassium may also be dangerous. • If you are on long-term therapy with this medication, your doctor may want you to carry a medical alert card.

Medroxyprogesterone Acetate progesterone hormone, see Provera progesterone hormone.

Meni-D antiemetic, see Antivert antiemetic.

Metaprel bronchodilator, see Alupent bronchodilator.

Methylphenidate HCl central nervous system stimulant, see Ritalin, Ritalin-SR central nervous system stimulants.

Methylprednisolone steroid hormone, see Medrol steroid hormone.

Meticorten steroid hormone, see prednisone steroid hormone.

Metoclopramide HCl gastrointestinal stimulant and antiemetic, see Reglan gastrointestinal stimulant and antiemetic.

Mevacor antihyperlipidemic

Ingredient: lovastatin
Dosage Form: Tablet: 10 mg; 20 mg; 40 mg
Use: In conjunction with diet to reduce elevated blood cholesterol levels
Minor Side Effects: Abdominal pain; altered sense of taste; constipation; cramps; decreased sexual desire; diarrhea; dizziness; flatulence; headache;

heartburn; itching; nausea; rash; stomach upset. Most of these side effects, if they occur, should subside as your body adjusts to the medication. Tell your doctor about any that are persistent or particularly bothersome.

Major Side Effects: Blurred vision; clouding of the eye; difficulty swallowing; fever; liver disorders; malaise (vague feeling of discomfort); muscle aches, cramps, pain, or weakness; tingling in the fingers or toes. Notify your doctor if you notice any major side effects.

Contraindications: This drug should not be used by persons who are allergic to it, by those with active liver disease, or by pregnant women. Consult your doctor if this drug has been prescribed for you and any of these conditions applies. • This drug is not recommended for use in children or nursing women.

Warnings: This drug must be used cautiously by persons with a history of liver disease. Periodic liver function tests are recommended during long-term therapy to assure that the drug is not affecting the liver. • This drug must be used with caution if you have developed a severe infection, uncontrolled seizures, or a severe blood disorder or if you are undergoing major surgery or trauma. Under such conditions, your doctor may temporarily discontinue your therapy with this medication. • This drug may interact with the anticoagulant warfarin. If you are currently taking warfarin, your dose may be monitored more frequently and an adjustment may be required. Make sure your doctor knows you are taking warfarin. • This drug may cause muscle pain, tenderness, or weakness associated with fever and fatigue. If you develop these symptoms while taking lovastatin, contact your doctor. These symptoms are most common in persons who are also taking immunosuppressive drugs, gemfibrozil, or nicotinic acid. Consult your doctor about concurrent use of these drugs. • There are reports that this drug may cause a clouding of the lens in the eye during long-term therapy. An eye examination is recommended before therapy is begun and then once each year thereafter.

Comments: This drug is best taken as a single dose with the evening meal. • When first taking this drug, you may experience stomach upset and gas. These effects usually disappear with continued use. Notify your doctor if they persist or worsen. • The full effects of this drug may not be evident for four to six weeks. Your doctor will want to monitor the effects of this drug by doing periodic blood tests. Ask your doctor to explain your cholesterol level and the goals of your therapy. Learn to monitor your progress. • This drug should be used only after diet therapy has proven ineffective. This drug is not a substitute for proper diet, exercise, and weight control. For maximum results, this drug must be used in conjunction with a diet that is low in saturated fat and cholesterol. You may be referred to a nutritionist for diet counseling.

Micro-K potassium replacement, see potassium replacement.

Micronase oral antidiabetic

Ingredient: glyburide
Equivalent Products: DiaBeta; Glynase PresTab (See Comments)
Dosage Form: Tablet: 1.25 mg; 2.5 mg; 5 mg
Use: Treatment of diabetes mellitus not controlled by diet and exercise alone

Minor Side Effects: Dizziness; fatigue; headache; heartburn; loss of appetite; nausea; stomach upset; sun sensitivity; weakness. Most of these side effects, if they occur, should subside as your body adjusts to the medication. Tell your doctor about any that are persistent or particularly bothersome.

Major Side Effects: Blood disorders; breathing difficulties; dark urine; diarrhea; fluid retention; itching; light-colored stools; low blood sugar; muscle cramps; rash; sore throat and fever; tingling in the hands and feet; unusual bleeding or bruising; vomiting; yellowing of the eyes or skin. Notify your doctor if you develop any major side effects.

Contraindications: This drug should not be used for the treatment of juvenile (insulin dependent) or unstable diabetes. This drug should not be used by diabetics subject to acidosis or ketosis or by diabetics with a history of diabetic coma. • Persons with severe liver, kidney, or thyroid disorders should not use this drug. • Avoid using this drug if you are allergic to sulfonylureas or sulfa drugs. Be sure your doctor knows if you have such an allergy. • In the presence of infections, fever, or severe trauma, your doctor may advise you to use insulin instead of this medication—at least during the acute stage.

Warnings: This drug should be used cautiously during pregnancy. If you are currently pregnant, or become pregnant while taking this drug, talk to your doctor about its use; insulin therapy may be indicated instead of the medication. • This drug should be used with caution by nursing women; children; and persons with liver, kidney, or thyroid disorders. • Thiazide diuretics and beta-blocking drugs commonly used to treat high blood pressure may interfere with your control of diabetes. • This drug interacts with steroids, estrogens, oral contraceptives, phenothiazines, phenytoin, isoniazid, thyroid hormones, aspirin, anti-inflammatories, and diuretics. If you are taking any drugs of these types, talk to your doctor about your use of glyburide. If you are not sure about the type or contents of your medications, consult your doctor or pharmacist. • Do not drink alcohol or take any other medications unless directed to do so by your doctor. Flushing or breathlessness can occur with the combination of alcohol and Micronase. Be especially careful with nonprescription cough and cold remedies. • Be sure you can recognize signs of low blood sugar (hypoglycemia) and know what to do if you begin to experience these symptoms. Signs of low blood sugar include chills, cold sweat, drowsiness, headache, nausea, nervousness, rapid pulse, tremors, and weakness. If these symptoms develop, eat or drink something containing sugar and call your doctor. Poor diet, malnutrition, strenuous exercise, and alcohol consumption may lead to low blood sugar. • While taking this drug, call your doctor if you develop an infection, fever, sore throat, rash, itching, unusual bleeding or bruising, dark urine, light-colored stools, or yellowing of the eyes or skin.

Comments: Take this drug at the same time every day. It is usually taken 30 minutes before breakfast unless directed otherwise. • Do not discontinue taking this medication without consulting your doctor. If stomach upset occurs, this drug may be taken with food. • Avoid prolonged or unprotected exposure to sunlight while taking this drug, as it makes you more sensitive to the sun's burning rays. • While taking this drug, test your urine and/or blood as prescribed. It is important that you understand what the results mean. • It is advised that persons taking this drug carry a medical alert card or wear a medical alert bracelet. • Studies have shown that a good diet and exercise program are extremely important in controlling diabetes. Discuss the use of this drug with your doctor. Persons taking this drug must carefully watch their diet and exercise program and avoid infection through good personal hygiene. • There are other drugs similar to this (Orinase, Diabinese, Glucotrol) that vary slightly in their activity. Certain persons who do not benefit from one oral antidiabetic agent of this type may find another one more effective. Discuss this and any other questions with your doctor. Glynase PresTab is available in tablet strengths of 1.5 mg and 3 mg.

Minitran transdermal antianginal, see nitroglycerin transdermal antianginal.

Minocin antibiotic

Ingredient: minocycline hydrochloride

Equivalent Products: Dynacin; Minocycline

Dosage Forms: Capsule: 50 mg; 100 mg. Tablet: 50 mg; 100 mg. Suspension (content per 5 ml teaspoon): 50 mg

Uses: Treatment of a wide variety of bacterial infections; treatment of severe acne

Minor Side Effects: Diarrhea; dizziness; drowsiness; increased sensitivity to sunlight; light-headedness; loss of appetite; nausea; upset stomach; vomiting. Most of these side effects, if they occur, should subside as your body adjusts to the medication. Tell your doctor about any that are persistent or particularly bothersome.

Major Side Effects: Anemia; breathing difficulties; dark urine; irritation of the mouth; itching; rash; rectal and vaginal itching; sore throat; staining of teeth in children; unusual bleeding or bruising; yellowing of the eyes or skin. Notify your doctor if you notice major side effects.

Contraindication: Anyone who has demonstrated an allergy to any of the tetracycline antibiotics, such as tetracycline, doxycycline, or oxytetracycline, should not take this drug. Consult your doctor immediately if this drug has been prescribed for you and you have such a history.

Warnings: This drug should be used cautiously by people who have liver or kidney diseases; by children under the age of eight; and by women who are pregnant or nursing. This drug can cause permanent discoloration of the teeth when taken by children under eight. When taken during the last half of pregnancy, it can cause permanent discoloration of the fetus's teeth. Be sure your doctor knows if any of these conditions applies to you. • This drug interacts with penicillin, lithium, antacids, laxatives, steroids, and anticoagulants. If you are currently taking any drugs of these types, consult your doctor about their use. If you are unsure of the type or contents of your medications, ask your doctor or pharmacist. • Do not take this drug within two hours of the time you take an antacid or within three hours of taking an iron preparation; both of these drugs interact with minocycline and make it ineffective. • This drug may affect tests for syphilis. Make sure your doctor knows you are taking this drug if you are scheduled for this test. • Complete blood cell counts and liver and kidney function tests should be done if you take this drug for a prolonged period. • Prolonged use of this drug may allow organisms that are not susceptible to it to grow and cause a severe infection. • Do not use this drug unless your doctor has specifically told you to do so. Be sure to follow the directions carefully and report any unusual reactions to your doctor at once. • This drug may impair your ability to perform tasks that require alertness, such as driving a car or operating potentially dangerous equipment.

Comments: Try to take this drug on an empty stomach (one hour before or two hours after a meal) with at least eight ounces of water. If you find the drug upsets your stomach, you may try taking it with food. • This drug is usually taken once or twice a day. It is most effective when taken at evenly spaced intervals throughout the day and night. Ask your doctor or pharmacist for help in planning a medication schedule. Never increase the dosage unless your doctor tells you to do so. • Take this drug for as long as prescribed, even if the symptoms have disappeared. Stopping treatment early may lead to reinfection. • Make sure that your prescription is marked with the drug's expiration date. Do not use this drug after the expiration date. Discard unused medication. • This drug may cause you to be especially sensitive to the sun, so avoid exposure to sunlight as much as possible. When outside, wear protective clothing and use an effective sunscreen.

Minocycline antibiotic, see Minocin antibiotic.

Mitran antianxiety, see Librium antianxiety.

morphine analgesic

Ingredient: morphine
Equivalent Products: Morphine Sulfate; MS Contin; MSIR; OMS Concentrate; RMS; Roxanol; Roxanol SR
Dosage Forms: Oral solution (content per 5 ml teaspoon): 10 mg; 20 mg; 100 mg. Rectal suppository: 5 mg; 10 mg; 20 mg; 30 mg. Sustained-release tablet: 15 mg; 30 mg; 60 mg; 100 mg. Tablet: 15 mg; 30 mg
Use: Relief of moderate to severe pain
Minor Side Effects: Blurred vision; constipation; dizziness; drowsiness; dry mouth; flushing; indigestion or gas; light-headedness; loss of appetite; nausea; sweating; vomiting. Most of these side effects, if they occur, should subside as your body adjusts to the medication. Tell your doctor about any that are persistent or particularly bothersome.
Major Side Effects: Abdominal pain; abnormal dreams; anxiety; confusion; delirium; depression; difficulty in breathing; excitation; fainting; false sense of well-being; fatigue; fear; irregular heartbeat; mood changes; painful or difficult urination; palpitations; rash; restlessness; sore throat and fever; tremors; weakness. Notify your doctor if you notice any major side effects.
Contraindications: This medication should not be used by persons with an allergy to narcotic analgesics or by those with acute bronchial asthma or certain other breathing disorders. Consult your doctor immediately if you have any of these conditions and this medication has been prescribed for you.
Warnings: Tell your doctor about unusual or allergic reactions you have had to any medications, especially to morphine or to other narcotic analgesics (such as codeine, hydrocodone, hydromorphone, meperidine, methadone, oxycodone, and propoxyphene). • Tell your doctor if you now have or have ever had acute abdominal conditions, asthma, brain disease, colitis, epilepsy, gallstones or gallbladder disease, head injuries, heart disease, kidney disease, liver disease, lung disease, mental illness, emotional disorders, enlarged prostate gland, thyroid disease, or urethral stricture. • Tell your doctor if you are pregnant. The effects of morphine during the early stages of pregnancy have not been thoroughly studied in humans. However, regular use of morphine in large doses during the later stages of pregnancy can result in addiction of the fetus, leading to withdrawal symptoms at birth. Also, tell your doctor if you are breast-feeding. Small amounts of this drug may pass into breast milk and cause excessive drowsiness in the infant. • Morphine has the potential for abuse and must be used with caution. Usually, it should not be taken on a regular schedule for longer than ten days (unless your doctor directs you to do so). Tolerance develops quickly; do not increase the dosage or stop taking the drug abruptly, unless you first consult your doctor. If you have been taking large amounts of this drug or have been taking it for long periods, you may experience a withdrawal reaction (muscle aches, diarrhea, gooseflesh, runny nose, nausea, vomiting, shivering, trembling, stomach cramps, sleep disorders, irritability, weakness, excessive yawning, or sweating) when you stop taking it. Your doctor may, therefore, want to reduce your dosage gradually. • If this drug makes you dizzy or drowsy, do not take part in any activity that requires alertness, such as driving a car or operating potentially dangerous machinery. • Before having surgery or any other medical or dental treatment, tell your doctor or dentist that you are taking this drug. • Concurrent use of morphine with other central nervous system depressants (such as alcohol, antihist-

amines, barbiturates, benzodiazepine tranquilizers, muscle relaxants, and phe-nothiazine tranquilizers), sedatives, or with tricyclic antidepressants can cause extreme drowsiness; avoid combining any of these drugs with morphine.

Comments: The sustained-release tablets should be swallowed whole; chewing, crushing, or crumbling them destroys their sustained-release activity and may increase side effects. • To avoid stomach upset, you can take mor-phine with food or milk. The oral solution form can be mixed with fruit juices to improve the taste. • This medication works best if taken at the onset of pain rather than once pain becomes intense. • To avoid dizziness when you stand, contract and relax the muscles in your legs for a few moments before rising. Do this by pushing one foot against the floor while raising the other foot slightly, alternating feet so that you are pumping your legs in a pedaling mo-tion. • Chew gum or suck on ice chips or a piece of hard candy to reduce mouth dryness. • If this drug causes constipation, increase the amount of fiber in your diet, exercise, and drink more water, unless your doctor directs you oth-erwise. • Store this and all medications out of the reach of children.

Morphine Sulfate analgesic, see morphine analgesic.

MS Contin analgesic, see morphine analgesic.

MSIR analgesic, see morphine analgesic.

Mycelex antifungal, see Lotrimin antifungal.

Mycostatin antifungal

Ingredient: nystatin
Equivalent Products: Nilstat; Nystatin; Nystex; O-V Statin
Dosage Forms: Cream; Ointment; Powder (per gram): 100,000 units. Oral suspension (per ml): 100,000 units. Oral tablet: 500,000 units. Oral troche: 200,000 units. Vaginal tablet: 100,000 units
Use: Treatment of fungal infections
Minor Side Effects: Oral forms: diarrhea; nausea; vomiting. Topical and vaginal forms: itching. Most of these side effects, if they occur, should subside as your body adjusts to the medication. Tell your doctor about any that are per-sistent or particularly bothersome.
Major Side Effect: Rash or irritation. Notify your doctor if you notice a major side effect.
Contraindication: This drug should not be used by people who are allergic to it. Contact your doctor immediately if this drug has been prescribed for you and you have such an allergy.
Warnings: This drug must be used carefully by pregnant or nursing women. If you suffer a rash or irritation from taking this drug, consult your doctor; use of the drug may be discontinued. • Avoid use around the eyes.
Comments: Continue taking this as long as directed even if symptoms dis-appear before that time to ensure the infection is gone. Stopping therapy too soon can lead to a reinfection. If symptoms to not improve or become worse while using this medication, contact your doctor. Oral use: If you are using the oral suspension, oral tablets, or oral troches to treat an infection in the mouth, rinse the drug around in your mouth as long as possible before swallowing. Do not crush or chew the oral tablets or troches; let them dissolve slowly in your mouth. The oral suspension must be shaken well before use. It need not be re-frigerated. • If you are using the topical cream or ointment form of this drug,

apply it after cleaning the area unless otherwise specified by your doctor. If you are using the powder form of this drug to treat a foot infection, sprinkle the powder liberally into your shoes and socks. • Moist lesions or sores are best treated with the powder form of this drug. • If you are using this drug to treat a vaginal infection, avoid sexual intercourse or ask your partner to wear a condom until treatment is completed; these measures will help prevent reinfection. • The vaginal tablets are supplied with an applicator that should be used to insert the tablets high into the vagina. • Unless instructed otherwise by your doctor, do not douche during the treatment period or for two to three weeks following your use of the vaginal tablets. Use the vaginal tablets continuously, including during your menstrual period, until your doctor tells you to stop. Be sure to complete a full course of therapy with this drug. • Wear cotton panties rather than those made of nylon or other nonporous materials while fungal infections of the vagina are being treated. • You may wish to wear a sanitary napkin while using the vaginal tablets to prevent soiling of your underwear.

Mykrox diuretic, see Zaroxolyn diuretic.

Naprosyn anti-inflammatory

Ingredient: naproxen

Equivalent Products: Aleve (see Comments); Anaprox (see Comments); Naproxen

Dosage Forms: Oral suspension (content per 5 ml teaspoon): 125 mg. Tablet: 250 mg; 375 mg; 500 mg

Uses: Relief of pain and swelling due to rheumatoid arthritis, osteoarthritis, tendonitis, bursitis, and acute gout; relief of mild to moderate pain; relief of menstrual pain

Minor Side Effects: Abdominal pain; bloating; constipation; diarrhea; dizziness; drowsiness; dry mouth; headache (mild to moderate); heartburn; insomnia; loss of appetite; nausea; nervousness; peculiar taste in mouth; sore mouth; sweating; vomiting; weakness. Most of these side effects, if they occur, should subside as your body adjusts to the medication. Tell your doctor about any that are persistent or particularly bothersome.

Major Side Effects: Black, tarry stools; breast enlargement (in both sexes); breathing difficulties; chest tightness; dark urine; depression; difficulty in urinating; easy bruising or bleeding; fluid retention; hair loss; hallucinations; hearing loss; itching; kidney disease; menstrual irregularities; palpitations; rash; ringing in the ears; sore throat; swelling of the hands or feet; tingling in hands or feet; ulcers; unusual weight gain; visual disturbances; yellowing of the eyes or skin. Notify your doctor if you notice any major side effects.

Contraindication: This drug should not be taken by people who are allergic to it or to aspirin or similar drugs. Consult your doctor immediately if this drug has been prescribed for you and you have such an allergy.

Warnings: This medication should be used with extreme caution by people who have a history of ulcers or of stomach or intestinal disorders. Make sure your doctor knows if you have or have had any of these conditions. • This drug should be used cautiously by persons with anemia, severe allergies, bleeding diseases, high blood pressure, liver disease, kidney disease, or certain types of heart disease. Be sure your doctor knows if any of these conditions applies to you. • This drug should be used only if clearly needed during pregnancy or while nursing. Discuss the risks and benefits with your doctor. • This drug interacts with anticoagulants, oral antidiabetics, barbiturates, diuretics, steroids, phenytoin, and aspirin. If you are currently taking any drugs of these types, consult your doctor or pharmacist about their use. If you are unsure about the type or contents of your medications, consult your doctor or pharmacist. • Avoid the use of alcohol while taking this medication. • While using this medication, avoid the use of nonprescription medication containing aspirin or ibuprofen, since they are similar in some actions to this drug. • This drug may cause drowsiness or blurred vision. Avoid activities that require alertness, such as driving a car or operating potentially dangerous equipment. Notify your doctor if you experience frequent indigestion or notice a change in the appearance of your urine or stools. • Notify your doctor if you experience a skin rash, vision changes, unusual weight gain, fluid retention, or a persistent headache while taking this drug.

Comments: Take this drug with food or milk to reduce stomach upset. • To be most effective in relieving symptoms of arthritis, this drug must be taken as prescribed. Do not take this medication only when you feel pain. It is important to take this drug continuously. You should note improvement in your symptoms soon after starting this drug, but it may take a few weeks for the full benefit to be apparent. • This drug is not a substitute for rest, physical therapy, or other measures recommended by your doctor to treat your condition. • Many different anti-inflammatory medications are available. If one is not effective or not well-tolerated, your doctor may have you try other ones. • A related drug (naproxen sodium), called Anaprox, converts in the body to Naproxen. The two drugs should not be taken together. Aleve, also naproxen sodium, is available without a prescription. Talk to your doctor or pharmacist about its use.

Naproxen anti-inflammatory, see Naprosyn anti-inflammatory

Nasacort intranasal steroid

Ingredient: triamcinolone acetonide

Dosage Form: Nasal spray (content per one actuation): 55 mcg

Use: For relief of symptoms of allergy, such as stuffy nose, runny nose, and sneezing, due to seasonal or perennial rhinitis

Minor Side Effects: Change in senses of taste and smell; dry throat; headache; light-headedness; mild, temporary nasal burning and stinging; nasal congestion; nasal irritation; nausea; nosebleed; sneezing; sore throat; watery eyes. Most of these side effects, if they occur, should subside as your body adjusts to the medication. Tell your doctor about any that are persistent or particularly bothersome.

Major Side Effects: Breathing trouble; nasal infection; rash; vomiting; wheezing. Notify your doctor if you notice a major side effect.

Contraindications: This drug should not be used by persons allergic to it or by persons who have an untreated nasal infection. Consult your doctor immediately if this drug has been prescribed for you and you have either of these conditions. • This drug is not recommended for use in children under twelve years of age.

Warnings: This drug must be used cautiously by persons with tuberculosis, viral infections, ocular herpes simplex, or nasal ulcers and by persons recovering from nasal trauma or surgery. Be sure your doctor knows if any of these conditions applies to you. • This drug is to be used in pregnant or nursing women only when clearly necessary. Discuss the benefits and risks with your doctor. • This drug must be used cautiously by persons receiving oral steroid therapy and persons being switched from oral steroid therapy to Nasalide. Report any increase in symptoms or feelings of weakness to your physician. A dosage adjustment may be necessary. • If symptoms do not improve within a few weeks or if they worsen with continued use, contact your doctor.

Comments: Take this drug exactly as prescribed. For maximum effect, it must be taken at regular intervals. It is not effective for immediate relief of symptoms. Although symptoms will improve in a few days, full relief may not be obtained for one to two weeks with continued use of this drug. Do not increase the dose. Taking more than prescribed leads to increased incidence of side effects. • If you are also using a decongestant spray, it is best to use the decongestant prior to the Nasacort. The decongestant will clear nasal passages, ensuring adequate penetration of this medication. • For best results, clear nasal passages of all secretions prior to using this drug. Shake the canister before using. To use, do not tilt your head back. Instead, tilt your head forward slightly and insert the nasal adapter into the nose keeping it upright. Close the other nostril. Avoid touching the inner nasal membranes. Depress the spray while breathing in gently through the nostril at the same time. Then breathe out through your mouth. After you have inhaled the prescribed number of times in one or both nostrils, gently sniff two or three times. Wipe the applicator clean with a tissue or rinse it under cold water if so directed. • Patient instructions explaining proper use of the nasal spray should be dispensed with the medication. Read and follow the instructions carefully for best results. If you have any questions about proper use of the nasal spray, ask your pharmacist. • Each Nasacort canister contains approximately 100 sprays.

Nasalcrom respiratory inhalant, see Intal antiasthmatic and antiallergic.

Nasalide intranasal steroid

Ingredient: flunisolide
Dosage Form: Spray (content per one actuation): 25 mcg
Use: For relief of symptoms of allergy, such as stuffy nose, runny nose, and sneezing, due to seasonal or perennial rhinitis
Minor Side Effects: Change in senses of taste and smell; dry throat; headache; light-headedness; mild, temporary nasal burning and stinging; nasal congestion; nasal irritation; nausea; nosebleed; sneezing; sore throat; watery eyes. Most of these side effects, if they occur, should subside as your body adjusts to the medication. Tell your doctor about any that are persistent or particularly bothersome.
Major Side Effects: Breathing trouble; nasal infection; rash; vomiting; wheezing. Notify your doctor if you notice a major side effect.
Contraindications: This drug should not be used by persons allergic to it or by persons who have an untreated nasal infection. Consult your doctor immediately if this drug has been prescribed for you and you have either of these conditions. • This drug is not recommended for use in children under six.
Warnings: This drug must be used cautiously by persons with tuberculosis, viral infections, ocular herpes simplex, or nasal ulcers and by persons recovering from nasal trauma or surgery. Be sure your doctor knows if any of these conditions applies to you. • This drug is to be used in pregnant or nursing women only when clearly necessary. Discuss the benefits and risks with your doctor. • This drug must be used cautiously by persons receiving oral steroid therapy and persons being switched from oral steroid therapy to Nasalide. Report any increase in symptoms or feelings of weakness to your physician. A dosage adjustment may be necessary. • If symptoms do not improve within a few weeks or if they worsen with continued use, contact your doctor.
Comments: Take this drug exactly as prescribed. For maximum effect, it must be taken at regular intervals. It is not effective for immediate relief of symptoms. Although symptoms will improve in a few days, full relief may not be obtained for one to two weeks with continued use of this drug. Do not in-

crease the dose. Taking more than prescribed leads to increased incidence of side effects. Adults should not exceed eight sprays in each nostril per day. The maximum recommended dose for children is four sprays per nostril per day. • If you are also using a decongestant spray, it is best to use the decongestant prior to the Nasalide. The decongestant will clear nasal passages, ensuring adequate penetration of Nasalide. • For best results, clear nasal passages of all secretions prior to using this drug. Shake the pump before using it. To use, do not tilt your head back. Instead, tilt your head forward slightly and insert the pump tube into the nose, keeping it upright. Close the other nostril. Avoid touching the inner nasal membranes. Push down on the plunger while breathing in gently through the nostril at the same time. Then breathe out through your mouth. After you have inhaled the prescribed number of times in one or both nostrils, gently sniff two or three times. Wipe the applicator clean with a tissue or rinse it under cold water if so directed. • Patient instructions explaining proper use of the nasal pump unit are available. Read and follow the instructions carefully for best results. If you have any questions about proper use of the pump unit, ask your pharmacist. • Each Nasalide pump unit contains approximately 200 sprays.

Neomycin/Polymyxin B Sulfate/Hydrocortisone ophthalmic steroid and antibiotic, see Cortisporin ophthalmic steroid and antibiotic.

Neomycin Sulfate-Polymyxin B Sulfate-Gramicidin ophthalmic antibiotic, see Neosporin ophthalmic antibiotic.

Neosporin ophthalmic antibiotic

Ingredients: gramicidin (solution only); neomycin sulfate; polymyxin B sulfate; alcohol (solution only); thimerosal (solution only); bacitracin (ointment only)

Equivalent Products: AK-Spore; Bacitracin Neomycin Polymyxin B; Neomycin Sulfate-Polymyxin B Sulfate-Gramicidin; Ocutricin

Dosage Forms: Ointment (content per gram): bacitracin, 400 units; neomycin sulfate, 3.5 mg; polymyxin B sulfate, 10,000 units. Solution (content per ml): gramicidin, 0.025 mg; neomycin sulfate, 1.75 mg; polymyxin B sulfate, 10,000 units; alcohol, 0.5%; thimerosal, 0.001%

Use: Short-term treatment of superficial bacterial infections of the eye

Minor Side Effects: Blurred vision; red eyes; temporary burning or stinging on contact. Most of these side effects, if they occur, should subside as your body adjusts to the medication. Tell your doctor about any that are persistent or particularly bothersome.

Major Side Effects: Eye irritation or pain; eyelid swelling; skin rash. Notify your doctor if you notice any major side effects.

Contraindication: This drug should not be taken by people with known sensitivity to any of its ingredients. Make sure your doctor knows if you have such a sensitivity. If you have a known sensitivity to thimerosal, consult your doctor or pharmacist; there are similar products that do not contain this preservative.

Warnings: Prolonged use of this drug may result in secondary infection. Use only as directed. • This drug should be used cautiously by people who have an injured cornea, kidney disease, inner ear disease, myasthenia gravis, or Parkinson's disease.

Comments: Blurred vision, stinging, or irritation may occur for a few minutes after the medication is applied; these effects should be temporary. If symptoms do not improve or if they become bothersome, contact your doctor. • Continue using this drug for the full period prescribed even if symptoms have subsided. Stopping therapy too soon can lead to ineffective treatment and a recurrence of the infection. If you miss a dose, apply it as soon as it is remembered unless it is near the time for the next dose. In that case, skip the missed dose and resume your usual dosing schedule. Do not double the dose to catch up. To administer eye drops, lie or sit down and tilt your head back. Carefully pull your lower eyelid down to form a pouch. Hold the dropper close to, but not touching, the eyelid, and place the prescribed number of drops into the pouch. Do not place the drops directly on the eyeball; you probably will blink and lose the medication. Close your eye and keep it shut for a few moments. To administer eye gel, lie or sit down and tilt your head back. Carefully pull your lower eyelid down to form a pouch. Gently squeeze the tube to release a small amount of the gel. With a sweeping motion, place the gel into the pouch. Do not place it directly on the eyeball; you probably will blink and lose the medication. Slowly roll your eyeball around to spread the gel. If you are using other eye medications in addition to the gel, use eye drops at least five minutes before using the gel. • Be careful about the contamination of medications used for the eyes. Wash your hands before administering eye medications. Do not touch the dropper or ointment tube to your eye. Do not wash or wipe the dropper before replacing it in the bottle. Close the bottle tightly to keep out moisture. Store at room temperature away from heat and direct sunlight. If the eye drops or gel become discolored or contain particles, discard the unused medication and begin using a fresh bottle or tube. Check the expiration date on the drug label and discard any unused drug after that date.

Nicoderm transdermal smoking deterrent

Ingredient: nicotine

Dosage Form: Transdermal patch (daily amount delivered by each patch): 7 mg; 14 mg; 21 mg. (see Comments)

Equivalent Products: Habitrol; Nicotrol; Prostep

Use: An aid to stop smoking

Minor Side Effects: Abdominal pain; constipation; diarrhea; dizziness; dry mouth; frequent urination; headache; insomnia; light-headedness; local irritation at patch site; nervousness; sweating. Most of these side effects, if they occur, should subside as your body adjusts to the medication. Tell your doctor about any that are persistent or particularly bothersome.

Major Side Effects: Breathing difficulties; burning, redness, or pain at patch site; cold sweats; false sense of well-being; faintness; flushing; rapid, pounding heart rate; vision disturbances. Notify your doctor if you notice any major side effects.

Contraindications: This drug should not be taken by nonsmokers; people with an allergy to nicotine; or those who have suffered a recent heart attack, have severe chest pain, or severe irregular heart rhythms. Consult your doctor immediately if any of these conditions applies to you.

Warnings: This drug should be used cautiously by persons with certain types of heart disease, thyroid disease, diabetes, hypertension, peptic ulcer disease, or certain skin disorders. Be sure your doctor knows if any of these conditions applies to you. • This drug should be used with caution in conjunction with other transdermal patches, caffeine, theophylline, beta blockers, furosemide, propoxyphene, antihypertensives, imipramine, insulin, glutethimide, and pentazocine. If you are currently taking any drugs of these types, consult your doctor about their use. If you are unsure of the type or contents of your medications, ask your doctor or pharmacist. • Use of this drug in adolescents and children who smoke has not been evaluated. • This drug con-

CONSUMER GUIDE®

tains nicotine, as do cigarettes; therefore, concurrent use can lead to an overdose. You must stop smoking completely while using this drug. If you do not stop smoking after four weeks, use of this drug should be discontinued. Because nicotine is addicting, the patches should be used for no longer than three months. In addition, the strength of the patch should be reduced after four to eight weeks of therapy. • If you experience severe or continuous skin reactions to the patches, discontinue use and consult your doctor.

Comments: Stop smoking completely before using this drug. • Remove the patch from the protective pouch and apply it to a clean, dry, nonhairy area on the upper part of the body or upper arm. Nicoderm, Habitrol, and Prostep patches are to remain in place for 24 hours. Apply the new patch just before removing the old one. Do not use the same patch for more than 24 hours. Nicotrol patches are applied each morning and taken off at bedtime. Be sure the application sites vary so as not to irritate the skin. Wash hands after applying and removing a patch. Avoid contact with eyes. • Discard patches carefully by folding them over and placing the old one in the pouch the new system was in. Keep this and all medications out of the reach of children and pets. • Patient information sheets are available for this drug. If one is not dispensed with your prescription, ask your pharmacist for it. Read the information carefully before taking this drug. • To be most effective, this drug is to be used in conjunction with a smoking cessation program. • Nicotine is similar in action to caffeine. Limit your consumption of coffee, tea, cola, chocolate, and other caffeine-containing products while using this drug. • Prostep patches are available in strengths of 11 mg and 22 mg. Nicotrol patches are available in strengths of 5 mg, 10 mg, and 15 mg. Store patches in a cool, dry area away from heat. Do not remove patches from their pouch until ready to use, since they may lose strength.

Nicorette smoking deterrent

Ingredient: nicotine resin complex
Dosage Form: Chewing gum (content per piece): 2 mg; 4 mg
Use: An aid to stop smoking
Minor Side Effects: Constipation; diarrhea; dizziness; dry mouth; gas pains; headache; hiccups; hoarseness; insomnia; jaw ache; light-headedness; mouth sores; sneezing; sore throat. Most of these side effects, if they occur, should subside as your body adjusts to the medication. Tell your doctor about any that are persistent or particularly bothersome.

Major Side Effects: Breathing difficulties; cold sweats; confusion; dental problems; faintness; false sense of well-being; flushing; rapid, pounding heart rate; visual disturbances; weakness. Notify your doctor if you develop any major side effects.

Contraindications: Nonsmokers; people who have recently suffered a heart attack; people with certain heart conditions, such as chest pain or severe arrhythmias; and pregnant and nursing women should consult their doctor if this drug has been prescribed for them.

Warnings: This drug must be used with caution by persons with certain types of heart disease, thyroid disease, diabetes, hypertension, or peptic ulcer disease. If any of these conditions applies to you, discuss the use of this drug with your doctor. • Use of this drug in adolescents or children who smoke has not been evaluated. • This drug interacts with caffeine, theophylline, imipramine, pentazocine, furosemide, propranolol, glutethimide, and propoxyphene. If you are taking any of these medicines, consult your doctor or pharmacist about their use. If you are unsure of the type or contents of your medications, ask your doctor or pharmacist. • Nicorette contains nicotine, as do cigarettes; therefore, concurrent use can lead to overdose. Stop smoking completely while taking this drug. • Because nicotine is known to be addictive, this drug is not recommended to be used for longer than six months. Dental problems may be exacerbated while using this drug. • Report any unusual effects, such as nausea, salivation, abdominal pain, confusion, or weakness, to your doctor.

Comments: Take this drug as directed by your doctor. Do not use more than recommended. If using the 2 mg strength, you should not chew more than 30 pieces of gum a day and if using the 4 mg strength, do not chew more than 20 pieces of gum a day. Most people require about 9 to 12 pieces a day during the first month of use. • The gum should be chewed slowly. Chewing the gum too quickly can cause symptoms similar to oversmoking (nausea, hiccups, and throat irritation). During chewing, you will be able to taste the nicotine or experience a slight tingling sensation in your mouth. Once this occurs, you should stop chewing until the taste is gone or the tingling stops. Then resume chewing the same piece of gum, and repeat the process for about half an hour. This method delivers the nicotine at a more constant rate. Avoid eating and drinking for 15 minutes before and during the time you chew nicotine gum, since these activities can interfere with the effects of this drug. It has been observed that those who chew the gum on a regular schedule, i.e., every two hours, are more likely to sucessfully quit smoking than those who just chew the gum when they need it. Talk to your doctor about this. After two to three months of therapy, gradually reduce the amount of gum you chew by one of the following methods, as dicussed with your doctor: Replace the 4 mg strength with the 2 mg strength; every five to seven days, reduce the number of pieces of gum you chew by one or more; decrease the chewing time for each piece from the usual 30 minutes to 15 minutes for five to seven days, then decrease the amount of gum chewed each day; chew each piece for longer than 30 minutes, but reduce the number of pieces used each day; every five to seven days, substitute a piece of sugarless gum for a piece of nicotine gum. Once you are chewing only one to two pieces a day, therapy can be stopped. • To be most effective, this drug is to be used in conjunction with a smoking cessation program by persons who have a desire to stop smoking. • Patient information sheets are available for Nicorette. If one is not dispensed with your prescription, ask your pharmacist for one. Read the information carefully before taking this drug. • Nicotine is similar in action to caffeine. Limit your consumption of coffee, tea, cola, chocolate, and other caffeine-containing products while using this drug. • As with all medications, remember to store this gum properly and keep it out of the reach of children; it is medicine, not candy. Discard of gum properly by first wrapping it in paper. Do not swallow the gum. Nicorette DS refers to the 4 mg strength.

Nicotrol, see Nicoderm transdermal smoking deterrent.

Nifedipine antihypertensive and antianginal, see Procardia, Procardia XL antihypertensive and antianginal.

Nilstat antifungal, see Mycostatin antifungal.

Nitro-Bid sustained-release antianginal, see nitroglycerin sustained-release antianginal.

Nitrocine Timecaps sustained-release antianginal, see nitroglycerin sustained-release antianginal.

Nitrocine transdermal antianginal, see nitroglycerin transdermal antianginal.

Nitrodisc transdermal antianginal, see nitroglycerin transdermal antianginal.

Nitro-Dur transdermal antianginal, see nitroglycerin transdermal antianginal.

Nitrofan antibacterial, see nitrofurantoin antibacterial.

nitrofurantoin antibacterial

Ingredient: nitrofurantoin

Equivalent Products: Furadantin; Furalan; Furan; Furanite; Macrobid; Macrodantin; Nitrofan; see Comments

Dosage Forms: Capsule: 25 mg (Macrodantin only); 50 mg; 100 mg (Macrodantin only). Liquid (content per 5 ml teaspoon): 25 mg. Tablet: 50 mg; 100 mg

Use: Treatment of bacterial urinary tract infections such as pyelonephritis, pyelitis, or cystitis

Minor Side Effects: Abdominal cramps; change in urine color; diarrhea; dizziness; drowsiness; headache; loss of appetite; nausea; vomiting. Most of these side effects, if they occur, should subside as your body adjusts to the medication. Tell your doctor about any that are persistent or bothersome.

Major Side Effects: Anemia; breathing difficulties; chest pain; chills; cough; dark urine; fever; hepatitis; irritation of the mouth; low blood pressure; muscle aches; numbness and tingling in face, fingers, or toes; rash; rectal and vaginal itching; superinfection; swelling of the hands and feet; symptoms of lung infection; transient hair loss; weakness; yellowing of eyes and skin. Notify your doctor if you notice any major side effects.

Contraindications: This drug should not be used by persons with severe kidney disease or little or no urine production. Be sure your doctor knows if either condition applies to you. • This drug should not be used by pregnant women at term or in infants under one month of age. • This drug should not be used by people who are allergic to it. Consult your doctor immediately if this drug has been prescribed for you and you have such an allergy.

Warnings: This drug should be used cautiously by people with kidney disease, anemia, diabetes, vitamin-B imbalance, electrolyte imbalance, and certain other debilitating diseases. Be sure your doctor knows if any of these conditions applies to you. • This drug should be used with caution by pregnant women, by women who may become pregnant, and by nursing mothers. • This drug should be used with caution by blacks and by ethnic groups of Mediterranean and Near Eastern origin, since cases of hemolytic anemia have been known to be brought about in a percentage of such persons while using this drug. • This drug may interact with nalidixic acid, norfloxacin, probenecid, magnesium trisilicate, and sulfinpyrazone. If you are currently taking any drugs of these types, consult your doctor. If you are unsure about the type or contents of your medications, ask your doctor or pharmacist. • This drug may interfere with certain blood and urine laboratory tests. Remind your doctor that you are taking this drug if you are scheduled for any tests. • This drug may cause false results with urine sugar tests. • This drug should be taken cautiously; it has been associated with lung problems. If such problems occur, your doctor will discontinue this drug and appropriate measures will be taken. • If you experience fever, chills, cough, chest pain, shortness of breath, rash, pallor, weakness, breathing difficulties, tingling of the fingers or toes, or signs of jaundice (yellowing of the eyes or skin), consult your doctor. • This drug may cause nerve damage and liver disease. If this drug is taken for prolonged periods, tests to monitor for these effects are recommended. Report any tingling sensations or loss of feeling in your extremities.

Comments: To reduce nausea and vomiting, take this drug with a meal or glass of milk. Shake the liquid well before pouring each dose. The liquid may be stored at room temperature. • This drug should be taken for as long as prescribed; stopping treatment early may result in reinfection. • It is best to take this medication at evenly spaced intervals around the clock. Ask your doctor or pharmacist to help you establish a practical dosing schedule. • If you have a urinary tract infection, you should drink at least nine or ten glasses of water each day, unless your doctor directs you otherwise. • This drug may cause your urine to become dark in color. Do not be alarmed. • Not all nitrofurantoin preparations are generic equivalents; consult your pharmacist about the use of generics. Macrodantin and Macrobid (which are not identical) contain macrocrystals of nitrofurantoin, which are better tolerated. They cause less nausea and less stomach distress than other nitrofurantoin products.

nitroglycerin sustained-release antianginal

Ingredient: nitroglycerin

Equivalent Products: Nitro-Bid; Nitrocine Timecaps; Nitroglyn; Nitrong

Dosage Forms: Time-release capsule: 2.5 mg; 6.5 mg; 9 mg; 13 mg. Time-release tablet: 2.6 mg; 6.5 mg; 9 mg

Use: Prevention of chest pain (angina) due to heart disease

Minor Side Effects: Dizziness; flushing of the face; headache; nausea; vomiting; weakness. Most of these side effects, if they occur, should subside as your body adjusts to the medication. Tell your doctor about any that are persistent or particularly bothersome.

Major Side Effects: Fainting; rapid, pounding heartbeat; rash; sweating. Notify your doctor if you notice any major side effects.

Contraindications: This drug should not be taken by people who are allergic to it or by people who have a head injury, low blood pressure, certain types of glaucoma, or severe anemia. Consult your doctor immediately if this drug has been prescribed for you and any of these conditions applies.

Warnings: This medication should be used cautiously by persons who have recently suffered a heart attack, by those with low blood pressure or glaucoma, and by pregnant or nursing women. Be sure your doctor knows if any of these conditions applies to you. • This drug should be used cautiously in conjunction with antihypertensive drugs and aspirin. If you are currently taking any of these drugs, consult your doctor about their use. If you are unsure about the types or contents of your medications, ask you doctor or pharmacist. • Do not drink alcohol unless your doctor has told you that you may as it can add to the side effects. • This drug may not continue to relieve chest pain after prolonged use; tolerance to nitroglycerin develops quickly. If this drug begins to seem less effective, consult your doctor, who may recommend a change in your dosing schedule. • This drug is not effective against an attack of angina that is already in progress. It must be taken consistently to prevent chest pain. • If you develop blurred vision, severe headaches, or dry mouth, contact your doctor.

Comments: The time-release forms of this drug must be swallowed whole; do not crush or break the capsules or tablets. • It is best to take the capsule form on an empty stomach with a full glass of water. • Do not stop taking this medication abruptly without consulting your doctor. • Side effects generally disappear as your body adjusts to the medication. • Headache is a common side effect. It generally occurs after taking a dose and lasts a short time. Headaches should be less noticeable with continued treatment. If they persist, contact your doctor. Aspirin or acetaminophen may help to relieve headaches, but do not take either without first consulting your doctor. • To avoid dizziness or light-headedness, contract and relax the muscles of your legs for a few moments before rising. Do this by pushing one foot against the floor while raising the other foot slightly, alternating feet so that you are pumping your legs. The tablets and capsules should be stored in their original containers, and the containers should be kept tightly closed. Do not keep outdated medication. Do not switch brands of nitroglycerin without consulting your doctor or pharmacist, as all products may not be exact equivalents.

nitroglycerin transdermal antianginal

Ingredient: nitroglycerin

Equivalent Products: Deponit; Minitran; Nitrocine; Nitrodisc; Nitro-Dur; Transderm-Nitro

Dosage Form: Transdermal patch systems (various strengths)

Use: Prevention of angina (chest pain) attacks due to heart disease

Minor Side Effects: Dizziness; flushing of face; headache; light-headedness; nausea; skin irritation. Most of these side effects, if they occur, should subside as your body adjusts to the medication. Tell your doctor about any that are persistent or particularly bothersome.

Major Side Effects: Blurred vision; fainting; skin rash; vomiting; weakness. Notify your doctor if you notice any major side effects.

Contraindications: This product should not be used by people who are allergic to nitrates or adhesive tape, or by those who have anemia, certain types of glaucoma, or head injuries. Consult your doctor if this drug has been prescribed for you and any of these conditions applies.

Warnings: This medication should be used cautiously by persons who have recently suffered a heart attack, by those with low blood pressure or glaucoma, and by pregnant or nursing women. Be sure your doctor is aware if any of these conditions applies to you. • This drug should be used cautiously in conjunction with antihypertensive drugs and aspirin. If you are currently taking any drugs of these types, consult your doctor about their use. If you are unsure about the types or contents of your medications, ask your doctor or pharmacist. • Do not drink alcohol without your doctor's approval, as it can add to side effects. • This drug may not continue to relieve chest pain after prolonged use; tolerance to nitroglycerin develops quickly. If this drug begins to seem less effective, consult your doctor. • This drug is not effective against an attack of angina that is already in progress. It must be used consistently to prevent chest pain. • If you develop blurred vision, severe headache, or dry mouth, contact your doctor.

Comments: This drug is supplied as a transdermal patch. Each patch is designed to continually release nitroglycerin over a 24-hour period. It may be necessary to clip hair prior to using these patches; hair may interfere with patch adhesion. • Do not apply patch to lower parts of arms or legs. Application sites should be changed slightly with each use to avoid skin irritation. Avoid placing patch on irritated or damaged skin. • You can shower or bathe while the patch is in place. If it loosens, apply a new patch. • It is recommended that you apply a new patch 30 minutes before removing the old one, if possible; this will ensure constant protection. Do not stop using these patches without consulting your doctor. • Store the patches in a cool, dry place. Do not refrigerate. • Patient instructions for application of these patches are available. Ask your pharmacist for them if they are not provided with your prescription. For maximum benefit, read and follow the instructions carefully. Different manufacturers use different delivery systems and adhesives. If you are not satisfied with the product you are currently using, discuss with your doctor or pharmacist the availability of other patches. • Side effects generally disappear as your body adjusts to the medication. If they persist or worsen, call your doctor. • Side effects generally disappear as your body adjusts to the medication. • Headache is a common side effect. It generally occurs after taking a dose and lasts a short time. Headaches should be less noticeable with continued treatment. If they persist, contact your doctor. Aspirin or acetaminophen may help to relieve headaches, but do not take either without first consulting your doctor. • To avoid dizziness or light-headedness when you stand, contract and relax the muscles of your legs for a few moments before rising. Do this by pushing one foot against the floor while raising the other foot slightly, alternating feet so that you are pumping your legs in a pedaling motion.

Nitroglyn sustained-release antianginal, see nitroglycerin sustained-release antianginal.

Nitrong sustained-release antianginal, see nitroglycerin sustained-release antianginal.

Nitrostat sublingual antianginal

Ingredient: nitroglycerin
Dosage Form: Sublingual tablet: 0.15 mg; 0.3 mg; 0.4 mg; 0.6 mg
Use: Relief of chest pain (angina) due to heart disease
Minor Side Effects: Dizziness; flushing of the face; headache; nausea; temporary burning or stinging of the tongue; vomiting. Most of these side effects, if they occur, should subside as your body adjusts to the medication. Tell your doctor about any that are persistent or particularly bothersome.
Major Side Effects: Fainting; rapid, pounding heart rate; sweating. Notify your doctor if you notice any major side effects.
Contraindications: This drug should not be used by people who are allergic to it; by those who have low blood pressure or severe anemia; or by those who have suffered a head injury or recent heart attack. Consult your doctor immediately if this drug has been prescribed for you and any of these conditions applies. People who have glaucoma should consult their doctor if this drug has been prescribed for them.
Warnings: Do not swallow this drug. The tablets must be placed under the tongue. Do not drink water or swallow for five minutes after taking this drug. • This drug should be used cautiously by pregnant women. Be sure your doctor knows if you are pregnant. • If you develop blurred vision or dry mouth, contact your doctor. • This drug interacts with alcohol and other agents that affect blood pressure. Consult your doctor about their use. If you are unsure of the type or contents of your medications, ask your doctor or pharmacist. • If you require more tablets than usual to relieve chest pain, contact your doctor. You may have developed a tolerance to the drug, or the drug may not be working effectively because of interference with other medication. • If this drug does not relieve pain or if pain arises from a different location or differs in severity, call your doctor immediately. • Before using this drug to relieve pain, be certain that the pain arises from the heart and is not due to another condition, such as a muscle spasm or indigestion.
Comments: Frequently chest pain will be relieved in two to five minutes simply by sitting down. • When you take this drug, sit down, lower your head, and breathe deeply. (See the chapter called Administering Medication Correctly to

be sure you are taking this drug properly. If you have any questions regarding the proper use of this medication, talk to your doctor.) If relief is not obtained in five minutes, take another tablet. Repeat in five minutes if necessary. Take no more than three tablets in 15 minutes. If relief still does not occur or if pain increases, call your doctor immediately or go to the nearest emergency treatment facility. • Side effects caused by this drug are most bothersome the first two weeks after starting therapy; they should subside as therapy continues. Headaches can usually be relieved by taking aspirin or acetaminophen, but do not take either without first consulting your doctor. If headaches are persistent or severe, contact your doctor. • This drug must be stored in a tightly capped glass container. Store the bottle in a cool, dry place. Never store the tablets in a metal box, plastic vial, or in the refrigerator or the bathroom medicine cabinet, as the drug may lose potency. The tablet usually causes a slight stinging sensation when placed under the tongue, although some individuals may not experience this effect. A lack of this sensation does not necessarily indicate a lack of potency. To ensure potency, discard unused tablets six months after the original container is opened. Replace with a fresh bottle. • Nitroglycerin is available in many different dosage forms. Discuss the various products with your doctor or pharmacist.

Nizoral antifungal

Ingredient: ketoconazole

Dosage Forms: Cream; Shampoo: 2%. Oral tablet: 200 mg

Use: Treatment of fungal infections; shampoo is used to reduce scaling due to dandruff

Minor Side Effects: Oral forms: dizziness; drowsiness; headache; nausea; stomach upset. Topical forms: itching. Most of these side effects, if they occur, should subside as your body adjusts to the medication. Tell your doctor about any that are persistent or particularly bothersome.

Major Side Effect: Oral forms: Blood disorders; dark urine; decreased sexual ability; depression; enlargement of breasts in both men and women; fever; itching; pale stools; skin rash; stomach pain; unusual weakness; vomiting; yellowing of the eyes or skin. Topical forms: dry skin; irritation; skin rash; stinging. Notify your doctor if you notice a major side effect.

Contraindication: This drug should not be used by people who are allergic to it. Contact your doctor immediately if this drug has been prescribed for you and you have such an allergy.

Warnings: This drug must be used carefully by pregnant or nursing women. Discuss the risks and benefits with your doctor. This drug should be used cautiously by people who have liver disease. Be sure your doctor knows if this condition applies to you. • This drug may interact with antacids, ulcer medications, antihistamines, steroids, theophylline, isoniazid, or rifampin. If you are currently taking any of these drug types, consult your doctor about their use. If you are unsure of the type or contents of your medications, ask your doctor or pharmacist. • This drug may make you dizzy or drowsy, especially during the first few days of therapy: This should subside as your body adjusts to the medication. If it does make you dizzy, avoid activities that require alertness, such as driving a car or operating potentially dangerous equipment, and limit your consumption of alcohol, which exaggerates this side effect. • Your doctor may want to see you regularly while you are taking this drug to check your response and to conduct liver function tests. • Contact your doctor if this drug causes fever, dark urine, pale stools, stomach pain, or vomiting. If you suffer a rash or irritation from using the cream or shampoo forms of this drug, consult your doctor. Use of the drug may be discontinued. • Avoid use of the ointment or shampoo around the eyes.

Comments: Continue taking this as long as directed even if symptoms disappear before that time to ensure the infection is gone. Stopping therapy too soon can lead to a reinfection. If symptoms to not improve or if they become worse while using this medication, contact your doctor. Take the oral tablets with food to minimize stomach upset. Avoid taking antacids within two hours of the tablets since the absorption of the drug may be affected. The shampoo may remove curls from hair that has been permanently waved. To use the shampoo, moisten hair and scalp with water. Apply about one teaspoonful (or enough to make lather) to wash scalp and hair. Gently massage over entire scalp for about one minute. Rinse with warm water. Repeat shampooing, leaving shampoo on scalp for three minutes. Rinse throughly and towel hair dry. Use twice a week or as directed. Once improvement is seen, this is used less often. • If you are using the topical cream form of this drug, apply it after cleaning the area unless otherwise specified by your doctor. Rub in gently as directed. Consult doctor if no improvement is seen or your condition worsens.

Nolex LA decongestant and expectorant, see Entex LA decongestant and expectorant.

Nolvadex chemotherapy agent

Ingredient: tamoxifen citrate
Dosage Form: Tablet: 10 mg
Use: Used alone or in combination with other drugs to treat breast and other forms of cancer

Minor Side Effects: Abdominal pain; change in food tastes; constipation; diarrhea; dizziness; headache; hot flashes; menstrual irregularities; nausea; vaginal discharge. Most of these side effects, if they occur, should subside as your body adjusts to the medication. Tell your doctor about any that are persistent or particularly bothersome.

Major Side Effects: Abnormal blood counts; blurred vision; bone pain; breathing trouble; changes in vision; confusion; depression; fever; fluid retention; leg pain; loss of appetite; rash; sleepiness; sore throat; swelling of the feet or ankles; vomiting; weakness; weight gain. Notify your doctor if you notice any major side effects.

Contraindication: This drug should not be taken by persons with an allergy to it. Consult your doctor immediately if you have such an allergy and this drug has been prescribed for you. • This drug should not be used during pregnancy or while breast-feeding. Discuss the risks and benefits with your doctor. It is recommended that appropriate contraceptive measures be taken while using this drug because of the risk of fetal harm.

Warnings: This drug should be used cautiously by people with abnormal blood counts, increased cholesterol or triglyceride levels, or increased calcium levels. Be sure your doctor knows if any of these conditions applies to you. • This drug should be used with caution in conjunction with oral anticoagulants; if you are currently taking any drugs of this type, consult your doctor about its use. If you are unsure of the type or contents of your medications, ask your doctor or pharmacist. • Use of this drug has not been studied in children. • Use of this drug has been associated with changes in vision. Report any vision changes to your doctor. • Notify your doctor if you develop breathing trouble, weakness, confusion, swelling of feet or ankles, weight gain, or bone pain while taking this drug. • Laboratory tests will be done periodically while you are taking this drug to monitor its effectiveness and check for side effects.

Comments: Take this drug exactly as prescribed, usually twice a day (morning and evening). Do not take it more often or stop taking it without consulting your doctor.

Norcet analgesic, see Vicodin, Vicodin ES analgesics.

Normodyne antihypertensive

Ingredient: labetalol hydrochloride
Equivalent Product: Trandate
Dosage Form: Tablet: 100 mg; 200 mg; 300 mg
Use: Treatment of high blood pressure
Minor Side Effects: Abdominal pain; altered sense of taste; bloating; blurred vision; constipation; dizziness (mild to moderate); drowsiness; dry eyes; dry mouth; gas; headache; heartburn; insomnia; light-headedness; loss of appetite; nasal congestion; nausea; scalp tingling; slowed heart rate; sweating. Most of these side effects, if they occur, should subside as your body adjusts to the medication. Tell your doctor about any that are persistent or particularly bothersome.
Major Side Effects: Blood disorders; breathing difficulties; change in vision; dark urine; decreased sexual ability; depression; difficulty in urinating; dizziness (severe); fever; impotence; mouth sores; numbness in fingers and toes; shortness of breath; skin rash; sore throat; swelling in hands and feet; yellowing of the eyes or skin. Notify your doctor if you notice any major side effects.
Contraindications: This drug should not be used by persons allergic to it or by those with a sensitivity to beta blockers. This drug should not be used by persons with bronchial asthma or certain types of heart disease (severe heart failure, bradycardia, shock). Consult your doctor immediately if this drug has been prescribed for you and any of these conditions applies.
Warnings: This drug must be used cautiously by persons with certain respiratory diseases, certain heart problems, diabetes, or liver disease. Be sure your doctor knows if any of these conditions applies to you. • This drug should be used with caution by pregnant or nursing women. • This drug must be used cautiously in conjunction with cimetidine, beta adrenergic agonists (used to treat bronchospasms), nitroglycerin, anesthetic agents, and other antihypertensive agents. If you are currently taking any drugs of these types, consult your doctor about their use. If you are unsure about the type or contents of your medications, ask your doctor or pharmacist. • Diabetics should be aware that this drug can mask signs of hypoglycemia, such as changes in heart rate and blood pressure. Routinely monitor urine or blood glucose while taking this drug. • Notify your doctor if you develop a sore throat, fever, bruising, shortness of breath, yellowing of the eyes or skin, dark urine, or difficulty urinating. • While taking this drug, limit your consumption of alcoholic beverages to minimize dizziness and light-headedness. • Do not take any nonprescription item for weight control, cough, cold, or sinus problems without first checking with your doctor; such items may contain ingredients that can increase blood pressure. • Do not suddenly stop taking this drug without first consulting your doctor. Chest pain—even heart attacks—may occur if this drug is suddenly stopped after prolonged use.
Comments: Take this drug as prescribed. Do not skip doses or take extra doses without your doctor's approval. Be sure to take your medication doses at the same time each day. It is important to continue taking this medication even if you do not feel sick. Most people with high blood pressure do not have symptoms and do not feel ill; therefore, it is easy to forget to take the medication. • This drug may be taken with food to prevent stomach upset. • Initially this drug

may cause dizziness, light-headedness, or drowsiness, which should disappear as therapy continues. If it persists or worsens, notify your doctor. To prevent light-headedness when standing, change positions slowly. Contract and relax the muscles of your legs for a few moments before rising. Do this by pushing one foot against the floor while raising the other foot slightly, alternating feet so that you are pumping your legs in a pedaling motion. • Transient scalp tingling has been reported by persons when the drug is first taken. This effect should disappear as therapy continues. • Learn how to monitor your pulse and blood pressure while taking this drug; discuss this with your doctor. As with all antihypertensive medications, they are most effective when used in conjunction with diet and lifestyle changes, such as exercise and stress reduction to control blood pressure. The medication does not bring about a cure for high blood pressure.

Noroxin antibiotic

Ingredient: norfloxacin
Dosage Form: Tablet: 400 mg
Uses: Treatment of urinary tract infections and sexually transmitted diseases in adults
Minor Side Effects: Abdominal pain; constipation; dizziness; drowsiness; dry mouth; fatigue; flatulence; headache; heartburn; nausea; sensitivity to sunlight; stomach upset. Most of these side effects, if they occur, should subside as your body adjusts to the medication. Tell your doctor about any that are persistent or particularly bothersome.
Major Side Effects: Blurred vision; breathing difficulties; chest pain; chills; confusion; depression; fever; hallucinations; hives; itchy skin; mouth sores; rapid, pounding heart rate; restlessness; skin rash; tremor; vaginal itching; vomiting. Notify your doctor if you notice any major side effects.
Contraindications: This drug is a quinolone antibiotic. It should not be taken by anyone who is allergic to it or to other quinolone antibiotics. Be sure your doctor knows if you have such an allergy. • This drug is not recommended for use in children or pregnant women. Discuss the risks and benefits of this drug with your doctor.
Warnings: This drug must be used with caution by nursing women. Discuss the benefits and risks with your doctor. • Persons with certain kidney problems should use this drug cautiously. Lower than normal doses may be necessary. • This drug should be used cautiously by persons with epilepsy, central nervous system disorders, or seizure disorders, because tremor, confusion, restlessness, and, very rarely, hallucinations and seizures have occurred. Make sure your doctor knows if you have any of these conditions or experience any of these effects. • This drug has been shown to interact with nitrofurantoin, probenecid, theophylline, and antacids. Do not take this drug within two hours of taking an antacid. If you are currently taking any drugs of these types, consult your doctor or pharmacist. If you are unsure of the type or contents of your medications, ask your doctor or pharmacist. • Notify your doctor if you experience breathing difficulties, fever, skin rash, chest pain, tremor, restlessness, or confusion while taking this medication. • This drug may cause dizziness, especially during the first few days of therapy. Use caution when engaging in activities that require alertness, such as driving a car or operating potentially dangerous equipment. • This drug can increase sensitivity to sunlight. Avoid prolonged sun exposure and wear protective clothing and an effective sunscreen when outdoors.
Comments: This drug is best if taken one hour before or two hours after a meal at evenly spaced intervals throughout the day and night. Ask your doctor

or pharmacist to help you devise a dosing schedule. • Take this drug for as long as prescribed, even if symptoms disappear before that time. If you stop taking the drug too soon, resistant bacteria are given a chance to continue growing, and the infection could recur. • Drink plenty of fluids while taking this drug. Try to drink eight to ten glasses of water, unless your doctor directs you otherwise. • Nausea, stomach upset, diarrhea, or headache may occur during the first few days of therapy. These effects should subside over time as your body adjusts to the medication. If they become severe or bothersome, notify your doctor.

Norpace, Norpace CR antiarrhythmics

Ingredient: disopyramide phosphate
Equivalent Product: Disopyramide Phosphate
Dosage Forms: Capsule: 100 mg; 150 mg. Controlled-release capsule (CR): 100 mg; 150 mg
Use: Treatment of some heart arrhythmias (irregular heartbeats)
Minor Side Effects: Abdominal pain; blurred vision; constipation; diarrhea; dizziness; dry mouth; dry nose, eyes, throat; fatigue; gas; headache; increased sensitivity to sunlight; loss of appetite; muscle pain; muscle weakness; nausea; nervousness; rash; sexual disturbances; vomiting. Most of these side effects, if they occur, should subside as your body adjusts to the medication. Tell your doctor about any that are persistent or particularly bothersome.
Major Side Effects: Abnormal thoughts; breathing difficulty; chest pain; dark urine; difficulty urinating; fainting; fever; fluid retention and weight gain; heart disorders; low blood pressure; low blood sugar; numbness or tingling sensation; palpitations; rapid pulse; shortness of breath; sore throat; yellowing of the eyes or skin. Notify your doctor if you notice any major side effects.
Contraindications: This drug should not be taken by persons who have certain types of severe heart disease or by those who are allergic to it. Consult your doctor immediately if this drug has been prescribed for you and either condition applies.
Warnings: This drug should be used with caution by pregnant or nursing women and by persons with glaucoma, myasthenia gravis, enlarged prostate, low blood sugar (hypoglycemia), malnutrition, urinary retention, low blood potassium (hypokalemia), liver disease, or kidney disease. Be sure your doctor knows if any of these conditions applies to you. • This drug should be used with caution in children. • This drug should be used cautiously in conjunction with certain other agents, such as quinidine or procainamide, phenytoin, barbiturates, carbamazepine, rifampin, beta blockers, and alcohol. If you are currently taking any drugs of these types, consult your doctor about their use. If you are unsure of the type or contents of your medications, ask your doctor or pharmacist. • Patients receiving more than one antiarrhythmic drug must be carefully monitored. • While taking this drug, do not take any nonprescription item for weight control, cough, cold, or sinus problems without first checking with your doctor. • Notify your doctor if you develop signs of jaundice (yellowing of the eyes or skin, dark urine).
Comments: The controlled-release form must be swallowed whole. Do not crush or chew it as the sustained action will be destroyed and the risk of side effects increased. This drug must be taken exactly as directed. Do not take extra doses or skip a dose. Do not stop taking this drug unless advised to do so by your physician. • This drug is best taken at evenly spaced intervals around the clock to assure a constant level of medication in your body. If you miss a dose, take it as soon as you remember unless it is near the time for the next dose. In that case, skip the missed dose and resume your normal dosing

schedule. Do not double the dose to catch up. • The controlled-release form of this drug, CR, is taken less frequentiy during the day. Sustained-release tablets should not be used for initial therapy but can be substituted once the dosage is stabilized. Consult your doctor about the use of this dosage form. • Chew gum or suck on ice chips or a piece of hard candy to reduce mouth dryness. • To minimize dizziness, rise from a lying or sitting position slowly. • Side effects, such as dry mouth, constipation, and blurred vision, should be temporary. If these symptoms persist, call your doctor. • Your doctor may want you to monitor your pulse and blood pressure while you are taking this medication; discuss this with your doctor. • This drug is similar in action to procainamide and to quinidine sulfate. All of these medications are used to help control the heart's rhythm.

Norpramin antidepressant

Ingredient: desipramine hydrochloride
Equivalent Products: Desipramine HCl; Pertofrane
Dosage Forms: Capsule (Pertofrane): 25 mg; 50 mg. Tablet (Norpramin and desipramine): 10 mg; 25 mg; 50 mg; 75 mg; 100 mg; 150 mg
Use: For relief of depression
Minor Side Effects: Agitation; anxiety; blurred vision; constipation; cramps; diarrhea; dizziness; drowsiness; dry mouth; fatigue; headache; heartburn; increased sensitivity to light; insomnia; loss of appetite; nausea; peculiar tastes; restlessness; vomiting; weakness; weight gain or loss. Most of these side effects, if they occur, should subside as your body adjusts to the medication. Tell your doctor about any that are persistent or particularly bothersome.
Major Side Effects: Chest pain; confusion; convulsions; dark urine; difficulty urinating; easy bleeding or bruising; enlarged or painful breasts (in both sexes); fainting; fever; fluid retention; hair loss; hallucinations; high or low blood pressure; impotence; loss of balance; mood changes; mouth sores; muscle stiffness; nervousness; nightmares; numbness in fingers or toes; palpitations; problems concentrating; psychosis; ringing in the ears; seizures; skin rash; sleep disorders; sore throat; stroke; sweating; tremors; uncoordinated movements; yellowing of the eyes or skin. Notify your doctor if you notice any major side effects.
Contraindications: This drug should not be taken by people who are allergic to it, by those who have recently had a heart attack, or by those who are taking monoamine oxidase inhibitors (ask your pharmacist if you are unsure). Consult your doctor immediately if this drug has been prescribed for you and any of these conditions applies. • This drug is not recommended for use by children under the age of 12.
Warnings: This drug should be used cautiously by pregnant or nursing women and by people with glaucoma (certain types), heart disease (certain types), high blood pressure, enlarged prostate, epilepsy, urine retention, liver disease, asthma, kidney disease, alcoholism, or hyperthyroidism. Be sure your doctor knows if any of these conditions applies to you. • Elderly persons should use this drug with caution because they are more sensitive to its effects. • This drug should be used cautiously by patients who are receiving electroshock therapy or those who are about to undergo surgery. • This drug interacts with alcohol, antihypertensives, amphetamine, barbiturates, cimetidine, clonidine, epinephrine, monoamine oxidase inhibitors, oral anticoagulants, phenylephrine, and depressants; if you are currently taking any drugs of these types, consult your doctor about their use. If you are unsure of the type or contents of your medications, ask your doctor or pharmacist. • To prevent oversedation, avoid the use of alcohol or other drugs that have sedative properties. • While

CONSUMER GUIDE®

taking this drug, do not take any nonprescription item for weight control, cough, cold, or sinus problems without first checking with your doctor. Be sure your doctor is aware of every medication you use; do not stop or start any other drug without your doctor's approval. • This drug may cause changes in blood sugar levels. Diabetics should monitor their blood sugar levels more frequently. • This drug may cause drowsiness; avoid tasks that require alertness, such as driving a car or operating potentially dangerous equipment. • Report any sudden mood changes to your doctor. • Notify your doctor if you develop signs of jaundice (yellowing of the eyes or skin, dark urine).

Comments: Take this medicine exactly as your doctor prescribes. Do not stop taking it without first checking with your doctor. • The effects of therapy with this drug may not be apparent for two to four weeks. • Dry mouth, blurred vision, drowsiness, or constipation may occur initially, but should subside as your body adjusts to the medication. • Your doctor may adjust your dosage frequently during the first few months of therapy in order to find the best dose for you. • Chew gum or suck on ice chips or a piece of hard candy to reduce mouth dryness • Avoid prolonged exposure to the sun while taking this drug, and wear protective clothing and a sunscreen when outdoors. • To avoid dizziness or light-headedness when you stand, contract and relax the muscles of your legs for a few moments before rising. Do this by pushing one foot against the floor while raising the other foot slightly, alternating feet so that you are pumping your legs in a pedaling motion. • Many people receive as much benefit from taking a single dose of this drug at bedtime as from taking multiple doses throughout the day. Talk to your doctor about this. • This drug is very similar in action to other tricyclic antidepressants. If one of these antidepressant drugs is ineffective or is not well tolerated, your doctor may want you to try one of the others in order to find the one that is best for you.

Nor-Tet antibiotic, see tetracycline hydrochloride antibiotic.

nortriptyline antidepressant, see Pamelor antidepressant.

Norvasc antihypertensive

Ingredient: amlodipine
Dosage Form: Tablet: 2.5 mg; 5 mg; 10 mg
Uses: Treatment of hypertension (high blood pressure); treatment of angina (chest pain)
Minor Side Effects: Bloating; blurred vision; constipation; cough; diarrhea; dizziness (mild); dry mouth; fatigue; flushing; frequent urination; headache; heartburn; loss of balance; muscle cramps; nasal congestion; nausea; nervousness; sweating; weakness. Most of these side effects, if they occur, should subside as your body adjusts to the medication. Tell your doctor about any that are persistent or particularly bothersome.
Major Side Effects: Breathing difficulties; chills; dizziness (severe); fainting; fever; rapid, pounding heart rate; sexual difficulties; skin rash; sore throat; swelling of ankles, feet, or lower legs. Notify your doctor if you notice any major side effects.
Contraindication: This drug should not be used by people who are allergic to it. Consult your doctor immediately if this drug has been prescribed for you and you have such an allergy.
Warnings: This drug should be used cautiously by people who have low blood pressure or heart disease (certain types) and by pregnant or nursing women. Be sure your doctor knows if any of these conditions applies to you. • This drug may interact with beta blockers, digoxin, phenytoin, quinidine, war-

farin, calcium supplements, and digitalis. If you are taking antihypertensive medication, the dose may have to be adjusted. If you are currently taking any of these drug types, consult your doctor about their use. If you are unsure of the type or contents of your medications, ask your doctor or pharmacist. • This drug may make you dizzy, especially during the first few days of therapy; this should subside as your body adjusts to the medication. If it does make you dizzy, avoid activities that require alertness, such as driving a car or operating potentially dangerous equipment, and limit your consumption of alcohol, which exaggerates this side effect. • Your doctor may want to see you regularly while you are taking this drug to check your response and to conduct liver function tests. • Contact your doctor if this drug causes severe or persistent dizziness, constipation, breathing difficulties, swelling of hands and feet, or irregular heartbeat.

Comments: Take this drug as directed, even if you feel well. Compliance is necessary to manage high blood pressure and prevent chest pain. • Swallow tablets whole without breaking or chewing them unless otherwise instructed by your physician. • Do not suddenly stop taking this drug, unless you consult with your doctor first. Your dosage may have to be decreased gradually. • This drug does not stop an attack of chest pain. It must be taken continuously to be effective. It may take several days before the effects of this drug are noticed. • Learn how to monitor your pulse and blood pressure; discuss this with your doctor. • If you feel dizzy or light-headed, sit or lie down for a while, get up slowly from a sitting or reclining position, and be careful on stairs. • Protect this drug from light and moisture. As with all antihypertensive medications, they are most effective when used in conjunction with diet and lifestyle changes, such as exercise and stress reduction to control blood pressure. The medication does not cure high blood pressure.

Nystatin antifungal, see Mycostatin antifungal.

Nystex antifungal, see Mycostatin antifungal.

Octicair otic steroid and antibiotic, see Cortisporin Otic steroid and antibiotic.

Ocu-Carpine ophthalmic glaucoma preparation, see Isopto Carpine ophthalmic glaucoma preparation.

Ocusert Pilo-20, Ocusert Pilo-40 ophthalmic glaucoma preparation, see Isopto Carpine ophthalmic glaucoma preparation.

Ocutricin ophthalmic antibiotic, see Neosporin ophthalmic antibiotic.

Ogen estrogen hormone

Ingredient: estropipate
Equivalent Product: Estropipate; Ortho-Est
Dosage Forms: Tablet: 0.625 mg; 1.25 mg; 2.5 mg; 5 mg. Vaginal cream (content per gram): 1.5 mg
Uses: Estrogen replacement therapy; treatment of symptoms of menopause; prevention of osteoporosis
Minor Side Effects: Abdominal cramps; bloating; breast tenderness; change in sexual desire; diarrhea; dizziness; headache (mild); increased sensitivity to sunlight; loss of appetite; nausea; vomiting; weight loss or gain. These side effects should subside as your body adjusts to the medication. Tell your doctor about any that are persistent.

Major Side Effects: Allergic rash; breathing difficulties; cervical changes; change in menstrual patterns; chest pain; dark urine; depression; fluid retention; fungal infections; increased blood pressure; loss of coordination; migraine; pain in calves; painful urination; severe headache; skin irritation; slurring of speech; swelling of the feet or ankles; vaginal itching; vaginal bleeding; vision changes; yellowing of the eyes or skin. Notify your doctor if you notice any major side effects.

Contraindications: This drug should not be taken by persons who have experienced an allergic reaction to estrogen. This drug should not be used by pregnant or nursing women, by persons with blood clotting disorders or a history of such disorders because of estrogen use, or by those persons with certain cancers or vaginal bleeding. Consult your doctor immediately if this drug has been prescribed for you and you have any of these conditions.

Warnings: Your pharmacist has a brochure that describes the benefits and risks involved with estrogen therapy. Your pharmacist is required by law to give you a copy each time you have your prescription filled. Read this material carefully. Discuss any concerns or questions you may have with your doctor or pharmacist. • This drug should be used cautiously by people who have asthma, diabetes, epilepsy, gallbladder disease, heart disease, high blood levels of calcium, high blood pressure, kidney disease, liver disease, migraine, porphyria, uterine fibroid tumors, or a history of depression and by nursing women. Be sure your doctor knows if any of these conditions applies to you. • This drug may retard bone growth and therefore should be used cautiously by young patients who have not yet completed puberty. • This drug interacts with oral anticoagulants, barbiturates, rifampin, ampicillin, some antibiotics, anticonvulsants, and steroids; if you are currently taking any drugs of these types, consult your doctor about their use. If you are unsure of the type or contents of your medications, ask your doctor or pharmacist. • This drug may alter the body's tolerance to glucose. Diabetics should monitor urine sugar or blood glucose and report any changes to their doctors. • Notify your doctor immediately if you experience abnormal vaginal bleeding, breast lumps, pain in the calves or chest, sudden shortness of breath, coughing up of blood, severe headaches, loss of coordination, changes in vision or skin color, or dark urine. • This drug may increase your sensitivity to sunlight. Avoid sun exposure and wear a sunscreen outdoors. • This drug may affect a number of laboratory tests; remind your doctor that you are taking it if you are scheduled for any tests. • You should have a complete physical examination at least once a year while you are taking this medication.

Comments: This drug is usually taken for 21 days followed by a seven day rest. • Compliance is mandatory with this drug. Take it exactly as prescribed. • If you miss a dose, take it as soon as it is remembered unless it is near the time for the next dose. If so, skip the missed dose and resume your normal dosing schedule. Do not double the dose in order to catch up. If more than one dose is missed, contact your doctor to establish a new dosing schedule. • Special applicators are available with the vaginal cream to ensure proper dosing. Fill the applicator with the cream. Insert the applicator high into the vagina unless otherwise directed, and gently depress the plunger to release the medication. Remove the applicator and wash it in warm, soapy water. Refer to the chapter on Administering Medication for details on the use of vaginal drug products. This drug is helpful in preventing estrogen-deficiency osteoporosis when used in conjunction with calcium supplements and exercise. It is important to ensure adequate intake of calcium while on estrogen therapy to reduce the risk of osteoporosis. Make sure your diet contains 1,000 to 1,500 mg calcium per day. If not, a calcium supplement may be recommended. Discuss the use of calcium with your doctor or pharmacist.

Omnipen antibiotic, see ampicillin antibiotic.

OMS Concentrate analgesic, see morphine analgesic.

oral contraceptives (birth control pills)

"Oral contraceptives" is a descriptive term.

Examples: Brevicon; Demulen; Desogen; Enovid; GenCept; Genora; Jenest; Levlen; Loestrin; Lo/Ovral; Micronor; Modicon; N.E.E.; Nelova; Nelulen; Norcept-E; Nordette; Norethin; Norinyl; Norlestrin; Nor-Q.D.; Ortho-Cept; Ortho-Cyclen; Ortho-Novum; Ortho-tri-cyclen; Ovcon; Ovral; Ovrette; Tri-Levlen; Tri-Norinyl; Triphasil

Dosage Form: Tablets in packages

Uses: Birth control; control of painful menstruation (dysmenorrhea)

Minor Side Effects: Abdominal cramps; acne; backache; bloating; change in appetite; change in sexual desire; diarrhea; dizziness; enlarged or tender breasts; fatigue; headache; hearing changes; intolerance to contact lenses; itching; nasal congestion; nausea; nervousness; vaginal irritation; vomiting. Most of these side effects should subside as your body adjusts to the medication. Tell your doctor about any that are persistent or particularly bothersome.

Major Side Effects: Birth defects; blood clots; breakthrough bleeding (spotting); breathing difficulty; cancer; cervical damage; cessation of menstruation; changes in menstrual flow; colitis; dark urine; depression; elevated blood sugar; eye damage; fluid retention; gallbladder disease; heart attack; high blood pressure; increase or decrease in hair growth; internal bleeding; joint aches; kidney damage; liver damage; lung damage; migraine; muscle stiffness and pain; numbness or tingling; pain during menstruation; pancreatic changes; rash; reduced ability to conceive after drug is stopped; skin color changes; stroke; swelling of the ankles or feet; tumor growth; weight changes; yeast infection; yellowing of the eyes or skin. Notify your doctor if you notice any major side effects.

Contraindications: This type of drug should not be used by women who smoke, by nursing women, or by women who have or have had certain types of heart disease, liver disease, blood disease, blood clots, clotting disorders, abnormal vaginal bleeding, strokes or mini-strokes, heart attack, or chest pain. This drug should not be used by women who have, have had, or may have breast cancer or certain other cancers or by women who have had liver tumors as a result of using drugs of this type. Women who may be pregnant should not take this drug. Be sure that your doctor knows if any of these conditions applies to you.

Warnings: This type of drug has been suspected to cause an increased risk of breast, ovarian, endometrial, and cervical cancer. Although no cause and effect relationship can be determined, you should inform your doctor if you have a family history of cancer before taking oral contraceptives. • This type of drug should be used cautiously by women over age 35, by persons who are overweight, smoke more than 15 cigarettes per day, have taken oral contraceptives for more than ten years, or have a family history of coronary artery disease. These are risk factors that increase the likelihood of side effects from this medication. • Oral contraceptives are known to cause an increased risk of heart attacks, stroke, liver disease, gallbladder disease, fluid retention, depression, clotting disorders, blood diseases, eye disease, cancer, birth defects, diabetes, high blood pressure, headache, bleeding disorders, and poor production of breast milk. • Caution should be observed while taking oral contraceptives if you have uterine tumors, mental depression, epilepsy, migraine, asthma, kidney disease, jaundice, or vitamin deficiency. Be sure your doctor knows if any of these conditions applies to you. • Notify your doctor if you develop signs of jaundice (yellowing of the eyes or skin, dark urine). • Oral contraceptives interact with oral anticoagulants, barbiturates, phenylbutazone, isoniazid, carbamazepine, primidone, chloramphenicol, phenytoin, ampicillin, tetracycline, rifampin, and steroids. Contact your doctor immediately if you are currently taking any drugs of these types. If you are unsure of the type or contents of your medications, ask your doctor or pharmacist. • Some women who have used oral contraceptives have had trouble becoming pregnant after they stopped using the drug. Most of these women had scanty or irregular menstrual periods before they started taking oral contraceptives. Possible subsequent difficulty in becoming pregnant is a matter that you should discuss with your doctor before using this drug. • You should have a complete physical, including a Pap smear, before you start taking oral contraceptives and then every year that you take them. Oral contraceptives affect a wide variety of lab tests. Be sure your doctor knows you are taking oral contraceptives if you are being tested or examined for any reason. • Little is known about the long-term effects of the use of this type of drug on pituitary, ovarian, adrenal, liver, or uterine function or on the immune system. • Use of this drug may make it difficult to tell when menopause occurs.

Comments: Take an oral contraceptive at the same time every day—either with a meal or at bedtime—so that you get into the habit of taking the pills. Effectiveness depends on strict adherence to a dosing schedule. If you skip one day, take a tablet for the day you missed as soon as you think of it and another tablet at the regular time. If you miss two days, take two tablets each day for the next two days, then continue with your normal schedule. If you miss more than two days, contact your doctor, and use supplemental contraceptive measures. • If you do not start to menstruate on schedule at the end of the pill cycle and you took all the pills as directed, begin the next cycle of pills at the prescribed time anyway. Many women taking oral contraceptives have irregular menstruation. Do not be alarmed, but consult your doctor. • Stop taking oral contraceptive tablets at least three months before you wish to become pregnant. Use another type of contraceptive during this three-month period. • Some oral contraceptive packets contain 28 tablets rather than the usual 20 or 21 tablets. The 28-tablet packets contain seven placebos (sugar pills) or iron tablets. The placebos help you remember to take a tablet each day even while you are menstruating, and the iron tablets help replace the iron that is lost in menstruation. • Nausea is common, especially during the first two or three months, but may be prevented by taking the tablets at bedtime. If nausea persists for more than three months, consult your doctor. • Although many brands of oral contraceptives are available, most differ in only minor ways, and you may have to try several brands before you find the product that is ideal for you. Three categories of oral contraceptives contain both estrogen and progestin: monophasic, biphasic, and triphasic. Monophasics contain a fixed dose of estrogen and progestin throughout the cycle. With the biphasics, the estrogen content remains the same while the progestin increases in the second half of the cycle. With the triphasics, the amount of both estrogen and progestin may vary throughout the cycle. The biphasics and triphasics are designed to more closely mimic the natural physiological process and thus limit side effects. Side effects are related to the potency of estrogen or progestin in the product. Your doctor may have you try several products to find the right balance of these two ingredients for you. • Some oral contraceptives contain progestin only (Micronor, Nor-QD, Ovrette). These products have a slightly higher failure rate than the estrogen/progestin combination products but have the advantage of fewer side effects, such as high blood pressure, headache, and swelling of feet and ankles. • With every prescription, your pharmacist will give you a booklet explaining birth control pills. Read this booklet carefully. It contains exact directions on how to use the medication correctly. • If you use oral contraceptives, you should not smoke cigarettes; smoking increases the risk of serious side effects. • You should visit your doctor for a checkup at least once a year while you are taking oral contraceptives. • Women over 35 have an increased risk of adverse effects from use of oral contraceptives. • Spotting or breakthrough bleeding may occur during the first months of use of this drug. Call your physician if it continues past the second month. • Use a supplemental method of birth control during the first month that you take oral contraceptives. • Oral contraceptives currently are considered the most effective reversible method of birth control. The table that follows shows various methods of birth control and their effectiveness.

Birth Control Method	Effectiveness*
Oral contraceptives	up to 3
Intrauterine device (IUD)	up to 6
Diaphragm (with cream or gel)	up to 20
Vaginal sponge	up to 27
Aerosol foam	up to 29
Condom	up to 36
Gel or cream	up to 36
Rhythm	up to 47
No contraception	up to 80

* Pregnancies per 100 woman years

Orasone steroid hormone, see prednisone steroid hormone.

Oretic diuretic, see hydrochlorothiazide diuretic.

Orinase oral antidiabetic

Ingredient: tolbutamide
Equivalent Product: Tolbutamide
Dosage Form: Tablet: 250 mg; 500 mg
Use: Treatment of diabetes mellitus not controlled by diet and exercise alone

Minor Side Effects: Cramps; dizziness; fatigue; headache; heartburn; loss of appetite; nausea; sensitivity to sunlight; stomach upset. Most of these side effects, if they occur, should subside as your body adjusts to the medication. Tell your doctor about any that are persistent or particularly bothersome.

Major Side Effects: Blood disorders; breathing difficulties; dark urine; diarrhea; easy bruising or bleeding; fluid retention; light-colored stools; low blood sugar; muscle cramps; rash; ringing in the ears; sore throat; tingling in hands and feet; tremor; vomiting; weakness; yellowing of the eyes or skin. Notify your doctor if you notice any major side effects.

Contraindications: This drug should not be used to treat juvenile (insulin-dependent) or unstable diabetes. Diabetics who are subject to acidosis or ketosis and diabetics with a history of repeated diabetic comas should not use this drug. This drug should not be used by people with severe renal impairment or by those with an allergy to sulfonylureas or sulfa drugs. In the presence of fever, severe trauma, or infections, insulin should be used instead, at least during the acute stage of the problem. If any of these conditions applies to you, inform your doctor.

Warnings: Tolbutamide may not be safe for use during pregnancy. If you are or might become pregnant, be sure to tell your doctor before taking this drug. • People with thyroid disease or kidney, heart, or liver damage and those who are malnourished must use this drug cautiously. Be sure your doctor knows if any of these conditions applies to you. • This drug interacts with anabolic steroids, anticoagulants, anticonvulsants, aspirin, chloramphenicol, guanethidine, propranolol, monoamine oxidase inhibitors, phenylbutazone, steroids, tetracycline, thiazide diuretics, and thyroid hormones; if you are currently taking any drugs of these types, consult your doctor about their use. If you are unsure of the type or contents of your medications, ask your doctor or pharmacist. • Thiazide diuretics (commonly used to treat high blood pressure) and beta-blocking drugs may interfere with control of your diabetes. If you are taking any drugs of either type, talk to your physician before you take this drug. If you are unsure of the type of your medications, ask your doctor or pharmacist. • Do not drink alcohol and do not take any other drugs while you are taking this drug unless your doctor tells you that you may. Be especially careful with nonprescription cold remedies. • Be sure you can recognize the symptoms of low blood sugar (hypoglycemia) and know what to do if you begin to experience these symptoms. You will have to be especially careful during the transition from insulin to tolbutamide. • Persons taking this drug should visit the doctor frequently during the first few weeks of therapy. They should check their urine or blood for sugar and ketones frequently as directed. (Be sure that you know how to test your urine or blood and that you know what the results mean.) Know how to recognize the first signs of low blood sugar. Signs of low blood sugar include chills; cold sweat; cool, pale skin; drowsiness; headache; nausea; nervousness; rapid pulse; tremors; weakness. If these symptoms develop, eat or drink something containing sugar and call your doctor. • Call your doctor if you develop an infection, fever, sore throat, unusual bleeding or bruising, yellowing of the eyes or skin, excessive thirst or urination, or dark urine while taking this drug.

Comments: Take this drug at the same time every day. Do not stop taking this drug unless told to do so by your doctor. • If this drug causes stomach upset, it may be taken with food. • Recent evidence indicates that not all generic forms of tolbutamide are equivalent. Ask your pharmacist for a product that is bioequivalent. • This drug makes you more sensitive to the sun. Avoid prolonged exposure to sunlight, and wear protective clothing and a sunscreen when outdoors. • This drug is not an oral form of insulin. • Studies have shown that a good diet and exercise program are extremely important in controlling diabetes. Oral antidiabetic drugs should only be used after diet and exercise alone have not proven adequate. Persons taking this drug should carefully watch their diet and exercise program and pay close attention to good personal hygiene. • It is advised that you carry a medical alert card or wear a medical alert bracelet indicating you are taking this medication. • There are other drugs that are similar to this one that vary slightly in activity (Diabinese, Glucotrol, Micronase). Certain persons who do not benefit from one type of oral antidiabetic may benefit from another.

Ortho-Est estrogen hormone, see Ogen estrogen hormone.

Orudis anti-inflammatory

Ingredient: ketoprofen
Equivalent Products: Ketoprofen; Oruvail
Dosage Forms: Capsule: 25 mg; 50 mg; 75 mg. Sustained-release capsule: 200 mg

Uses: Treatment of signs and symptoms of arthritis; relief of menstrual pain; relief of mild to moderate pain or swelling

Minor Side Effects: Abdominal cramps; bloating; change in taste; constipation; diarrhea; dizziness; drowsiness; dry mouth; headache (mild to moderate); heartburn; light-headedness; loss of appetite; mouth sores; nausea; stomach upset; vomiting. Most of these side effects, if they occur, should subside as your body adjusts to the medication. Tell your doctor about any that are persistent or particularly bothersome.

Major Side Effects: Anemia; blood in stools; blood in urine; breathing difficulties; chest pain; chest tightness; headache (severe); itchy skin; painful or difficult urination; palpitations; rapid heartbeat; ringing in the ears; skin rash; ulcer; unusual bruising or bleeding; visual disturbances; yellowing of the eyes or skin. Notify your doctor if you notice any major side effects.

Contraindication: This drug should not be taken by anyone allergic to it or to aspirin or similar drugs. Consult your doctor immediately if this drug has been prescribed for you and you have any such allergies.

Warnings: This drug should be used with extreme caution by people who have a history of ulcers or stomach or intestinal disorders. Peptic ulcers and gastrointestinal bleeding have been reported in persons taking anti-inflammatory drugs. Make sure your doctor knows if you have or have had any of these conditions. Notify your doctor if you experience frequent indigestion or notice blood in your stools or urine. • This drug should be used cautiously by persons with anemia, severe allergies, bleeding diseases, high blood pressure, liver disease, kidney disease, or certain types of heart disease. Be sure your doctor knows if any of these conditions applies to you. • This drug should be used only if clearly needed during pregnancy or while nursing. Discuss the risks and benefits with your doctor. • This drug is not recommended for use in children under 12 years of age since safety and efficacy have not been established in this age group. • This drug interacts with anticoagulants, oral antidiabetics, fenoprofen, phenylbutazone, diuretics, steroids, phenytoin, and aspirin. If you are currently taking any drugs of these types, consult your doctor about their use. If you are unsure about the type or contents of your medications, consult your doctor or pharmacist. • Avoid the use of aspirin and alcohol while taking this medication. • This drug may cause drowsiness, dizziness, or light-headedness; avoid activities that require alertness, such as driving a car or operating potentially dangerous equipment. • Notify your doctor if you experience a skin rash, vision changes, weight gain, fluid retention, blood in stools, or a severe headache while taking this drug. • While using this medication, avoid the use of nonprescription medication containing aspirin since it is similar in some actions to this drug.

Comments: Take this drug with food or milk to reduce stomach upset. The sustained relase form of this drug, Oruvail, must be swallowed whole. Do not crush or chew it as the long action will be destroyed and the risk of side effects increased. Oruvail is taken only once a day, whereas the regular capsules are taken three to four times a day. • This drug has been shown to be as effective as aspirin in the treatment of arthritis, but aspirin is still the drug of choice for treating arthritis. To be most effective in relieving symptoms of arthritis, this drug must be taken as prescribed. Do not take this only when you feel the pain. It is important to take this drug continuously. You should note improvement in your symptoms soon after starting this drug, but it may take a few weeks for the full benefit to be apparent. • This drug is not a substitute for rest, physical therapy, or other measures recommended by your doctor to treat your condition. • Many different anti-inflammatory medications are available. If one is not effective or not well tolerated, other ones may be tried.

CONSUMER GUIDE®

Oruvail anti-inflammatory, see Orudis anti-inflammatory.

Otic-Care otic steroid and antibiotic, see Cortisporin Otic steroid and antibiotic.

OtiTricin otic steroid and antibiotic, see Cortisporin Otic steroid and antibiotic.

Otobiotic Otic steroid and antibiotic, see Cortisporin Otic steroid and antibiotic.

Otocort Otic steroid and antibiotic, see Cortisporin Otic steroid and antibiotic.

Otomycin-HPN Otic steroid and antibiotic, see Cortisporin Otic steroid and antibiotic.

Otosporin otic steroid and antibiotic, see Cortisporin Otic steroid and antibiotic.

O-V Statin antifungal, see Mycostatin antifungal.

oxycodone hydrochloride, oxycodone terephthalate, and aspirin analgesic, see Percodan analgesic.

Pamelor antidepressant

Ingredient: nortriptyline hydrochloride
Equivalent Products: Aventyl HCl; nortriptyline
Dosage Forms: Capsule: 10 mg; 25 mg; 50 mg; 75 mg. Solution (content per 5 ml teaspoon): 10 mg
Use: Relief of symptoms of mental depression
Minor Side Effects: Abdominal cramps; agitation; anxiety; blurred vision; change in appetite; change in sense of taste; change in sex drive; constipation; diarrhea; dizziness; drowsiness; dry mouth; gas; headache; increased sensitivity to sunlight; insomnia; light-headedness; nausea; nervousness; reduced concentration; sweating; tremor; vomiting; weight loss or gain. Most of these side effects, if they occur, should subside over a period of time as your body adjusts to the medication. Tell your doctor about any that are persistent or particularly bothersome.
Major Side Effects: Chest pain; confusion; convulsions; dark urine; delusions; disorientation; excitement; fever; hair loss; impotence; incoordination; memory loss; mood changes; mouth sores; nightmares; numbness or tingling in the feet or hands; palpitations; panic; rapid pulse; ringing in the ears; sleep disorders; swollen glands; uncoordinated movements; unusual bleeding or bruising; yellowing of the eyes or skin. Notify your doctor if you notice any major side effects.
Contraindications: This medication should not be used by people who are allergic to it or by those who have recently had a heart attack. This medication should not be used by those who are currently taking monoamine oxidase inhibitors or who have taken such a drug within the past two weeks. Consult your doctor immediately if this drug has been prescribed for you and any of these conditions applies.
Warnings: This drug should be used cautiously by people who have heart disease (certain types), glaucoma (certain types), high blood pressure, an en-

larged prostate, epilepsy, liver disease, or hyperthyroidism. Be sure your doctor knows if any of these conditions applies to you. • This drug should be used with caution in persons receiving electroshock therapy or those about to undergo surgery. • Elderly persons should use this drug with caution. Reduced doses may be prescribed for persons in this age group. • This drug should be used only if clearly needed during pregnancy. Discuss the risks and benefits with your doctor. • This drug appears in breast milk. Consult your doctor before nursing while taking this medication. • This drug has been found to interact with barbiturates, benzodiazepines, cimetidine, estrogens, clonidine, epinephrine, oral anticoagulants, and other antidepressants. If you are currently taking any medications of these types, consult your doctor about their use. If you are unsure about the type or contents of your medication, ask your doctor or pharmacist. Inform your doctor of any medications (prescription or nonprescription) you are taking or plan to take during treatment with this drug. • Smoking effects this drug. Be sure your doctor knows if you smoke. This drug causes drowsiness and dizziness; avoid tasks that require alertness, such as driving a car or operating potentially dangerous equipment. To prevent excessive drowsiness, avoid use of alcohol or other depressant medications.

Comments: Take this drug with food or a full glass of water if stomach upset occurs. • Continue to take this medication as prescribed. Do not suddenly stop taking this drug without your doctor's approval. • Dizziness, light-headedness, headache, and blurred vision are common during the first few days of therapy. These effects should subside as your body adjusts to the drug. • Some improvement in the symptoms of depression should be seen within one week of beginning treatment, but it may take three to four weeks before optimal results are achieved. Your doctor may adjust your dose frequently during the first few months to find the best dose for you. • Chew gum or suck on ice chips or a piece of hard candy to relieve dry mouth. • To avoid dizziness or light-headedness, contract and relax the muscles of your legs for a few moments before rising. Do this by pushing one foot against the floor while raising the other foot slightly, alternating feet so that you are pumping your legs in a pedaling motion. • This drug may increase sensitivity to sunlight; avoid prolonged exposure to sunlight, wear protective clothing, and use an effective sunscreen. • Many people receive as much benefit from taking a single dose of this drug at bedtime as from taking multiple doses throughout the day. Talk to your doctor about this dosage plan. • This drug is similar in action to other tricyclic antidepressants. If this drug is ineffective or not well tolerated, your doctor may have you try another.

Panacet analgesic, see Vicodin, Vicodin ES analgesic.

Panasol-S steroid hormone, see prednisone steroid hormone.

Panmycin antibiotic, see tetracycline hydrochloride antibiotic.

Panwarfin anticoagulant, see Coumadin anticoagulant.

Par Glycerol C cough suppressant and expectorant, see Tussi-Organidin cough suppressant and expectorant.

Partuss LA decongestant and expectorant, see Entex LA decongestant and expectorant.

PCE antibiotic, see erythromycin antibiotic.

Pediazole antibiotic

Ingredients: erythromycin ethylsuccinate; sulfisoxazole acetyl

Equivalent Products: Erythromycin and Sulfisoxazole; Eryzole

Dosage Form: Oral Suspension (content per 5 ml teaspoon): erythromycin ethylsuccinate, 200 mg and sulfisoxazole, 600 mg

Use: Treatment of ear infections (predominantly those in children)

Minor Side Effects: Abdominal pain; diarrhea; dizziness; headache; increased sensitivity to sunlight; insomnia; loss of appetite; nausea; stomach upset; vomiting. Most of these side effects, if they occur, should subside as your body adjusts to the medication. Tell your doctor about any that are persistent or particularly bothersome.

Major Side Effects: Aching muscles or joints; allergic skin rash; blood disorders; dark urine; depression; difficulty in swallowing; difficulty urinating; fatigue; fever; hallucinations; hearing impairment; itching; mouth sores; ringing in the ears; sore throat and fever; superinfection; unusual bleeding or bruising; yellowing of the eyes or skin. Notify your doctor of any major side effects.

Contraindications: This drug should not be used by persons who are allergic to either erythromycin or sulfa drugs, infants less than two months old, pregnant women at term, or nursing women. Contact your doctor immediately if this drug has been prescribed and any of these conditions applies.

Warnings: This drug must be used cautiously by pregnant women and by persons with liver or kidney disease or a history of severe allergies or asthma. Make sure your doctor knows if any of these conditions applies to you. • If you develop a sore throat, fever, dark urine, or yellowing of the skin or eyes while taking this drug, call your doctor immediately. • If a skin rash develops, discontinue taking the drug and contact your doctor. • Your doctor may want to test your blood periodically if you are taking this drug (or any sulfa drug) for an extended period of time. Prolonged use of this drug may allow uncontrolled growth of organisms that are not susceptible to it. • Do not use this drug unless your doctor has specifically told you to do so.

Comments: Take this drug as prescribed. For best results, this drug should be taken at evenly spaced intervals around the clock. Continue taking it for the number of days indicated, even if the symptoms disappear within that time. • This medication must be stored in the refrigerator. Shake well before using. • Discard any unused portion after 14 days. • While taking this drug, it is recommended that you drink plenty of fluids each day. • Avoid unprotected exposure to sunlight, as this drug may make you more sensitive to the sun's effects.

Pediotic otic steroid and antibiotic, see Cortisporin Otic steroid and antibiotic.

penicillin G potassium antibiotic

Ingredient: penicillin G potassium

Equivalent Product: Pentids

Dosage Forms: Liquid; Tablet (various dosages)

Use: Treatment of a wide variety of bacterial infections

Minor Side Effects: Diarrhea; heartburn; nausea; stomach upset. Most of these side effects, if they occur, should subside as your body adjusts to the medication. Tell your doctor about any that are persistent or particularly bothersome.

Major Side Effects: Black tongue; bloating; breathing difficulties; chills; cough; fever; irritation of the mouth; muscle aches; rash; rectal and vaginal itching; severe diarrhea; sore throat; superinfection; unusual bruising or bleeding; vomiting. Notify your doctor if you notice any major side effects.

Contraindication: This drug should not be taken by people who are allergic to any penicillin or cephalosporin antibiotic. Consult your doctor immediately if this drug has been prescribed for you and you have such an allergy.

Warnings: This drug should be used cautiously by people who have kidney disease, asthma, or other significant allergies. Be sure your doctor knows if you have any type of allergy. • This drug interacts with aspirin, probenecid, phenylbutazone, indomethacin, sulfinpyrazone, chloramphenicol, erythromycin, and tetracycline; if you are currently taking any drugs of these types, consult your doctor about their use. If you are unsure of the type or contents of your medications, ask your doctor or pharmacist. • This drug may affect the potency of oral contraceptives. Consult your doctor about using supplementary contraceptive measures while you are taking this drug. • This drug is readily destroyed by acids in the stomach; do not take this medication with fruit juice or carbonated beverages. It is best taken with water or milk. • Severe allergic reactions to this drug—indicated by breathing difficulties, rash, fever, and chills—have been reported but are rare when the drug is taken orally. If you experience any of these symptoms while taking this drug, contact your doctor. • Diabetics using Clinitest urine test may get a false high sugar reading while taking this drug. Change to Clinistix, Diastix, or Tes-Tape urine test to avoid this problem. • Prolonged use of this drug may allow uncontrolled growth of organisms that are not susceptible to it. • Do not use this drug unless your doctor has specifically told you to do so. Be sure to follow the directions carefully and report any unusual reactions to your doctor at once. • Complete blood cell counts and liver and kidney function tests should be done if you take this drug for a prolonged period.

Comments: Take this drug on an empty stomach (one hour before or two hours after a meal) with a full glass of water. • It is best to take this drug at evenly spaced times throughout the day and night. Your doctor or pharmacist will help you set up a dosing schedule. • This drug should be taken for the full prescribed period, even if symptoms disappear within that time; stopping treatment early can lead to reinfection. • The liquid form of this drug should be stored in the refrigerator. This drug should not be frozen. Any unused portion should be discarded after 14 days. Shake well before using. • This drug is very similar to penicillin V potassium phenoxymethyl (see next profile) and they can often be used interchangeably. Penicillin G potassium is less effective than penicillin potassium phenoxymethyl when taken with acidic fluids, such as fruit juice. • This drug is similar in nature and action to amoxicillin and ampicillin.

penicillin V potassium (penicillin VK) antibiotic

Ingredient: penicillin potassium phenoxymethyl

Equivalent Products: Beepen VK; Betapen-VK; Ledercillin VK; Pen-V; Pen-Vee K; Robicillin VK; V-Cillin K; Veetids

Dosage Forms: Liquid (content per 5 ml teaspoon): 125 mg; 250 mg. Tablet: 125 mg; 250 mg; 500 mg

Use: Treatment of a wide variety of bacterial infections

Minor Side Effects: Diarrhea; heartburn; nausea; stomach upset. Most of these side effects, if they occur, should subside as your body adjusts to the medication. Tell your doctor about any that are persistent or particularly bothersome.

Major Side Effects: Black tongue; bloating; breathing difficulties; chills; cough; fever; irritation of the mouth; muscle aches; rash; rectal and vaginal itching; severe diarrhea; sore throat; superinfection; unusual bruising or bleeding; vomiting. Notify your doctor if you notice any major side effects.

Contraindication: This drug should not be used by people allergic to any penicillin or cephalosporin antibiotic. Consult your doctor immediately if this drug has been prescribed for you and you have such an allergy.

Warnings: This drug should be used cautiously by people who have kidney disease or asthma or other significant allergies. Be sure your doctor knows if any of these conditions applies to you. • This drug interacts with chloramphenicol, probenecid, aspirin, phenylbutazone, indomethacin, sulfinpyrazone, erythromycin, and tetracycline; if you are currently taking any drugs of these types, consult your doctor about their use. If you are unsure of the type or contents of your medications, ask your doctor or pharmacist. • This drug may affect the potency of oral contraceptives. Consult your doctor about using supplementary contraceptive measures while you are taking this drug. • Severe allergic reactions to this drug—indicated by breathing difficulties, rash, fever, and chills—have been reported but are rare when the drug is taken orally. Consult your doctor if you develop any of these symptoms while taking this drug. • Diabetics using Clinitest urine test may get a false high sugar reading while taking this drug. Change to Clinistix, Diastix, or Tes-Tape urine test to avoid this problem. • Prolonged use of this drug may allow uncontrolled growth of organisms that are not susceptible to it. • Do not use this drug unless your doctor has specifically told you to do so. Be sure to follow directions carefully and report any unusual reactions to your doctor at once.

Comments: Take this drug on an empty stomach (one hour before or two hours after a meal). • It is best to take this drug at evenly spaced times throughout the day and night. Your doctor or pharmacist will help you set up a dosing schedule. • This drug should be taken for the full prescribed course, even if symptoms disappear within that time; stopping treatment early can lead to reinfection. • The liquid form of this drug should be stored in the refrigerator. This medication should never be frozen. Any unused portion should be discarded after 14 days. Shake well before use. • Penicillin VK tablets should be stored at room temperature in a tightly closed container. • "Penicillin V" is another name for this drug. • This drug has approximately the same antibacterial activity as the less expensive product, penicillin G. However, this drug is more stable in the stomach and may be worth the extra cost. • This drug is similar in nature and action to amoxicillin and ampicillin. Keep this and all medications out of the reach of children.

Pentids antibiotic, see penicillin G potassium antibiotic.

Pen-V antibiotic, see penicillin V potassium (penicillin VK) antibiotic.

Pen-Vee K antibiotic, see penicillin V potassium (penicillin VK) antibiotic.

Pepcid antisecretory and antiulcer

Ingredient: famotidine
Dosage Forms: Oral suspension (content per 5 ml teaspoon): 40 mg. Tablet: 20 mg; 40 mg
Uses: Treatment of ulcers and hypersecretory conditions; prevention of recurrent ulcers; treatment of gastroesophageal reflex disease
Minor Side Effects: Acne; altered sense of taste; blurred vision; constipation; decreased sexual desire; diarrhea; dizziness; dry mouth; dry skin; fatigue; flushing; headache; itching; muscle pain; nausea; somnolence; stomach upset. Most of these side effects, if they occur, should subside as your body adjusts to the medication. Tell your doctor about any that are particularly bothersome.

Major Side Effects: Anorexia; anxiety; blood disorders; breathing difficulties; depression; hair loss; palpitations; rash; tingling in the hands or feet; vomiting. Notify your doctor if you notice any major side effects.

Contraindication: This drug should not be taken by anyone who is allergic to it. Consult your doctor if this drug has been prescribed for you and you have such an allergy.

Warnings: This drug must be used with caution by pregnant or nursing women. Discuss the benefits and risks with your doctor. • This drug is not recommended for use in children. • Elderly persons and persons with kidney disease should use this drug cautiously; lower than normal doses may be required. • This drug has not been shown to interact with other medications; however, check with your doctor or pharmacist before taking any other medication in addition to this drug.

Comments: • This drug is usually taken twice a day or once daily at bedtime. • The oral suspension must be shaken well before use. • For best results with ulcers, this drug must be taken as directed for four to eight weeks, even if you feel better during that time. • Lifestyle changes may be recommended in addition to this medication to assist in the prevention and treatment of ulcers. Dietary changes, exercise programs, smoking cessation, and stress-reduction programs may be beneficial. • This drug is very similar in action to Zantac, Axid, and Tagamet. Discuss these medications with your doctor in order to identify the best product for you.

Percocet analgesic

Ingredients: acetaminophen; oxycodone hydrochloride

Equivalent Products: acetaminophen with oxycodone; Roxicet; Roxilox (see Comments); Tylox

Dosage Form: Tablet: acetaminophen, 325 mg and oxycodone hydrochloride, 5 mg (see Comments)

Use: For relief of moderate to severe pain

Minor Side Effects: Blurred vision; constipation; dizziness; drowsiness; fatigue; light-headedness; loss of appetite; nausea; restlessness; sedation; sweating; vomiting; weakness. Most of these side effects, if they occur, should subside as your body adjusts to the medication. Tell your doctor about any that are persistent or particularly bothersome.

Major Side Effects: Anxiety; breathing difficulties; dark urine; difficult or painful urination; false sense of well-being; hallucinations; light-colored stools; palpitations; rash; yellowing of the eyes or skin. Notify your doctor if you notice any major side effects.

Contraindication: This drug should not be used by persons allergic to either acetaminophen or narcortic pain relievers. Consult your doctor immediately if this drug has been prescribed for you and you have such an allergy.

Warnings: This drug should be used cautiously by pregnant women, the elderly, children, persons with liver or kidney disease, persons with Addison's disease, epilepsy, and in the presence of head injury or acute abdominal conditions. Be sure your doctor knows if any of these conditions applies to you. • This drug interacts with narcotic analgesics, tranquilizers, phenothiazines, sedatives, and hypnotics. If you are currently taking any drugs of these types, consult your doctor about their use. If you are unsure about the type or contents of your medications, ask your doctor or pharmacist. • Because this drug causes sedation, it should not be used with other sedative drugs or alcohol. • Avoid tasks requiring alertness, such as driving a car or operating potentially dangerous equipment. • This drug contains a narcotic, oxycodone HCl; therefore, it can be habit-forming and must be used with caution. Tolerance may develop quickly. Do not increase your dose or take this drug more often than pre-scribed without first consulting your doctor. Products containing narcotics are usually not used for more than seven to ten days. • Notify your doctor if you de-velop signs of jaundice (yellowing of the eyes or skin, dark urine) or experience breathing difficulties while taking this medication. • While taking this medicine, be cautious of taking nonprescription medicines containing acetaminophen.

Comments: Take this as directed. If stomach upset occurs, take this drug with food or milk. • Side effects of this drug may be somewhat relieved by lying down. To prevent constipation, eat a high-fiber diet and drink plenty of water while taking this medication. Pain relievers are most effective in preventing pain rather than stopping it once it has occurred. • Percocet is similar to Perco-dan, the difference being that Percocet contains acetaminophen and Percodan contains aspirin. • Roxicet is also available in liquid form, which contains the same amount (per 5 ml teaspoon) of acetaminophen and oxycodone as do the tablets. Roxilox has the same ingredients as Percocet but a different strength of acetaminophen: 500 mg.

Percodan analgesic

Ingredients: aspirin; oxycodone hydrochloride; oxycodone terephthalate
Equivalent Products: oxycodone hydrochloride, oxycodone terephthalate, and aspirin; Roxiprin (see Comments)
Dosage Form: Tablet: aspirin, 325 mg; oxycodone hydrochloride, 4.50 mg; oxycodone terephthalate, 0.38 mg
Use: Relief of moderate to severe pain
Minor Side Effects: Blurred vision; constipation; dizziness; drowsiness; dry mouth; flushing; itching; light-headedness; loss of appetite; nausea; sedation; sweating; vomiting. Most of these side effects, if they occur, should subside as your body adjusts to the medication. Tell your doctor about any that are persis-tent or particularly bothersome.
Major Side Effects: Anxiety; bloody stools; breathing difficulties; chest tight-ness; dark urine; difficulty urinating; easy bruising or bleeding; false sense of well-being; hallucinations; kidney disorders; low blood sugar; odd movements; palpitations; rapid or slow heartbeat; rash; ringing in the ears; tremors; ulcer; yellowing of the eyes or skin. Notify your doctor if you notice any major side ef-fects.
Contraindication: This drug should not be taken by people who are allergic to aspirin or narcotic pain relievers. Consult your doctor immediately if this drug has been prescribed for you and you have such an allergy.
Warnings: This drug should be used cautiously by pregnant women, the el-derly, children, and debilitated persons. It should be used cautiously by per-sons with anemia, colitis, lung disease, gallbladder disease, bleeding disor-ders, peptic ulcer, abdominal disease, head injuries, liver disease, kidney disease, thyroid disease, or prostate disease. Be sure your doctor knows if any of these conditions applies to you. • This drug must be used cautiously in con-junction with alcohol, methotrexate, 6-mercaptopurine, oral antidiabetics, phenytoin, oral anticoagulants, aspirin, or gout medications (probenecid, sulfin-pyrazone). If you are unsure of the type or contents of your medications, ask your doctor or pharmacist. • Because this drug contains oxycodone, a narcotic, it can be habit-forming and must be used with caution. Tolerance may develop quickly; do not increase the dose of this drug without first consulting your doc-tor. • Products containing narcotics are usually not used for more than seven to ten days. • This drug may cause drowsiness; avoid tasks requiring alertness, such as driving a car or operating potentially dangerous equipment. • To pre-vent oversedation, avoid the use of alcohol or other drugs that have sedative

properties. • If your ears feel strange, if you hear buzzing or ringing, or if your stomach hurts, your dosage may need adjustment. Call your doctor. • Notify your doctor if you develop a rash or experience breathing difficulties. • Avoid the use of nonprescription medicines that contain aspirin.

Comments: Take this as directed. Take this drug with food or milk to lessen stomach upset. • Side effects caused by this drug may be somewhat relieved by lying down. To prevent constipation, eat a high-fiber diet and drink plenty of water while taking this medication. Pain relievers are most effective in preventing pain rather than stopping it once it has occurred. • There are half-strength forms of this drug available (only the oxycodone components are half strength). One is called Percodan-Demi. There is also a generic form available.

Peridex mouth rinse

Ingredient: chlorhexidine gluconate
Dosage Forms: Oral Rinse: chlorhexidine gluconate, 0.12%; alcohol, 11.6%
Use: Treatment of gingivitis (red, swollen, bleeding gums)
Minor Side Effects: Altered taste; minor irritation; mouth sores. Most of these side effects, if they occur, should subside as your body adjusts to the medication. Tell your doctor about any that are persistent or particularly bothersome.
Major Side Effect: Increased staining of teeth. Notify your doctor if you notice a major side effect.
Contraindication: This drug should not be taken by persons allergic to it or who have an alcohol sensitivity. Consult your doctor immediately if you have such an allergy.
Warnings: This drug should be used cautiously by pregnant and nursing women and children under 18 years of age. Be sure your doctor knows if you fit any of these categories. • This drug should be used with caution in conjunction with disulfiram because of alcohol content; if you are currently taking this drug, consult your doctor about its use. If you are unsure of the type or contents of your medications, ask your doctor or pharmacist. • This drug is a mouth rinse and should not be swallowed. Ingestion can cause stomach upset, nausea, and alcohol intoxication, especially in children. • Notify your dentist if staining of the teeth occurs. The stains can usually be removed.
Comments: Use this medication as directed, usually twice a day after brushing your teeth. Take one capful undiluted, and swish it around in your mouth for 30 seconds, then spit it out. Do not swallow it. • For best results, this medication is to be used in conjunction with a dental program. It is recommended that you visit your dentist every six months.

Persantine anticoagulant

Ingredient: dipyridamole
Equivalent Product: Dipyridamole
Dosage Form: Tablet: 25 mg; 50 mg; 75 mg
Uses: With Coumadin anticoagulant, for prevention of blood clot formation; may also be used after a heart attack to improve outcome
Minor Side Effects: Cramps; dizziness; fainting; fatigue; flushing; headache; nausea; weakness. Most of these side effects, if they occur, should subside as your body adjusts to the medication. Tell your doctor about any that are persistent or particularly bothersome.
Major Side Effects: Rash; worsening of chest pain (mainly at start of therapy). Notify your doctor if you notice a major side effect.
Contraindications: None known.

Warnings: This drug should be used cautiously by pregnant or nursing women and by patients with low blood pressure. This drug may cause allergic-type reactions, particularly in persons with aspirin hypersensitivity. Be sure your doctor knows if any of these conditions applies to you. • Your doctor may wish to perform periodic blood tests to determine the effectiveness of this drug. • This drug is often used as a "blood thinner"; it prevents clots from forming and keeps blood flowing freely. While taking this drug, you will bleed longer than normal after a cut or scrape; be aware of this. Contact your doctor immediately if you sustain a severe cut or injury.

Comments: This drug should be taken with a full glass of liquid on an empty stomach (one hour before or two hours after a meal) and only in the prescribed amount. • The effects of this drug may not become apparent for at least two months. • Do not suddenly stop taking this medication without consulting your doctor. • To avoid dizziness or light-headedness when you stand, contract and relax the muscles of your legs for a few moments before rising. Do this by pushing one foot against the floor while raising the other foot slightly, alternating feet so that you are pumping your legs. • Not all generic forms of this drug are identical. Consult your doctor or pharmacist about the use of a generic product.

Pertofrane antidepressant, see Norpramin antidepressant.

Phenameth antihistamine, see Phenergan, Phenergan with Codeine antihistamine.

Phenaphen with Codeine analgesic, see acetaminophen with codeine analgesic.

Phenergan, Phenergan with Codeine antihistamine

Ingredients: promethazine hydrochloride; codeine phosphate (Phenergan with Codeine only); alcohol (syrup only)

Equivalent Products: Phenergan: Phenameth; Promethazine HCl; Prothazine. Phenergan with Codeine: Pherazine with Codeine; Promethazine HCl with Codeine; Prometh with Codeine

Dosage Forms: Phenergan: Liquid (content per 5 ml teaspoon): promethazine hydrochloride, 6.25 mg and alcohol, 7%. Tablet: promethazine hydrochloride, 12.5 mg; 25 mg; 50 mg. Suppository: promethazine hydrochloride, 12.5 mg; 25 mg; 50 mg. Phenergan with Codeine: Liquid (content per 5 ml teaspoon): codeine phosphate, 10 mg; promethazine hydrochloride, 6.25 mg; alcohol, 7%

Uses: Cough suppressant; for relief of allergy symptoms; prevention and treatment of motion sickness and nausea and vomiting

Minor Side Effects: Blurred vision; constipation; diarrhea; dizziness; drowsiness; dry mouth, nose, and throat; headache; heartburn; insomnia; loss of appetite; nasal congestion; nausea; nervousness; rash; restlessness; sun sensitivity; sweating; trembling; vomiting; weakness. Most of these side effects, if they occur, should subside as your body adjusts to the medication. Tell your doctor about any that are persistent or particularly bothersome.

Major Side Effects: Breathing difficulties; confusion; convulsions; dark urine; difficulty in urinating; disturbed coordination; excitation; low blood pressure; muscle spasms; nightmares; rapid, pounding heart rate; palpitations; rash from exposure to sunlight; severe abdominal pain; sore throat; yellowing of the eyes and skin. Notify your doctor if you notice any major side effects.

Contraindications: This drug should not be taken by nursing mothers, newborns, people who are allergic to any of its components or to narcotic analgesics, or those taking monoamine oxidase inhibitors (ask your pharmacist if you are unsure). Consult your doctor immediately if any of these conditions applies.

Warnings: This drug should be used cautiously by people who have glaucoma (certain types), asthma, high blood pressure, central nervous system disorders (such as seizures), colitis, gallbladder disease, liver disease, ulcers, blood vessel or heart disease, kidney disease, thyroid disease, bowel or bladder obstruction, prostate trouble, or diabetes. Be sure your doctor knows if any of these conditions applies to you. • This drug interacts with amphetamine, anticholinergics, levodopa, antacids, and trihexyphenidyl; if you are currently taking any drugs of these types, consult your doctor about their use. If you are unsure of the type or contents of your medications, ask your doctor or pharmacist. • To prevent oversedation, avoid the use of alcohol or other drugs that have sedative properties. • While taking this drug, do not take any nonprescription substance for weight control, cough, cold, or sinus problems without first checking with your doctor. • This drug may affect the results of certain laboratory tests. Remind your doctor that you are taking this drug if you are scheduled for any tests. • The codeine-containing form of this product has the potential to be habit-forming and must be used with caution. It usually should not be taken for more than five days without some improvement of symptoms nor for longer than ten days at a time if prescribed for use on a regular basis. Tolerance may develop quickly; do not increase the dosage without consulting your doctor. An overdose usually sedates an adult but may cause excitation leading to convulsions and death in a child. • This drug may cause drowsiness; avoid tasks that require alertness, such as driving a car or operating potentially dangerous equipment. • Notify your doctor if you develop signs of jaundice (yellowing of the eyes or skin, dark urine). • If this drug makes you dizzy or drowsy, avoid tasks requiring alertness.

Comments: Take this drug as directed. • If you need an expectorant, you need more moisture in your environment. The use of a vaporizer or humidifier may be beneficial. Consult your doctor. You should also drink nine to ten glasses of water daily. • Chew gum or suck on ice chips or a piece of hard candy to reduce mouth dryness. • This drug may make you more sensitive to the sun; avoid prolonged sun exposure, and wear protective clothing and an effective sunscreen when outdoors.

Phenergan VC, Phenergan VC with Codeine expectorants

Ingredients: phenylephrine hydrochloride; promethazine hydrochloride; codeine phosphate (Phenergan VC with Codeine only); alcohol

Equivalent Products: Phenergan VC: Pherazine VC; Promethazine HCl VC; Prometh VC Plain. Phenergan VC with Codeine: Mallergan VC with Codeine; Pherazine VC with Codeine; Promethazine HCl VC with codeine; Prometh VC with Codeine

Dosage Form: Phenergan VC: Liquid (content per 5 ml teaspoon): phenylephrine hydrochloride, 5 mg; promethazine hydrochloride, 6.25 mg; alcohol, 7%. Phenergan VC with Codeine: Liquid (content per 5 ml teaspoon): codeine phosphate, 10 mg; phenylephrine hydrochloride, 5 mg; promethazine hydrochloride, 6.25 mg; alcohol, 7%

Uses: Relief of coughing, congestion, and other symptoms of allergies or the common cold

Minor Side Effects: Blurred vision; constipation; diarrhea; dizziness; drowsiness; dry mouth, nose, and throat; headache; heartburn; insomnia; loss of appetite; nasal congestion; nausea; nervousness; rash; restlessness; sun sensitivity; sweating; trembling; vomiting; weakness. Most of these side effects, if they occur, should disappear as your body adjusts to the medication. Tell your doctor about any that are persistent or particularly bothersome.

Major Side Effects: Breathing difficulties; confusion; convulsions; dark urine; difficulty in urinating; disturbed coordination; excitation; low blood pressure; muscle spasms; nightmares; rapid, pounding heartbeat; rash from exposure to sunlight; severe abdominal pain; sore throat; yellowing of the eyes and skin. Notify your doctor if you notice any major side effects.

Contraindications: This drug should not be taken by nursing mothers, by newborns, by people who are allergic to any of its components or to narcotic analgesics, and by those taking monoamine oxidase inhibitors (ask your doctor if you are unsure about what medications you are taking). Consult your doctor immediately if any of these conditions applies.

Warnings: This drug should be used cautiously by people who have glaucoma (certain types), asthma, high blood pressure, seizure disorders, colitis, gallbladder disease, liver disease, ulcers, blood vessel or heart disease, kidney disease, thyroid disease, bowel or bladder obstruction, prostate trouble, or diabetes. Be sure your doctor knows if any of these conditions applies to you. • This drug interacts with amphetamine, anticholinergics, levodopa, guanethidine, antacids, and trihexyphenidyl; if you are currently taking any drugs of these types, consult your doctor about their use. If you are unsure of the type or contents of your medications, ask your doctor or pharmacist. • To prevent oversedation, avoid the use of alcohol or other drugs that have sedative properties. • While taking this drug, do not take any nonprescription item for weight control, cough, cold, or sinus problems without first checking with your doctor. • This drug may affect the results of certain laboratory tests. Remind your doctor that you are taking this drug if you are scheduled for any tests. • The codeine-containing form of this product has the potential to be habit-forming and must be used with caution. It usually should not be taken for more than five days without improvement of symptoms, nor for longer than ten days at a time if prescribed for use on a regular basis. Tolerance may develop quickly; do not increase the dosage without consulting your doctor. An overdose usually sedates an adult but may cause excitation leading to convulsions and death in a child. • This drug may cause drowsiness; avoid tasks that require alertness, such as driving a car or operating potentially dangerous equipment. • Notify your doctor of signs of jaundice (yellowing of the eyes or skin, dark urine).

Comments: Take this drug as directed. • If you need an expectorant, you need more moisture in your environment. The use of a vaporizer or humidifier may be beneficial, consult your doctor. You should also drink nine to ten glasses of water daily. • Chew gum or suck on ice chips or a piece of hard candy to reduce mouth dryness. • This drug may make you more sensitive to the sun; avoid prolonged sun exposure, and wear protective clothing and an effective sunscreen when outdoors.

phenobarbital sedative and anticonvulsant

Ingredient: phenobarbital
Equivalent Product: Solfoton
Dosage Forms: Capsule; Liquid; Tablet (various dosages)
Uses: Control of convulsions; anxiety or tension relief; short-term sleeping aid
Minor Side Effects: Diarrhea; dizziness; drowsiness; headache; muscle pain; nausea; stomach upset; vomiting. Most of these side effects, if they occur, should subside as your body adjusts to the medication. Tell your doctor about any that are persistent or particularly bothersome.

Major Side Effects: Breathing difficulties or other allergic reactions; chest tightness; confusion; depression; easy bruising; excitation; fainting; fever; loss of coordination; low blood pressure; mouth sores; nose bleed; skin rash; slow or fast heart rate; slurred speech; sore throat; unusual behavior. Notify your doctor if you notice any major side effects.

Contraindications: This drug should not be used by people who are allergic to it, by those who have porphyria or severe respiratory disease, or by those with a history of drug abuse. Consult your doctor immediately if any of these conditions applies.

Warnings: This drug should be used cautiously by people who have liver or kidney disease or certain lung diseases, by women who are pregnant or nursing, and by children. Be sure your doctor knows if any of these conditions applies to you. • This drug interacts with alcohol, central nervous system depressants, griseofulvin, oral contraceptives, cyclophosphamide, digitalis rifampin, chloramphenicol, theophylline, aminophylline, oral anticoagulants, phenytoin, steroids, sulfonamides, tetracycline, and antidepressants; if you are currently taking any drugs of these types, consult your doctor about their use. If you are unsure of the type or contents of your medications, ask your doctor or pharmacist. • This drug may cause drowsiness; avoid tasks that require alertness, such as driving a car or operating potentially dangerous equipment. • To prevent oversedation and serious adverse reactions, avoid the use of alcohol or other drugs that have sedative properties while taking this drug. • This drug has the potential to be habit-forming and must be used with caution. Tolerance may develop quickly; do not increase the dose without first consulting your doctor. • Do not stop taking this drug without first consulting your doctor. If you have been taking the drug for a long time, the dose should be reduced gradually. • Children may respond to this drug differently than adults; they may become excited, irritable, and aggressive. • Periodic laboratory tests may be necessary if you are taking this drug for prolonged periods. • Notify your doctor if you develop fever, mouth sores, sore throat, or unusual bleeding or bruising while taking this drug.

Comments: Take this drug exactly as prescribed. Try to take it at the same time every day so you remember to take it. If you miss a dose, take it as soon as you remember unless it is near the time for the next dose. In that case, skip the missed dose and resume your usual dose schedule. Do not double up the dose to catch up. • If this drug is being used as a sleep aid, it should not be taken for longer than two weeks. It is also important to try relaxation techniques in addition to drug therapy. • If this drug is being used for seizure control, you should wear a medical alert tag or carry a card in your wallet stating your dosing schedule.

Phenylfenesin LA decongestant and expectorant, see Entex LA decongestant and expectorant.

Pheylpropanolamine HCl and Guaifensin decongestant and expectorant, see Entex LA decongestant and expectorant.

Phenytoin Sodium anticonvulsant, see Dilantin anticonvulsant.

Pherazine VC, Pherazine VC with Codeine expectorants, see Phenergan VC, Phenergan VC with Codeine expectorants.

Pherazine with Codeine antihistamine, see Phenergan, Phenergan with Codeine antihistamine.

Pilocar ophthalmic glaucoma preparation, see Isopto Carpine ophthalmic glaucoma preparation.

Pilocarpine HCl ophthalmic glaucoma preparation, see Isopto Carpine ophthalmic glaucoma preparation.

Piloptic-1 ophthalmic glaucoma preparation, see Isopto Carpine ophthalmic glaucoma preparation.

Piloptic-2 ophthalmic glaucoma preparation, see Isopto Carpine ophthalmic glaucoma preparation.

Pilostat ophthalmic glaucoma preparation, see Isopto Carpine ophthalmic glaucoma preparation.

Polycillin antibiotic, see ampicillin antibiotic.

Polymox antibiotic, see amoxicillin antibiotic.

Potasalan potassium replacement, see potassium replacement.

potassium replacement

Ingredient: potassium salts (see Comments)
Equivalent Products: Cena-K; Effer-K; Effervescent Potassium; Gen-K; K + 8; K + 10; Kaochlor; Kaon; Kaon-Cl; Kato; Kay Ciel; Kaylixir; K + Care; K-Dur; K-G; K-Lease; K-Lor; Klor-Con; Klor-Con/EF; Klorvess; Klotrix; K-Lyte; K-Lyte/Cl; K-Lyte DS; K-Norm; Kolyum; K-Tab; Micro-K; Potasalan; Rum-K; Slow-K; Ten-K; Tri-K; Twin-K
Dosage Forms: Controlled-release capsule; Controlled-release tablet; Effervescent tablet; Liquid; Powder (various dosages)
Use: Prevention or treatment of potassium deficiency, especially that caused by diuretics
Minor Side Effects: Diarrhea; gas; nausea; stomach pains. Most of these side effects, if they occur, should subside as your body adjusts to the medication. Tell your doctor about any that are persistent or particularly bothersome.
Major Side Effects: Breathing difficulties; confusion; dark, tarry stools; numbness or tingling in arms or legs; rapid, pounding heart rate; rash; ulcer; vomiting. Notify your doctor if you notice any major side effects.
Contraindications: This drug should not be used by people who have severe kidney disease, high blood levels of potassium, or Addison's disease. This drug should not be used by those allergic to it. Consult your doctor immediately if any of these conditions applies to you.
Warnings: This drug should be used cautiously by people who have heart disease (certain types), intestinal blockage, peptic ulcer, or acute dehydration. Pregnant or nursing women should use this drug only if clearly needed. Be sure your doctor knows if any of these conditions applies to you. • This drug should be taken cautiously by digitalized patients, and such patients should be monitored by ECG for heart problems. • This drug interacts with amiloride, captopril, spironolactone, and triamterene; if you are currently taking any drugs of these types, consult your doctor about their use. If you are unsure of the type or contents of your medications, ask your doctor or pharmacist. • Follow your doctor's dosage instructions exactly and do not stop taking this medication without first consulting your doctor. • Supplements of potassium should be administered with caution since the amount of potassium deficiency may be diffi-

cult to determine accurately; too much potassium can also be dangerous. Potassium intoxication, however, rarely occurs in patients with normal kidney function. • If you develop severe nausea and vomiting, black stools, abdominal pain, tingling of the hands or feet, or unusual weakness while taking this drug, call your doctor.

Comments: This drug should be taken with food or after meals to prevent upset stomach. • The liquid and powder forms of this drug are to be added to one-half or one full glass of cold water, then swallowed. The effervescent tablet form of this drug must be completely dissolved in a full glass of water before being swallowed. Do not crush or chew the slow-release tablets; this form of the drug must be swallowed whole with a full glass of water. • Some of the slow-release tablets have an insoluble wax core designed to dissolve the drug slowly. You may notice a core in your stool. Do not be alarmed. • Potassium supplements usually have a low rate of patient compliance. People usually take them infrequently, or they stop taking them altogether. If a potassium product is prescribed for you, be sure to take the medication exactly as directed and do not stop taking it without first consulting your doctor. • There are many forms of this drug available. Discuss the various forms with your doctor or pharmacist to find the one that best suits you. • Some of these products are sugar-free. • Ask your doctor about using a salt substitute in addition to, or instead of, potassium chloride. • Potassium replacement products and potassium supplements are available as various salts of potassium, such as potassium chloride, potassium gluconate, potassium citrate, potassium bicarbonate, and potassium acetate. The therapeutic effect of potassium is the same regardless of the salt. The only difference is in the amount of potassium that the various salts contain. For example, if you compare potassium chloride to an equal amount of potassium gluconate, the chloride contains more potassium than the gluconate. Therefore, in order to ensure that you are getting an adequate amount of potassium from the replacement product, do not change potassium salts without first checking with your doctor or pharmacist. • Ask your doctor whether you should include potassium-rich foods in your diet. Foods rich in potassium include meat, bananas, oranges, raisins, dates, prunes, avocados, broccoli, watermelon, brussels sprouts, lentils, and spinach.

Pramosone topical steroid and anesthetic

Ingredients: pramoxine hydrochloride; hydrocortisone

Equivalent Products: Analpram-HC; Enzone; Epifoam; ProctoCream-HC; Zone-A Forte

Dosage Forms: Cream; Lotion; Ointment: hydrocortisone, 1% and pramoxine, 1%; hydrocortisone, 2.5% and pramoxine, 1%

Uses: For temporary relief of discomfort, irritation, itching, and pain due to skin disorders caused by minor wounds, bruises, prickly heat, diaper rash, sunburn, insect bites, plant poisoning (poison ivy), eczema, psoriasis, allergies, and other skin conditions

Minor Side Effects: Burning or stinging sensation; redness of skin. Most of these side effects, if they occur, should subside as your body adjusts to the medication. Tell your doctor about any that are persistent or particularly bothersome.

Major Side Effects: Blistering; itching; peeling of skin; rash; swelling or tenderness of skin. Notify your doctor if you notice any major side effects.

Contraindications: This drug should not be used by persons allergic to either of its ingredients or to local anesthetics. Consult your doctor immediately if this drug has been prescribed for you and you have such an allergy. • This drug should not be used in or near the eyes. • This drug should not be used for treatment of most bacterial, fungal, or viral infections of the skin or in areas where blood circulation is markedly impaired. Be sure your doctor knows if any of these conditions applies to you. This medication should not be used on burns or infections, unless directed, as it may slow the healing process.

Warnings: Use this medication sparingly and with caution on children and the elderly. • Pregnant women should use this medication with caution and only if clearly necessary. • Use this medication with caution in persons with known drug sensitivities or when the skin in the area is severely traumatized or broken. If irritation, rash, or swelling occurs, discontinue use and notify your doctor. • Use of an occlusive dressing or bandage will increase the absorption of the drug. Use a dressing only if directed to do so by your doctor. If this medication is being used on a child's diaper area, avoid tight-fitting diapers and plastic pants, which increase absorption of the drug. • This product is for external use only. • Do not apply this medication to large areas of the body. Avoid using this medication for prolonged periods and do not apply it more frequently than directed. Additional benefits are not achieved with larger amounts of medication. If the condition does not improve after three days, discontinue use of the product and contact your doctor.

Comments: Wash or soak the affected area before applying the medication; this helps increase penetration. Wash your hands immediately after applying this medication. Avoid contact with the eyes. • The cream or lotion may be applied to gauze or a bandage before being applied to the skin. A thin layer of medication rubbed into the skin lightly is all that is necessary to achieve benefit; do not use a bandage or wrap unless directed to do so. • The ointment form is best for use on dry skin. The lotion is preferred for application to hairy areas.

Pravachol antihyperlipidemic

Ingredient: simvastatin
Dosage Form: Tablet: 10 mg; 20 mg
Use: In conjunction with diet to reduce elevated blood cholesterol levels
Minor Side Effects: Abdominal pain; altered sense of taste; constipation; cramps; decreased sexual desire; diarrhea; dizziness; flatulence; headache; heartburn; itching; nausea; rash; stomach upset. Most of these side effects, if they occur, should subside as your body adjusts to the medication. Tell your doctor about any that are persistent or particularly bothersome.
Major Side Effects: Blurred vision; clouding of the eye; difficulty swallowing; fever; liver disorders; malaise (vague feeling of discomfort); muscle aches, cramps, pain, or weakness; tingling in the fingers or toes. Notify your doctor if you notice any major side effects.
Contraindications: This drug should not be used by persons who are allergic to it, by those with active liver disease, or by pregnant women. Consult your doctor if this drug has been prescribed for you and any of these conditions applies. • This drug is not recommended for use in children or nursing women.
Warnings: This drug must be used cautiously by persons with a history of liver disease. Periodic liver function tests are recommended during long-term therapy to assure that the drug is not affecting the liver. • This drug must be used with caution if you have developed a severe infection, uncontrolled seizures, or a severe blood disorder or if you are undergoing major surgery or trauma. Under such conditions, your doctor may temporarily discontinue your therapy with this medication. • This drug may interact with the anticoagulant warfarin. If you are currently taking warfarin, your dose may be monitored more frequently and an adjustment may be required. Make sure your doctor knows you are taking warfarin. • This drug may cause muscle pain, tenderness, or weakness associated with fever and fatigue. If you develop these symptoms

while taking lovastatin, contact your doctor. These symptoms are most common in persons who are also taking immunosuppressive drugs, gemfibrozil, or nicotinic acid. Consult your doctor about concurrent use of these drugs. • There are reports that this drug may cause a clouding of the lens in the eye during long-term therapy. An eye examination is recommended before therapy is begun and then once each year thereafter.

Comments: This drug is best taken as a single dose at bedtime. • When first taking this drug, you may experience stomach upset and gas. These effects usually disappear with continued use. Notify your doctor if they persist or worsen. • The full effects of this drug may not be evident for four to six weeks. Your doctor will want to monitor the effects of this drug by doing periodic blood tests. Ask your doctor to explain your cholesterol level and the goals of your therapy. Learn to monitor your progress. • This drug should be used only after diet therapy has proven ineffective. This drug is not a substitute for proper diet, exercise, and weight control. For maximum results, this drug must be used in conjunction with a diet that is low in saturated fat and cholesterol. You may be referred to a nutritionist for diet counseling.

Prednicen-M steroid hormone, see prednisone steroid hormone.

prednisone steroid hormone

Ingredient: prednisone

Equivalent Products: Deltasone; Liquid Pred; Meticorten; Orasone; Panasol-S; Prednicen-M; Sterapred

Dosage Forms: Oral Solution; Syrup (content per 5 ml teaspoon): 5 mg. Tablet: 1 mg; 2.5 mg; 5 mg; 10 mg; 20 mg; 50 mg

Uses: Treatment of endocrine or rheumatic disorders; asthma; blood diseases; certain cancers; eye disorders; gastrointestinal disturbances, such as ulcerative colitis; respiratory diseases; inflammations, such as arthritis, dermatitis, and poison ivy; allergic conditions

Minor Side Effects: Dizziness; headache; increased hair growth; increased susceptibility to infection; increased sweating; indigestion; insomnia; menstrual irregularities; muscle weakness; nervousness; reddening of the skin on the face; restlessness; thin skin; weight gain. Most of these side effects, if they occur, should subside as your body adjusts to the medication. Tell your doctor about any that are persistent or particularly bothersome.

Major Side Effects: Abdominal enlargement; blurred vision; bone loss; bruising; cataracts; convulsions; diabetes; false sense of well-being; fluid retention; fracture; fungal infections of mouth and vagina; glaucoma; growth impairment in children; heart failure; high blood pressure; impaired healing of wounds; mood changes; mouth sores; muscle wasting; nightmares; peptic ulcer; potassium loss; salt retention; weakness. Notify your doctor if you notice any major side effects.

Contraindications: This drug should not be taken by people who are allergic to it or by those who have systemic fungal infections. Consult your doctor if this drug has been prescribed for you and either of these conditions applies.

Warnings: This drug should be used very cautiously by people who have had tuberculosis and by those who have thyroid disease, liver disease, severe ulcerative colitis, diabetes, seizures, a history of ulcers, kidney disease, high blood pressure, a bone disease, or myasthenia gravis. Be sure your doctor knows if any of these conditions applies to you. Diabetics who are taking this drug should monitor blood glucose carefully. • This drug has not been proven safe for use during pregnancy. • Growth of children may be affected by this drug. • This drug interacts with aspirin, barbiturates, diuretics, rifampin, cy-

CONSUMER GUIDE®

clophosphamide, estrogens, indomethacin, oral anticoagulants, antidiabetics, and phenytoin; if you are currently taking any drugs of these types, consult your doctor about their use. If you are unsure of the type or contents of your medications, ask your doctor or pharmacist. • While you are taking this drug you should not be vaccinated or immunized as your response will be inhibited by this drug. • This drug may cause glaucoma or cataracts, high blood pressure, high blood sugar, fluid retention, or potassium loss. Blood pressure, body weight, and vision should be checked at regular intervals if you are taking this drug for prolonged periods. • This drug may mask signs of an infection or cause new infections to develop. • Stomach X rays are advised for persons with suspected or known ulcers. It is best to limit alcohol consumption while taking this drug. Alcohol may aggravate stomach problems. • Depending on the dose and the duration of steroid treatment, you may need to receive higher dosages if you are subjected to stress such as serious infection, injury, or surgery. • Report mood swings or depression to your doctor. • Do not stop taking this medication without consulting your doctor. Depending on the dose and the duration of steroid treatment, your dose may have to be reduced gradually. Never increase the dose or take the drug for a longer time than prescribed without consulting your doctor.

Comments: Take this drug exactly as directed. Do not take extra doses or skip a dose without first consulting your doctor. For long-term treatment, taking the drug every other day may be permitted. Ask your doctor about alternate-day dosing. • Often, taking the entire daily dose at one time (about eight A.M.) gives the best results. • This drug is often taken on a decreasing-dosage schedule (four times a day for several days, then three times a day, etc.). • To prevent stomach upset, take this drug with food or a snack. • To help avoid potassium loss while using this drug, take your dose with a glass of fresh or frozen orange juice or eat a banana each day. The use of a salt substitute also helps prevent potassium loss. Do not change your diet, however, without consulting your doctor. Too much potassium may also be dangerous. • If you are using this drug chronically, you should wear or carry a notice that you are taking a steroid.

Premarin estrogen hormone

Ingredients: conjugated estrogens
Equivalent Product: Conjugated Estrogens
Dosage Forms: Tablet: 0.3 mg; 0.625 mg; 0.9 mg; 1.25 mg; 2.5 mg. Vaginal cream (per gram): 0.625 mg
Uses: Estrogen replacement therapy; treatment of symptoms of menopause; treatment of prostatic cancer in men, uterine bleeding, and some cases of breast cancer; and prevention of osteoporosis
Minor Side Effects: Bloating; breast tenderness; change in sexual desire; cramps; diarrhea; dizziness; headache (mild); increased sensitivity to sunlight; loss of appetite; nausea; swelling of ankles and feet; vomiting; weight gain or loss. Most of these side effects, if they occur, should subside as your body adjusts to the medication. Tell your doctor about any that are persistent or particularly bothersome.
Major Side Effects: Allergic rash; breathing difficulties; cervical damage; change in menstrual patterns; chest pain; dark urine; depression; diabetes; eye damage; fluid retention; fungal infections; high blood pressure; loss of coordination; migraine; pain in calves; painful urination; severe headache; skin color changes; slurred speech; unusual bleeding; vaginal itching; vision changes; yellowing of the eyes or skin. Notify your doctor in the event that you notice any major side effects.

Contraindications: This drug should not be used by persons with an allergy to estrogen, by pregnant women, by people who have blood clotting disorders or a history of such disorders due to estrogen use, or by those who have certain cancers or vaginal bleeding. In most cases, this drug should not be used by people who have breast cancer. Consult your doctor immediately if this drug has been prescribed for you and any of these conditions applies.

Warnings: Your pharmacist has a brochure that describes the benefits and risks involved with estrogen therapy. Your pharmacist is required by law to give you a copy each time you have your prescription filled. Read this material carefully. Discuss any concerns you have with your doctor or pharmacist. • This drug should be used cautiously by people who have asthma, diabetes, epilepsy, gallbladder disease, heart disease, high blood levels of calcium, high blood pressure, kidney disease, liver disease, migraine, porphyria, uterine fibroid tumors, a history of depression, and by nursing women. Be sure your doctor knows if any of these conditions applies to you. • This drug may retard bone growth and therefore should be used cautiously by young patients who have not yet completed puberty. • This drug interacts with oral anticoagulants, barbiturates, rifampin, ampicillin, anticonvulsants, some antibiotics, and steroids; if you are currently taking any drugs of these types, consult your doctor about their use. If you are unsure of the type or contents of your medications, ask your doctor or pharmacist. • This drug may alter the body's tolerance to glucose. Diabetics should monitor urine sugar or blood glucose and report any changes to their doctors. • Notify your doctor immediately if you experience abnormal vaginal bleeding, breast lumps, pains in the calves or chest, sudden shortness of breath, coughing up of blood, severe headaches, loss of coordination, changes in vision or skin color, or dark urine. • This drug may increase your sensitivity to sunlight. Avoid prolonged sun exposure, and wear a sunscreen when outdoors. • This drug may affect a number of laboratory tests; remind your doctor that you are taking it if you are scheduled for any tests. • You should have a complete physical examination at least once a year while you are on this medication.

Comments: This drug is usually taken for 21 days followed by a seven-day rest. • Compliance is mandatory with this drug. Take it exactly as prescribed. • If you miss a dose, take it as soon as it is remembered unless it is near the time for the next dose. If so, skip the missed dose and resume your normal dosing schedule. Do not double the dose in order to catch up. If more than one dose is missed, contact your doctor to establish a new dosing schedule. • Special applicators are available with the vaginal cream to ensure proper dosing. Fill the applicator with the cream. Insert the applicator high into the vagina unless otherwise directed and gently depress the plunger to release the medication. Remove the applicator and wash it in warm, soapy water. Refer to the chapter on Administering Medication for details on the use of vaginal drug products. This drug is helpful in preventing estrogen-deficiency osteoporosis when used in conjunction with calcium supplements and exercise. It is important to ensure adequate intake of calcium while on estrogen therapy to reduce the risk of osteoporosis. Make sure your diet contains 1,000 to 1,500 mg of calcium per day. If not, a calcium supplement may be recommended. Discuss the use of calcium with your doctor or pharmacist.

Prilosec antisecretory

Ingredient: omeprazole
Dosage Form: Sustained-release capsule: 20 mg
Uses: Treatment of gastroesophageal reflux disease; treatment of hypersecretory conditions

Minor Side Effects: Abdominal pain; back pain; bloating; change in food tastes; constipation; cough; diarrhea; dizziness; drowsiness; dry skin; headache; itching; loss of appetite; nausea; tiredness; vomiting; weakness. Most of these side effects, if they occur, should subside as your body adjusts to the medication. Tell your doctor about any that are persistent or particularly bothersome.

Major Side Effects: Back pain; chills; fever; joint pain; muscle cramps; rapid, pounding heartbeat; rash; ringing in the ears; sore throat; swelling of the feet or ankles. Notify your doctor if you notice any major side effects.

Contraindications: This drug should not be taken by people who are allergic to it. Consult your doctor immediately if you have such an allergy. • This drug is not recommended for use in children since safety and efficacy in this age group have not been adequately studied.

Warnings: This drug should be used by pregnant or nursing women only if clearly needed. • This drug should be used with caution in conjunction with ampicillin, diazepam, iron salts, ketoconazole, phenytoin, and warfarin. If you are currently taking any drugs of these types, consult your doctor about their use. If you are unsure of the type or contents of your medications, ask your doctor or pharmacist. • This drug should not be used longer than eight weeks without doctor's approval. Long term use may be associated with increased risk of stomach tumors. • Notify your doctor if you develop chills, fever, back pain, or sore throat while taking this medication. • Headache, nausea, and stomach upset may occur when first taking this medication. If it continues, inform your doctor.

Comments: Take this drug before meals as directed. • Swallow the capsule whole. Do not crush or chew it. • Do not increase your dose or take this more often than prescribed.

Principen antibiotic, see ampicillin antibiotic.

Prinivil antihypertensive

Ingredient: losinopril
Equivalent Product: Zestril
Dosage Form: Tablet: 5 mg; 10 mg; 20 mg; 40 mg
Use: Treatment of high blood pressure
Minor Side Effects: Cough; decreased sexual desire; diarrhea; dizziness; drowsiness; fatigue; flushing; frequent urination; gas; headache; indigestion; light-headedness; nasal congestion; nausea; stomach upset; vomiting. Most of these side effects, if they occur, should subside as your body adjusts to the medication. Tell your doctor about any that are persistent or particularly bothersome.

Major Side Effects: Blood disorders; blurred vision; breathing trouble; chest pain; chills; decreased sexual ability; difficulty urinating; fainting; fast pulse; fever; fluid retention; joint pain; muscle aches; nosebleed; palpitations; rash; shortness of breath; sore throat; tingling of the fingers or toes. Notify your doctor if you notice any major side effects.

Contraindications: This drug should not be taken by people who are allergic to it. Consult your doctor immediately if you have such an allergy. • This drug should not be used by any woman who is pregnant, who thinks she is pregnant, or who intends to become pregnant while taking this. Use of this drug during pregnancy has resulted in fetal abnormalities. Notify your doctor immediately if you suspect you are pregnant.

Warnings: This drug should be used cautiously by the elderly, nursing women, children, and by people with kidney diseases or blood disorders. Be sure your doctor knows if any of these conditions applies to you. • This drug should be used with caution with other medicines including any other antihypertensive drugs, diuretics, digoxin, lithium, indomethacin, allopurinol, or potassium supplements. If you are unsure of the type or contents of your medications, ask your doctor. • While taking this drug, do not take any nonprescription item for weight control, cough, cold, allergy, or sinus problems without first checking with your doctor; such items may contain ingredients that can increase blood pressure. • While taking this drug, you should limit your consumption of alcoholic beverages, which can increase dizziness and other side effects. • Because initial therapy with this drug may cause dizziness and fainting, your doctor will probably start you on a low dose and gradually increase it. • This drug causes drowsiness and light-headedness, especially during the first few days of use and when the dose is increased; avoid tasks requiring alertness, such as driving or operating potentially dangerous equipment.

Comments: Take this drug exactly as directed. Do not take extra doses or skip a dose without consulting your doctor first. • Do not discontinue taking this medication unless your doctor directs you to do so. It is important to continue taking this medication even if you do not feel sick. Most people with high blood pressure do not have symptoms and do not feel ill; therefore, it is easy to forget or stop taking the medication. • Mild side effects (e.g., nasal congestion, headache) are most noticeable during the first two weeks of therapy and become less bothersome as your body adjusts to the medication. • Taking this medication at bedtime may make the side effects more tolerable. • To avoid dizziness or light-headedness when you stand, contract and relax the muscles of your legs for a few moments before rising. Do this by pushing one foot against the floor while raising the other foot slightly, alternating feet so that you are pumping your legs in a pedaling motion. If you are taking this drug and begin therapy with another antihypertensive drug, your doctor may reduce the dose, then recalculate it over the next couple of weeks. Dosage adjustments will be made based on your response. As with all antihypertensive medications, they are most effective when used in conjunction with diet and lifestyle changes, such as exercise and stress reduction to control blood pressure. The medication does not cure high blood pressure. • Learn how to monitor your pulse and blood pressure while taking this drug; discuss this with your doctor.

Procainamide HCl antiarrhythmic, see Pronestyl, Pronestyl SR antiarrhythmic.

Procan SR antiarrhythmic, see Pronestyl, Pronestyl SR antiarrhythmic.

Procardia, Procardia XL antihypertensive and antianginal

Ingredient: nifedipine
Equivalent Products: Adalat; Nifedipine
Dosage Forms: Capsule: 10 mg; 20 mg. Sustained-release tablet (XL): 30 mg; 60 mg; 90 mg
Uses: Treatment of various types of angina (chest pain); Procardia XL is used in the treatment of hypertension (high blood pressure)
Minor Side Effects: Bloating; blurred vision; constipation; cough; dizziness (mild); flushing; frequent urination; giddiness; headache; heartburn; heat sensation; loss of balance; muscle cramps; nasal congestion; nausea; nervousness; sleep disturbances; sweating; tremors; weakness. Most of these side effects, if they occur, should subside as your body adjusts to the medication. Tell your doctor about any that are persistent or particularly bothersome.

Major Side Effects: Breathing difficulties; chills; confusion; dizziness (severe); fainting; fever; low blood pressure; mood changes; rapid, pounding heart rate; sexual difficulties; skin rash; sore throat; swelling of ankles, feet, or lower legs. Get in touch with your doctor without delay in the event that you notice any major side effects.

Contraindication: This drug should not be used by people who are allergic to it. Consult your doctor immediately if this drug has been prescribed for you and you have such an allergy.

Warnings: This drug should be used cautiously by people who have low blood pressure or heart disease (certain types) and by pregnant or nursing women. Be sure your doctor knows if any of these conditions applies to you. • This drug may interact with beta blockers, digoxin, phenytoin, quinidine, warfarin, calcium supplements, and digitalis. If you are taking antihypertensive medication, the dose may have to be adjusted. If you are currently taking any of these drug types, consult your doctor about their use. If you are unsure of the type or contents of your medications, ask your doctor or pharmacist. • This drug may make you dizzy, especially during the first few days of therapy; this should subside as your body adjusts to the medication. If it does make you dizzy, avoid activities that require alertness, such as driving a car or operating potentially dangerous equipment, and limit your consumption of alcohol, which exaggerates this side effect. • Your doctor may want to see you regularly while you are taking this drug to check your response and to conduct liver function tests. • Contact your doctor if this drug causes severe or persistent dizziness, constipation, breathing difficulties, swelling of hands and feet, or irregular heartbeat.

Comments: Take this drug as directed, even if you feel well. Compliance is necessary to prevent chest pain or manage high blood pressure. This drug will not stop an attack of chest pain that is already in progress. • Swallow the capsule whole without breaking or chewing it unless otherwise instructed by your physician. Procardia XL must be swallowed whole. Crushing or chewing the drug will destroy the prolonged action, increasing the risk of side effects. The empty tablet shell may be found in your stool, but it is no cause for concern. • Do not suddenly stop taking this drug, unless you consult with your doctor first. Your dosage may have to be decreased gradually. • It may take several days before the effects of this drug are noticed. • Learn how to monitor your pulse and blood pressure; discuss this with your doctor. • If you feel dizzy or lightheaded, sit or lie down for a while; get up slowly from a sitting or reclining position, and be careful on stairs. • Protect this drug from light and moisture. As with all antihypertensive medications, they are most effective when used in conjunction with diet and lifestyle changes, such as exercise and stress reduction to control blood pressure. The medication does not provide a cure for high blood pressure.

Prochlorperazine antiemetic and antipsychotic, see Compazine anticmctic and antipsychotic

ProctoCream-HC topical steroid and anesthetic, see Pramosone topical steroid and anesthetic.

Promethazine HCl, Promethazine HCl with codeine antihistamine, see Phenergan, Phenergan with Codeine antihistamine.

Promethazine HCl VC, Promethazine HCl VC with codeine expectorants, see Phenergan VC, Phenergan VC with Codeine expectorants.

Prometh VC Plain expectorant, see Phenergan VC, Phenergan VC with Codeine expectorants.

Prometh VC with Codeine expectorant, see Phenergan VC, Phenergan VC with Codeine expectorants.

Prometh with Codeine antihistamine, see Phenergan, Phenergan with Codeine antihistamine.

Pronestyl, Pronestyl SR antiarrhythmic

Ingredient: procainamide hydrochloride
Equivalent Products: Procainamide HCl; Procan SR
Dosage Forms: Capsule: 250 mg; 375 mg; 500 mg. Sustained-release tablet: 250 mg; 500 mg; 750 mg; 1,000 mg (see Comments). Tablet: 250 mg; 375 mg; 500 mg
Use: Treatment of some heart arrhythmias (irregular heartbeats)
Minor Side Effects: Bitter taste in the mouth; diarrhea; dizziness; dry mouth; flushing; headache; itching; loss of appetite; nausea; stomach upset; vomiting. Most of these side effects, if they occur, should subside as your body adjusts to the medication. Tell your doctor about any that are persistent or particularly bothersome.
Major Side Effects: Bruising; chest pains; chills; confusion; depression; fatigue; fever; giddiness; hallucinations; low blood pressure; mouth sores; muscle aches; pain in the joints; palpitations; rash; sore throat; unusual behavior; weakness. Notify your doctor if you notice any major side effects.
Contraindications: This drug should not be taken by people who are allergic to it or to some local anesthetics. The drug should not be taken by people who have myasthenia gravis or certain types of heart disease. Be sure to notify your doctor if you have any of these conditions.
Warnings: People who have liver or kidney disease or certain types of heart disease should use this drug with caution. Be sure your doctor knows if any of these conditions applies to you. • This drug may interact with other heart drugs, diuretics, lidocaine, and cimetidine. If you are taking any drugs of these types, ask your doctor about their use. If you are unsure about the type or contents of your medications, ask your doctor or pharmacist. • Alcohol consumption may affect the way the body handles this drug. Use caution if you consume alcohol while taking this drug. While taking this drug, do not take any nonprescription item for weight control, cough, cold, or sinus problems without first checking with your doctor. • Notify your doctor if you experience soreness around the mouth, throat, or gums; unexplained fever; a head cold or respiratory infection; or joint pain or stiffness. • Contact your doctor if this drug causes severe or persistent dizziness, constipation, nausea, shortness of breath, swelling of hands and feet, or irregular heartbeat. • Your doctor may want to check your blood levels of this drug periodically. Blood levels indicate the effectiveness of the dosage.
Comments: It is best to take this drug on an empty stomach (one hour before or two hours after meals). However, if this drug causes stomach upset, it may be taken with food or milk. • Do not crush or chew any of the dosage forms of this drug; they must be swallowed whole. Follow your doctor's dosage instructions carefully; it is especially important that this drug be taken on schedule. It should be taken at evenly spaced intervals around the clock. Do not take extra doses, and do not skip a dose without first consulting your doctor. If you miss a dose, take it as soon as you remember unless it is near the time for the next dose. In that case, skip the missed dose and resume your

normal dosing schedule. Do not double the dose to catch up. Sustained-release tablets require less frequent dosing than the regular tablets. Sustained-release tablets should not be used for initial therapy but can be substituted once the dosage is stabilized. Consult your doctor about the use of this dosage form. • Chew gum or suck on ice chips or a piece of hard candy to reduce mouth dryness. • To minimize dizziness, rise from a lying or sitting position slowly. Do not be alarmed if you notice an empty tablet in your bowel movements. This is the core of the tablet, which is made of wax. Since it is not digestible, it is excreted from the body. • Your doctor may want you to monitor your pulse and blood pressure while you are taking this medication; discuss this with your doctor.

Propacet 100 analgesic, see Darvocet-N analgesic.

Propine ophthalmic glaucoma preparation

Ingredient: dipivefrin hydrochloride
Dosage Form: Solution: 0.1%
Use: Treatment of open-angle glaucoma
Minor Side Effects: Aching brow; blurred vision; burning; headache; increased sensitivity of the eyes to glare or sunlight; poor night vision; stinging; twitching eyelids. Most of these side effects, if they occur, should subside as your body adjusts to the medication. Tell your doctor about any that are persistent or particularly bothersome.

Major Side Effects: Irregular heartbeat; nervousness; rapid heart rate; sweating; vision changes. Notify your doctor if you become aware of any major side effects.

Contraindications: This drug should not be taken by anyone who is allergic to it. Consult your doctor immediately if this drug has been prescribed for you and you have such an allergy. • This drug is not recommended for use in children under 12 years of age, since safety and efficacy have not been established in this age group.

Warnings: This drug should be used with caution by people who have heart disease, high blood pressure, hyperthyroidism, diabetes, or asthma. Since this drug contains sulfites, persons sensitive to sulfites may develop allergic reactions to the medication. Make sure your doctor knows if you have or have had any of these conditions. • Soft contact lenses should not be worn while using this drug, as lenses may be discolored. • This drug should be used only if clearly needed during pregnancy or while nursing. • This drug should be used with caution in elderly persons, since they may be more sensitive to the side effects. • This drug may interact with anesthetics and antidepressants. If you are currently taking any drugs of these types, inform your doctor. If you are unsure about the type or contents of your medications, check with your doctor or pharmacist. • Report any vision changes to your doctor.

Comments: Learn the proper technique for administering eye drops. Wash your hands before using the medication. To avoid contamination of the eye drops, do not touch the dropper to your eye. Do not wash or wipe the dropper before replacing it in the bottle. To administer eye drops, tilt your head back. Gently pull down lower lid to form a pouch. Hold the dropper above the eye and place the prescribed number of drops into the pouch. Close eyes and keep them shut for a few moments. Try not to blink or rub your eyes. If you miss a dose, apply it as soon as it is remembered unless it is near the time for the next dose. In that case, skip the missed dose and resume your usual dosing schedule. Do not double the dose to catch up. • Temporary stinging, burning, or blurred vision may occur when drops are first put into the eyes. If these effects persist or worsen, notify your doctor. • Because this drug can increase sensitivity to bright light, wear sunglasses to protect your eyes. • Close cap tightly and store in a cool, dark place. • Discard the eye drops if the solution turns brown or if it contains particles, and begin using a fresh bottle or tube. Check the expiration date on the drug label, and discard any unused drug after that date.

propoxyphene napsylate and acetaminophen analgesic, see Darvocet-N analgesic.

Propranolol and Hydrochlorothiazide diuretic and antihypertensive, see Inderide, Inderide LA diuretic and antihypertensive.

propranolol antihypertensive and antianginal

Ingredient: propranolol hydrochloride
Equivalent Product: Inderal
Dosage Forms: Solution (content per ml): 4 mg; 8 mg; 80 mg. Sustained-release capsule: 60 mg; 80 mg; 120 mg; 160 mg. Tablet: 10 mg; 20 mg; 40 mg; 60 mg; 80 mg; 90 mg (see Comments)
Uses: Treatment of chest pain (angina), certain abnormal heart rhythms (arrhythmias), thyroid disorders or tremor; prevention of heart attacks, high blood pressure (hypertension), or migraine headaches
Minor Side Effects: Abdominal cramps; blurred vision; constipation; dry mouth; fatigue; gas; insomnia; light-headedness; loss of appetite; nausea; sweating; vomiting; weakness. Most of these side effects, if they occur, should subside as your body adjusts to the medication. Tell your doctor about any that are persistent or particularly bothersome.
Major Side Effects: Breathing difficulties; cold hands and feet; decreased sexual ability; depression; diarrhea; difficulty in urinating; dizziness; fever; hair loss; hallucinations; nightmares; rash; ringing in the ears; slow pulse; slurred speech; sore throat; tingling in fingers; unusual bruising; visual disturbances. Notify your doctor if you notice any major side effects.
Contraindications: This drug should not be used by persons with bronchial asthma or certain types of heart problems or by persons allergic to it. Be sure your doctor knows if any of these conditions applies to you.
Warnings: This drug should be used with caution by persons with certain respiratory problems, diabetes, certain types of heart problems, liver and kidney diseases, hypoglycemia, or thyroid disease. Be sure your doctor knows if any of these conditions applies to you. • Diabetics taking this medication should watch for signs of altered blood glucose levels. • This drug should be used cautiously by pregnant women. • This drug should be used with care during anesthesia. If possible, this drug should be withdrawn 48 hours prior to major surgery. • This drug should be used cautiously when insulin, digoxin, reserpine, cimetidine, theophylline, or aminophylline are taken. • While taking this drug, do not take any nonprescription item for weight control, cough, cold, or sinus problems without first checking with your doctor; such medications may contain ingredients that can increase blood pressure. • Do not suddenly stop taking this drug unless directed to do so by your doctor. Your doctor will reduce your dosage gradually or substitute another drug if this medication is no longer to be used. • Notify your doctor if breathing difficulties, dizziness, or diarrhea develop.
Comments: Be sure to take your medication doses at the same time each day. It is best to take this with food. • Your doctor may want you to take your pulse and blood pressure every day while you take this medication. Discuss

CONSUMER GUIDE®

this with your doctor. • This drug may make you more sensitive to the cold; dress warmly. • This drug is of value in preventing further heart attacks among patients who have already suffered a heart attack. • The sustained-release capsule form of this drug is available under the name Inderal LA, which requires less frequent dosing. Consult your doctor about its use.

Prostep transdermal smoking deterrent, see Nicoderm transdermal smoking deterrent.

Prothazine antihistamine, see Phenergan, Phenergan with Codeine antihistamine.

Proventil bronchodilator, see Ventolin bronchodilator.

Provera progesterone hormone

Ingredient: medroxyprogesterone acetate
Equivalent Products: Amen; Curretab; Cycrin; Medroxyprogesterone Acetate
Dosage Form: Tablet: 2.5 mg; 5 mg; 10 mg
Uses: Treatment of abnormal menstrual bleeding, difficult menstruation, or lack of menstruation
Minor Side Effects: Acne; bloating; breast tenderness; change in sex drive; difficulty sleeping; dizziness; hair growth; headache; nausea; sensitivity to the sun. Most of these side effects, if they occur, should subside as your body adjusts to the medication. Tell your doctor about any that are persistent or particularly bothersome.
Major Side Effects: Birth defects (if used during pregnancy); cervical damage; change in menstrual patterns; dark urine; depression; fainting; fluid retention; hair loss; itching; pain in calves; rash; spotting or breakthrough or unusual vaginal bleeding; vision changes; weight gain or loss; yellowing of the eyes or skin. Notify your doctor if you notice any major side effects.
Contraindications: This drug should not be taken by people who have cancer of the breast or genitals, clotting disorders or a history of clotting disorders, vaginal bleeding of unknown cause, or liver disease; by those who are pregnant, especially during the first trimester; or by those who have had a stroke. The drug should not be used by anyone with a history of missed abortion (retention of a dead fetus in the uterus for a number of weeks). This drug should not be used if you are allergic to it. Consult your doctor immediately if this drug has been prescribed for you and any of these conditions applies. • This drug should not be used as a test to determine pregnancy.
Warnings: This drug should be used cautiously by nursing women and by people who have gallbladder disease, epilepsy, migraine, asthma, heart or kidney disease, depression, or diabetes. Be sure your doctor knows if any of these conditions applies to you. • Watch for early signs of clotting disorders, loss of vision, or headache; report any such signs to your doctor immediately. • Notify your doctor if any unusual vaginal bleeding occurs. • If you take this drug and later discover that you are pregnant, consult your doctor immediately. • Before you begin to take this drug, you should have a complete physical examination, including a Pap smear. • This drug may mask the signs of menopause. • This drug may affect the results of many laboratory tests and other medical examinations. Be sure your doctor knows you are taking this drug if you are being tested for any medical condition. • Notify your doctor if you develop signs of jaundice (yellowing of the eyes or skin, dark urine), pain in the calves, sudden severe headache, or vision changes while taking this drug.

Comments: Take this drug with food if stomach upset occurs. This medication is usually taken in cycles. Withdrawal menstrual bleeding occurs within three to seven days of stopping a cycle. • Your pharmacist has a brochure that describes this drug. Your pharmacist is required by law to give you a copy each time you have your prescription filled. Read this material carefully. Discuss the risks and benefits of this medication with your doctor. • Do not change brands of this drug without consulting your doctor or pharmacist; the products may not be equally effective for your condition.

Prozac antidepressant

Ingredient: fluoxetine hydrochloride
Dosage Forms: Capsule: 10 mg; 20 mg. Liquid (content per 5 ml teaspoon): 20 mg
Use: Treatment of mental depression
Minor Side Effects: Abdominal cramps; anxiety; change in appetite; change in sexual drive; constipation; diarrhea; dizziness; drowsiness; dry mouth; gas; headache; insomnia; light-headedness; nausea; nervousness; reduced concentration; sweating; tremor; trouble sleeping; vomiting. Most of these side effects, if they occur, should subside as your body adjusts to the medication. Tell your doctor about any that are persistent or particularly bothersome.
Major Side Effects: Chest pain; chills; cough; fever; frequent or painful urination; hives; mood or behavior changes; muscle aches; painful or difficult breathing; rapid, pounding heartbeat; sexual dysfunction; sinus infection; skin rash; sore throat; vision changes. Notify your doctor if you notice any major side effects.
Contraindication: This drug should not be used by people who are allergic to it. Consult your doctor immediately if this drug has been prescribed for you and you have such an allergy.
Warnings: This drug should be used cautiously by people who have severe liver or kidney disease; unstable heart disease; head injury; or history of seizures, suicide attempts, or drug abuse. Be sure your doctor knows if any of these conditions applies to you. • Elderly persons should use this drug with caution. • This drug should be used only if clearly needed during pregnancy. Discuss the risks and benefits with your doctor. • It is not known if this drug appears in breast milk. Consult your doctor before breast-feeding while taking this medication. • This drug is not recommended for use in children under 18 years of age since safety and efficacy have not been established in this age group. • This drug has been found to interact with diazepam, warfarin, digoxin, monoamine oxidase inhibitors, desipramine, and nortriptyline. If you are currently taking any medications of these types, consult your doctor about their use. If you are unsure about the type or contents of your medications, ask your doctor or pharmacist. Inform your doctor of any medications (prescription or nonprescription) you are taking or plan to take during treatment with this drug. • This drug may cause drowsiness and dizziness; avoid tasks requiring alertness, such as driving a car or operating potentially dangerous equipment. To prevent excessive drowsiness, avoid the use of alcohol or other depressant medication while taking this drug. • This medication may cause a rash or hives. If you experience either of these symptoms, inform your doctor. Notify your doctor of any changes in mood or behavior that occur while taking this drug.
Comments: Take this drug with food or a full glass of water if stomach upset occurs. • Continue to take this medication as prescribed. Do not suddenly stop taking this drug without your doctor's approval. • Some improvement should be seen within one week, but it may take three to four weeks before optimal results are achieved. • Nausea, dizziness, headache, light-headedness, and anx-

iety are common during the first few days of therapy. These effects should sub-side as your body adjusts to the drug. • Chew gum or suck on ice chips to help relieve dry mouth. • To avoid dizziness or light-headedness, contract and relax the muscles of your legs for a few moments before rising. Do this by pushing one foot against the floor while raising the other foot slightly, alternating feet so that you are pumping your legs in a pedaling motion. This drug has been found to be effective in the treatment of depression when taken as directed. Serious side effects can result from improper use. Your condition will be monitored closely while you are taking this drug. Prozac should be used only by the person for whom it was prescribed and for the specific condition only. The use of Prozac to change personality or self esteem is not without risk. Use of this drug must be carefully evaluated by your doctor.

Quibron-T bronchodilator, see theophylline bronchodilator.

Reglan gastrointestinal stimulant and antiemetic

Ingredient: metoclopramide
Equivalent Products: Maxolon; Metoclopramide HCl
Dosage Forms: Syrup (per 5 ml teaspoon): 5 mg. Tablet: 5 mg; 10 mg
Uses: Relief of the symptoms associated with diabetic gastric stasis or gastric reflux; treatment of nausea and vomiting associated with cancer chemotherapy

Minor Side Effects: Diarrhea; dizziness; drowsiness; fatigue; headache; insomnia; nausea; restlessness. Most of these side effects, if they occur, should subside as your body adjusts to the medication. Tell your doctor about any that are persistent or particularly bothersome.

Major Side Effects: Anxiety; depression; involuntary movements of the face, mouth, jaw, and tongue; menstrual irregularities; muscle spasms; trembling; uncoordinated movements. Notify your doctor if you notice any major side effects.

Contraindications: This drug should not be used by persons with pheochromocytoma, epilepsy or seizure disorders, or in the presence of gastrointestinal bleeding, obstruction, or perforation. Reglan should not be prescribed for persons who are allergic to it. Consult your doctor if this drug has been prescribed for you and any of these conditions applies.

Warnings: This drug should be used cautiously by children and by nursing mothers. • This drug should be used with extreme caution during pregnancy. Talk to your doctor about the use of this medication if you are pregnant. • Persons with previously detected breast cancer should be monitored closely while using this drug. An increase in breast cancer has been found in laboratory rats who were given large doses of this drug for a prolonged period. These findings have not been duplicated in humans. • Diabetics who require insulin should use this drug cautiously, as the dosage or timing of the insulin may need adjustment. Discuss this with your doctor. • This drug interacts with narcotic analgesics, anticholinergics, alcohol, sedatives, hypnotics, and tranquilizers. If you are currently taking any drugs of these types, consult your doctor about their use. If you are unsure, ask your doctor or pharmacist. • Because this drug causes stimulation of the gastrointestinal tract, talk to your doctor about the effect this may have on any other medications you are taking. For some drugs, the timing of doses may need to be adjusted. • This drug may cause motor restlessness, uncoordinated movements, or fine tremors of the tongue. Contact your doctor immediately if you notice any of these symptoms. If you experience involuntary movements of the face, hands, legs, or eyes, call your doctor. • Because this drug may cause drowsiness, avoid tasks that require alertness, such as driving a car or operating potentially dangerous equipment, for a few hours after taking each dose.

Comments: This medication is usually taken 30 minutes before each meal. For maximum benefit, take this drug exactly as prescribed. Do not take extra doses or skip doses without first consulting your doctor.

Relafen anti-inflammatory

Ingredient: nabumetone
Dosage Form: Tablet: 500 mg; 750 mg
Use: Relief of pain and swelling due to arthritis
Minor Side Effects: Bloating; blurred vision; constipation; diarrhea; dizziness; drowsiness; gas; headache; heartburn; insomnia; nausea; nervousness; stomach upset; vomiting; weakness. Most of these side effects, if they occur, should subside as your body adjusts to the medication. Tell your doctor about any that are persistent or particularly bothersome.
Major Side Effects: Black or tarry stools; breathing difficulties; chest pain; depression; difficulty urinating; easy bruising or bleeding; fluid retention; itching; rapid weight gain; rash; ringing in the ears; sore throat; swelling of the hands or feet especially at night; ulcers; visual disturbances. Notify your doctor if you notice any major side effects.
Contraindications: This drug should not be taken by people who are allergic to it or to aspirin or similar drugs. Consult your doctor immediately if this drug has been prescribed for you and you have such an allergy.
Warnings: This drug should be used with extreme caution by patients with upper gastrointestinal tract disease, peptic ulcer, heart disease (certain types), high blood pressure, kidney disease, or bleeding diseases. Be sure your doctor knows if any of these conditions applies to you. • Use of this drug by pregnant women, nursing mothers, and children under two years of age is not recommended. • This drug should be used cautiously in conjunction with aspirin, diuretics, oral anticoagulants, oral antidiabetics, phenytoin, and probenecid. If you are currently taking any drugs of these types, consult your doctor. If you are unsure of the type or contents of your medications, ask your doctor or pharmacist. • Do not take aspirin or alcohol while taking this drug without first consulting your doctor. • This drug may cause drowsiness; avoid tasks that require alertness, such as driving a car or operating potentially dangerous equipment. • Notify your doctor if skin rash; itching; black, tarry stools; swelling of the hands or feet; or persistent headache occurs. • Persons taking this drug for prolonged periods should have regular eye examinations.
Comments: If this drug upsets your stomach, take it with food, milk or antacids. • You should note improvement of your condition soon after you start using this drug; however, full benefit may not be obtained for one to two weeks. It is important not to stop taking this drug even though symptoms have diminished or disappeared. Do not take it only when you feel pain. Its benefit is based on continued, regular use. • This drug is not a substitute for rest, physical therapy, or other measures recommended by your doctor to treat your condition. • This drug is similar in action to other anti-inflammatory agents, such as Indocin, Naprosyn, Lodine, and ibuprofen. If one of these drugs is not well tolerated, your doctor may have you try the others in order to find the drug that is best for you.

Repan analgesic, see Fioricet analgesic.

Reposans-10 antianxiety, see Librium antianxiety.

Respbid bronchodilator, see theophylline bronchodilator.

Restoril sedative and hypnotic

Ingredient: temazepam
Equivalent Product: Temazepam
Dosage Form: Capsule: 15 mg; 30 mg
Use: Short-term relief of insomnia
Minor Side Effects: Blurred vision; constipation; decreased sex drive; diarrhea; dizziness; drowsiness; dry mouth; heartburn; lethargy; light-headedness; loss of appetite; relaxed feeling. Most of these side effects, if they occur, should subside as your body adjusts to the medication. Tell your doctor about any that are persistent or particularly bothersome.
Major Side Effects: Confusion; depression; hallucinations; impaired coordination; memory loss; nightmares; rapid, pounding heartbeat; tremors; weakness. Notify your doctor if you notice any major side effects.
Contraindications: This drug should not be used by persons allergic to it or by pregnant women. Consult your doctor immediately if this drug has been prescribed for you and either of these conditions applies.
Warnings: This drug should be used with caution by depressed people, nursing mothers, persons under the age of 18, and people with liver or kidney diseases or psychosis. Be sure your doctor knows if any of these conditions applies to you. • Because this drug has the potential to be habit-forming, it must be used with caution, especially by those with a history of drug dependence. Tolerance may develop quickly; do not increase the dose or take this drug more often than prescribed without first consulting your doctor. If you have been taking this drug for a long time, do not stop taking it suddenly unless directed to do so by your doctor. Your doctor may gradually reduce your dosage. • When this drug is combined with other sedative drugs or alcohol, serious adverse reactions may develop. Therefore, avoid the use of alcohol, other sedatives, or central nervous system depressants while you are taking this medication. If you are currently taking any drugs of these types, consult your doctor about their use. If you are unsure of the type or contents of your medications, ask your doctor or pharmacist. • This drug causes drowsiness; avoid tasks that require alertness, such as driving a car or operating potentially dangerous equipment. • The elderly are more sensitive to this drug, so smaller doses are often prescribed for them.
Comments: Take this drug one-half to one hour before bedtime unless otherwise prescribed. • After you stop taking this drug, your sleep may be disturbed for a few nights. If you feel groggy the day after taking this drug, talk to your doctor about using a smaller dose or a different sedative so you get a restful night's sleep but can still function and think clearly the next day.

Retin-A acne preparation

Ingredient: tretinoin (retinoic acid; vitamin A acid)
Dosage Forms: Cream: 0.025%; 0.05%; 0.1%. Gel: 0.025%; 0.01%. Liquid: 0.05%
Uses: Topical application in treatment of acne vulgaris; may also be used in the treatment of skin cancer or other skin conditions as determined by your doctor
Minor Side Effects: Heightened sensitivity to sunlight; localized rash; peeling; red, irritated skin; stinging. These side effects, if they occur, should subside as your body adjusts to the medication. Tell your doctor if they are persistent or particularly bothersome.
Major Side Effects: Blistering or crusting of the skin; pain; temporary change in skin color. Notify your doctor if you notice any major side effects.

Contraindication: This drug should not be used by people who are allergic to it. Consult your doctor immediately if this drug has been prescribed for you and you have such an allergy.

Warnings: This drug should be used with extreme caution by persons suffering from eczema. • This drug should be used during pregnancy only if clearly needed. Consult your doctor about use of this drug during breast-feeding. • This drug should not be used in conjunction with other acne preparations, particularly peeling agents containing sulfur, resorcinol, benzoyl peroxide, or salicylic acid. • Medicated or abrasive soaps, cosmetics that have a strong drying effect, and locally applied products containing high amounts of alcohol, spices, or lime should be used with caution because of a possible negative interaction with the drug. Cosmetics that do not have a strong drying effect may be used during therapy with this medication; however, thoroughly remove cosmetics before applying the medication. • While using this drug, exposure to sunlight (or sunlamps), wind, and/or cold should be minimized or totally avoided to prevent skin irritation. Wear protective clothing and an effective sunscreen when outdoors. If you are sunburned, wait for the sunburn to heal before using this product. • Applying this product more often than recommended will not hasten improvement of the condition and is likely to cause further irritation. • If redness, peeling, or pain continue or become worse, notify your doctor as soon as possible.

Comments: Clean and dry affected area. Apply lightly. The liquid form of this drug may be applied with a fingertip, gauze pad, or cotton swab. If gauze or cotton is used, do not oversaturate so that the liquid runs onto areas that are not intended for treatment. • Wash your hands immediately after applying this drug. • This drug should be kept away from the eyes, the mouth, the angles of the nose, and the mucous membranes. • A temporary feeling of warmth or a slight stinging may be noted following application of this drug. This effect is normal and not dangerous. • During the early weeks of using this drug, there may be an apparent increase in skin lesions. This is usually not a reason to discontinue its use; however, your doctor may wish to modify the concentration of the drug. Therapeutic effects may be noted within two to three weeks although more than six weeks may be required before definite benefits are seen. • There are claims that Retin-A can help prevent premature aging of the skin and help eliminate wrinkles. This drug is not approved for such a purpose. More studies are needed to evaluate these claims. You may want to discuss this with your doctor.

Ritalin, Ritalin-SR central nervous system stimulants

Ingredient: methylphenidate hydrochloride
Equivalent Product: Methylphenidate HCl
Dosage Forms: Sustained-release tablet: 20 mg. Tablet: 5 mg; 10 mg; 20 mg
Uses: Treatment of hyperactivity in children; treatment of narcolepsy

Minor Side Effects: Dizziness; drowsiness; headache; insomnia; loss of appetite; nausea; nervousness; weakness. Most of these side effects, if they occur, should subside as your body adjusts to the medication. Tell your doctor about any that are persistent or particularly bothersome.

Major Side Effects: Chest pain; easy bruising; fever; hair loss; heart irregularities; high or low blood pressure; hives; joint pain; mood changes; rapid, pounding heartbeat; rash; seizures; sore throat; uncoordinated movements; unusual behavior; vomiting. In addition, children may experience: abdominal pain; impairment of growth; weight loss. Notify your doctor if you notice any major side effects.

Contraindications: This drug should not be taken by persons with marked anxiety, tension, or agitation, since it may aggravate these symptoms. This drug should not be taken by people who are allergic to it or by people with glaucoma. This drug should not be taken by people who have tics or by people who have Tourette's syndrome or a family history of the disorder. Consult your doctor immediately if this drug has been prescribed for you and any of these conditions applies.

Warnings: This drug is not recommended for use by children under six years of age since suppression of growth has been reported with long-term use. The long-term effects of this drug on children have not been well established. Your doctor may want to stop the medication periodically to determine effectiveness. Treatment is usually discontinued after puberty. • This drug should be used cautiously by persons with severe depression, epilepsy, high blood pressure, or eye disease. Be sure your doctor knows if any of these conditions applies to you. • This drug should not be used for the prevention or treatment of normal fatigue. • This drug should be used with caution by pregnant women and women of childbearing age. • This drug should be used cautiously by people with a history of drug dependence or alcoholism. Do not increase the dose of this drug without consulting your doctor. Chronic abuse of this drug can lead to tolerance and psychological dependence. • This drug interacts with guanethidine, monoamine oxidase inhibitors, antidepressants, anticoagulants, anticonvulsants, and phenylbutazone. If you are currently taking any drugs of these types, consult your doctor about their use. If you are unsure of the type or contents of your medications, ask your doctor or pharmacist. • While taking this drug, do not take any nonprescription substance for weight control, cough, cold, or sinus problems without first checking with your doctor. • Do not stop taking this drug without consulting your doctor. • Periodic blood tests are recommended for patients on long-term therapy with this drug.

Comments: Take this medication as directed. It may be taken 30 minutes before meals if stomach upset occurs. • The sustained-release tablets, Ritalin-SR, must be swallowed whole; do not crush or chew them as the long action will be destroyed and the risk of side effects increased. To avoid sleeplessness, this drug should not be taken later than six P.M. • This drug may mask symptoms of fatigue and pose serious danger; never take this drug as a stimulant to keep you awake. • If your child's teacher tells you that your child is hyperactive, take the child to a physician for a complete physical and evaluation. Discuss the risks and benefits of this therapy and other available options with your physician. • If a child needs to take a dose of this drug at noontime, make arrangements with the school nurse.

RMS analgesic, see morphine analgesic.

Robicillin VK antibiotic, see penicillin V potassium (penicillin VK) antibiotic.

Robimycin antibiotic, see erythromycin antibiotic.

Robitet antibiotic, see tetracycline hydrochloride antibiotic.

Roxanol, Roxanol SR analgesic, see morphine analgesic.

Roxicet analgesic, see Percocet analgesic.

Roxilox analgesic, see Percocet analgesic.

Roxiprin analgesic, see Percodan analgesic.

Rum-K potassium replacement, see potassium replacement.

Ru-Vert-M antiemetic, see Antivert antiemetic.

Rymed-TR decongestant and expectorant, see Entex LA decongestant and expectorant.

Scabene pediculicide and scabicide, see Kwell pediculicide and scabicide.

Seldane antihistamine

Ingredient: terfenadine
Dosage Form: Tablet: 60 mg
Use: Relief of allergy symptoms (including insect stings), such as watery eyes, sneezing, itching, hives
Minor Side Effects: Blurred vision; constipation; diarrhea; drowsiness; dry mouth, nose, and throat; excitation; headache; increased frequency of urination; insomnia; loss of appetite; muscle pain; nasal stuffiness; nausea; nightmares; sedation; sun sensitivity; sweating; vomiting; weight gain. Most of these side effects, if they occur, should subside as your body adjusts to the medication. Tell your doctor about any that are persistent or particularly bothersome.
Major Side Effects: Breathing difficulties; chest pain; confusion; depression; difficulty in urinating; dizziness; faintness; irregular heartbeat; menstrual disorders; rapid, pounding heartbeat; rash; ringing in the ears; tingling of hands and feet; thinning of hair; tremors. Notify your doctor of any major side effects.
Contraindications: This drug should not be taken by people who are allergic to it, by persons taking monoamine oxidase inhibitors, or by nursing mothers. Consult your doctor immediately if any of these conditions applies to you. • This drug is not recommended for use in infants or children under 12 years of age. • This drug should not be used to treat asthma or lower respiratory tract symptoms.
Warnings: This drug must be used cautiously by persons with glaucoma (certain types), ulcers (certain types), thyroid disease, certain urinary difficulties, enlarged prostate, or heart disease (certain types). Be sure your doctor knows if any of these conditions applies to you. • Elderly persons may be more likely than others to experience side effects, especially sedation, and should use this drug with caution. • The sedative effects of this drug are enhanced by alcohol and other central nervous system depressants. This drug can effect your response to eyrthromycin, theophylline, heart medications, and antibiotics. If you are currently taking drugs of these types, consult your doctor about their use. If you are unsure about the type or contents of your medications, ask your doctor or pharmacist. • This medication may cause irregular heart rhythms, especially at high doses. Do not increase your dose or take other drugs with this without consulting your doctor. Notify your doctor if you experience faintness, dizziness, or an irregular heartbeat. • Because this drug may cause drowsiness, avoid tasks requiring alertness, such as driving a car or operating potentially dangerous equipment. • While taking this medication, do not take any nonprescription substance for weight control, cough, cold, or sinus problems without first consulting your doctor or pharmacist. • If taken for prolonged periods, you may become tolerant to the effects of this drug. Do not increase your dose. Another type of antihistamine may be substituted if necessary for a short period.

Comments: If stomach upset occurs, try taking each dose with food or milk. • Chew gum or suck on ice chips or a piece of hard candy to relieve mouth dryness. • This drug may make you more sensitive to the effects of the sun. Wear protective clothing and use a sunscreen when outdoors. • Seldane offers the advantage of causing less drowsiness and sedation than other antihistamines. It is similar to Hismanal.

Septra, Septra DS antibacterials, see Bactrim, Bactrim DS antibacterials.

Sinemet, Sinemet CR antiparkinson drug

Ingredients: carbidopa; levodopa
Equivalent Product: Carbidopa & Levodopa
Dosage Form: Tablet: Sinemet-10/100: carbidopa, 10 mg and levodopa, 100 mg; Sinemet-25/100: carbidopa, 25 mg and levodopa, 100 mg; Sinemet-25/250: carbidopa, 25 mg and levodopa, 250 mg; Sinemet CR: carbidopa, 50 mg and levodopa, 200 mg
Use: Treatment of symptoms of Parkinson's disease
Minor Side Effects: Abdominal pain; agitation; anxiety; bitter taste in the mouth; constipation; diarrhea; discoloration or darkening of the urine; dizziness; dry mouth; excessive salivation; faintness; fatigue; fluid retention; flushing; headache; hiccups; hot flashes; increased sexual interest; insomnia; loss of appetite; low blood pressure; nausea; sweating; vision changes; vomiting; weakness. Most of these side effects, if they occur, should subside as your body adjusts to the medication. Tell your doctor about any that are persistent or particularly bothersome.
Major Side Effects: Aggressive behavior; blood disorders; burning of the tongue; confusion; convulsions; delusions; depression; difficulty swallowing; difficulty urinating; double vision; euphoria; gastrointestinal bleeding; grinding of teeth; hallucinations; high blood pressure; involuntary movements; irregular heartbeats; jaw stiffness; loss of balance; loss of hair; mental changes; nightmares; numbness; rapid, pounding heartbeat; persistent erection; skin rash; suicidal tendencies; tremors; ulcer; weight gain or loss. Notify your doctor if you notice any major side effects.
Contraindications: This drug should not be taken by people with narrow-angle glaucoma or hypersensitivity to either of the drug's ingredients. This drug should not be taken by people with certain cancers or skin diseases. • You must stop taking monoamine oxidase inhibitors at least two weeks prior to starting therapy with this drug. Be sure your doctor knows about all the medications you take. Consult your doctor immediately if any of these conditions applies.
Warnings: This drug should be used with caution by people with heart, lung, kidney, liver, or glandular diseases; epilepsy; diabetes; low blood pressure; asthma; or ulcers. Be sure your doctor knows if any of these conditions applies to you. • Pregnant women, nursing mothers, and children should use this drug with caution. • This drug should be taken with caution by people who are taking drugs to treat high blood pressure. When this drug is started, dosage adjustment of the antihypertensive drug may be required. • This drug interacts with hypoglycemics, monoamine oxidase inhibitors, antipsychotics, phenytoin, papaverine, adrenergics, and antidepressants. If you are currently taking any drugs of these types, consult your doctor about their use. If you are unsure about the type or contents of your medications, ask your doctor or pharmacist. • When this drug is administered to patients currently taking levodopa (L-dopa), the levodopa must be discontinued at least eight hours before. • This drug may cause dizziness or drowsiness; avoid tasks that require alertness, such as dri-

ving a car or operating potentially dangerous equipment. • Consult your doctor if you experience a drastic mood change or if you notice any involuntary movements of the hands or tongue. • Periodic evaluations of liver, blood, heart, and kidney function are recommended during extended therapy with this drug.

Comments: Take this drug with food or milk to lessen stomach upset. • It may take several weeks before the full effect of this drug is evident. You must take this continuously to ensure maximum effectiveness. Do not increase your dose or stop taking this without first consulting your doctor. • If dizziness or light-headedness occurs when you stand, contract and relax the muscles of your legs for a few moments before rising. Do this by pushing one foot against the floor while raising the other foot slightly, alternating feet so that you are pumping your legs in a pedaling motion. • This drug causes beneficial effects in Parkinson's disease similar to levodopa. Because of its carbidopa content, lower doses of levodopa contained in the tablet give better results than if the levodopa were taken alone. During long term use (two to three years), this medication may suddenly become less effective. Your doctor may suggest a "drug holiday" in which the medication is stopped for a few days, then the dose gradually increased. Consult your doctor if you think the drug is losing its effectiveness.

Slo-bid bronchodilator, see theophylline bronchodilator.

Slo-Phyllin bronchodilator, see theophylline bronchodilator.

Slow-K potassium replacement, see potassium replacement.

Sofarin anticoagulant, see Coumadin anticoagulant.

Solfoton sedative and anticonvulsant, see phenobarbital sedative and anticonvulsant.

Sorbitrate antianginal, see Isordil antianginal.

S-P-T thyroid hormone, see thyroid hormone.

Stagesic analgesic, see Vicodin, Vicodin ES analgesics.

Sterapred steroid hormone, see prednisone steroid hormone.

sulfamethoxazole and trimethoprim, sulfamethoxazole and trimethoprim DS antibacterials, see Bactrim, Bactrim DS antibacterials.

Sulfatrim, Sulfatrim DS antibacterials, see Bactrim, Bactrim DS antibacterials.

Sumycin antibiotic, see tetracycline hydrochloride antibiotic.

Suprax antibiotic

Ingredient: cefixime
Dosage Forms: Tablets: 200 mg; 400 mg. Liquid (content per 5 ml teaspoon): 100 mg
Use: Treatment of a wide variety of bacterial infections, including ear, respiratory, skin, and urinary tract infections
Minor Side Effects: Diarrhea; fatigue; heartburn; loss of appetite; mouth sores; nausea; vomiting. Most of these side effects, if they occur, should sub-

side as your body adjusts to the medication. Tell your doctor about any that are persistent or particularly bothersome.

Major Side Effects: Breathing difficulties; dark urine; fever; kidney disease; rash; rectal or vaginal itching; severe diarrhea; superinfection; tingling in hands and feet; unusual bleeding and bruising; yellowing of the eyes or skin. Notify your doctor if you notice any major side effects.

Contraindication: This is a cephalosporin antibiotic. This drug should not be used by people who are allergic to it or to other cephalosporin antibiotics. It is generally believed that about ten percent of all people who are allergic to penicillin will be allergic to an antibiotic like this as well. Consult your doctor immediately if this drug has been prescribed for you and you have such an allergy.

Warnings: This drug should be used cautiously by people who are allergic to penicillin or who have other allergies; by women who are pregnant or nursing; and by people with kidney disease. Be sure your doctor knows if any of these conditions applies to you. • This drug should be used cautiously in newborns. • Prolonged use of this drug may allow organisms that are not susceptible to it to grow wildly. Do not use this drug unless your doctor has specifically told you to do so. Be sure to follow directions carefully and report any unusual reactions to your doctor at once. • This drug should be used cautiously in conjunction with diuretics, oral anticoagulants, and probenecid. • This drug may interfere with some blood tests. Be sure your doctor knows you are taking it. • Notify your doctor if you develop signs of jaundice (yellowing of the eyes or skin, dark urine) while taking this drug. • Diabetics using Clinitest urine test may get a false high sugar reading. Change to Clinistix, Tes-Tape, Diastix or Chemstrip uG urine test to avoid this problem.

Comments: Take this drug with food or milk if stomach upset occurs. • Finish all of the medication, even if you begin to feel better. Stopping therapy too soon may lead to reinfection. • This medication works best if a constant level of the drug is kept in the body. To do this, take each dose as prescribed at evenly spaced intervals around the clock. Your doctor or pharmacist can help you establish a dosing schedule. The liquid form of this drug should be stored in the refrigerator. Any unused portion should be discarded after 14 days. Shake well before using.

Sustaire bronchodilator, see theophylline bronchodilator.

Symadine antiviral and antiparkinson, see Symmetrel antiviral and antiparkinson.

Symmetrel antiviral and antiparkinson

Ingredient: amantadine hydrochloride
Equivalent Products: Amantadine HCl; Symadine
Dosage Forms: Capsule: 100 mg. Syrup (content per 5 ml teaspoon): 50 mg
Uses: Symptomatic treatment of Parkinson's disease; prevention and treatment of respiratory illness due to flu
Minor Side Effects: Anxiety; blurred vision; constipation; dizziness; dry mouth; fatigue; headache; irritability; light-headedness; loss of appetite; nausea; slurred speech; vomiting. Most of these side effects, if they occur, should subside as your body adjusts to the medication. Tell your doctor about any that are persistent or particularly bothersome.
Major Side Effects: Blood disorders; changes in vision; depression; difficulty in urinating; fluid retention; psychiatric disorders; rash; shortness of

breath; swelling of the hands and feet; unusual behavior; weakness; weak pulse. Notify your doctor if you notice any major side effects.

Contraindication: This drug should not be used by persons who are allergic to it. Consult your doctor immediately if this drug has been prescribed for you and you have such an allergy.

Warnings: This drug must be used with caution by persons with seizure disorders, heart failure, kidney disease, liver disease, or psychiatric disorders and by pregnant or nursing women. Be sure your doctor knows if any of these conditions applies to you. • This drug interacts with central nervous system stimulants, anticholinergics, and levodopa. If you are currently taking any drugs of these types, consult your doctor about their use. If you are unsure of the type or contents of your medications, consult your doctor or pharmacist. • This drug is not recommended for use in children less than one year of age. • If you are taking this drug for Parkinson's disease, do not suddenly stop taking it without consulting your doctor; stopping treatment early can lead to a worsening of symptoms. • This drug may become ineffective after long periods of use. If this occurs, your doctor may have you stop taking the drug for a short period. When you start taking the drug again, it should be effective. If you must take this drug for a prolonged period, discuss this type of therapy with your doctor. • This drug may cause dizziness, blurred vision, or light-headedness; avoid tasks that require alertness, such as driving a car or operating potentially dangerous equipment. • While taking this drug, limit your consumption of alcoholic beverages in order to minimize dizziness. • Notify your doctor if you experience shortness of breath, difficulty in urinating, mood changes, or swelling of the extremities while taking this drug.

Comments: This drug is used for prevention of respiratory tract illness due to influenza A virus in persons with a high risk of contracting it, such as persons with chronic medical problems. If this drug is being used for prevention of respiratory illness, begin therapy as soon as possible after contact has been made with a person having the influenza virus. Therapy should be continued for at least ten days. If this is used to treat "the flu," therapy should be started as soon as possible after symptoms occur and continue for one to two days after symptoms disappear, usually five to seven days. • If this drug is used to treat symptoms of Parkinson's disease, it may take a few weeks before benefits are noticed. • To prevent dizziness and light-headedness when you stand, contract and relax the muscles of your legs for a few moments before rising. Do this by pushing one foot against the floor while raising the other foot slightly. Alternate feet so that you are pumping your legs in a pedaling motion.

Synthroid thyroid hormone

Ingredient: levothyroxine sodium

Equivalent Products: Levothroid; Levothyroxine Sodium; Levoxine (see Comments)

Dosage Form: Tablet: 0.025 mg; 0.05 mg; 0.075 mg; 0.088 mg; 0.1 mg; 0.112 mg; 0.125 mg; 0.15 mg; 0.175 mg; 0.2 mg; 0.3 mg

Use: Thyroid-hormone replacement therapy

Minor Side Effects: Change in appetite; headache; irritability; vomiting. Most of these side effects, if they occur, should subside as your body adjusts to the medication. Tell your doctor about any that are persistent or particularly bothersome.

Major Side Effects: In overdose: Chest pain; diarrhea; fever; heat intolerance; insomnia; leg cramps; menstrual irregularities; nervousness; rapid, pounding heartbeat; shortness of breath; sweating; trembling; weight loss. Notify your doctor if you notice any major side effects.

Contraindications: Although there are no absolute contraindications to this drug, special care should be taken if it is used by persons who have recently had a heart attack and those with defective adrenal glands or an overactive thyroid gland. Tell your doctor if any of these conditions applies to you.

Warnings: This drug should be used cautiously by people who have heart disease, high blood pressure, or diabetes. Be sure your doctor knows if any of these conditions applies to you. • This drug interacts with cholestyramine, digitalis, oral anticoagulants, oral antidiabetics, oral contraceptives, epinephrine, and phenytoin; if you are currently taking any drugs of these types, consult your doctor about their use. If you are unsure of the type or contents of your medications, ask your doctor or pharmacist. • While taking this drug, do not take any nonprescription item for weight control, cough, cold, or sinus problems without first checking with your doctor. • If you are taking digitalis in addition to this drug, watch carefully for symptoms of decreased digitalis effects (e.g., heart failure, water retention, weakness), and notify your doctor immediately if they occur. • Because this medication is used to supplement or replace thyroid hormone produced by the body, side effects are most often related to the dose. Thus, most side effects can be controlled by dosage adjustment. Be sure to follow your doctor's dosage instructions exactly. Consult your doctor if you experience side effects. • Periodic laboratory tests will be done while you are taking this drug to evaluate your response and guide any dosage adjustments. • This drug should not be used to treat obesity. Using this drug in conjunction with appetite suppressants is particularly dangerous.

Comments: Compliance with the prescribed therapy is essential. Follow your dosing instructions exactly. Get into the habit of taking this drug at the same time every day, usually once a day before breakfast. • Do not stop taking this drug without first consulting your doctor. • Not all levothyroxine products are true equivalents. Do not switch brands without consulting your doctor or pharmacist; a dosage adjustment may be necessary. Thyroid hormone replacement therapy is usually continued for life. Learn about the thyroid gland and the symptoms of hypothyroidism (low thyroid hormone) versus hyperthyroidism (high thyroid hormone). Talk to your doctor, as this understanding will make you more informed regarding your therapy.

Tagamet antisecretory and antiulcer

Ingredient: cimetidine
Dosage Forms: Liquid (content per 5 ml teaspoon): 300 mg; Tablet: 200 mg; 300 mg; 400 mg; 800 mg
Uses: Treatment of duodenal and gastric ulcer; long-term treatment of excessive gastric acid secretion; prevention of recurrent ulcers; treatment of gastroesophageal reflux disease
Minor Side Effects: Diarrhea; dizziness; drowsiness; fatigue; headache; muscle pain. Most of these side effects, if they occur, should subside as your body adjusts to the medication. Tell your doctor about any that are persistent or particularly bothersome.
Major Side Effects: Blood disorders; breast enlargement (when taken in extremely high doses over a prolonged period); confusion; dark urine; difficulty in urinating; easy bruising; fever; hair loss; impotence (when taken in extremely high doses over a prolonged period); numbness or tingling in the hands or feet; rash; slow pulse; sore throat; weakness; yellowing of the eyes or skin. Notify your doctor if you notice any major side effects.
Contraindication: This drug should not be taken by anyone who is allergic to it. Consult your doctor if this drug has been prescribed for you and you have such an allergy.

Warnings: This drug should be used with caution by pregnant women or women who may become pregnant and by nursing mothers. • This drug is not recommended for use by children under 16 years of age unless your doctor feels the benefits outweigh any potential risks. Elderly persons may be more likely to develop certain side effects to this medication. • This drug should be used with caution by people with liver or kidney disease, or organic brain syndrome. Be sure your doctor knows if any of these conditions applies to you. • This drug may interact with theophylline, aminophylline, phenytoin, beta blockers, blood thinners, digoxin, anticoagulants, ketoconazole, and certain tranquilizers. If you are currently taking any drugs of these types, consult your doctor about their use. If you are unsure about the type or contents of your medications, ask your doctor or pharmacist. • Be sure your doctor is aware of all the medications you take, including those not requiring a prescription. Antacid therapy may be continued while taking this drug, but the two drugs should not be taken at the same time. For maximum benefit, stagger the doses of antacid and Tagamet by at least two hours. • Notify your doctor if you develop signs of jaundice (yellowing of the eyes or skin, dark urine). • This drug may cause changes in blood cells; therefore, periodic blood tests may be requested by your doctor if you take this medication for prolonged periods.

Comments: This drug is usually taken throughout the day. It should be taken with, or immediately following, a meal. • When used as a preventive, the medication may be taken as a single dose at bedtime. • This drug should not be crushed or chewed because cimetidine has a bitter taste and an unpleasant odor. • Take this drug for the prescribed period, even if you feel better, to ensure adequate results. The liquid form of this drug contains 2.8 percent alcohol. • Lifestyle changes may be recommended in addition to this medication to assist in the prevention and treatment of ulcers. Dietary changes, exercise, smoking cessation, and stress reduction may be beneficial. • This drug is similar but not equivalent in action to Zantac, Axid, and Pepcid. Talk to your doctor about these drugs to see if they may be less expensive alternatives.

Tavist-D antihistamine and decongestant

Ingredients: phenylpropanolamine hydrochloride; clemastine fumarate

Dosage Form: Sustained-release tablet: phenylpropanolamine hydrochloride, 75 mg and clemastine fumarate, 1.34 mg

Uses: Relief of hay fever, upper respiratory tract congestion, and allergy symptoms, such as sneezing, runny nose, teary eyes, and nasal congestion

Minor Side Effects: Anxiety; blurred vision; chills; constipation; diarrhea; dizziness; drowsiness; dry mouth, throat, and nose; fatigue; headache; irritability; loss of appetite; nasal congestion; nausea; nervousness; restlessness; ringing or buzzing in the ears; sedation; stomach upset; sun sensitivity; sweating; tremors; weakness. Most of these side effects, if they occur, should subside as your body adjusts to the medication. Tell your doctor about any that are persistent or particularly bothersome.

Major Side Effects: Breathing difficulty; confusion; convulsions; difficulty in urinating; high blood pressure; loss of coordination; low blood pressure; menstrual changes; rapid, pounding heartbeat; rash; sore throat and fever; tightness in the chest; tingling in the hands and feet; unusual bleeding or bruising. Notify your doctor if you notice any major side effects.

Contraindications: This drug should not be taken by people who are allergic to either of its components, persons taking monoamine oxidase inhibitors, nursing mothers, or persons with severe high blood pressure or coronary artery disease. Consult your doctor immediately if any of these conditions applies to you. • This drug is not recommended for use in children under 12 years of age. • This drug should not be used to treat asthma or lower respiratory tract symptoms.

Warnings: This drug must be used cautiously by persons with glaucoma (certain types), ulcers (certain types), thyroid disease, diabetes, certain urinary difficulties, enlarged prostate, and certain heart diseases. Be sure your doctor knows if any of these conditions applies to you. • This drug should be used only if clearly needed during pregnancy. • Elderly persons may be more likely than others to experience side effects, especially sedation, and should use this drug with caution. • The sedative effects of this drug are enhanced by alcohol and other central nervous system depressants. If you are currently taking any drugs of these types, consult your doctor about their use. If you are unsure about the type or contents of your medications, ask your doctor or pharmacist. • While taking this drug, do not take any nonprescription item for weight control, cough, cold, or sinus problems without first consulting your doctor or pharmacist; such items may contain ingredients similar to this drug. • This drug may cause drowsiness; avoid tasks requiring alertness, such as driving a car or operating potentially dangerous equipment.

Comments: These tablets must be swallowed whole. Do not crush or chew them, as the sustained action will be lost and side effects will be increased. Take this medication as prescribed; never take it more frequently or increase your dose unless instructed to do so by your doctor; a serious overdose may result. • If stomach upset occurs, try taking each dose with food or milk. • Chew gum or suck on ice chips or a piece of hard candy to reduce mouth dryness. • Because this medication reduces sweating, avoid excessive work or exercise in hot weather and drink plenty of fluids. • This medication can make you more sensitive to sunlight; avoid prolonged exposure, wear protective clothing, and use an effective sunscreen when outdoors. • There are many drugs of this type on the market that vary slightly in ingredients and amounts. Some are available without a prescription. Your doctor or pharmacist can help select an antihistamine and decongestant medication best for you.

Tebamide antiemetic, see Tigan antiemetic.

Tegretol anticonvulsant

Ingredient: carbamazepine
Equivalent Products: Carbamazepine; Epitol
Dosage Forms: Chewable tablet: 100 mg. Oral suspension (content per 5 ml teaspoon): 100 mg. Tablet: 200 mg
Uses: Treatment of seizure disorders; relief of trigeminal neuralgia pain or other conditions as determined appropriate by your doctor
Minor Side Effects: Agitation; blurred vision; constipation; diarrhea; dizziness; double vision; drowsiness; dry mouth; eye discomfort; headache; loss of appetite; muscle or joint pain; nausea; restlessness; sensitivity to sunlight; sweating; unsteadiness; vomiting; weakness. Most of these side effects, if they occur, should subside as your body adjusts to the medication. Tell your doctor about any that are persistent or particularly bothersome.
Major Side Effects: Abdominal pain; blood disorders; breathing difficulties; chills; confusion; dark urine; depression; difficulty in urinating; easy bruising or bleeding; fainting; fever; hair loss; hallucinations; impotence; loss of balance; mouth sores; numbness or tingling; pale stools; rapid, pounding heart rate; ringing in the ears; skin rash; sore throat; swelling of hands or feet; twitching; yellowing of the eyes or skin. Notify your doctor of any major side effects.
Contraindications: This drug should not be used by people who are allergic to it or to tricyclic antidepressants. This drug should not be taken by anyone

who has bone marrow depression or who has taken a monoamine oxidase inhibitor within the past two weeks. Consult your doctor immediately if this drug has been prescribed for you and any of these conditions applies.

Warnings: This drug should be used cautiously by pregnant or nursing women and by people who have glaucoma, blood disorders, kidney or liver disease, or heart disease. Be sure your doctor knows if any of these conditions applies to you. • This drug interacts with oral anticoagulants, digitalis, erythromycin, troleandomycin, oral contraceptives, pain killers, tranquilizers, and other anticonvulsants. If you are currently taking any drugs of these types, consult your doctor about their use. If you are unsure of the type or contents of your medications, ask your doctor or pharmacist. Do not use any other medicines—prescription or nonprescription— without first checking with your doctor. This drug alters the response to thyroid function tests. Be sure to remind your doctor that you are taking this drug if you are scheduled for any tests. • This drug may cause dizziness or drowsiness, especially during the first few weeks of therapy; avoid tasks that require alertness, such as driving or operating potentially dangerous equipment. • Notify your doctor if you develop a sore throat, mouth sores, fever, chills, unusual bruising, pale stools, dark urine, yellowing of the eyes or skin, or edema (swelling) while taking this medication.

Comments: If this drug causes stomach upset, take it with food. • It is important that all doses of this medication are taken on time. • Do not stop taking this drug suddenly and do not increase the dosage without your doctor's approval. • While taking this drug, your doctor will want to see you regularly for blood tests, liver and kidney function tests, and eye examinations. • This drug increases your sensitivity to sunlight; limit your exposure to the sun, wear protective clothing and sunglasses, and use an effective sunscreen when outdoors. • Chew gum or suck on ice chips or a piece of hard candy to reduce mouth dryness. • It is recommended that persons taking this medication carry a medical alert card or wear a medical alert bracelet. • This drug is not to be used to treat ordinary pain. It is only effective in treating pain from trigeminal neuralgia.

Teline antibiotic, see tetracycline hydrochloride antibiotic.

Temazepam sedative and hypnotic, see Restoril sedative and hypnotic.

Tenex antihypertensive

Ingredient: guanfacine hydrochloride
Dosage Form: Tablet: 1 mg
Use: Treatment of high blood pressure
Minor Side Effects: Abdominal pain; change in taste; constipation; cough; diarrhea; dizziness; drowsiness; dry mouth; frequent urination; gas; headache; itching; nasal congestion; nausea; nervousness; sedation; tiredness; vomiting; weakness. Most of these side effects, if they occur, should subside as your body adjusts to the medication. Tell your doctor about any that are persistent or particularly bothersome.

Major Side Effects: Blurred vision; breathing trouble; chest pain; decreased sexual ability; depression; difficulty urinating; fainting; fast pulse; fever; fluid retention; leg cramps; joint pain; muscle aches; nosebleed; rapid, pounding heartbeat; rash; ringing in the ears; shortness of breath; tingling of the fingers or toes. Notify your doctor if you notice any major side effects.

Contraindication: This drug should not be taken by people who are allergic to it. Consult your doctor immediately if you have such an allergy.

Warnings: This drug should be used with caution by persons with kidney disease, liver disease, or certain types of heart disease. Be sure your doctor knows if any of these conditions applies to you. • This drug should be used only if clearly needed in pregnant women or nursing mothers. Discuss the risks and benefits with your doctor. • This drug is not recommended for use in children under 12 years of age since safety and efficacy have not been established in this age group. • This drug interacts with antianxiety drugs, sleep medications, narcotic pain relievers, antidepressants, antipsychotic drugs, and other hypertensive drugs. If you are currently taking any drugs of these types, consult your doctor about their use. If you are unsure of the type or contents of your medications, ask your doctor of pharmacist. • While taking this drug, do not take any nonprescription item for weight control, cough, cold, allergy, or sinus problems without first checking with your doctor; such items may contain ingredients that can increase blood pressure. • While taking this drug, you should limit your consumption of alcoholic beverages, which can increase dizziness and other side effects. • Because initial therapy with this drug may cause dizziness and fainting, the medication is usually taken at bedtime. • Do not drive a car or operate potentially dangerous equipment if dizziness occurs.

Comments: Take this drug exactly as directed. Do not take extra doses or skip a dose without consulting your doctor first. • Do not discontinue taking this medication unless your doctor directs you to do so. It is important to continue taking this medication even if you do not feel sick. Most people with high blood pressure do not have symptoms and do not feel ill; therefore, it is easy to forget to take the medication. • Mild side effects (e.g., nasal congestion, headache) are most noticeable during the first two weeks of therapy and become less bothersome as your body adjusts to the medication. • To avoid dizziness or light-headedness when you stand, contract and relax the muscles of your legs for a few moments before rising. Do this by pushing one foot against the floor while raising the other foot slightly, alternating feet so that you are pumping your legs in a pedaling motion. • For best effects, this medication is usually taken in conjunction with a diuretic drug (water pill). • Learn how to monitor your pulse and blood pressure while taking this drug; discuss this with your doctor. As with all antihypertensive medications, they are most effective when used in conjunction with diet and lifestyle changes, such as exercise and stress reduction to control blood pressure. The medication does not cure high blood pressure.

Ten-K potassium replacement, see potassium replacement.

Tenormin antihypertensive and antianginal

Ingredient: atenolol
Equivalent Product: Atenolol
Dosage Form: Tablet: 25 mg; 50 mg; 100 mg
Uses: Treatment of high blood pressure (hypertension) and angina (chest pain); prevention of irregular heartbeat after a heart attack
Minor Side Effects: Abdominal pain; anxiety; bloating; blurred vision; constipation; dizziness (mild); drowsiness; dry eyes, mouth, or skin; headache; heartburn; increased sensitivity to cold; insomnia; light-headedness; nasal congestion; nausea; sweating; vivid dreams; vomiting; weakness. Most of these side effects, if they occur, should subside as your body adjusts to the medication. Tell your doctor about any that are persistent or particularly bothersome.
Major Side Effects: Blood disorders; breathing difficulties; cold hands and feet; confusion; decreased sexual ability; depression; diarrhea; difficulty in urinating; dizziness (severe); fever; hallucinations; mouth sores; nightmares;

numbness and tingling in the fingers and toes; rash; ringing in the ears; slow heartbeat; swelling in the hands or feet; unusual bleeding or bruising. Notify your doctor if you notice any major side effects.

Contraindications: This drug should not be used by people who are allergic to atenolol or any other beta blocker. This drug may interact with monoamine oxidase inhibitors. Consult your doctor if you are taking any drugs of this type. If you are unsure about the type or contents of your medications, ask your doctor or pharmacist. • This drug should not be used by persons who have certain types of heart disease (e.g., slow heart rate, heart failure).

Warnings: This drug should be used with caution by persons with certain respiratory problems, diabetes, certain heart problems, liver or kidney diseases, hypoglycemia, or certain types of thyroid disease. Be sure your doctor knows if any of these conditions applies to you. • This drug should be used cautiously by pregnant women and by women of childbearing age. • Before having surgery, including dental surgery, be sure to tell the doctor or dentist that you are taking this medication. • This drug should be used cautiously when reserpine, cimetidine, theophylline, aminophylline, phenytoin, or digoxin is taken. • Diabetics should be aware that this drug may mask signs of low blood sugar, such as changes in heart rate and blood pressure. If you are diabetic, you will need to monitor your blood glucose level more closely, especially when first taking this drug. • While taking this drug, do not take any nonprescription item for weight control, cough, cold, or sinus problems without first checking with your doctor or pharmacist; such items may contain ingredients that can increase blood pressure. • Notify your doctor if dizziness (severe), diarrhea, depression, breathing difficulties, sore throat, or unusual bruising develops. • This drug may cause drowsiness, blurred vision, or light-headedness, especially during the first few days of therapy as your body adjusts to it. Use caution when engaging in activities that require alertness, such as driving a car or operating potentially dangerous equipment. • This drug is a potent medication; do not stop taking it abruptly, unless your doctor directs you to do so. Chest pain—even heart attacks—can occur if administration of this medicine is stopped suddenly.

Comments: Take this drug as directed. Do not take extra doses or skip a dose without first consulting your doctor. • Be sure to take your medication at the same time each day. It is important to continue taking this medication even if you do not feel sick. Most people with high blood pressure do not have symptoms and do not feel ill; therefore, it is easy to forget to take the medication. • This drug may cause you to become more sensitive to the cold; dress warmly. • Your doctor may want you to take your pulse and blood pressure every day while you are taking this medication. Learn what your normal values are and what they should be; discuss this with your doctor. As with all antihypertensive medications, they are most effective when used in conjunction with diet and lifestyle changes, such as exercise and stress reduction to control blood pressure. The medication does not cure high blood pressure. • There are many beta blockers available. Your doctor may have you try different ones if this drug is ineffective.

Terazol vaginal antifungal

Ingredient: terconazole
Dosage Form: Vaginal cream: 0.4%; 0.8%. Vaginal suppositories: 80 mg
Use: Treatment of vaginal fungal infections
Minor Side Effects: Headache, itching. Most of these side effects, if they occur, should subside as your body adjusts to the medication. Tell your doctor about any that are persistent or particularly bothersome.

Major Side Effect: Rash or irritation. Notify your doctor if you notice a major side effect.

Contraindication: This drug should not be used by people who are allergic to it. Contact your doctor immediately if this drug has been prescribed for you and you have such an allergy.

Warnings: This drug must be used carefully by pregnant or nursing women. If you suffer a rash or irritation from taking this drug, consult your doctor; use of the drug may be discontinued.

Comments: Continue taking this as long as directed even if symptoms disappear before that time to ensure the infection is gone. Stopping therapy too soon can lead to a reinfection. If symptoms to not improve or become worse while using this medication, contact your doctor. • If you are using this drug to treat a vaginal infection, avoid sexual intercourse or ask your partner to wear a condom until treatment is completed; these measures will help prevent reinfection. • The vaginal suppositories are supplied with an applicator used to insert them high into the vagina. • Unless instructed otherwise by your doctor, do not douche during the treatment period or for two to three weeks following your use of this medication. Use this continuously, including during your menstrual period, until your doctor tells you to stop. Be sure to complete a full course of therapy with this drug. • Wear cotton panties rather than those made of nylon or other nonporous materials while fungal infections of the vagina are being treated. • You may wish to wear a sanitary napkin while using the vaginal tablets to prevent soiling of your underwear.

Tetracap antibiotic, see tetracycline hydrochloride antibiotic.

tetracycline hydrochloride antibiotic

Ingredient: tetracycline hydrochloride

Equivalent Products: Achromycin V; Ala-Tet; Nor-Tet; Panmycin; Robitet; Sumycin; Teline; Tetracap; Tetralan; Tetram

Dosage Forms: Capsule: 100 mg; 250 mg; 500 mg. Liquid (content per 5 ml teaspoon): 125 mg. Tablet: 250 mg; 500 mg

Uses: Treatment of acne and a wide variety of bacterial infections; treatment of Lyme disease

Minor Side Effects: Diarrhea; increased sensitivity to sunlight; loss of appetite; nausea; stomach cramps and upset; vomiting. Most of these side effects, if they occur, should subside as your body adjusts to the medication. Tell your doctor about any that are persistent or particularly bothersome.

Major Side Effects: Anemia; black tongue; blurred vision; breathing difficulties; mouth irritation; rash; rectal and vaginal itching; severe headache; sore throat; staining of teeth in children; unusual bleeding or bruising; yellowing of the eyes or skin. Notify your doctor if you notice any major side effects.

Contraindication: This drug should not be taken by people who are allergic to any tetracycline antibiotic such as doxycycline or minocycline. Consult your doctor immediately if this drug has been prescribed for you and you have such an allergy.

Warnings: This drug may cause permanent discoloration of the teeth if used during tooth development; therefore, it should not be used by pregnant or nursing women or in infants and children under nine years of age unless absolutely necessary. This drug should be used cautiously by people who have liver or kidney disease or diabetes. Be sure your doctor knows if any of these conditions applies to you. • This drug interacts with antacids, laxatives, barbiturates, carbamazepine, lithium, diuretics, digoxin, oral contraceptives, penicillin, and phenytoin; if you are currently taking any drugs of these types, consult your doctor about their use. If you are unsure of the type or contents of your medications, ask your doctor or pharmacist. • Milk, other dairy products, and antacids interfere with the body's absorption of this drug, so separate taking this drug and any dairy product or antacid by at least two hours. Do not take this drug at the same time as any iron preparation; their use should be separated by at least two hours. • This drug may affect syphilis tests; if you are being treated for this disease, make sure that your doctor knows you are taking this drug. • If you are taking an anticoagulant in addition to this drug, remind your doctor. • Prolonged use of this drug may allow organisms that are not susceptible to it to grow wildly. Do not use this drug unless your doctor has specifically told you to do so. Be sure to follow the directions carefully and report any unusual reactions to your doctor at once. • Complete blood cell counts and liver and kidney function tests should be done if you take this drug for a prolonged period.

Comments: Ideally, you should take this drug on an empty stomach (one hour before or two hours after a meal). If this drug causes stomach upset, you may take it with food. Take it with at least eight ounces of water. • This drug should be taken for as long as prescribed, even if symptoms disappear within that time. Stopping treatment too soon can lead to reinfection. • This drug is most effective when taken at evenly spaced intervals throughout the day and night. Ask your doctor or pharmacist for help in planning a medication schedule. • The liquid form of this drug should be stored in the refrigerator and must be shaken before use. • Any unused medication should be discarded. Make sure your prescription is marked with the drug's expiration date. Do not use tetracycline after that date, as it can cause serious side effects. • This drug may cause you to be especially sensitive to the sun, so avoid exposure to sunlight as much as possible. When outside, wear protective clothing and use an effective sunscreen. • Tetracycline is also available in a topical solution that is used to treat acne.

Tetralan antibiotic, see tetracycline hydrochloride antibiotic.

Tetram antibiotic, see tetracycline hydrochloride antibiotic.

T-Gen antiemetic, see Tigan antiemetic.

T-Gesic analgesic, see Vicodin, Vicodin ES analgesics.

Theo-24 bronchodilator, see theophylline bronchodilator.

Theobid bronchodilator, see theophylline bronchodilator.

Theochron bronchodilator, see theophylline bronchodilator.

Theoclear-80 bronchodilator, see theophylline bronchodilator.

Theo-Dur bronchodilator, see theophylline bronchodilator.

Theolair bronchodilator, see theophylline bronchodilator.

theophylline bronchodilator

Ingredient: anhydrous theophylline
Equivalent Products: Accurbron; Aerolate; Aquaphyllin; Asmalix; Bronkodyl; Constant-T; Elixomin; Elixophyllin; Lanophyllin; Quibron-T; Resp-

bid; Slo-bid; Slo-Phyllin; Sustaire; Theo-24; Theobid; Theochron; Theoclear-80; Theo-Dur; Theolair; Theo-Sav; Theospan; Theostat 80; Theovent; Theo-X; T-Phyl; Uniphyl

Dosage Forms: Capsule; Liquid; Tablet; Time-release capsule; Time-release tablet (various strengths) (see Comments)

Use: Symptomatic relief and prevention of bronchial asthma and other lung diseases

Minor Side Effects: Dizziness; flushing; heartburn; insomnia; irritability; loss of appetite; nausea; nervousness; paleness. Most of these side effects, if they occur, should subside as your body adjusts to the medication. Tell your doctor about any that are persistent or particularly bothersome.

Major Side Effects: Black, tarry stools; breathing difficulties; chest pain; confusion; convulsions; gastrointestinal disturbances (diarrhea, vomiting); headache; high blood sugar; increased urination; irregular heartbeat; muscle twitches; rapid, pounding heartbeat; rash; ulcer; weakness. Notify your doctor if you notice any major side effects.

Contraindication: This drug should not be taken by people who are allergic to it. Consult your doctor immediately if you have such an allergy.

Warnings: This drug should be used cautiously by newborns, pregnant women, and the elderly and by people who have peptic ulcer, liver disease, chronic obstructive lung disease, certain types of heart disease, kidney disease, low or high blood pressure, or thyroid disease. Be sure your doctor knows if any of these conditions applies to you. • This drug may aggravate an ulcer; call your doctor if you experience stomach pain, vomiting, or restlessness. • This drug should be used with caution in conjunction with furosemide, reserpine, chlordiazepoxide, cimetidine, oral anticoagulants, phenobarbital, certain antibiotics, disulfiram, ephedrine, lithium carbonate, propranolol, and other xanthines, such as caffeine, dyphylline, or aminophylline; if you are currently taking any drugs of these types, consult your doctor about their use. If you are unsure of the type or contents of your medication, ask your doctor or pharmacist. • Before receiving an influenza vaccine, tell your doctor you are taking this drug. • While taking this drug, do not use any nonprescription item for asthma without first checking with your doctor. • Avoid drinking alcohol, coffee, tea, cola drinks, cocoa, or other beverages that contain caffeine. Caffeine produces side effects that are similar to those of this drug. • Cigarette smoking may affect this drug's action. Be sure your doctor knows you smoke. Also, do not suddenly stop smoking without informing your doctor. • This drug may interfere with certain blood and urine laboratory tests. Remind your doctor you are taking this drug before undergoing tests. • If your symptoms do not improve, if they get worse, or if you experience chest pain or breathing trouble while using this drug, contact your doctor. • Your doctor may want to check the amount of drug in your blood in order to ensure its effectiveness. Ask your doctor to explain what the blood level means, and learn how to keep track of your blood levels.

Comments: Take this drug exactly as your doctor has prescribed. The time-release forms must be swallowed whole; do not chew or crush them. If you are unable to swallow the capsule, open the capsule and mix its contents with jelly or applesauce, and swallow the mixture without chewing. • Be sure to take your dose at exactly the right time each day. It is best to take this drug on an empty stomach one hour before or two hours after a meal (unless otherwise prescribed by your doctor). • While taking this drug, drink at least eight glasses of water every day. • Do not switch brands of this medication without first checking with your doctor or pharmacist, as your dosage may need to be adjusted with another brand.

Theo-Sav bronchodilator, see theophylline bronchodilator.

Theospan bronchodilator, see theophylline bronchodilator.

Theostat 80 bronchodilator, see theophylline bronchodilator.

Theovent bronchodilator, see theophylline bronchodilator.

Theo-X bronchodilator, see theophylline bronchodilator.

Thyrar thyroid hormone, see thyroid hormone.

thyroid hormone

Ingredient: thyroid
Equivalent Products: Armour Thyroid; S-P-T; Thyrar; (see Comments)
Dosage Forms: Capsule; Enteric-coated tablet; Tablet (various dosages)
Use: Thyroid-hormone replacement therapy
Minor Side Effects: Change in appetite; diarrhea; headache; irritability. Most of these side effects, if they occur, should subside as your body adjusts to the medication. Tell your doctor about any that are persistent or particularly bothersome.
Major Side Effects: In overdose: chest pain; fever; heat intolerance; insomnia; leg cramps; menstrual irregularities; nervousness; rapid, pounding heartbeat; shortness of breath; sweating; trembling; vomiting; weight loss. Notify your doctor if you notice any major side effects.
Contraindications: There are no absolute contraindications for this drug, but special care should be taken if it is used by persons who have recently had a heart attack or who have an overactive thyroid gland or malfunctioning adrenal glands. Be sure to inform your doctor if any of these conditions applies to you.
Warnings: This drug should be used cautiously by people who have heart disease, high blood pressure, kidney disease, or diabetes. Be sure your doctor knows if any of these conditions applies to you. • This drug interacts with cholestyramine, epinephrine, digitalis, phenytoin, oral contraceptives, oral anticoagulants, and antidiabetics; if you are currently taking any drugs of these types, consult your doctor about their use. If you are unsure of the type or contents of your medications, ask your doctor or pharmacist. • While taking this drug, do not take any nonprescription item for weight control, cough, cold, or sinus problems without first checking with your doctor. • If you are taking digitalis in addition to this drug, watch carefully for symptoms of increased digitalis effects (e.g., nausea, blurred vision, palpitations), and notify your doctor immediately if any of these symptoms occur. • Periodic laboratory tests will be done while you are taking this drug in order to evaluate your response to them and guide dosage adjustments. • This drug should not be used to treat obesity. Using this drug in conjunction with appetite suppressants is particularly dangerous. Because this medication is used to supplement or replace thyroid hormone produced by the body, side effects are most often related to the dose. Thus, most side effects can be controlled by dosage adjustment. Be sure to follow your doctor's dosage instructions exactly.
Comments: Compliance with prescribed therapy is essential with this drug. Get into the habit of taking the drug at the same time each day, usually before breakfast. • Do not stop taking this drug without consulting your doctor. • Although many thyroid products are on the market, they are not all bioequivalent; that is, they may not all be absorbed into the bloodstream at the same rate or

have the same overall activity. To make sure you are receiving an equivalent product, don't change brands of this drug without first consulting your doctor or pharmacist. Thyroid hormone replacement therapy is usually continued for life. Learn about the thyroid gland and the symptoms of hypothyroidism (low thyroid hormone) versus hyperthyroidism (high thyroid hormone). Talk to your doctor, as this understanding will make you more informed regarding your therapy.

Tigan antiemetic

Ingredient: trimethobenzamide hydrochloride

Equivalent Products: Tebamide; T-Gen; Triban; Trimazide; Trimethobenzamide

Dosage Forms: Capsule: 100 mg; 250 mg. Pediatric suppository: 100 mg. Suppository: 200 mg

Use: Prevention and treatment of nausea and vomiting

Minor Side Effects: Blurred vision; diarrhea; dizziness; drowsiness; dry mouth; headache. Most of these side effects, if they occur, should subside as your body adjusts to the medication. Tell your doctor about any that are persistent or particularly bothersome.

Major Side Effects: Back pain; blurred vision; convulsions; dark urine; depression; disorientation; mouth sores; muscle cramps; rash; tremors; unusual hand or face movements; vomiting; yellowing of the eyes or skin. Notify your doctor if you notice any major side effects.

Contraindications: This drug should not be taken by people who are allergic to it or to local anesthetics such as lidocaine. Consult your doctor immediately if this drug has been prescribed for you and you have such an allergy. • The suppository form of this drug should not be given to newborn infants.

Warnings: This drug should be used with extreme caution in children for the treatment of vomiting. This drug is not recommended for treatment of uncomplicated vomiting in children; its use should be limited to prolonged vomiting of known cause. • This drug should be used cautiously by pregnant or nursing women. • This drug should be used with caution by patients (especially children and the elderly or debilitated) who have fever, viral infection, intestinal infection, or dehydration; or by persons with heart disease, glaucoma, kidney disease, ulcers, or prostate trouble. Be sure your doctor knows if any of these conditions applies to you. • To avoid excessive sedation, avoid taking alcohol and other depressive drugs while taking this drug. If you are unsure of the type or contents of your medications, ask your doctor or pharmacist. • This drug may cause drowsiness; avoid tasks that require alertness, such as driving a car or operating potentially dangerous equipment. • Notify your doctor if you develop signs of jaundice (yellowing of the eyes or skin, dark urine).

Comments: Capsules may be ineffective if vomiting has begun; suppositories should be used in such cases. • Chew gum or suck on ice chips or a piece of hard candy to reduce mouth dryness. • If severe vomiting is not relieved in 24 to 48 hours, contact your doctor.

Timolol Maleate antihypertensive, see Blocadren antihypertensive.

Timoptic, Timoptic-XE ophthalmic glaucoma preparations

Ingredient: timolol maleate

Dosage Form: Drop (content per ml): 0.25%; 0.5%

Uses: Treatment of some types of chronic glaucoma and ocular hypertension

Minor Side Effects: Mild eye irritation; temporary blurred vision. These side effects, if they occur, should subside as your body adjusts to the medication. Tell your doctor if they persist or are particularly bothersome.

Major Side Effects: Major side effects are rare when this product is used correctly. However, rare occurrences of anxiety, confusion, depression, difficulty breathing, dizziness, drowsiness, generalized rash, indigestion, loss of appetite, nausea, weakness, and slight reduction of the resting heart rate have been observed in some users of this drug. Notify your doctor if you notice any major side effects.

Contraindication: This drug should not be used by people who are allergic to it. Consult your doctor immediately if this drug has been prescribed for you and you have such an allergy.

Warnings: This drug should be used with caution by people with bronchial asthma, lung disease, diabetes, emphysema, hyperthyroidism, myasthenia gravis, certain types of heart disease, or narrow-angle glaucoma. Be sure your doctor knows if any of these conditions applies to you. • This drug is not recommended for use by children as the safety and efficacy in children have not been established. • If you are pregnant, be sure your doctor knows about your condition before you take this drug. This drug should be used only if clearly needed during pregnancy or while breast-feeding. • This drug should be used with caution in conjunction with quinidine, verapamil, or epinephrine. • People who are also taking beta blockers by mouth should use this drug with caution. If you are presently taking any drugs of this type, consult your doctor about their use. If you are unsure of the type or contents of your medications, ask your doctor or pharmacist.

Comments: Unlike other drugs used to treat glaucoma, this agent needs to be administered only once (Timoptic-XE) or twice a day (Timoptic). To administer eye drops, lie or sit down and tilt your head back. Carefully pull your lower eyelid down to form a pouch. Hold the dropper close to, but not touching, the eyelid, and place the prescribed number of drops into the pouch. Do not place the drops directly on the eyeball; you probably will blink and lose the medication. Close your eye and keep it shut for a few moments. If you miss a dose, apply it as soon as it is remembered unless it is near the time for the next dose. In that case, skip the missed dose and resume your usual dosing schedule. Do not double the dose to catch up. • Be careful about the contamination of drops used for the eyes. Wash your hands before using eye drops. Do not touch dropper to your eye. Do not wash or wipe the dropper before replacing it in the bottle. Close the bottle tightly to keep out moisture. Store at room temperature away from heat and direct sunlight. If the eye drops become discolored or contain particles, discard the unused medication and begin using a fresh bottle. Check the expiration date on the drug label and discard any unused drug after that date. • This product is also available in a white plastic ophthalmic dispenser with a controlled-drop tip, called an Ocumeter. Your pharmacist can give you details on this product. • This medication may sting at first, but this is normal and usually goes away after continued use. Like other eye drops, this drug may cause some temporary clouding or blurring of vision. This symptom will go away quickly. • If you are using more than one type of eye product, wait at least five minutes between administration of different medications.

Tobrex ophthalmic antibiotic

Ingredient: tobramycin
Dosage Forms: Ointment (per gram); Solution (per ml): tobramycin, 0.3%
Use: Short-term treatment of superficial bacterial infections of the eye

Minor Side Effects: Headache; mild eye irritation; redness; stinging; tearing; temporary blurred vision. Most of these side effects, if they occur, should subside as your body adjusts to the medication. Tell your doctor about any that are persistent or particularly bothersome.

Major Side Effects: Decreased vision; eyelid swelling; eye pain; itching. Notify your doctor if you notice any major side effects.

Contraindications: This drug should not be used by persons allergic to tobramycin or aminoglycoside antibiotics. Consult your doctor immediately if this drug has been prescribed for you and you have such an allergy.

Warnings: This drug must be used cautiously by pregnant women. • Nursing mothers who must take this drug should stop nursing. • Use this drug only for the condition for which it was prescribed. • Upon instillation of this drug, there may be mild and temporary burning and stinging. Vision may also be blurred for a short time. If the effects continue or worsen, contact your doctor. • Symptoms should improve within a few days. If they persist or worsen, contact your doctor.

Comments: Use this exactly as prescribed for as long as prescribed, even if symptoms disappear within that time. Stopping therapy early can lead to another infection. If you miss a dose, apply it as soon as it is remembered unless it is near the time for the next dose. In that case, skip the missed dose and resume your usual dosing schedule. Do not double the dose to catch up. To administer eye drops, lie or sit down and tilt your head back. Carefully pull your lower eyelid down to form a pouch. Hold the dropper close to, but not touching, the eyelid, and place the prescribed number of drops into the pouch. Do not place the drops directly on the eyeball; you probably will blink and lose the medication. Close your eye and keep it shut for a few moments. To administer eye gel, lie or sit down and tilt your head back. Carefully pull your lower eyelid down to form a pouch. Gently squeeze the tube to release a small amount of the gel. With a sweeping motion, place the gel into the pouch. Do not place it directly on the eyeball; you probably will blink and lose the medication. Slowly roll your eyeball around to spread the gel. If you are using other eye medications in addition to the gel, use eye drops at least five minutes before using the gel. • Be careful about the contamination of medications used for the eyes. Wash your hands before administering eye medications. Do not touch the dropper or ointment tube to your eye. Do not wash or wipe the dropper before replacing it in the bottle. Close the bottle tightly to keep out moisture. Store at room temperature away from heat and direct sunlight. If the eye drops or gel become discolored or contain particles, discard the unused medication and begin using a fresh bottle or tube. Check the expiration date on the drug label and discard any unused drug after that date.

Tofranil antidepressant

Ingredient: imipramine hydrochloride
Equivalent Products: Imipramine HCl; Janimine
Dosage Form: Tablet: 10 mg; 25 mg; 50 mg (see Comments)
Uses: Control of bed-wetting (in children); relief of depression

Minor Side Effects: Agitation; anxiety; blurred vision; change in sex drive; constipation; cramps; diarrhea; dizziness; drowsiness; dry mouth; fatigue; headache; heartburn; increased appetite; increased sensitivity to light; insomnia; nausea; peculiar tastes in the mouth; restlessness; stomach upset; sweating; vomiting; weakness; weight loss or gain. Most of these side effects, if they occur, should subside as your body adjusts to the medicine. Tell your doctor about any that are persistent or particularly bothersome.

Major Side Effects: Chest pain; confusion; convulsions; dark urine; delusions; difficulty in urinating; enlarged or painful breasts (in both sexes); fainting; fever; fluid retention; hair loss; hallucinations; high or low blood pressure; impotence; loss of balance; mood changes; mouth sores; nervousness; nightmares; numbness in fingers or toes; rapid, pounding heartbeat; rapid pulse; rash; reduced concentration; ringing in the ears; sleep disorders; sore throat; testicular swelling; tremors; uncoordinated movements; unusual bleeding or bruising; yellowing of the eyes or skin. Notify your doctor if you notice any major side effects.

Contraindications: This drug should not be taken by people who are allergic to it or by anyone who has recently had a heart attack. This drug should not be taken by people who are using monoamine oxidase inhibitors or have used such medications within the past two weeks (ask your pharmacist if you are unsure). Consult your doctor immediately if this drug has been prescribed for you and any of these conditions applies.

Warnings: This drug should be used cautiously by the elderly and by people who have glaucoma, high blood pressure, enlarged prostate, porphyria, intestinal blockage, heart disease (certain types), epilepsy, thyroid disease, liver or kidney disease, or a history of urinary retention problems. Pregnant or nursing women, people who receive electroshock therapy, and those who use drugs that lower blood pressure should also use this drug cautiously. Be sure your doctor knows if any of these conditions applies to you. • Elderly persons should use this drug with caution. Reduced doses may be prescribed for persons in this age group. • This drug must be used cautiously by children. It is not recommended for use in children under six years of age. • This drug interacts with alcohol, amphetamines, antihypertensives, barbiturates, central nervous system depressants, cimetidine, clonidine, anticholinergics, epinephrine, guanethidine, methylphenidate hydrochloride, monoamine oxidase inhibitors, oral anticoagulants, and phenylephrine; if you are currently taking any drugs of these types, consult your doctor about their use. If you are unsure of the type or contents of your medications, ask your doctor or pharmacist. Smoking affects this drug. Be sure your doctor knows if you smoke. • While taking this drug, do not take any nonprescription item for weight control, cough, cold, or sinus problems without first checking with your doctor. • If you are going to have any type of surgery, be sure your doctor knows that you are taking this drug; the drug should be discontinued before surgery. (Consult your doctor before stopping the drug.) • Notify your doctor if you experience abrupt changes in mood or if you have a sore throat with fever. • Notify your doctor if you develop signs of jaundice (yellowing of the eyes or skin, dark urine). • This drug may cause drowsiness; avoid tasks that require alertness, such as driving a car or operating potentially dangerous equipment. • To prevent excessive drowsiness, avoid the use of alcohol or other drugs that have sedative properties. • Do not stop taking this drug suddenly without consulting your doctor. It may be necessary to reduce your dosage gradually.

Comments: Take this medication exactly as prescribed. • This drug may be taken with food to lessen stomach upset. • If this drug is being used to control bed-wetting, it should be taken one hour before bedtime. • The effects of therapy with this drug may not be apparent for at least two weeks. Your doctor may adjust your dosage frequently during the first few months of therapy in order to find the best dose for you. • Many people receive as much benefit from taking a single dose of this drug at bedtime as from taking multiple doses throughout the day. Talk to your doctor about this dosage plan. • This drug may cause you to be especially sensitive to the sun, so avoid exposure to sunlight as much as possible, and wear protective clothing and an effective sunscreen when outdoors. • To avoid dizziness or light-headedness when you stand, contract and relax the muscles of your legs for a few moments before rising. Do this by pushing one foot against the floor while raising the other foot slightly, alternating feet so that you are pumping your legs in a pedaling motion. • Chew gum or suck on ice chips or a piece of hard candy to reduce mouth dryness. • Tofranil antidepressant is also available in capsules that contain larger doses of the drug than the tablets. The capsule form, called Tofranil-PM, should not be used by children because the greater potency increases the risk of overdose. • This drug is similar in action to other tricyclic antidepressants. If this drug is ineffective or not well tolerated, your doctor may have you try another.

Tolbutamide oral antidiabetic, see Orinase oral antidiabetic.

Tolectin anti-inflammatory

Ingredient: tolmetin sodium
Dosage Forms: Capsule: 400 mg. Tablet: 200 mg; 600 mg
Use: Relief of pain and swelling due to arthritis
Minor Side Effects: Bloating; blurred vision; constipation; diarrhea; dizziness; drowsiness; gas; headache; heartburn; insomnia; nausea; nervousness; stomach upset; vomiting; weakness. Most of these side effects, if they occur, should subside as your body adjusts to the medication. Tell your doctor about any that are persistent or particularly bothersome.
Major Side Effects: Black or tarry stools; breathing difficulties; chest pain; depression; difficulty urinating; easy bruising or bleeding; fluid retention; itching; rapid weight gain; rash; ringing in the ears; sore throat; swelling of the hands or feet, especially at night; ulcers; visual disturbances. Notify your doctor if you notice any major side effects.
Contraindications: This drug should not be taken by people who are allergic to it or to aspirin or similar drugs. Consult your doctor immediately if this drug has been prescribed for you and you have such an allergy.
Warnings: This drug should be used with extreme caution by patients with upper gastrointestinal tract disease, peptic ulcer, heart disease (certain types), high blood pressure, kidney disease, or bleeding diseases. Be sure your doctor knows if any of these conditions applies to you. • Use of this drug by pregnant women, nursing mothers, and children under two years of age is not recommended. • This drug should be used cautiously in conjunction with aspirin, diuretics, oral anticoagulants, oral antidiabetics, phenytoin, and probenecid. If you are currently taking any drugs of these types, consult your doctor. If you are unsure of the type or contents of your medications, ask your doctor or pharmacist. • Do not take aspirin or alcohol while taking this drug without first consulting your doctor. • This drug may cause drowsiness; avoid tasks that require alertness, such as driving a car or operating potentially dangerous equipment. • Notify your doctor if skin rash; itching; black, tarry stools; swelling of the hands or feet; or persistent headache occur. • Persons taking this drug for prolonged periods should have regular eye examinations.
Comments: If this drug upsets your stomach, take it with food, milk, or antacids (except sodium bicarbonate). • You should note improvement of your condition soon after you start using this drug; however, full benefit may not be obtained for one to two weeks. It is important not to stop taking this drug even though symptoms have diminished or disappeared. Do not take it only when you feel pain. Its benefit is based on continued, regular use. • This drug is not a substitute for rest, physical therapy, or other measures recommended by your doctor to treat your condition. • This drug is similar in action to other anti-inflammatory agents, such as Indocin, Naprosyn, Lodine, and ibuprofen. If one of

these drugs is not well tolerated, your doctor may have you try the others in order to find the drug that is best for you.

Toprol XL antihypertensive and antianginal, see Lopressor antihypertensive and antianginal.

Toradol analgesic

Ingredient: ketorolac
Dosage Form: Tablet: 10 mg
Use: Relief of mild to moderate pain
Minor Side Effects: Bloating; blurred vision; constipation; diarrhea; dizziness; drowsiness; gas; headache; heartburn; insomnia; nausea; nervousness; stomach upset; vomiting; weakness. Most of these side effects, if they occur, should subside as your body adjusts to the medication. Tell your doctor about any that are persistent or particularly bothersome.

Major Side Effects: Black or tarry stools; breathing difficulties; chest pain; depression; difficulty urinating; easy bruising or bleeding; fluid retention; itching; rapid weight gain; rash; ringing in the ears; sore throat; swelling of the hands or feet, especially at night; ulcers; visual disturbances. Notify your doctor if you notice any major side effects.

Contraindications: This drug should not be taken by people who are allergic to it or to aspirin or anti-inflammatory drugs. Consult your doctor immediately if this drug has been prescribed for you and you have such an allergy.

Warnings: This drug should be used with extreme caution by patients with upper gastrointestinal tract disease, peptic ulcer, heart disease (certain types), high blood pressure, kidney disease, or bleeding diseases. Be sure your doctor knows if any of these conditions applies to you. • Use of this drug by pregnant women, nursing mothers, and children is not recommended. • This drug should be used cautiously in conjunction with aspirin, diuretics, oral anticoagulants, oral antidiabetics, phenytoin, and probenecid. If you are currently taking any drugs of these types, consult your doctor. If you are unsure of the type or contents of your medications, ask your doctor or pharmacist. • Do not take aspirin or alcohol while taking this drug without first consulting your doctor. • This drug may cause drowsiness; avoid tasks that require alertness, such as driving a car or operating potentially dangerous equipment. • If you feel dizzy or light-headed, sit or lie down for a while; get up slowly from a sitting or reclining position, and be careful on stairs. • Notify your doctor if skin rash; itching; black, tarry stools; swelling of the hands or feet; or persistent headache occur. • Persons taking this drug for prolonged periods should have eye examinations on a regular basis.

Comments: If this drug upsets your stomach, take it with food, milk or antacids. Take this medication as directed. Do not increase your dose, take this more often or continue taking this for longer than prescribed. This medication should only be used for the condition for which it was prescribed. Do not use this to treat just any pain. • This drug is not a substitute for rest, physical therapy, or other measures recommended by your doctor to treat your condition. • This drug is similar in action to anti-inflammatory agents, such as Indocin, Naprosyn, Lodine, and ibuprofen. If one of these drugs is not well tolerated, your doctor may have you try the others in order to find the drug that is best for you.

Totacillin antibiotic, see ampicillin antibiotic.

T-Phyl bronchodilator, see theophylline bronchodilator.

Trandate antihypertensive, see **Normodyne** antihypertensive.

Transderm-Nitro transdermal antianginal, see nitroglycerin transdermal antianginal.

Tranxene antianxiety and anticonvulsant

Ingredient: clorazepate dipotassium
Equivalent Products: Clorazepate Dipotassium; Gen-XENE
Dosage Forms: Capsule: 3.75 mg; 7.5 mg; 15 mg. Sustained-action tablet: 11.25 mg; 22.5 mg. Tablet: 3.75 mg; 7.5 mg; 15 mg
Uses: Treatment of anxiety disorders and symptoms of anxiety; relief of symptoms of withdrawal from alcohol addiction; treatment of seizure disorders
Minor Side Effects: Constipation; decreased sexual desire; diarrhea; dizziness; drowsiness; dry mouth; fatigue; headache; heartburn; insomnia; irritability; loss of appetite; nausea; nervousness; sweating; yellowing of skin or eyes. Most of these side effects, if they occur, should subside as your body adjusts to the medication. Tell your doctor about any that are persistent or particularly bothersome.
Major Side Effects: Blurred vision; breathing difficulties; confusion; dark urine; depression; difficulty swallowing; difficulty urinating; double vision; drooling; fever; hallucinations; low blood pressure; menstrual irregularities; rapid, pounding heartbeat; rash; slow heartbeat; slurred speech; sore throat; tremors; yellowing of the eyes or skin. Notify your doctor if you become aware of any major side effects.
Contraindications: This drug should not be taken by people who are allergic to it or by those who have acute narrow-angle glaucoma. Consult your doctor immediately if this drug has been prescribed for you and either condition applies.
Warnings: This drug is not recommended for use by people who are severely depressed, those who have severe mental illness, or those under the age of nine. This drug should be used cautiously by people with a history of drug dependence; by pregnant or nursing women; by the elderly or debilitated; and by people with impaired liver or kidney function, lung disease, epilepsy, porphyria, or myasthenia gravis. Be sure your doctor knows if any of these conditions applies to you. • This drug should not be taken with alcohol or other central nervous system depressants such as narcotic pain relievers or sedatives; serious adverse reactions may develop. This drug should be used cautiously in conjunction with cimetidine, phenytoin, or oral anticoagulants. If you are currently taking any drugs of these types, consult your doctor about their use. If you are unsure about the type or contents of your medications, ask your doctor or pharmacist. • Do not take it with an antacid, which may retard absorption of the drug. Space dosing of this drug and an antacid by 30 minutes. • This drug may cause drowsiness, especially during the first few days of therapy; avoid tasks that require alertness, such as driving a car or operating potentially dangerous equipment. • Notify your doctor if you develop signs of jaundice (yellowing of the eyes or skin, dark urine).
Comments: Take this medication with food or a full glass of water to lessen stomach upset. • Do not stop taking this drug suddenly without first consulting your doctor. If you have been taking this drug regularly, your dosage will have to be reduced gradually according to your doctor's directions. • This drug has the potential to become habit-forming and must be used with caution. Do not increase the dose without first consulting your doctor. • Never take the sustained-action tablets more frequently than your doctor prescribes; a serious overdose may result. • Chew gum or suck on ice chips or a piece of hard

candy to reduce mouth dryness. • This drug may be used to relieve nervousness. It is effective for this purpose, but it is important to try to remove the cause of the anxiety as well.

Trental hemorrheologic (blood flow promoter)

Ingredient: pentoxifylline
Dosage Form: Sustained-release tablet: 400 mg
Use: Promotes blood flow in the treatment of certain blood vessel diseases
Minor Side Effects: Bloating; blurred vision; brittle fingernails; constipation; diarrhea; dizziness; drowsiness; dry mouth; earache; headache; nasal congestion; nausea; stomach upset; taste disturbances; thirst; tremors; weakness; weight change. Most of these side effects, if they occur, should subside as your body adjusts to the medication. Tell your doctor about any that are persistent or particularly bothersome.

Major Side Effects: Bleeding or bruising; blood disorders; breathing difficulties; chest pain; confusion; dark urine; earache; faintness; fluid retention; flushing; hallucinations; low blood pressure; nosebleed; rapid, pounding heartbeat; palpitations; rash; sleeping disorders; sore throat; swollen neck glands; yellowing of the eyes or skin. Notify your doctor if you notice any major side effects.

Contraindications: This drug should not be used by persons allergic to it or to caffeine, theophylline, or theobromine. Consult your doctor immediately if this drug has been prescribed for you and you have any such allergy. • This drug is not recommended for use by children under 18 years of age or by nursing mothers.

Warnings: This drug must be used cautiously by pregnant women and persons with coronary artery disease or kidney disease. Consult your doctor if any of these conditions applies to you. • This drug may interact with antihypertensive medications. This medication should be used cautiously by persons taking warfarin, aspirin, or salicylates. If you are currently taking any drugs of these types, consult your doctor about their use. If you are unsure about the type or contents of your medications, ask your doctor or pharmacist. • While you are taking this drug, do not take any nonprescription medications without checking with your doctor or pharmacist. • Notify your doctor if you develop signs of jaundice (yellowing of the eyes or skin, dark urine).

Comments: This drug is taken with food unless otherwise prescribed. • The tablets are sustained release and must be swallowed whole; do not crush or chew them. • It may take two to four weeks before the effects of this drug are evident. Therapy is usually continued for at least eight weeks. • Side effects should subside with continued treatment. If they persist or become bothersome, contact your physician. An alteration in dosage may alleviate side effects. Do not, however, stop taking this drug or change the dose without your doctor's advice.

Triamterene with hydrochlorothiazide diuretic and antihypertensive, see Dyazide and Maxzide diuretic and antihypertensive.

Triban antiemetic, see Tigan antiemetic.

Tri-K potassium replacement, see potassium replacement.

Trimazide antiemetic, see Tigan antiemetic.

Trimethobenzamide antiemetic, see Tigan antiemetic.

Trimox 250 antibiotic, see amoxicillin antibiotic.

Trimox 500 antibiotic, see amoxicillin antibiotic.

Trinalin antihistamine and decongestant

Ingredients: pseudoephedrine sulfate; azatadine maleate
Dosage Form: Sustained-release tablet: pseudoephedrine sulfate, 120 mg and azatadine maleate, 1 mg
Use: For the relief of symptoms of hay fever, allergy, and upper respiratory tract congestion
Minor Side Effects: Anxiety; blurred vision; constipation; diarrhea; dizziness; drowsiness; dry mouth; headache; insomnia; irritability; nausea; rash; reduced sweating; sedation; stomach upset; weakness. Most of these side effects, if they occur, should subside as your body adjusts to the medication. Tell your doctor about any that are persistent or particularly bothersome.
Major Side Effects: Abdominal cramps; breathing difficulties; chest pain; confusion; difficulty urinating; headache; high blood pressure; loss of coordination; low blood pressure; rapid, pounding heartbeat; sore throat; unusual bleeding or bruising. Notify your doctor if you notice any major side effects.
Contraindications: This drug should not be used to treat asthma or symptoms of lower respiratory infections. This drug should not be taken by persons allergic to it or to other antihistamines. If you are allergic to antihistamines, check with your doctor or pharmacist before taking this drug. • This drug should not be used by persons with narrow-angle glaucoma, urinary retention, hyperthyroidism, severe hypertension, or severe heart disease or by persons concurrently taking monoamine oxidase inhibitors (ask your pharmacist if you are unsure). Consult your doctor immediately if this drug has been prescribed for you and any of these conditions applies. • This drug should not be taken by children under 12 years of age. • This drug should be used with extreme caution during pregnancy. Discuss the benefits and risks with your doctor. • Use of this drug by nursing mothers is not recommended.
Warnings: This drug should be used cautiously by persons with peptic ulcer, blood vessel disease, high blood pressure, or diabetes and by persons taking digitalis or oral anticoagulants. If you are unsure of the type or contents of your medications, ask your doctor or pharmacist. • This drug must be used cautiously by persons over 60 years of age who may be more likely to experience dizziness, sedation, and low blood pressure. • To prevent oversedation, avoid the use of alcohol and other drugs having sedative properties. • While taking this drug, do not take any nonprescription item for weight control, cough, cold, or sinus problems without first checking with your doctor or pharmacist; such items may contain ingredients similar to this drug. • Because this drug causes drowsiness, avoid tasks that require alertness, such as driving a car or operating potentially dangerous equipment.
Comments: Because this is a sustained-release product, the tablets must be swallowed whole; do not crush or chew them. • Never increase your dose or take this drug more frequently than prescribed; a serious overdose could result. • Chew gum or suck on ice chips or a piece of hard candy to reduce mouth dryness. • Because this drug reduces sweating, avoid excessive work or exercise in hot weather. • If this drug causes stomach upset, take it with food. • There are many drugs of this type on the market that vary slightly in ingredients and amounts. Some are available without a prescription. Your doctor or pharmacist can help select an antihistamine and decongestant medication best for you.

Tussi-Organidin cough suppressant and expectorant

Ingredients: codeine phosphate; iodinated glycerol
Equivalent Products: Iodinated glycerol and codeine; Iophen-C; Iotuss; Par Glycerol C (see Comments)
Dosage Form: Liquid (content per 5 ml teaspoon): codeine phosphate, 10 mg and iodinated glycerol, 30 mg; (see Comments)
Use: Symptomatic relief of cough
Minor Side Effects: Acne flare-up; blurred vision; constipation; dizziness; drowsiness; headache; nausea; stomach upset; vomiting. Most of these side effects, if they occur, should subside as your body adjusts to the medication. Tell your doctor in the event that any side effects appear that are persistent or particularly bothersome.
Major Side Effects: Breathing difficulties; difficulty swallowing; false sense of well-being; impaired coordination; rash; thyroid gland enlargement. Notify your doctor if you notice any major side effects.
Contraindications: This drug should not be used by pregnant or nursing women, newborns, or persons sensitive (allergic) to codeine, narcotic pain relievers, or iodides. Call your doctor immediately if any of these conditions applies.
Warnings: This drug should be used cautiously by persons with a history or any evidence of thyroid disease and by children with cystic fibrosis. Be sure your doctor knows if either of these conditions applies. • This drug interacts with lithium and antithyroid drugs. If you are currently taking any drugs of these types, consult your doctor about their use. If you are unsure about the type or contents of your medications, ask your doctor or pharmacist. • To avoid oversedation, avoid alcohol and other central nervous system depressants while taking this drug. • Codeine has the potential to be habit-forming and must be used with caution. Do not take this drug more frequently than prescribed, and do not increase the dose without consulting your doctor. • While taking this medication, do not take any nonprescription item for weight control, coughs, colds, or sinus problems without first checking with your doctor or pharmacist. • If you develop a rash while taking this medication, stop using it and call your doctor; you may be sensitive to the drug. • This drug may cause a flare-up of acne in adolescents. • This drug may cause drowsiness; avoid tasks that require alertness, such as driving a car or operating other potentially dangerous equipment.
Comments: An expectorant helps to break up and clear mucous plugs. If you need an expectorant, you need more moisture in your environment. Use of a vaporizer or humidifier may be helpful. Also, drink nine to ten glasses of water daily. • Tussi-Organidin DM is very similar in action to this product. The DM formulation contains dextromethorphan instead of codeine phosphate, a narcotic. Dextromethorphan is an ingredient that works as a cough suppressant. This may be an alternative to persons sensitive to the effects of narcotics.

Twin-K potassium replacement, see potassium replacement.

Tylenol with Codeine analgesic, see acetaminophen with codeine analgesic.

Tylox analgesic, see Percocet analgesic.

UAD Otic steroid and antibiotic, see Cortisporin Otic steroid and antibiotic.

ULR-LA decongestant and expectorant, see Entex LA decongestant and expectorant.

Ultracef antibiotic, see Duricef antibiotic.

Uniphyl bronchodilator, see theophylline bronchodilator.

Uroplus DS, Uroplus SS antibacterials, see Bactrim and Bactrim DS antibacterials.

Utimox antibiotic, see amoxicillin antibiotic.

Valisone topical steroid hormone

Ingredient: betamethasone valerate
Equivalent Products: betamethasone valerate; Betatrex; Beta-Val
Dosage Forms: Cream: 0.01%; 0.1%. Lotion: 0.1%. Ointment: 0.1%
Use: Relief of skin inflammation associated with conditions such as dermatitis, eczema, and poison ivy

Minor Side Effects: Acne; burning sensation; dryness; irritation of the affected area; itching; rash; redness. Most of these side effects, if they occur, should subside as your body adjusts to the medication. Tell your doctor about any that are persistent or particularly bothersome.

Major Side Effects: Blistering; increased hair growth; loss of skin color; secondary infection; skin wasting. Notify your doctor if you notice any major side effects.

Contraindications: This drug should not be used by people who are allergic to it or by those with severe circulatory system disorders or infections of the skin. This drug should not be used in the ear if the eardrum is perforated. Consult your doctor immediately if this drug has been prescribed for you and any of these conditions applies.

Warnings: This drug should be used with caution during pregnancy. • If irritation develops when using this drug, immediately discontinue use and notify your doctor. • These products are not for use in the eyes or other mucous membranes. • Do not use this product with an occlusive wrap unless your doctor directs you to do so. Systemic absorption of this drug will be increased if extensive areas of the body are treated, particularly if occlusive bandages are used. If it is necessary for you to use this drug under a wrap, follow your doctor's instructions exactly; do not leave the wrap in place longer than specified. If this drug is being used in the diaper area, avoid tight-fitting diapers or plastic pants, which can increase absorption of the drug. • Use this product to treat only the condition for which it was prescribed. Using topical steroids to treat an infection may worsen the infection.

Comments: Use this drug exactly as prescribed. Do not use it more often or for a longer period than your doctor prescribes. • The ointment form is probably better for dry or scaling skin. If the affected area is extremely dry or is scaling the skin may be gently washed and patted dry. The skin should be left slightly moist when the medication is applied. • A mild, temporary stinging sensation may occur after this medication is applied. If this persists, contact your doctor. • If the condition worsens while using this drug, notify your doctor.

Valium antianxiety, anticonvulsant, and muscle relaxant

Ingredient: diazepam
Equivalent Products: Diazepam; Valrelease

Dosage Forms: Solution (content per ml): 1 mg; 5 mg. Sustained-release capsule: 15 mg (see Comments). Tablet: 2 mg; 5 mg; 10 mg

Uses: Relief of anxiety symptoms and anxiety disorders, muscle spasms, convulsive disorders, and symptoms of withdrawal from alcohol addiction

Minor Side Effects: Constipation; depression; diarrhea; dizziness; drowsiness; dry mouth; fatigue; headache; heartburn; increased salivation; loss of appetite; nausea; sweating; vomiting; weakness. Most of these side effects, if they occur, should subside over a period of time as your body adjusts to the medication. Be sure to inform your doctor about any that are persistent or particularly bothersome.

Major Side Effects: Blurred vision; breathing difficulties; confusion; dark urine; difficulty urinating; double vision; excitement; fever; hallucinations; low blood pressure; menstrual irregularities; rapid, pounding heartbeat; rash; slurred speech; sore throat; stimulation; tremors; uncoordinated movements; yellowing of the eyes or skin. Notify your doctor if you notice any major side effects.

Contraindications: This drug should not be given to children under six months of age. • This drug should not be taken by persons with certain types of glaucoma or by people who are allergic to it. Consult your doctor immediately if either condition applies to you.

Warnings: This drug should be used cautiously by people with epilepsy, respiratory problems, myasthenia gravis, porphyria, a history of drug abuse or psychotic disorder, or impaired liver or kidney function; by pregnant women; by children; and by the elderly or debilitated. Be sure your doctor knows if any of these conditions applies to you. Tell your doctor if you are breast-feeding an infant. This medication can pass into breast milk and cause excessive drowsiness, slowed heartbeat, and breathing difficulties in nursing infants. • This drug should be used cautiously in conjunction with cimetidine, oral anticoagulants, and phenytoin. If you are unsure about the types or contents of your medications, consult your doctor or pharmacist. • This drug should not be taken simultaneously with alcohol or other central nervous system depressants such as sedatives or narcotic pain relievers; serious adverse reactions may develop. • Do not stop taking this drug without informing your doctor. If you have been taking the drug regularly and wish to discontinue use, you must decrease the dose gradually, following your doctor's instructions. • This drug may cause drowsiness; avoid tasks that require alertness, such as driving a car or operating potentially dangerous equipment. If the drowsiness becomes severe or if you are lethargic, contact your doctor. There are other drugs that are similar in action to this one that may or may not cause this "hang-over" effect since they are shorter acting; talk to your doctor about the alternatives. • This drug has the potential to be habit-forming and must be used with caution. Tolerance may develop quickly; do not increase the dose without first consulting your doctor. • Notify your doctor if you develop signs of jaundice (yellowing of the eyes or skin, dark urine).

Comments: To lessen stomach upset, take with food or a full glass of water. • The sustained-release form must be swallowed whole; do not crush or chew the capsule. • The sustained-release form of this drug is available under the name Valrelease. • Chew gum or suck on ice chips or a piece of hard candy to reduce mouth dryness. • This drug is used to relieve anxiety. It is effective for this purpose, but it is important to make an effort to understand the cause of the anxiety as well.

Valrelease antianxiety, anticonvulsant, and muscle relaxant, see Valium antianxiety, anticonvulsant, and muscle relaxant.

CONSUMER GUIDE®

Vancenase, Vancenase AQ intranasal steroid and antiallergy

Ingredient: beclomethasone
Equivalent Products: Beconase; Beconase AQ
Dosage Forms: Nasal spray: 0.042%. Nasal inhaler (content per metered dose): 42 mcg
Uses: Treatment of allergic symptoms, such as runny nose, nasal congestion, post nasal drip, and sneezing, due to seasonal or chronic rhinitis; management of nasal polyps
Minor Side Effects: Change in senses of taste and smell; dry throat and nasal passages; headache; light-headedness; nasal burning and stinging; nasal congestion; nasal irritation; nausea; nosebleed; sneezing; sore throat; watery eyes. Most of these side effects, if they occur, should subside as your body adjusts to the medication. Tell your doctor about any that are persistent or particularly bothersome.
Major Side Effects: Breathing trouble; hives; nasal infection; rash; weakness. Notify your doctor if you notice any major side effects.
Contraindications: This drug should not be used by persons allergic to it or by persons who have an untreated nasal infection. Consult your doctor immediately if this drug has been prescribed for you and you have either of these conditions. • This drug is not recommended for use in children who are under six years of age.
Warnings: This drug must be used cautiously by persons with tuberculosis, viral infections, ocular herpes simplex, or nasal ulcers and by persons recovering from nasal trauma or surgery. Be sure your doctor knows if any of these conditions applies to you. • This drug is to be used in pregnant or nursing women only if clearly needed. Discuss the risks and benefits with your doctor. • This drug must be used cautiously by persons receiving oral steroid therapy and persons being switched from oral therapy to intranasal therapy. Report any increase in symptoms or feelings of weakness or fatigue to your doctor. A dosage adjustment may be necessary. In times of stress or under acute medical conditions, it may be necessary to supplement this medication with oral steroid therapy. It is recommended that you carry a medical identification card indicating you are taking this medication. • If symptoms do not improve within a few weeks or if they worsen with continued use, contact your doctor.
Comments: Take this drug exactly as prescribed. For maximum effect, it must be taken at regular intervals. It is not effective for immediate relief of symptoms. Although symptoms will improve in a few days, full benefit may not be obtained for one to two weeks of continuous use. • Do not stop taking this drug or increase your dose without your doctor's approval. Increasing the dose leads to an increase in side effects. • For best results, clear nasal passages of all secretions prior to using this drug. If you are also using a nasal decongestant spray, use the decongestant prior to this drug. The decongestant will help clear nasal passages ensuring adequate penetration of this drug. To use nasal medication, shake the container first. Do not tilt your head back. Instead, tilt your head forward slightly and insert the sprayer into one of your nostrils. Avoid touching the inner membrane, and keep the container in an upright position. Close the other nostril. Then squeeze the canister as you breath in gently through the open nostril. Continue to squeeze the sprayer until you have withdrawn it from your nose: This will prevent nasal mucus and bacteria from entering the plastic bottle and contaminating its contents. Then breathe out through your mouth. After you have used the prescribed number of sprays or inhalations in one or both nostrils, gently sniff two or three times. Wipe the applicator clean with a tissue or rinse it under cold water if so directed. • Patient instructions explaining the proper use of the nasal inhaler and nasal spray are

available and should be dispensed with your prescriptions. Ask your pharmacist for the information. Read it carefully and follow the instructions closely for best results. If you have any questions about the use of the nasal inhaler or nasal spray, ask your pharmacist. • Each spray and inhaler contains approximately 200 sprays.

Vanceril inhaled antiasthmatic

Ingredient: beclomethasone dipropionate
Equivalent Product: Beclovent
Dosage Form: Pressurized inhaler for oral use (content per one actuation from mouthpiece): 42 mcg
Use: Control of chronic asthma
Minor Side Effects: Coughing; dry mouth; dry throat; hoarseness; rash. Most of these side effects, if they occur, should subside as your body adjusts to the medication. Tell your doctor about any that are persistent or particularly bothersome.
Major Side Effects: Breathing difficulties; depression; mouth sores; muscle aches and pains; nosebleeds; sore throat or infections of the mouth or throat; weakness. Notify your doctor if you notice any major side effects.
Contraindications: This drug is a steroid. It should not be used in the initial treatment of severe asthma attacks where immediate measures are required, since it does not produce immediate effects. This drug should not be used by people who are allergic to it or by those who have reacted adversely to other steroids. It should not be used in the presence of a systemic fungal infection. Be sure your doctor knows if you have any of these infections.
Warnings: Pregnant women, nursing mothers, women of childbearing age, and children under the age of six should use this drug with caution. Consult your doctor immediately if this drug has been prescribed for you and any of these conditions applies. • If you have been taking oral steroids to control your asthma, conversion to therapy with this inhaled drug will have to be accomplished slowly. You will have to exercise special caution if you develop an infection, need to have surgery, or experience other injury. Talk with your doctor about this transition, and make sure you understand what you must do. You should carry a card with you that explains how your asthma is being treated in case an emergency arises and you are unable to explain it yourself. • This drug is not for rapid relief of an asthma attack (bronchospasm). If you have an asthma attack and your dilator drugs do not help, call your doctor. • The dosage of this drug should be monitored very carefully. Taking more of this drug than is recommended will probably not give you more relief over the long term. • If you develop mouth sores or a sore throat while taking this medication, call your doctor.
Comments: Use this drug exactly as prescribed. Do not use it more often than prescribed. Full benefit from this drug may not be apparent for two to four weeks. • Shake the canister well before use. • Rinsing your mouth before and after inhalation of this drug is advised in order to reduce irritation and dryness of mouth and throat. To use the inhaler, place the inhaler device two finger-widths away from the mouth. With your head tipped back slightly, depress the inhaler while taking a slow, deep breath. Hold it for ten seconds, then breathe out slowly. If more than one inhalation is used, wait at least one minute between inhalations. • Your pharmacist should dispense patient instructions with this drug that explain administration technique. • If you use a bronchodilator with this drug, use the bronchodilator first, wait a few minutes, then use this drug. This method has been shown to be the most effective and to have the least potential for toxicity. • The contents of one canister of this drug should

CONSUMER GUIDE®

provide at least 200 oral inhalations. • This drug is sealed in the canister under pressure. Do not puncture the canister. Do not store the canister near heat or an open flame. • This drug is not useful during acute asthma attacks. It is used to prevent attacks.

Vanex LA decongestant and expectorant, see Entex LA decongestant and expectorant.

Vaseretic diuretic and antihypertensive

Ingredient: hydrochlorothiazide; enalapril
Dosage Form: Tablet: Vaseretic 10-25: hydrochlorothiazide, 25 mg and enalapril, 10 mg
Uses: Treatment of high blood pressure and removal of fluid from tissues
Minor Side Effects: Constipation; cramps; cough; deceased sexual desire; diarrhea; dizziness; drowsiness; fatigue; flushing; frequent urination; gas; headache; heartburn; indigestion; light-headedness; loss of appetite; nasal congestion; nausea; stomach upset; sun sensitivity; vomiting. Most of these side effects, if they occur, should subside as your body adjusts to the medication. However, tell your doctor about any that are persistent or particularly bothersome to you.
Major Side Effects: Blurred vision; breathing trouble; bruising; chest pain; chills; dark urine; decreased sexual ability; difficulty urinating; elevated blood sugar; fainting; fast pulse; fever; fluid retention; joint pain; muscle aches; muscle spasm; nosebleed; palpitations; shortness of breath; skin rash; sore throat; thirst; tingling of the fingers or toes; yellowing of the eyes or skin. Notify your doctor if you notice any major side effects.
Contraindications: This drug should not be taken by people who are allergic to either ingredient or to sulfa drugs, by people with kidney disease, or by people who are unable to urinate. Consult your doctor immediately if this medication has been prescribed for you and any of these conditions applies. • This drug should not be used by any woman who is pregnant, who thinks she is pregnant, or who intends to become pregnant while taking this. Use of this drug during pregnancy has resulted in fetal abnormalities. Notify your doctor immediately if you suspect you are pregnant.
Warnings: This drug should be used cautiously by the elderly, nursing women, children, and by people with kidney trouble, liver disease, diabetes, or blood disorders. Be sure your doctor knows if any of these conditions applies to you. • This drug should be used with caution in conjunction with other medicines. Inform your doctor if you are taking any other antihypertensive drugs, diuretics, digoxin, lithium, indomethacin, allopurinol, or potassium supplements. If you are unsure of the type or contents of your medications, ask your doctor or pharmacist. • While taking this drug, do not take any nonprescription item for weight control, cough, cold, allergy, or sinus problems without first checking with your doctor; such items may contain ingredients that can increase blood pressure. • While taking this drug, you should limit your consumption of alcoholic beverages, which can increase dizziness and other side effects. • This drug causes drowsiness and light-headedness, especially during the first few days of use; avoid tasks requiring alertness, such as driving a car or operating potentially dangerous equipment. • Notify your doctor if you develop dark urine or yellowing of the skin or eyes. It may be a sign of jaundice indicating a possible change in the dose. This medication increases sensitivity to the sun. Avoid prolonged sun exposure and wear a protective sunscreen when outdoors.
Comments: Take this drug exactly as directed. Do not take extra doses or skip a dose without consulting your doctor first. • Do not discontinue taking this

medication unless your doctor directs you to do so. It is important to continue taking this medication even if you do not feel sick. Most people with high blood pressure do not have symptoms and do not feel ill; therefore, it is easy to forget or stop taking the medication. • Mild side effects (e.g., nasal congestion, headache) are most noticeable during the first two weeks of therapy and become less bothersome as your body adjusts to the medication. • Taking this medication at bedtime may make the side effects more tolerable. Talk to your doctor about the dose schedule. • To avoid dizziness or light-headedness when you stand, contract and relax the muscles of your legs for a few moments before rising. Do this by pushing one foot against the floor while raising the other foot slightly, alternating feet so that you are pumping your legs in a pedaling motion. • Diuretics are also called water pills. Diuretics help eliminate extra fluid that may build up, especially in the feet, causing swelling. As a result, this medication causes frequent urination. Expect this effect. • Learn how to monitor your pulse and blood pressure while taking this drug; discuss this with your doctor or pharmacist. As with all antihypertensive medications, they are most effective when used in conjunction with diet and lifestyle changes, such as exercise and stress reduction to control blood pressure. The medication does not cure high blood pressure. • Combination or fixed-dose medications are usually not prescribed as the first choice in the treatment of high blood pressure. Patients should receive each ingredient alone, and if the response is adequate to the fixed dose contained in this product, then this combination medication can be substituted. The advantage of a combination product is added convenience to the patient.

Vasotec antihypertensive

Ingredient: enalapril maleate
Dosage Form: Tablet: 2.5 mg; 5 mg; 10 mg; 20 mg
Uses: Treatment of high blood pressure; management of heart failure
Minor Side Effects: Cough; decreased sexual desire; diarrhea; dizziness; fatigue; flushing; headache; insomnia; light-headedness; nasal congestion; nausea; sleep disturbances; stomach upset; sweating; taste disturbances. Most of these side effects, if they occur, should subside as your body adjusts to the medication. Tell your doctor about any that are persistent or particularly bothersome.

Major Side Effects: Blood disorders; blurred vision; breathing difficulties; chest pain; decreased sexual ability; depression; fever; impotence; irregular pulse; itching; low blood pressure; muscle aches or cramps; nervousness; rapid, pounding heartbeat; rash; sore throat; swelling of face, lips, and tongue; tingling in fingers and toes; vomiting. Notify your doctor if you notice any major side effects.

Contraindications: This drug should not be used by any woman who is pregnant, who thinks she is pregnant, or who intends to become pregnant. Use of this drug during pregnancy has resulted in fetal abnormalities. Notify your doctor immediately if you suspect you are pregnant. • This drug should not be used by persons who are allergic to it or to similar drugs such as captopril or lisinopril. Remind your doctor that you have such an allergy if this drug has been prescribed for you.

Warnings: This drug should be used cautiously by nursing mothers, persons with kidney disease, and diabetics. Be sure your doctor knows if any of these conditions applies to you. • Persons taking this drug in conjunction with other antihypertensive or heart medications should use it cautiously, especially during initial therapy. Dosage adjustments may be required to prevent blood pressure from dropping too low. • This drug must be used cautiously with

CONSUMER GUIDE®

agents that increase serum potassium, such as spironolactone, triamterene, amiloride, potassium supplements, and salt substitutes containing potassium. If you are currently taking any drugs of these types, consult your doctor about their use. Dosages may need to be adjusted. Your doctor may wish to test your blood periodically to check the potassium level. While taking this drug, you should limit your consumption of alcoholic beverages, which can increase dizziness and other side effects. • It is recommended that persons taking this drug for a prolonged period have periodic blood tests to monitor the effects of therapy. • Contact your doctor immediately if you notice swelling of the face, lips, tongue, or eyes, or have breathing difficulties while taking this drug. • If this medication makes you dizzy, avoid driving a car or operating potentially dangerous equipment. • Notify your doctor if you develop signs of an infection (sore throat, fever) while taking this drug. • Notify your doctor if you develop severe or persistent vomiting or diarrhea while taking this drug, since they can lead to dehydration. • If you have high blood pressure, do not take any nonprescription item for weight control, cough, cold, or sinus problems without consulting your doctor or pharmacist; such items can increase blood pressure. • Avoid prolonged work or exercise in hot weather, since excessive sweating can intensify the effects of this drug.

Comments: Take this drug as prescribed. Do not skip doses or take extra doses without consulting your doctor. • This drug may be taken with food if stomach upset occurs. • Do not stop taking this drug without consulting your doctor. It is important to continue taking this medication even if you do not feel sick. Most people with high blood pressure do not have symptoms and do not feel ill; therefore, it is easy to forget to take the medication. • Side effects of this drug are usually mild and transient. During the first few days you may experience light-headedness, which should subside as therapy continues. If light-headedness continues or becomes more pronounced, contact your doctor. • To avoid dizziness or light-headedness, contract and relax the muscles of your legs for a few moments before rising. Do this by pushing one foot against the floor while raising the other foot slightly, alternating feet so that you are pumping your feet in a pedaling motion. • Learn how to monitor your pulse and blood pressure while taking this drug. As with all antihypertensive medications, they are most effective when used in conjunction with diet and lifestyle changes, such as exercise and stress reduction to control blood pressure. The medication does not cure high blood pressure.

V-Cillin K antibiotic, see penicillin V potassium (penicillin VK) antibiotic.

Veetids antibiotic, see penicillin V potassium (penicillin VK) antibiotic.

Ventolin bronchodilator

Ingredient: albuterol
Equivalent Products: Albuterol; Proventil
Dosage Forms: Capsules for inhalation (Rotacaps): 200 mcg. Inhaler (content per actuation): 90 mcg. Solution for inhalation: 0.083%; 0.5%. Syrup (content per 5 ml teaspoon): 2 mg. Tablet: 2 mg; 4 mg. (see Comments)
Use: Prevention of bronchospasm in the treatment of asthma, bronchitis, or emphysema
Minor Side Effects: Dry mouth and throat; headache; hyperactivity; increased appetite; increased blood pressure; insomnia; nausea; nervousness; restlessness; stomach upset; sweating; tremor; unusual taste in mouth; weakness. Most of these side effects, if they occur at all, should gradually subside

over a period of time as your body makes an adjustment to the medication. Be sure to inform your physician about any that are persistent or particularly bothersome.

Major Side Effects: Breathing difficulties; chest pain; confusion; difficulty urinating; dizziness; flushing; irritability; muscle cramps; palpitations; rapid, pounding heartbeat; trembling; vomiting. Notify your doctor if you notice any major side effects.

Contraindication: This drug should not be taken by people who are allergic to it.

Warnings: This drug should be used with caution by people who have diabetes, high blood pressure, heart disease (certain types), or thyroid disease and by pregnant or nursing women. Be sure your doctor knows if any of these conditions applies to you. • This drug is not recommended for use in children under two years of age. • This drug has been shown to interact with amphetamines, monoamine oxidase inhibitors, antidepressants, beta blockers, and epinephrine. If you are currently using any drugs of these types, consult your doctor. If you are unsure of the type or contents of your medications, ask your doctor or pharmacist. • If your symptoms do not improve, if they get worse, or if you experience chest pain or breathing difficulties while using this drug, contact your doctor. Prolonged or excessive use of this drug may reduce its effectiveness. Take this drug as prescribed. Do not take it more often than prescribed, increase your dose, or stop taking it without first consulting your physician. It may be necessary to temporarily stop using this drug for a short period to ensure its effectiveness. • Excessive use can increase the risk of side effects or reduce the effectiveness of this medication. Notify your doctor if you experience dizziness or chest pain, or if you feel that the medication is not effective.

Comments: If stomach upset occurs, take the syrup or tablets with food or milk. • The Rotacaps are for use in a special inhaler. DO NOT SWALLOW THE CAPSULES. The contents of the capsules are to be inhaled. Make sure your doctor or pharmacist has demonstrated the use of the Rotacaps for you. • If you are using the inhaler or the Rotacaps form, make sure you know how to use it properly. Ask your pharmacist for an instruction sheet on the use of this product. • Shake the canister well before use. • Rinsing your mouth before and after inhalation of this drug is advised in order to reduce irritation and dryness of mouth and throat. To use the inhaler, place the inhaler device two fingerwidths away from the mouth. With you head tipped back slightly, depress the inhaler while taking a slow, deep breath. Hold it for ten seconds, then breathe out slowly. If two inhalations per dose are prescribed, wait at least one minute between inhalations for maximum effectiveness. • Your pharmacist should dispense patient instructions with this drug that explain administration technique. The contents of one canister of this drug should provide approximately 200 oral inhalations. Keep spray away from eyes. The drug is sealed in the canister under pressure. Store away from heat or open flame. Do not puncture, break, or burn the container. • Chew gum or suck on ice chips or a piece of hard candy to reduce mouth dryness. • Proventil is also available as a 4 mg extended-release tablet. As with all medications, store properly and keep out of the reach of children.

Verapamil HCI antianginal and antihypertensive, see Isoptin, Isoptin SR antianginal, antihypertensive and antiarrhythmic.

Verelan antianginal and antihypertensive, see Isoptin, Isoptin SR antianginal, antihypertensive, and antiarrhythmic.

Vicodin, Vicodin ES analgesics

Ingredients: hydrocodone bitartrate; acetaminophen

Equivalent Products: Amacodone; Anexsia; Anodynos-DHC; Bancap HC; Co-Gesic; Dolacet; Duocet; Duradyne DHC; Hydrocet; Hydrocodone Bitatrate and Acetaminophen; Hydrogesic; Hy-Phen; Lorcet; Lorcet-HD; Lorcet Plus; Lortab; Margesic; Medipain 5; Norcet; Panacet; Stagesic; T-Gesic; Zydone

Dosage Form: Tablet: Vicodin: hydrocodone bitartrate, 5 mg and acetaminophen, 500 mg; Vicodin ES: hydrocodone bitartrate, 7.5 mg and acetaminophen, 750 mg

Use: Relief of moderate to severe pain

Minor Side Effects: Anxiety; constipation; dizziness; drowsiness; fatigue; light-headedness; loss of appetite; nausea; sedation; stomach upset; sweating; vomiting; weakness. Most of these side effects, if they occur, should subside as your body adjusts to the medication. Tell your doctor about any that are persistent or particularly bothersome.

Major Side Effects: Breathing difficulties; confusion; dark urine; difficulty in urinating; excitation; false sense of well-being; fear; hallucinations; mood changes; rapid, pounding heartbeat; rash; restlessness; tremors; unpleasant emotions; yellowing of the eyes or skin. Notify your doctor if you notice any major side effects.

Contraindications: This drug should not be used by persons allergic to either of its components or to certain other narcotic analgesics. Consult your doctor immediately if this drug has been prescribed for you and you have such an allergy.

Warnings: This drug should be used cautiously by pregnant women; the elderly; children; persons with liver or kidney disease, Addison's disease, or prostate disease; and in the presence of head injury or acute abdominal conditions. Be sure your doctor knows if any of these conditions applies to you. • This drug interacts with narcotic analgesics, tranquilizers, phenothiazines, sedatives, and hypnotics. If you are currently taking any of these drugs, consult your doctor about their use. If you are unsure of the type or contents of your medications, ask your doctor or pharmacist. • Because this drug causes sedation, it should not be used with other sedative drugs or with alcohol. • Avoid tasks requiring alertness, such as driving a car or operating potentially dangerous equipment, while taking this drug. • This drug contains the narcotic hydrocodone; therefore, it can be habit-forming and must be used with caution. Do not increase your dosage or take this medication more often than prescribed without first consulting your doctor. • Products containing narcotics are usually not used for more than seven to ten days. • Notify your doctor if you develop signs of jaundice (yellowing of the eyes or skin, dark urine). • Be cautious about taking nonprescription medicines containing acetaminophen.

Comments: Take this medication as directed. Do not increase your dose or take this more often than prescribed. If stomach upset occurs, take this drug with food or milk. • To prevent constipation, drink plenty of water and eat a high-fiber diet while taking this medication. Pain relievers are usually more effective in preventing pain than treating it once it occurs.

Vistaril antianxiety and antihistamine, see Atarax antianxiety and antihistamine.

Voltaren anti-inflammatory

Ingredient: diclofenac sodium

Dosage Form: Coated tablet: 25 mg; 50 mg; 75 mg

Use: Relief of pain, inflammation, and swelling due to arthritis; relief of moderately painful conditions and menstrual pain

Minor Side Effects: Change in sense of taste; constipation; diarrhea; drowsiness; dry mouth; gas; headache; heartburn; loss of appetite; nausea; stomach upset; vomiting. Most of these side effects, if they occur, should subside as your body adjusts to the medication. Tell your doctor about any that are persistent or particularly bothersome.

Major Side Effects: Blood in urine; bloody or black tarry stools; breathing difficulties; chest pain; chest tightness; fluid retention; itchy skin; mouth sores; painful or difficult urination; rapid, pounding heartbeat; ringing in the ears; severe stomach cramps; skin rash; unusual bleeding or bruising; unusual weight gain; visual disturbances; yellowing of the eyes or skin. Notify your doctor if you notice any major side effects.

Contraindications: This drug should not be taken by anyone who is allergic to it or to aspirin or similar drugs. Consult your doctor immediately if this drug has been prescribed for you and you have any such allergies.

Warnings: This medication should be used with extreme caution by people who have a history of ulcers or of stomach or intestinal disorders. Make sure your doctor knows if you have or have had any of these conditions. Notify your doctor if you experience frequent indigestion or notice a change in the appearance of your urine or stools. • This drug should be used cautiously by persons with anemia, severe allergies, bleeding diseases, high blood pressure, liver disease, kidney disease, or certain types of heart disease. Be sure your doctor knows if any of these conditions applies to you. • This drug should be used only if clearly needed during pregnancy or while nursing. Discuss the risks and benefits with your doctor. • This drug is not recommended for use in children under 12 years of age since safety and efficacy have not been established in this age group. • This drug interacts with anticoagulants, oral antidiabetics, barbiturates, diuretics, steroids, phenytoin, and aspirin. If you are currently taking any drugs of these types, consult your doctor or pharmacist about their use. If you are unsure about the type or contents of your medications, consult your doctor or pharmacist. • Avoid the use of alcohol while taking this medication. • While using this medication, avoid the use of nonprescription medication containing aspirin or ibuprofen, since they are similar in some actions to this drug. • This drug may cause drowsiness or blurred vision. Avoid activities that require alertness, such as driving a car or operating potentially dangerous equipment. • Notify your doctor if you experience a skin rash, vision changes, unusual weight gain, fluid retention, or a persistent headache.

Comments: Take this drug with food or milk to reduce stomach upset. • To be most effective in relieving symptoms of arthritis, this drug must be taken as prescribed. Do not take this medication only when you feel pain. It is important to take this drug continuously. You should note improvement in your symptoms soon after starting this drug, but it may take a few weeks for the full benefit to be apparent. • This drug is not a substitute for rest, physical therapy, or other measures recommended by your doctor to treat your condition.

Wyamycin S antibiotic, see erythromycin antibiotic.

Wymox antibiotic, see amoxicillin antibiotic.

Xanax antianxiety

Ingredient: alprazolam
Equivalent Product: Alprazolam

Dosage Forms: Tablet: 0.25 mg; 0.5 mg; 1 mg; 2 mg. Oral solution (content per 5 ml teaspoonful): 0.5 mg. Oral drops (content per 1 ml): 1 mg.

Uses: Relief of anxiety disorders and anxiety associated with depression; treatment of panic disorder

Minor Side Effects: Blurred vision; change in sex drive; constipation; diarrhea; dizziness; drowsiness; dry mouth; fatigue; headache; heartburn; irritability; nervousness; stomach pains; sweating; weakness. Most of these side effects, if they occur, should subside as your body adjusts to the medication. Tell your doctor about any that are persistent or particularly bothersome.

Major Side Effects: Breathing difficulties; clumsiness; confusion; dark urine; depression; difficulty urinating; hallucinations; menstrual changes; nervousness; rapid heartbeat; rash; shakiness; sleeping difficulties; slurred speech; sore throat; tremor; uncoordinated movements; yellowing of the eyes or skin. Notify your doctor if you notice any major side effects.

Contraindications: This drug should not be used by persons allergic to it or to other benzodiazepines or by persons with acute narrow-angle glaucoma. Consult your doctor immediately if this drug has been prescribed for you and either condition applies.

Warnings: This drug should be used cautiously by pregnant or nursing women, elderly people, children, and people with kidney or liver disease or psychiatric illness. Be sure your doctor knows if any of these conditions applies to you. • This drug should be used cautiously with psychotropic medications, antidepressants, pain medications, anticonvulsants, antihistamines, alcohol, or other central nervous system depressants. If you are currently taking any drugs of these types, consult your doctor about their use. If you are unsure of the type or contents of your medications, ask your doctor or pharmacist. • To prevent oversedation, avoid the use of alcohol or other drugs with sedative properties. • Do not stop taking this drug suddenly without first consulting your doctor. If you have been taking this drug for a long time, your dosage should gradually be reduced, according to your doctor's directions. • This drug has the potential to become habit-forming and must be used with caution. Tolerance may develop; do not increase the dose of this medication without first consulting your doctor. • If you are taking this drug for an extended duration, your doctor may require you to have periodic blood and liver-function tests. • This drug may cause drowsiness; avoid tasks that require alertness, such as driving a car or operating potentially dangerous equipment. • Notify your doctor if you develop signs of jaundice (yellowing of the eyes or skin, dark urine).

Comments: To lessen stomach upset, take this medication with food or with a full glass of water. • The full effects of this drug may not become apparent for three to four days. • Chew gum or suck on ice chips or a piece of hard candy to reduce mouth dryness. • This drug is currently used by many people to relieve anxiety. Although it is effective for this purpose, it is important to try to understand the cause of the anxiety as well.

Zantac antisecretory and antiulcer

Ingredient: ranitidine

Dosage Forms: Syrup (content per ml): 15 mg. Tablet: 150 mg; 300 mg

Uses: Treatment of ulcers and hypersecretory conditions; prevention of recurrent ulcers; treatment of gastroesophageal reflux disease

Minor Side Effects: Constipation; decreased sexual desire; diarrhea; difficulty sleeping; dizziness; dry mouth; dry skin; fatigue; headache; insomnia; nausea; sedation; stomach upset; sweating; taste disturbances. Most of these side effects, if they occur, should subside as your body adjusts to the medication. Tell your doctor about any that are persistent or particularly bothersome.

Major Side Effects: Agitation; blood disorders; confusion; depression; diffi-culty urinating; impotence; irregular pulse; muscle aches; numbness or tingling in the hands or feet; rapid, pounding heartbeat; rash; weakness; weak pulse. Notify your doctor if you notice any major side effects.

Contraindication: This drug should not be taken by anyone who is allergic to it. Consult your doctor if you have such an allergy.

Warnings: This drug must be used with caution by pregnant or nursing women, elderly people, and people with liver or kidney diseases. Elderly per-sons may be more likely to develop certain side effects to this medication. If this drug has been prescribed for you and any of these conditions applies, con-sult your doctor. • Safety of this drug for use in children has not yet been estab-lished; therefore, it is not recommended for children under 12. • This drug has not been shown to affect the concurrent use of other medications. However, check with your doctor or pharmacist before taking any other drugs.

Comments: To ensure best results, this drug must be taken continuously for as long as your doctor prescribes, even if you feel better. • This drug may be used in conjunction with antacids to relieve pain. For maximum effect, stagger the doses of Zantac and antacids by at least two hours. • This drug must be used in conjunction with lifestyle changes, including stress reduction, exercise, smoking cessation, and dietary changes. The liquid form of this drug contains 7.5 percent alcohol. • This drug is very similar in action to Tagamet, Axid, and Pepcid. Talk to your doctor about these medications to determine the least ex-pensive alternative.

Zartan antibiotic, see Keflex antibiotic.

Zaroxolyn diuretic

Ingredient: metolazone
Equivalent Product: Mykrox
Dosage Form: Tablet: 0.5 mg; 2.5 mg; 5 mg; 10 mg
Uses: Removal of fluid from body tissues; treatment of high blood pressure
Minor Side Effects: Bitter taste in mouth; bloating; chills; constipation; diar-rhea; dizziness; drowsiness; fatigue; headache; heartburn; loss of appetite; nausea; rash; restlessness; sensitivity to sunlight; stomach upset; vomiting; weakness. Most of these side effects, if they occur, should subside as your body adjusts to the medication. Tell your doctor about any that are persistent or particularly bothersome.

Major Side Effects: Blood disorders; blurred vision; breathing difficulties; chest pain; clotting disorders; cramps; dark urine; dehydration; dry mouth; easy bruising or bleeding; fainting; fever; low blood pressure; mood changes; mus-cle spasm; palpitations; rash; sore throat; tingling in the fingers and toes; yel-lowing of the eyes or skin. Notify your doctor in the event that you notice any major side effects.

Contraindications: This drug should not be used by people who are allergic to it or by those with anuria (inability to urinate) or liver disease. If this drug has been prescribed for you and any of these conditions applies, call your doctor at once. • This drug is not recommended for use by children.

Warnings: If you are allergic to sulfa drugs or thiazide diuretics, you may also be allergic to this drug. Talk to your doctor before you take this drug. • This drug should be used cautiously by pregnant women and by people with diabetes, kidney disease, or gout. Be sure your doctor knows if any of these conditions applies to you. • Nursing mothers who must take this drug should stop nursing. • This drug should be used cautiously with digitalis, nonsteroidal anti-inflammatory drugs, and lithium. • If you are taking digitalis in addition to this drug, watch carefully for symptoms of increased digitalis toxicity (nausea, blurred vision, palpitations), and notify your doctor immediately if they occur. • While taking this product, limit your consumption of alcoholic beverages in order to prevent dizziness or light-headedness. • If you have high blood pressure, do not take any nonprescription item for weight control, cough, cold, or sinus problems without first checking with your doctor; such medications may contain ingredients that can increase blood pressure. • Persons taking this drug along with other high blood pressure medications may need to have their dosages carefully monitored. It may be necessary to reduce the dose of the other drug(s). • Remind your doctor that you are taking this drug if you are scheduled for surgery. • This drug may cause a serious loss of potassium from the body, so it is often prescribed along with a potassium supplement. Watch for signs of potassium loss (dry mouth, thirst, weakness, muscle pain or cramps, nausea, or vomiting), and call your doctor if any occur. • This drug may affect kidney function tests. Be sure your doctor knows you are taking this drug if you are scheduled for such tests. • Periodic laboratory tests should be performed while you are taking this drug. • Notify your doctor if you develop signs of jaundice (yellowing of the eyes or skin, dark urine). • This drug can increase your skin's sensitivity to the sun. Avoid prolonged sun exposure, and use a sunscreen when outdoors.

Comments: This drug must be taken exactly as directed. Do not take extra doses or skip a dose without first consulting your doctor. It is important to continue taking this medication even if you do not feel sick. Most people with high blood pressure do not have symptoms and do not feel ill; therefore, it is easy to forget to take the medication. • If this drug causes stomach upset, take it with food or milk. • Diuretics are also called water pills. Diuretics help eliminate extra fluid that may build up, especially in the feet, causing swelling. As a result, this drug causes frequent urination. Expect this effect; do not be alarmed. Try to avoid taking this drug at bedtime. • To help prevent potassium loss, you can take this product with a glass of fresh or frozen orange juice or eat a banana every day. The use of a salt substitute also helps prevent potassium loss. Do not change your diet, however, without consulting your doctor. Too much potassium can also be dangerous. Your doctor may want to check your blood potassium levels periodically while you are taking this drug. • To avoid dizziness or light-headedness when you stand, contract and relax the muscles of your legs for a few moments before rising. Do this by pushing one foot against the floor while raising the other foot slightly, alternating feet so that you are pumping your legs in a pedaling motion. The light-headed feeling is more likely to occur in persons who combine this drug with other high blood pressure drugs, alcohol, sedatives, or narcotics. • Learn how to monitor your pulse and blood pressure while taking this medication; discuss this with your doctor. As with all antihypertensive medications, they are most effective when used in conjunction with diet and lifestyle changes, such as exercise and stress reduction to control blood pressure. The medication does not bring about a cure for high blood pressure.

Zestril antihypertensive, see Prinivil antihypertensive.

Zocor antihyperlipidemic

Ingredient: simvastatin
Dosage Form: Tablet: 5 mg; 10 mg; 20 mg; 40 mg
Use: In conjunction with diet to reduce elevated blood cholesterol levels
Minor Side Effects: Abdominal pain; altered sense of taste; constipation; cramps; decreased sexual desire; diarrhea; dizziness; flatulence; headache;

heartburn; itching; nausea; rash; stomach upset. Most of these side effects, if they occur, should subside as your body adjusts to the medication. Tell your doctor about any that are persistent or particularly bothersome.

Major Side Effects: Blurred vision; clouding of the eye; difficulty swallowing; fever; liver disorders; malaise (vague feeling of discomfort); muscle aches, cramps, pain, or weakness; tingling in the fingers or toes. Notify your doctor if you notice any major side effects.

Contraindications: This drug should not be used by persons who are allergic to it, by those with active liver disease, or by pregnant women. Consult your doctor if this drug has been prescribed for you and any of these conditions applies. • This drug is not recommended for use in children or nursing women.

Warnings: This drug must be used cautiously by persons with a history of liver disease. Periodic liver function tests are recommended during long-term therapy to assure that the drug is not affecting the liver. • This drug must be used with caution if you have developed a severe infection, uncontrolled seizures, or a severe blood disorder or if you are undergoing major surgery or trauma. Under such conditions, your doctor may temporarily discontinue your therapy with this medication. • This drug may interact with the anticoagulant warfarin. If you are currently taking warfarin, your dose may be monitored more frequently and an adjustment may be required. Make sure your doctor knows you are taking warfarin. • This drug may cause muscle pain, tenderness, or weakness associated with fever and fatigue. If you develop these symptoms while taking lovastatin, contact your doctor. These symptoms are most common in persons who are also taking immunosuppressive drugs, gemfibrozil, or nicotinic acid. Consult your doctor about concurrent use of these drugs. • There are reports that this drug may cause a clouding of the lens in the eye during long-term therapy. An eye examination is recommended before therapy is begun and then once each year thereafter.

Comments: This drug is best taken as a single dose with the evening meal. • When first taking this drug, you may experience stomach upset and gas. These effects usually disappear with continued use. Notify your doctor if they persist or worsen. • The full effects of this drug may not be evident for four to six weeks. Your doctor will want to monitor the effects of this drug by doing periodic blood tests. Ask your doctor to explain your cholesterol level and the goals of your therapy. Learn to monitor your progress. • This drug should be used only after diet therapy has proven ineffective. This drug is not a substitute for proper diet, exercise, and weight control. For maximum results, this drug must be used in conjunction with a diet that is low in saturated fat and cholesterol. You may be referred to a nutritionist for diet counseling.

Zoloft antidepressant

Ingredient: sertraline hydrochloride
Dosage Form: Tablet: 50 mg; 100 mg
Uses: Treatment of mental depression; also used to treat obsessive-compulsive disorder

Minor Side Effects: Abdominal cramps; anxiety; change in appetite; change in sexual drive; constipation; diarrhea; distorted sense of taste; dizziness; drowsiness; dry mouth; gas; headache; insomnia; light-headedness; nausea; nervousness; reduced concentration; sweating; tremor; trouble sleeping; vomiting. Most of these side effects, if they occur, should subside as your body adjusts to the medication. Tell your doctor about any that are persistent or particularly bothersome.

Major Side Effects: Chest pain; chills; confusion; cough; fever; frequent or painful urination; hives; mood or behavior changes; muscle aches; painful or difficult breathing; rapid, pounding heartbeat; ringing in the ears; sexual dysfunction; skin rash; sore throat; vision changes. Notify your doctor if you notice any major side effects.

Contraindication: This drug should not be used by people who are allergic to it. Consult your doctor immediately if this drug has been prescribed for you and you have such an allergy.

Warnings: This drug should be used cautiously by people who have severe liver or kidney disease; unstable heart disease; head injury; or history of seizures, suicide attempts, or drug abuse. Be sure your doctor knows if any of these conditions applies to you. • Elderly persons should use this drug with caution. • This drug should be used only if clearly needed during pregnancy. Discuss the risks and benefits with your doctor. • It is not known if this drug appears in breast milk. Consult your doctor before breast-feeding while taking this medication. • This drug is not recommended for use in children under 18 years of age since safety and efficacy have not been established in this age group. • This drug has been found to interact with diazepam, warfarin, monoamine oxidase inhibitors, lithium, and tolbutamide. If you are currently taking any medications of these types, consult your doctor about their use. If you are unsure about the type or contents of your medications, ask your doctor or pharmacist. Inform your doctor of any medications (prescription or nonprescription) you are taking or plan to take during treatment with this drug. • This drug may cause drowsiness and dizziness; avoid tasks requiring alertness, such as driving a car or operating potentially dangerous equipment. To prevent excessive drowsiness, avoid the use of alcohol or other depressant medication while taking this drug. • This medication may cause a rash or hives. If you experience either of these symptoms, inform your doctor. Notify your doctor of any changes in mood or behavior changes that occur while taking this drug.

Comments: Take this drug with food or a full glass of water if stomach upset occurs. • Continue to take this medication as prescribed. Do not suddenly stop taking this drug without your doctor's approval. • Some improvement should be seen within one week, but it may take three to four weeks before optimal results are achieved. • Nausea, dizziness, headache, light-headedness, and anxiety are common during the first few days of therapy. These effects should subside as your body adjusts to the drug. • Chew gum or suck on ice chips to help relieve dry mouth. To avoid dizziness or light-headedness, contract and relax the muscles of your legs for a few moments before rising. Do this by pushing one foot against the floor while raising the other foot slightly, alternating feet so that you are pumping your legs in a pedaling motion. This drug has been found to be effective in the treatment of depression when taken as directed. Serious side effects can result from improper use. Your condition will be monitored closely while you are taking this drug.

Zone-A Forte topical steroid and anesthetic, see Pramosone topical steroid and anesthetic.

Zovirax antiviral

Ingredient: acyclovir

Dosage Forms: Capsule: 200 mg. Ointment: 5%. Tablet: 400 mg; 800 mg. Oral suspension (content per 5 ml teaspoon): 200 mg

Uses: Management of herpes infections and treatment of herpes zoster (shingles)

Minor Side Effects: Capsule, Tablet: Bad taste in mouth; dizziness; fatigue; headache; loss of appetite; nausea; rash; vomiting. Ointment: Temporary pain, burning, stinging, itching, or rash after application. Most of these side effects, if they occur, should subside as your body adjusts to the medication. Tell your doctor about any that are persistent or particularly bothersome.

Major Side Effects: Blood disorders; muscle cramps; sore throat. Notify your doctor if you notice any major side effects.

Contraindication: This drug should not be used by anyone who is allergic to it. Consult your doctor immediately if this drug has been prescribed for you and you have such an allergy.

Warnings: This drug should be used with extreme caution during pregnancy; discuss the benefits and risks with your doctor. • Nursing women should also use Zovirax with caution, since small amounts of the drug pass into breast milk. • Use of this drug in children under two years of age is not recommended. • Take this drug exactly as prescribed. Notify your doctor if lesions appear more frequently or become worse. • The ointment is intended for use on the skin only and should not be used in or around the eyes.

Comments: To achieve full effect, this drug must be used as prescribed. Continue taking this drug for the prescribed period, even if symptoms disappear before that time. Do not use more than is prescribed. • The ointment is usually applied six times a day for a one-week period. Apply it as soon as possible after symptoms of a herpes infection begin, and use a rubber glove to apply the ointment in order to avoid spreading the infection. With genital herpes, avoid sexual intercourse when visible lesions are present. • The ointment may cause temporary burning, itching, and stinging. Notify your doctor if these symptoms worsen or persist. • This drug should be stored in a cool, dry place. • Patient information is available on this drug. If you don't receive an information sheet with your prescription, ask your pharmacist for one. • This drug will not cure or prevent a herpes infection but may relieve pain associated with the viral infection and may shorten its duration. Notify your doctor if the frequency and severity of recurrences does not improve.

Zydone analgesic, see Vicodin, Vicodin ES analgesics.

Zyloprim antigout drug

Ingredient: allopurinol
Equivalent Product: Allopurinol
Dosage Form: Tablet: 100 mg; 300 mg
Uses: Treatment of gout; reduction of uric acid levels in the blood

Minor Side Effects: Diarrhea; drowsiness; headache; nausea; stomach upset; vomiting. Most of these side effects, if they occur, should subside as your body adjusts to the medication. Tell your doctor about any that are persistent or particularly bothersome.

Major Side Effects: Acute gouty attacks; blood disorders; bruising; chills; fatigue; fever; kidney or liver damage; loss of hair; muscle ache; numbness or tingling sensations; paleness; rash; sore throat; visual disturbances. Notify your doctor if you notice any major side effects.

Contraindications: This drug should not be used by nursing mothers or by persons who have had a severe reaction to it. Consult your doctor immediately if this drug has been prescribed for you and any of these conditions applies.

Warnings: This drug should be used with caution by pregnant women; children; persons with blood disease, liver disease, or kidney disease; and people receiving other antigout drugs. Be sure your doctor knows if any of these conditions applies to you. • This drug should be used cautiously in conjunction with ampicillin, azathioprine, cyclophosphamide, mercaptopurine, oral anticoagulants, theophylline, or thiazides. If you are currently taking any drugs of these types, consult your doctor about their use. If you are unsure about the type or contents of your medications, ask your doctor or pharmacist. • Avoid large doses of vitamin C while taking this drug. The combination may increase the risk of kidney stone formation. • While you are on this drug, do not drink alcohol without first checking with your doctor. • Periodic determination of liver and kidney function and complete blood counts should be performed during therapy with this drug, especially during the first few months. • Some investigators have reported an increase in gout attacks during the early stages of use of this drug. • Drowsiness may occur as a result of using this drug; avoid tasks that require alertness, such as driving a car or operating potentially dangerous equipment. • This drug should be discontinued at the first sign of skin rash or any sign of adverse reaction. Notify your doctor immediately if reactions occur.

Comments: To lessen stomach upset, take this drug with food. Take each dose with a full glass of water. • Drink at least eight glasses of water each day to help minimize the formation of kidney stones. • If one tablet of this drug is prescribed three times a day, ask your doctor if a single dose (either three 100 mg tablets or one 300 mg tablet) can be taken as a convenience. • It is common in the treatment of gout for persons beginning to take this drug to also take colchicine for the first three months. Colchicine helps minimize painful attacks of gout. • The effects of therapy with this drug may not be apparent for at least two weeks.

Glossary

adrenergic—a substance that mimics the effects of adrenaline by stimulating the part of the nervous system that controls involuntary actions such as blood vessel contraction, sweating, etc.; used in the treatment of low blood pressure, asthma, shock, glaucoma, and respiratory congestion

adverse reaction—an unwanted, undesirable, possibly dangerous effect that results from the use of a drug

amphetamine—a substance that acts as a central nervous system stimulant; increases blood pressure and reduces appetite; used as an anorectic (to reduce appetite) and to treat attention deficit disorder (hyperactivity)

analgesic—having pain-relieving properties; a pain-relieving substance, may be narcotic or nonnarcotic

anesthetic—causing loss of feeling and sensation; a substance that causes loss of feeling and sensation

anorectic—a substance that decreases the appetite; usually a sympathomimetic amine, an amphetamine, or a related drug

antacid—a drug that neutralizes excess acidity, usually of the stomach; most frequently used to relieve gastrointestinal distress and to treat peptic ulcers

anthelmintic—an anti-infective used to kill worms infecting the body

antianginal—a substance used to relieve or prevent the chest pain known as angina

antiarrhythmic—a drug that improves abnormal heart rhythms

antiasthmatic—a drug used to improve breathing and relieve symptoms of asthma

antibacterial—a drug that destroys or prevents the growth of certain bacteria

antibiotic—a drug that destroys or prevents the growth of bacteria and/or fungi; can be derived from a mold or produced synthetically

anticholinergic—a drug that blocks the passage of certain nervous impulses; used to treat Parkinson's disease, to relieve motion sickness, to reduce acid production in the stomach, to relieve spasms of the intestines, and to treat diarrhea

anticoagulant—a substance that prevents the clotting of blood; also called blood-thinner

anticonvulsant—a substance used to treat or prevent seizures or convulsions

antidepressant—a substance used to treat symptoms of depression; drugs currently used as antidepressants are generally tricyclic antidepressants, monoamine oxidase inhibitors, or amphetamines

antidiabetic—a drug used to treat diabetes mellitus that is not controlled by diet and exercise alone

antidiarrheal—a drug used to treat diarrhea; may work by altering the contents of the bowel or by slowing the action of the bowel

antidote—a substance that counteracts or terminates the action of an ingested poison

antiemetic—an agent that prevents or relieves nausea and vomiting

antifungal—a drug that destroys and prevents the growth and reproduction of fungi

antihistamine—a drug used to relieve the symptoms of an allergy; works by blocking the effects of histamine

antihyperlipidemic—a drug used in conjunction with diet to reduce elevated serum (blood) cholesterol and/or triglyceride levels, which are associated with an increased risk of coronary heart disease

CONSUMER GUIDE®

antihypertensive—a drug that counteracts or reduces high blood pressure

anti-infective—an agent used to treat an infection by microorganisms (bacteria, viruses, or fungi), protozoa, or worms

anti-inflammatory—a drug that counteracts or suppresses inflammation; also relieves pain (aspirin has anti-inflammatory properties)

antinauseant—a drug used to relieve nausea; most work by blocking the transmission of nerve impulses that stimulate vomiting; antiemetic

antispasmodic—a drug that relieves spasms (violent, involuntary muscular contractions or sudden constrictions of a passage or canal); antispasmodics are typically used to treat dysfunctions of the gastrointestinal tract, the gallbladder, or the urinary system

antitussive—a drug used to relieve coughing; may be narcotic

antiulcer—a drug to treat or prevent ulcers

barbiturates—a class of drugs used as sedatives or hypnotics; such drugs can be addictive

beta blocker—an adrenergic used to slow the heart rate, reduce blood pressure, prevent the chest pain known as angina, and relieve migraine headaches

bronchodilator—a drug used to help breathing; works by relaxing bronchial muscles, thereby expanding the air passages of the lungs

calcium channel blocker—a drug that affects muscle contraction and nerve impulses in the heart; dilates (expands) the coronary arteries and inhibits spasms, allowing greater amounts of oxygen to reach the heart; used to reduce chest pain (angina) and high blood pressure and to relieve abnormal heart rate

central nervous system depressant—a drug that acts on the brain to decrease energy and concentration

central nervous system stimulant—a drug that acts on the brain to increase energy and alertness

chemotherapy agents—drugs used in the treatment of cancer; also known as antineoplastic agents

contraindications—conditions for which a drug should not be used; conditions in which the benefits of a given drug would be outweighed by its negative effects

decongestant—a drug that relieves congestion in the upper respiratory system; sympathomimetic amines are used as decongestants

digitalis—a drug used to improve heart rhythm or increase the output of the heart in heart failure; slows the heart rate and increases the force of contraction

diuretic—a drug that acts on the kidneys to cause an increase in urine flow; often used in the treatment of high blood pressure; also called water pill

emetic—a substance that causes vomiting

euphoria—a general false sense of well-being; mood alteration

expectorant—a drug used to increase the secretion of mucus in the respiratory system, thus making it easier to "bring up" phlegm from the lungs

gastric—pertaining to the stomach

generic—not protected by trademark

histamine—a substance produced by the body in an allergic reaction; causes dilation of blood vessels, constriction of smooth muscles in the lungs, and the stimulation of gastric secretions

hormone—a chemical substance produced by glands in the body; regulates the action of certain organs

hypnotic—a drug that is used to induce sleep

indications—uses for a drug that are approved by the government

keratolytic—an agent that softens and promotes peeling of the outer layer of the skin

mineral—an inorganic element found in foods; a variety of minerals, including iron and calcium, are necessary for normal body function

monoamine oxidase (MAO) inhibitor—a drug used to treat severe depression; acts by inhibiting the production of enzymes called monoamine oxidases

narcotic—a drug derived from the opium poppy; used to relieve pain and coughing; addictive

occlusive dressing—a plastic bandage or wrap that prevents the passage of air

ophthalmic—any medication administered through the eye

otic—pertaining to the ear

palpitations—rapid, pounding heartbeats; a feeling of throbbing in the chest

pediculicide—a preparation used to treat a person infested with lice

phenothiazine—a drug used to relieve certain psychological disorders; also used as an antinauseant

salicylates—a class of drugs prepared from the salts of salicylic acid; the most commonly used pain relievers in the United States

scabicide—a preparation used to treat a person infested with scabies

sedative—a drug given to reduce nervousness and promote calm, thereby inducing sleep

side effect—any effect from a drug other than that for which the drug is taken; minor side effects are usually expected and are not usually life-threatening; major side effects are rare but signal the need for a doctor's attention

smooth muscle relaxant—a drug that causes the relaxation of smooth muscle tissue (i.e., muscle tissue, such as that in the lungs, stomach, and bladder) that performs functions not under voluntary control

steroid—any one of a group of compounds secreted primarily by the adrenal glands; used to treat allergic or inflammatory reactions

sulfa drug—an antibacterial drug belonging to the chemical group sulfonamides

superinfection—an infection that occurs during the course of treatment for another infection

sympathomimetic amine—a drug that raises blood pressure, acts as a decongestant, improves air passage into the lungs, and decreases the appetite

thyroid preparation—a drug used to correct thyroid hormone deficiency; may be natural or synthetic; affects the biochemical activity of all body tissues and increases the rate of cellular metabolism

topical—applied directly on the skin rather than taken orally, injected, or administered in other ways

toxic—poisonous, harmful, possibly lethal

tranquilizer—a drug that, when taken in normal doses, calms part of the brain without affecting clarity of mind or consciousness

transdermal—a method of administering medication by means of a patch for absorption through the skin and into the bloodstream

tricyclic antidepressant—a drug used to suppress symptoms of depression; differs slightly in chemical structure from the phenothiazines

uricosuric—a drug that promotes the excretion of uric acid in the urine; used to prevent gout attacks

vaccine—a medication containing weakened or killed germs that stimulates the body to develop an immunity to those germs

vasoconstrictor—a drug that constricts blood vessels, thereby increasing blood pressure and decreasing blood flow

vasodilator—a drug that expands blood vessels to increase blood flow or to lower blood pressure

vitamin—a natural element present in foods that is vital to normal body functions

Index

CONSUMER GUIDE®